Teacher Edition

Strategies for Writers

Level F

Authors

Leslie W. Crawford, Ed.D.
Georgia College & State University

Rebecca Bowers Sipe, Ed.D.
Eastern Michigan University

Consulting Author

Ken Stewart
Master Teacher
Bexley Middle School
Bexley, Ohio

Zaner-Bloser

Strategies for Writers

A proven-effective, research-based program that powers the writing process and provides students with the tools for developing lifelong skills and success in all areas of writing. Strategies from the program can be immediately applied throughout all of a student's classwork.

Correlates to Your State Standards

► *Strategies for Writers* is correlated to your state standards to make lesson planning easy.

► The *Strategies for Writers* online lesson planner integrates the state standards into your daily plans automatically.

Integrates Six Traits of Effective Writing

► The Six Traits of Writing are incorporated into every unit.

► Detailed guidelines assist students in revising, editing, and effectively assessing their work.

Rubric-Based Instruction

► Assessment is rubric-based, so students know exactly what they need to do to succeed.

► Rubrics provide clear guidelines for students to assess their own and other students' writing.

Flexible Units

► Units can be taught in any order.

► The Teacher Edition contains a variety of activities to reinforce **writing across the curriculum**.

► **Grammar** is introduced early in each unit with multiple opportunities provided for instruction and practice.

Test-Writing Practice

► Each unit contains a chapter designed specifically to help improve high-stakes test results.

Descriptive Essay
Rubric

The traits of a good descriptive essay from page 106 have been used to make the rubric below. By using 1, 2, 3, or 4 check marks to judge each trait, you can decide how well any descriptive essay was written.

	Excelling ✓✓✓✓	Achieving ✓✓✓	Developing ✓✓	Beginning ✓
Information/Organization	The essay is about one subject and is well organized.	The essay is mostly about one subject and is mostly well organized.	The essay is about more than one subject and is loosely organized.	The essay needs to be about one subject and needs to be organized.
Voice/Audience	The description is clear, vivid, and interesting.	The description is mostly clear, vivid, and interesting.	The description is fairly clear and interesting.	The description needs to be clear and interesting.
Content/Ideas	Metaphors are well chosen and add to the description.	Some metaphors are included and add to the description.	A few metaphors are included, but they are not well chosen.	The description needs metaphors.
Word Choice/Clarity	Lively, interesting words are used throughout the essay.	Many lively and interesting words are used in the essay.	Some lively and interesting words are used.	Few lively or interesting words are used.
Sentence Fluency	Each paragraph has a topic sentence supported by detail sentences.	Most paragraphs have a topic sentence supported by detail sentences.	Some paragraphs have a topic sentence supported by detail sentences.	Few paragraphs have a topic sentence supported by detail sentences.
Grammar/Mechanics	Spelling, punctuation, and appositives are correct.	There are few errors in spelling, punctuation, and appositives.	There are some errors in spelling, punctuation, and appositives.	There are many errors in spelling, punctuation, and appositives.

108 **Descriptive Writing** ■ Descriptive Essay

Level F Student Edition shown

Independent Study
Research Proven
by Marzano and Associates, Inc.

Students who used *Strategies for Writers* outperformed students who used other programs. See page 16 for more details.

Strategies for Writers is a complete writing source that provides students with the tools for developing lifelong skills and success in all areas of writing—including test-taking situations!

Student Edition provides a powerful source for learning to write within the four modes of writing—narrative, descriptive, expository, and persuasive.

► **Student-friendly** format.

► **Level appropriate student guides** clearly define expectations and model good writing strategies to motivate students, step-by-step, through the writing process.

► **Test-writing practice** is integrated into every unit to build student confidence and boost test scores.

► **Integrated Grammar/Mechanics activities** help students develop essential skills, foundational to writing.

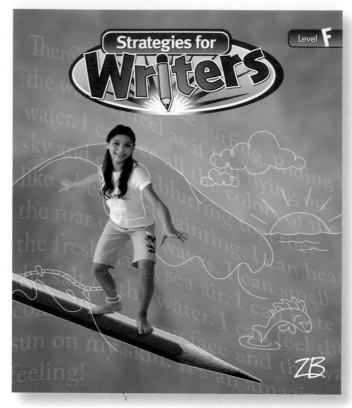

Level F Student Edition

Teacher Edition presents each unit in a clear, easy-to-follow format for flexible instruction.

► **Time Management charts** assist busy teachers with daily planning.

► **Differentiated instruction** is emphasized through helpful suggestions and tips to meet the needs of all students.

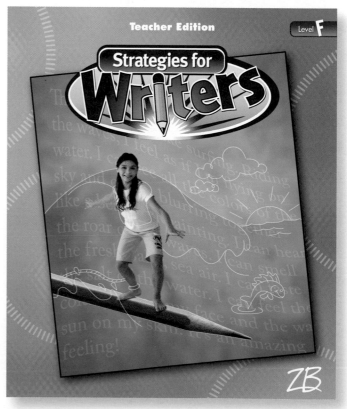

Level F Teacher Edition

Strategy Practice Book provides guided practice for the strategies taught in each unit.

Transparencies include blank graphic organizers and writing models for proofreading practice and additional grammar instruction and practice.

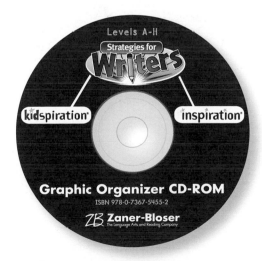

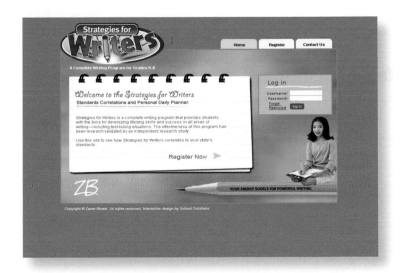

Kidspiration™ & Inspiration™ Graphic Organizer CD-ROM offers students additional practice using graphic organizer templates for building writing success.

Online Lesson Planner correlates daily lesson plans to **your state standards** online at **www.zaner-bloser.com/sfw**.

The Six Traits of Effective Writing

Strategies for Writers integrates the six traits of effective writing in instruction and assessment.

Writing Traits are explained throughout each unit and applied to each genre of writing.

Guides topic focus and text construction ➤

Supports writer's voice and awareness of audience ➤

Promotes richness and interest of content ➤

Develops clarity and appropriateness of language ➤

Supports text fluency and flow ➤

Integrates the conventions of writing ➤

Descriptive Essay
Writing Traits

What makes a good descriptive essay? My teacher says that good writing has the six traits below. I'll try to include them all in my essay.

Information/ Organization	The essay is about one subject. The essay is well organized.
Voice/ Audience	The description is clear, vivid, and interesting.
Content/ Ideas	Metaphors are well chosen and add to the description.
Word Choice/ Clarity	Lively, interesting words are used throughout the essay.
Sentence Fluency	Each paragraph has a topic sentence supported by detail sentences.
Grammar/ Mechanics	Spelling, punctuation, and appositives are correct.

I wonder how well Anna Yuishmal used these traits in her descriptive essay. Let's read and find out on the next page.

106 **Descriptive Writing** ■ Descriptive Essay

Level F Student Edition shown

Descriptive Essay
Rubric

The traits of a good descriptive essay from page 106 have been used to make the rubric below. By using 1, 2, 3, or 4 check marks to judge each trait, you can decide how well any descriptive essay was written.

	Excelling ✓✓✓✓	Achieving ✓✓✓	Developing ✓✓	Beginning ✓
Information/ Organization	The essay is about one subject and is well organized.	The essay is mostly about one subject and is mostly well organized.	The essay is about more than one subject and is loosely organized.	The essay needs to be about one subject and needs to be organized.
Voice/ Audience	The description is clear, vivid, and interesting.	The description is mostly clear, vivid, and interesting.	The description is fairly clear and interesting.	The description needs to be clear and interesting.
Content/ Ideas	Metaphors are well chosen and add to the description.	Some metaphors are included and add to the description.	A few metaphors are included, but they are not well chosen.	The description needs metaphors.
Word Choice/ Clarity	Lively, interesting words are used throughout the essay.	Many lively and interesting words are used in the essay.	Some lively and interesting words are used.	Few lively or interesting words are used.
Sentence Fluency	Each paragraph has a topic sentence supported by detail sentences.	Most paragraphs have a topic sentence supported by detail sentences.	Some paragraphs have a topic sentence supported by detail sentences.	Few paragraphs have a topic sentence supported by detail sentences.
Grammar/ Mechanics	Spelling, punctuation, and appositives are correct.	There are few errors in spelling, punctuation, and appositives.	There are some errors in spelling, punctuation, and appositives.	There are many errors in spelling, punctuation, and appositives.

108 Descriptive Writing ■ Descriptive Essay

Clearly Organized Rubrics

Rubrics are clearly organized, mode- and genre-specific guides that let students know exactly what is expected and help them evaluate their progress.

► Rubrics help students clearly understand writing terminology and assessment criteria.

► The rubric in each chapter is specific to the mode and genre being taught.

► Students learn to use the rubric by applying it to deconstruct an exemplary model.

► Throughout the chapter, the writing strategies being taught support the points of the rubric.

Level F Student Edition shown

The Student Edition

A flexible instructional plan guides the students through the four modes of writing.

1. Narrative
2. Descriptive
3. Expository
4. Persuasive

A student guide walks students, step-by-step, through the writing process.

NARRATIVE writing tells a story to the reader.

Hi, there! I'm Marco. I'm learning about narrative writing in school, and I really think I'm going to like this stuff. I share stories with my friends all the time. They always tell me I should write them down, and now I'll get the chance to do it!

IN THIS UNIT

1. Eyewitness Account
2. Historical Episode
3. Short Story
4. Writing for a Test

6 Narrative Writing

Level F Student Edition shown

Strategies for Writers

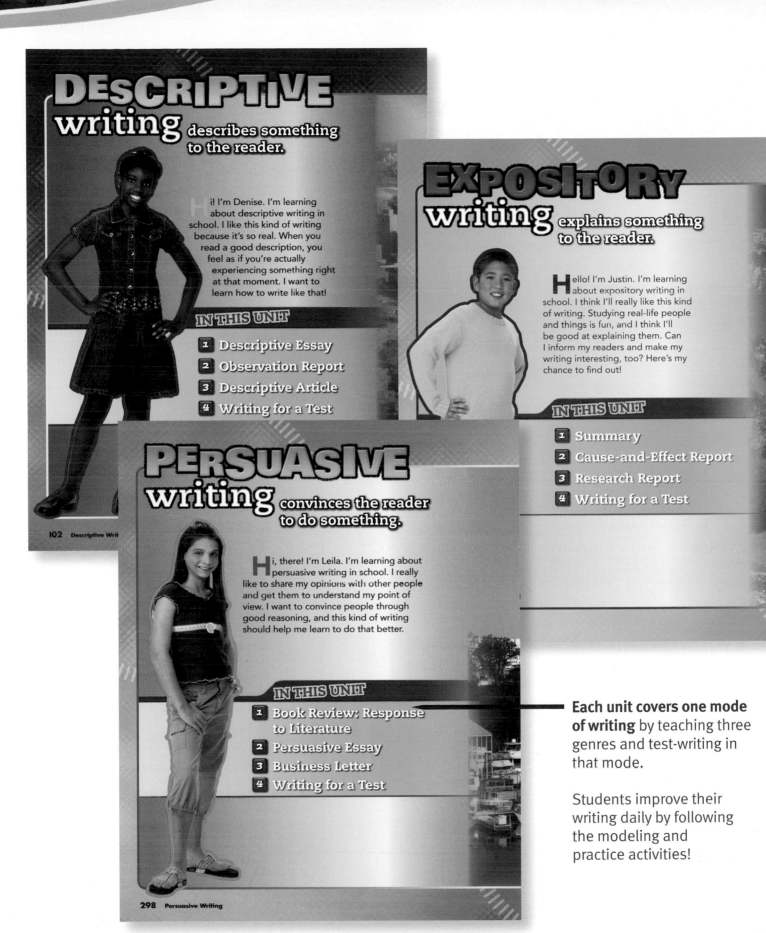

DESCRIPTIVE
writing describes something to the reader.

Hi! I'm Denise. I'm learning about descriptive writing in school. I like this kind of writing because it's so real. When you read a good description, you feel as if you're actually experiencing something right at that moment. I want to learn how to write like that!

IN THIS UNIT

1. Descriptive Essay
2. Observation Report
3. Descriptive Article
4. Writing for a Test

102 Descriptive Writing

EXPOSITORY
writing explains something to the reader.

Hello! I'm Justin. I'm learning about expository writing in school. I think I'll really like this kind of writing. Studying real-life people and things is fun, and I think I'll be good at explaining them. Can I inform my readers and make my writing interesting, too? Here's my chance to find out!

IN THIS UNIT

1. Summary
2. Cause-and-Effect Report
3. Research Report
4. Writing for a Test

PERSUASIVE
writing convinces the reader to do something.

Hi, there! I'm Leila. I'm learning about persuasive writing in school. I really like to share my opinions with other people and get them to understand my point of view. I want to convince people through good reasoning, and this kind of writing should help me learn to do that better.

IN THIS UNIT

1. Book Review: Response to Literature
2. Persuasive Essay
3. Business Letter
4. Writing for a Test

298 Persuasive Writing

Each unit covers one mode of writing by teaching three genres and test-writing in that mode.

Students improve their writing daily by following the modeling and practice activities!

Level F Student Edition shown

The Writing Process

Independent Study • Research Proven • by Marzano and Associates, Inc.

In *Strategies for Writers,* each step of the process is explicitly taught and clearly modeled.

Writing Strategies
are presented to help students meet each point of the rubric.

Writing a Descriptive Essay

Prewriting Organize Ideas

Information/Organization
The essay is well organized.

Writing Strategy Use a Spider Map to organize my notes.

The rubric stresses that my essay should be well organized. My notes are organized by senses, but I see that most of my details are in the "see" category. I need to break my notes into more categories.

A Spider Map will help me organize my notes better. I can make each leg a different category of details, like what I can see of the cat in the photograph, what I can see of the fish, and so on.

When I get my notes organized into several categories, I will be able to write my essay so that it flows smoothly, without jumping around.

Writer's Term
Spider Map
A **Spider Map** organizes information about a topic. The topic is written in the center circle. Each "leg" is one category of details.

114 Descriptive Writing ■ Descriptive Essay

Level F Student Edition shown

SPIDER MAP

looks like inside bowl
ears—pink shark fins
eyes—blue and black marbles in pink ovals
nose—pale pink
whiskers—white
see—cat

cat's nose—velvety
fish's tail—gauzy, delicate
ears—fluffy inside
whiskers—sharp
feel

2 tiny bubbles from mouth
black ink dot for eye
plump, shiny yellow on cat's nose
see—goldfish

cat saying, "Mmmm!"
fish saying, "Uh-oh!"
hear

bubble
open on top
curved edges
white gravel
see—bowl

Practice!
Now it's your turn. Organize your notes by using a Spider Map. Make sure each "leg" of your Spider Map has one category of sensory details.

Reflect
How did I do? Did I organize my notes in a logical way? Will this help me write a good descriptive essay?

Descriptive Writing ■ Descriptive Essay **115**

Writer's Terms
are defined to make the language of writing easy to understand.

Practice! is provided for each writing trait and strategy.

Strategies for Writers

Grammar/Mechanics practice is seamlessly integrated throughout each chapter for streamlined instruction.

Seamless Integration

Grammar/Mechanics Practice! provides additional activities to support grammar instruction.

Editing Proofread Writing

Grammar/Mechanics Spelling, punctuation, and appositives are correct.

Writing Strategy Check that I have used appositives correctly.

Writer's Term

Appositives
An **appositive** is a word or phrase that follows a noun and helps to identify or describe the noun.

Wow! I'm almost finished! Now I need to check my essay for mistakes in spelling and punctuation. I have to check another skill, too: using appositives correctly. Sometimes I forget the commas, but I'm getting better with practice.

[DRAFT] [added commas to fix error in appositive]

When you look at the picture, you can imagine what the cat and the fish are thinking and saying. The cat, a silent and sly hunter, is thinking about the ~~juicy~~ orange goldfish. The cat murmurs, "Mmmm!" and the fi:

Appositives

An appositive is a word or phrase that follows a noun and helps identify or describe it. Appositives are usually separated from the rest of the sentence by commas.

Examples: Dolly, **my cat,** came to our house as a stray.
My neighbor's dogs, **two boxers,**

Practice the Rule

Number your paper 1–10. For the first group of sentences below, write the noun and the appositive that follows.

1. Here are some tips, or guidelines, for getting good photographs of your pets.
2. The first tip, and the most important one, is to study your pet.
3. Find your pet's favorite spot, the place where it likes to spend most of its tin
4. For example, Bubba, my shaggy sheepdog, likes to hang out on the braided rug in the den.
5. Observe your pet's typical behavior, what he or she does every day.

In this group of sentences, notice the underlined nouns or pronouns. On your paper, write an appositive that you could use for each underlined word.

6. Our neighbor, ___, likes to take pictures of his dog.
7. His best picture, ___, won a prize last year.
8. Our neighbor's daughter, ___, takes the dog for walks.
9. They usually head for their favorite spot, ___.
10. Our neighbor has many pictures of the two of them, ___, at the park.

Apply the Rule

Read this descriptive essay about two cats. Write the essay on your paper, correcting any errors in appositives.

My Tigers

Tigers don't make good pets, but tiger cats or tabbies, do. A tabby is a striped shorthair or breed of cat. I have two tabbies, and I love them!

Hansel, the male cat is a butterscotch tabby with lemon-drop eyes. He loves to watch the world from his favorite spot our picture window. I's long, white whiskers twitch when he sees birds outside, and his il is a snake that can't keep still. When Thunder our neighbor's hihuahua, wanders into our yard, Hansel bats at the window with e soft paw. I don't think Hansel the king of the beasts likes Thunder espassing in his domain!

Hansel's sister, Gretel, is a chocolate-cinnamon tabby. She likes to lie beside me her favorite person and be petted. As I stroke the silk

Apply the Rule

Read this descriptive essay about two cats. Write the essay on your paper, correcting any errors in appositives.

Hansel and Gretel are named for the storybook characters the ones who are abandoned in the woods. My cats look like they live in the candy house because they are so chubby and sweet.

Level F Student Edition shown

Test Writing

Every unit contains a *Writing for a Test* chapter to provide practice for high-stakes testing.

Planning My Time

Before giving us a writing test prompt, my teacher tells us how much time we'll have to complete the test. Since I'm already familiar with the writing process, I can think about how much total time I have and then divide it up into the different parts of the writing process. If the test takes an hour, here's how I can organize my time. Planning your time will help you, too!

Step 4: Editing 10 minutes

Step 1: Prewriting 25 minutes

Step 3: Revising 10 minutes

Student guides model the application of writing strategies to test-writing situations for better results on high-stakes tests.

Plan for Success

► **Time planning** is taught to help students manage their time for test writing success.

Using the Writing Prompt

Stages of the **Writing Process** are used in a test-taking scenario.

Student guides examine a **test-writing prompt** and model how to respond to the task.

Writing a Descriptive Test

Prewriting Study the Writing Prompt

Writing Strategy   Study the writing prompt to be sure I know what to do.

When I am handed a test, the first thing I do is study the writing prompt so I will know what to do. The writing prompt usually has three parts. The parts probably won't be labeled, so you'll have to identify them on your own, like I did with my writing prompt. Locate and label the setup, task, and scoring guide on your writing prompt. Circle key words in the setup and the tasks that tell what kind of writing you need to do and who your audience will be. Here, I circled the setup in blue and the task in orange. I'm going to write my test for my teacher, since the writing prompt doesn't identify who the reader is.

My Writing Test Prompt

Setup — Think about an event that you attended or witnessed that really stands out in your mind.

Task — Write an essay describing the event in detail.

Be sure your writing

Scoring Guide
- is organized so that your essay flows smoothly.
- has a clear purpose and is appropriate for your audience.
- includes specific details about your subject.
- is colorful and interesting.
- stays on topic.
- contains correct grammar, punctuation, capitalization, and spelling.

182   **Descriptive Writing** ■ Descriptive Test

Strategies for Writers

Level F Student Edition shown

Writing a Descriptive Essay

Prewriting Gather Information

Information/Organization The essay is about one subject.

Writing Strategy Choose a picture and make notes about its sensory details.

Practice the Strategy Choose a picture that you have seen. Gather information by jotting down notes about sensory details you notice in the picture.

Additional activities provide further practice for learning essential writing skills.

After each writing process step is modeled, students may use their *Strategy Practice Book* for additional guided practice.

My Notes for My Descriptive Es...

Copyright © Zaner-Bloser, Inc.

Writing a Descriptive Essay

Prewriting Organize Ideas

Information/Organization The essay is well organized.

Writing Strategy Use a Spider Map to organize my notes.

Practice the Strategy Organize your ideas by including the notes you took on page 19 into a Spider Map.

SPIDER MAP

Copyright © Zaner-Bloser, Inc.

20 Descriptive Writing ■ Descriptive Essay

Level F Strategy Practice Book shown

Time Management Charts

Make lesson planning easy!

▶ **Time Management charts** assist with flexible planning.

▶ **Online Lesson Planner** provides seamless integration of **your state standards** at:

www.zaner-bloser.com/sfw

Learning Objectives and Daily Activities are clearly stated.

Descriptive Essay Time Management

WEEK 1

Day 1	Day 2	Day 3	Day 4	Day 5
Learning Objectives				
Students will: • study the components of a descriptive essay.	Students will: • learn how to gather information for a descriptive essay.	Students will: • practice gathering information for their own descriptive essays.	Students will: • learn how to make a Spider Map to organize their notes.	Students will: • practice organizing their notes into a Spider Map.
Activities				
• Discuss the elements and traits of a descriptive essay (Student pages 104–106). • Use the rubric to study the model (Student pages 107–111).	• Read and discuss **Prewriting: Gather Information** (Student pages 112–113).	• Brainstorm ideas and choose an interesting subject to share. • Work with a partner to gather information for descriptive essays.	• Read and discuss **Prewriting: Organize Ideas** (Student pages 114–115).	• Look at notes for a descriptive essay. • Make a Spider Map to organize the notes.

WEEK 2

Day 1	Day 2	Day 3	Day 4	Day 5
Learning Objectives				
Students will: • learn how to use vivid imagery to help the reader visualize the picture.	Students will: • practice writing their drafts.	Students will: • learn how to add effective metaphors that add to the description.	Students will: • practice adding effective metaphors.	Students will: • learn how to replace dull words with interesting words.
Activities				
• Read and discuss **Drafting: Write a Draft** (Student pages 116–117).	• Use a Spider Map to write a draft.	• Read and discuss **Revising: Extend Writing** (Student page 118).	• Add metaphors to help the readers visualize the subject.	• Read and discuss **Revising: Clarify Writing** (Student page 119).

WEEK 3

Day 1	Day 2	Day 3	Day 4	Day 5
Learning Objectives				
Students will: • practice replacing dull words with more interesting words.	Students will: • learn how topic sentences should be supported by detail sentences.	Students will: • learn how to use appositives correctly.	Students will: • practice editing their drafts for spelling, punctuation, and capitalization.	Students will: • learn different ways to publish their descriptive essays.
Activities				
• Reread draft, looking for dull words. • Replace dull words with lively, interesting words.	• Read and discuss **Editing: Check Sentences** (Student page 120). • Make sure draft includes detail sentences that relate to the topic sentence in every paragraph.	• Read and discuss **Editing: Proofread Writing** (Student page 121). • Make sure appositives are used correctly.	• Fix any spelling, punctuation, or capitalization errors in draft. • Fix any misused appositives.	• Read and discuss **Publishing: Share Writing** (Student page 124).

* To complete the chapter in fewer days, teach the learning objectives and activities for two days in one day.

This planning chart, correlated to your state's writing standards, is available on-line at http://www.zaner-bloser.com/sfw.

Descriptive Writing ■ Descriptive Essay **91**

Level F Teacher Edition shown

Strategies for **Writers**

Writing Across the Curriculum offers ideas that connect writing with other content areas.

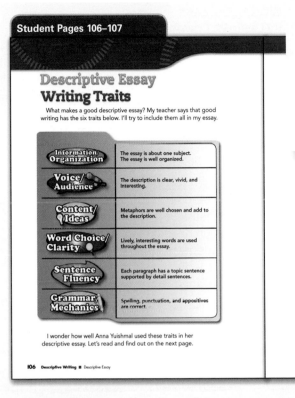

Writing Across the Curriculum

Science In Denise's draft, she describes how the water changes what you see, making the cat's face look huge and as if it is inside the fishbowl. Ask students to think about lessons that they have had in science in order to figure out why the cat's face looks so big on the other side of the glass. They may wish to research this on their own or ask a science teacher about it. Have each student write an explanation of why the cat's face appears as it does in the photo. Then ask for student volunteers to read aloud their explanations. You may even wish to have students try to replicate the effect by using a glass or bowl of water.

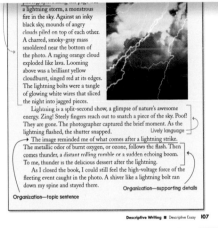

Teaching tips provide useful ideas.

Writing Traits
(Student pages 106–107)

Descriptive Essay

Explain to your students what a metaphor is. You may wish to use an example such as *The swimmer's hair had turned a shade of green that reminded me of the skin of a Granny Smith apple.* Explain that a good descriptive essay will include metaphors to help the audience get a clearer picture. Point out that if you wanted to make the sentence even more lively, you could add more interesting words, such as *The swimmer's pale blonde hair had turned a shade of [green that remin]ded me of the skin of a Granny Smith apple.* [Using] metaphors and lively, interesting [words help] to make a descriptive essay come to life

[With] students the traits of a descriptive essay [on page] 106. As students study the strategies for [descriptive] essays in this chapter, they will refer [to writing] traits. Note that a good descriptive essay [includes all] of the traits listed on this page.

Tell the students that you will be looking at a model writing sample that includes these traits. Ask them to pay attention to the traits as they read the essay "A Striking Image."

Differentiating Instruction

Support To help students understand metaphors, write the name of a familiar object on the board, such as *skyscraper*. Ask them for words that describe a skyscraper. **tall, glass, huge, imposing, dominating** Then help students think of other objects with similar features, such as *a giant*. Guide them to write a metaphor that compares the two. **The skyscraper was a glass giant.** Point out that students should not use the words *like* or *as*. They might want to use this template sentence: *The [blank] was a [blank].* Have the students practice using metaphors by completing sentences using this template.

Differentiating Instruction provides options and activities to meet the needs of all learners, including English-Language Learners.

Descriptive Writing ■ Descriptive Essay **93**

Level F Teacher Edition shown

School-Home Connection Letters provide a quick and easy way to communicate with families.

Research

Evidence-Based Research

Students who used *Strategies for Writers* outperformed students who used other programs.

An independent study, conducted by Marzano and Associates, Inc., measured the impact of *Strategies for Writers* (SFW) on the improvement of students' writing performance. Below is a brief synopsis from the first year's investigation, conducted in 2003–2004.*

- Given any group of 100 students, when 50 are taught using *Strategies for Writers* and 50 are taught using OTHER† materials and/or methodologies, students using SFW outperform students using OTHER materials 49 out of 50 times on writing tests.

- There are no differences in student performance among grade levels. *Strategies for Writers* consistently produces a 49 to 1 ratio result.

- It doesn't matter whether a school is urban or suburban. *Strategies for Writers* students score higher on holistic writing tests than students taught with OTHER materials or methodologies.

- In general, this independent first-year (2003–2004) evidence-based research study found that using *Strategies for Writers* produces superior writing scores (on standardized or state tests) compared to those scores produced by students using other writing materials and methodologies.

* The above data has been excerpted from the complete final report of the first-year evaluation (2003–2004) of the *Strategies for Writers* program. The complete report, conducted by **Marzano and Associates, Inc.,** can be found on the Zaner-Bloser Web site **www.zaner-bloser.com**.

† OTHER represents a variety of methods and materials.

Foundational Research

Strategies for Writers Research-Based Program for Writing Success
By Leslie W. Crawford, Ed.D.

In the last decade of the twentieth century, concerted effort in the field of literacy began to achieve an approach that would balance instruction between skills and process. With this in mind, *Strategies for Writers* was designed to embed strategies within a process approach to writing (Collins, 1998; Collins & Collins, 1996; Englert, 1990; and Harris & Graham, 1992).
Strategy instruction
- makes students aware of when, how, and why strategies work (Harris & Pressley, 1991; and Poindexter & Oliver, 1999).
- teaches students to think carefully and strategically about writing instruction (Christenson, 2002).
- focuses on developing writers who are able to write independently using the processes of writing (Englert, 1990).
- gives students the support needed to overcome difficulties in writing (Danoff, Harris, & Graham, 1993).

Rubrics include elements and criteria that provide students the scaffolds needed for judging and revising their work (Hillocks, 1986; James, Abbott, & Greenwood, 2001). Experience using rubrics leads students to become effective evaluators of their compositions.

Strategies for Writers Research Base for the Use of Rubrics
By Rebecca B. Sipe, Ed.D.

When used as instructional tools, rubrics
- help students become more thoughtful about their work as they engage in ongoing peer and self-assessments (Goodrich, 1996; Andrade, 1997, 2000).
- provide a platform of technical vocabulary to help students think about important aspects of their writing regardless of the genre. Terms like *purpose*, *audience*, and *organization* become part of the class vocabulary because teachers frequently start with established rubrics and then modify or expand these rubrics as the class discusses the important aspects of writing (DeLisle-Walker, 1996; Wolf & Wolf, 2002; Wolf & Gearhart, 1994; Wyngaard & Gehrke, 1996; Marzano, 2000; Skillings & Ferrell, 2000; Allington, Johnston, & Day, 2002). Used in this way, rubrics provide excellent tools for:
  1. engaging the students in a class discussion of writing elements (which are also sometimes called *domains* or *traits*).
  2. building student understanding of the qualities of good writing.
  3. supporting student writing.
  4. guiding students as they evaluate their own writing (Wyngaard & Gehrke, 1996; Strickland & Strickland, 1998).

Table of Contents

NARRATIVE writing

DESCRIPTIVE writing

(Continued on page 18)

DESCRIPTIVE writing (Continued)

EXPOSITORY writing

EXPOSITORY writing (Continued)

PERSUASIVE writing

NARRATIVE
writing strategies

NARRATIVE writing tells a story to the reader.

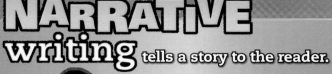

Hi, there! I'm Marco. I'm learning about narrative writing in school, and I really think I'm going to like this stuff. I share stories with my friends all the time. They always tell me I should write them down, and now I'll get the chance to do it!

IN THIS UNIT

1. Eyewitness Account
2. Historical Episode
3. Short Story
4. Writing for a Test

Name: Marco
Home: Arizona
Hobbies: rodeos, raising calves, reading about history
Favorite Book: *Walker's Crossing*, by Phyllis Reynolds Naylor
Favorite Food: macaroni and cheese

IN THIS UNIT

Eyewitness Account This genre opens the door to narrative writing by encouraging students to write about something that happened in real life.

Historical Episode This genre gives students an opportunity to weave fact and fiction together to create a story based on an actual time, place, event, or person in history.

Short Story This genre gives students a chance to use their imaginations to come up with interesting plots and believable characters.

Narrative Test Students will learn and practice how to read a narrative test prompt and how to plan their time. They will also learn and practice writing strategies for successful test-writing in the narrative mode.

Meet Marco

The student guide for this chapter is Marco, a boy from Arizona. Have students look at Marco's background and hobbies and ask them what kinds of stories he might have to tell. Explain to students that Marco's writing throughout this unit will be related to his own experiences. That will help to make his writing special and real. Encourage students to use their own backgrounds, knowledge, interests, and personalities as they write. Narrative writing tells stories, and your students will have many interesting, unique, and authentic stories to tell.

Internet TIPS for the Writing Classroom

by Julie Coiro, Ph.D.
University of Connecticut

Locating Resources: Search Engines for Adults and Students

For adults looking for specific information quickly, one search engine to try first is Google at **http://www.google.com**. It has a huge database that very quickly scans sites and returns a list of relevant Web sites with a short annotation and a link. The articles are listed in rank order, with the most popular and relevant at the top. Your students may also wish to use Google, but you will want to select the "Google Safe Search" option from the preferences menu to block inappropriate Web sites.

Other popular search engines for adults include Yahoo at **http://www.yahoo.com**, Alta Vista at **http://www.altavista.com**, MSN at **http://www.msn.com**, and Dogpile at **http://www.dogpile.com**.

A number of exceptional search engines and Web portals have been designed with the needs and interests of a younger audience in mind. A few of the most popular are listed below:

- **Kids Click** at **http://www.kidsclick.org** was created by librarians and organizes 5,000 Web sites into more than 600 categories.

- **AOL at School** at **http://www.aolatschool.com** searches a database of educator-reviewed classroom materials for students in grades K–12.

- **Kids Net.Au** at **http://www.kids.net.au** is designed for children, parents, and teachers. It links to reference materials, including a thesaurus, dictionary, and encyclopedia.

- **Fact Monster** at **http://www.factmonster.com** is a Web site for kids that combines the contents of reference materials with other educational resources.

- **Enchanted Learning** at **http://www.enchantedlearning.com/Home.html** provides access to a huge database guaranteed to spark writing ideas.

- **TekMom Search Tools for Students** at **http://tekmom.com/search/index.html** links readers to research tools designed with young learners in mind.

Critical Evaluation: Evaluating Reliability

As children begin using the Internet as a source for information, it is important that they realize Web sites do not go through the same editing process as books before they get published. Students need to expect that they may find information on the Internet that has mistakes or that has been created as a joke. One strategy you may wish to discuss with your students involves evaluating the **reliability** of online information.

For educational purposes, a reliable Web site is one created by a person or people with a reputation for publishing high quality, truthful information for children. It is critical that students be prepared to investigate who created a Web site, why it was created, and what authority the creators have to publish the information.

All quality information Web sites should have an "About Us" page that tells more about the authors, their qualifications, contact information, and their purpose for creating the site. You can find this information at a link labeled "Who We Are" or "About Us" on the starting page of a Web site. All of the biography Web sites listed on page 23 include such links. You may wish to explore a few of these Web sites as a class activity.

To begin, select two or three Web sites and use a digital projector to view each site with your students. Scroll up and down the homepage to look for the "About Us" link. Once you have found the link, discuss the answers to these questions:

a) Who created the information?

b) What is the purpose of this Web site?

c) When was the information updated?

d) What qualifications does the author have?

e) Would you use the information at this Web site in your own biographic sketch? Why or why not?

Encourage students to consider questions each time they visit a Web site. Answers will often provide the insights needed to critically evaluate whether or not the information is reliable and worthy of use.

Communicating Globally: Publishing Biographic Sketches

The Internet provides wonderful models for publishing for a public audience. You can create your own class project Web site to display your students' writing in a format that fits their interests. Here are three Web sites to get you thinking about the possibilities.

- *The Children's Encyclopedia of Women* was first published in 1988 by Terry Hongell's 3rd and 4th graders from Sleepy Hollow, New York. It is published as part of the Pocantico Hill School's Web site. Each year, students add new content to the collection. It is truly an example of the power of online publishing. **http://www2.lhric.org/pocantico/womenenc/womenenc.htm**

- A second project titled *Different People, Different Countries, Same Dream* was published as a telecollaboration among elementary school students in India, Israel, and the United States. The students helped design this interactive Web site and they continue to exchange their biographic sketches of leaders of different cultures. This Web site was created for a contest sponsored by The Global Virtual Classroom at **http://www.virtualclassroom.org**, an initiative designed to empower, enable, and connect students around the world using Internet technology. **http://gvctemp01.virtualclassroom.org**

- A third project, *Images of Greatness: The Lives of Twelve Enduringly Famous Individuals*, was created by a group of fourth and fifth graders from Brisas Elementary School in Chandler, Arizona. The students organized their twelve short biographic sketches in an amazing table that charts the similarities and differences among the contributions of these famous individuals. The Web site also contains a "Quotations Quiz" about these great achievers. **http://www.kyrene.k12.az.us/schools/brisas/sunda/great/great.htm**

Supporting and Extending Writing: Sparking Writing Ideas

There are many Web sites that offer opportunities for students to link their writing to topics such as science, math, social studies, art, and physical education. Here are a few online biography collections your students may wish to visit:

- **Biographies for Kids: Famous Leaders for Young Readers** at **http://gardenofpraise.com/leaders.htm** includes stories of men and women to inspire students with their courage, determination, and honesty.

- **Explorers of the Millenium: The Greatest Adventurers of the Past Thousand Years** at **http://library.thinkquest.org/4034** is an award-winning Thinkquest Junior Web site designed by fourth and fifth graders in Illinois. Its Hall of Fame features 29 explorers along with an Explorer Quiz and Timeline.

- **Women of the Century** at **http://school.discovery.com/schooladventures/womenofthecentury**, sponsored by DiscoverySchool.com, features a collection of biographies about women in space, science, arts, government, sports, and exploration.

- **Mr. Nussbaum's Famous People Biographies For Kids** at **http://www.mrnussbaum.com/bio.htm** was designed by a teacher in Virginia.

- The **Inventor of the Week Archive** at **http://Web.mit.edu/invent/i-archive.html**, created by the Massachusetts Institute of Technology, is dedicated to honoring the unsung heroes who have helped improve our lives through invention.

- **The HistoryMakers African American History Archive** at **http://www.thehistorymakers.com/** includes biographical information about African Americans who have influenced history.

- **Thomson Gale Resources** maintains an informative database of famous African Americans at **http://www.gale.com/free_resources/bhm/bio/index.htm** and famous Hispanics throughout history at **http://www.gale.com/free_resources/chh/bio**.

Eyewitness Account Overview

In this chapter, students will learn how to write an eyewitness account. They will learn the elements of an eyewitness account—narrator, order, tone, and the 5 W's—and some reasons for writing an eyewitness account. Students will then use an eyewitness account rubric to deconstruct and evaluate a model writing sample.

Next, students will follow the student guide as he goes through the writing stages—prewriting, drafting, revising, editing, and publishing. As Marco learns new writing strategies in each step, students will be directed to practice the strategies in their own writing. Students will talk about an incident that they have witnessed and then turn their notes on the account into a 5 W's chart. They will write a draft using

details from their 5 W's chart. In the revision stage, students will practice adding words or phrases that create a dramatic tone in their writing. Then, they will replace common words in their drafts with more interesting words. In the editing stage, students will learn how to use a variety of sentence beginnings. They will then edit their drafts for spelling, punctuation, and capitalization errors, and check to be sure there are no sentence fragments or run-on sentences. Finally, students will write a final draft for publishing.

You may wish to send to families the School-Home Connection Letter for this chapter, located at the end of this unit in the Teacher Edition.

Eyewitness Account Writing Traits

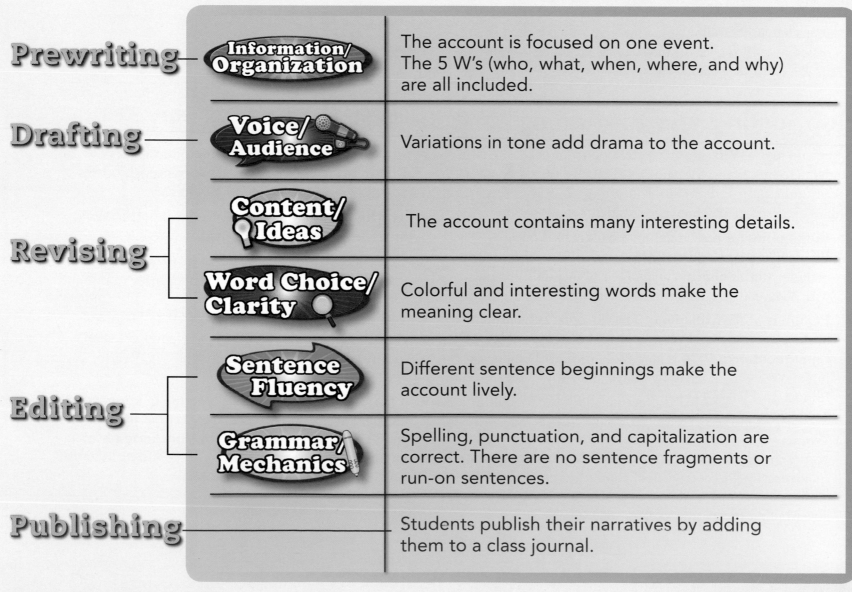

Prewriting	Information/Organization	The account is focused on one event. The 5 W's (who, what, when, where, and why) are all included.
Drafting	Voice/Audience	Variations in tone add drama to the account.
Revising	Content/Ideas	The account contains many interesting details.
	Word Choice/Clarity	Colorful and interesting words make the meaning clear.
Editing	Sentence Fluency	Different sentence beginnings make the account lively.
	Grammar/Mechanics	Spelling, punctuation, and capitalization are correct. There are no sentence fragments or run-on sentences.
Publishing		Students publish their narratives by adding them to a class journal.

Eyewitness Account Time Management

WEEK 1

	Day 1	Day 2	Day 3	Day 4	Day 5
Learning Objectives	Students will: • learn the components of an eyewitness account.	Students will: • learn how to gather information for an eyewitness account.	Students will: • practice gathering information for their own eyewitness accounts.	Students will: • learn how to make a 5 W's Chart to organize their notes.	Students will: • practice organizing their own notes into a 5 W's Chart.
Activities	• Discuss the elements and traits of an eyewitness account (Student pages 8–10). • Use the rubric to study the model (Student pages 11–15).	• Read and discuss **Prewriting: Gather Information** (Student page 16).	• Brainstorm ideas and choose an eyewitness account to share. • Work with a partner to gather information for the eyewitness accounts.	• Read and discuss **Prewriting: Organize Ideas** (Student page 17).	• Make a 5 W's Chart to organize notes.

WEEK 2

	Day 1	Day 2	Day 3	Day 4	Day 5
Learning Objectives	Students will: • learn how to pull the reader in at the beginning with interesting details.	Students will: • practice writing their own drafts.	Students will: • learn how varying tone can add more drama.	Students will: • practice adding words or details to create a dramatic tone.	Students will: • learn how to add colorful or interesting words to make the meaning clear.
Activities	• Read and discuss **Drafting: Write a Draft** (Student page 18).	• Use 5 W's Chart to write a draft.	• Read and discuss **Revising: Extend Writing** (Student page 20).	• Add words or phases that will create interest in the writing.	• Read and discuss **Revising: Clarify Writing** (Student page 21).

WEEK 3

	Day 1	Day 2	Day 3	Day 4	Day 5
Learning Objectives	Students will: • practice replacing common words in their drafts with more interesting words.	Students will: • learn how different sentence beginnings can make their accounts lively.	Students will: • learn how to fix sentence fragments and run-on sentences.	Students will: • practice editing their drafts for spelling, punctuation, and capitalization.	Students will: • learn different ways to publish their eyewitness accounts.
Activities	• Reread drafts, looking for common words. • Replace common words with colorful words.	• Read and discuss **Editing: Check Sentences** (Student page 22). • Make sure drafts use a variety of sentence beginnings, such as descriptive phrases.	• Read and discuss **Editing: Proofread Writing** (Student page 23). • Make sure drafts do not contain any sentence fragments or run-on sentences.	• Fix any spelling, punctuation, or capitalization errors in drafts. • Fix any sentence fragments and run-on sentences in drafts.	• Read and discuss **Publishing: Share Writing** (Student page 26).

To complete the chapter in fewer days, teach the learning objectives and activities for two days in one day.

This planning chart, correlated to your state's writing standards, is available on-line at http://www.zaner-bloser.com/sfw.

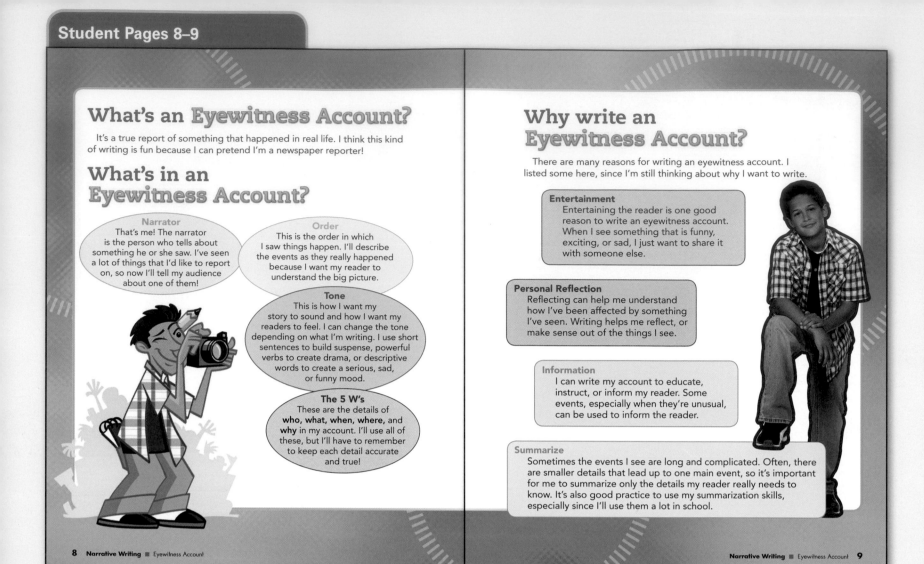

Define the Genre
(Student page 8)

Eyewitness Account

Discuss the definition of eyewitness account with students. Ask a student to describe an event that he or she saw during the past week. Prompt him or her to provide details. Explain that the student is giving an eyewitness account of the event. Point out that when students report the details of something they witnessed in real life, they are using the eyewitness account genre.

Elements of the Genre

Eyewitness Account

Read and discuss the elements of an eyewitness account with the students. Explain that these elements can also be found in news stories they might read on the front page of a newspaper. Have the students think about a current event and discuss how each of these elements might be present in a story about that current event.

Authentic Writing
(Student page 9)

Eyewitness Account

Read and discuss with students the reasons for writing an eyewitness account on Student page 9. Point out that all writing has a purpose. Writers write for many reasons and for a variety of audiences, and these authentic purposes help to shape the writing. Someone writing to entertain may use a tone that conveys humor or excitement. A writer who is writing for personal reflection may focus on feelings and thoughts. A person who is writing to inform may include many facts and explanations to educate, instruct, or inform his/her reader. Encourage students to think about their reasons for writing an eyewitness account and how these reasons will affect the tone and focus of their writing.

Eyewitness Account
Writing Traits

My teacher told me there are six traits of good writing. But what makes a good eyewitness account? I will use the traits that are listed below to help me write my report.

Information/ Organization	The account is focused on one event. The 5 W's (who, what, when, where, and why) are all included.
Voice/ Audience	Variations in tone add drama to the account.
Content/ Ideas	The account contains many interesting details.
Word Choice/ Clarity	Colorful and interesting words make the meaning clear.
Sentence Fluency	Different sentence beginnings make the account lively.
Grammar/ Mechanics	Spelling, punctuation, and capitalization are correct. There are no sentence fragments or run-on sentences.

I can use Joe Torelli's eyewitness account on the next page as a model for my own writing. Later, we'll see how Joe used these traits to help him write his account!

Eyewitness Account Model

THE GREAT CIRCUS PARADE
by Joe (Bongo the Clown) Torelli

Narrator

Last week I was amazed, astounded, flabbergasted, and stupefied! I saw wild animals, dozens of circus wagons and bands, hundreds of horses, and thousands of people in costumes. I, Bongo the Clown, fell under the spell of the Great Circus Parade.

Why As a professional clown, I had to see the parade. Every July, it winds three miles through downtown Milwaukee, Wisconsin. From near and far, people come to see the spectacle. *Who What When Where* **5 W's**

The day I attended was cloudless and bright; a faint breeze floated in from Lake Michigan. A drum troop at the start of the parade stirred up the crowd. Following close behind, young men in knickers pedaled high-wheeled bicycles, and mounted police waved from their saddles. By the time the clown snake charmers arrived, the parade was in full swing. *Order*

The clowns were funny, but I was more impressed by the historic circus wagons. Each one showed off a dazzling color scheme. As the wheels turned, yellow and orange webbing between the spokes swirled like sunbursts. Huge draft horses with fancy brass harnesses hauled most of the wagons, some weighing more than a ton. Magnificent bandwagons carried musicians playing grand old tunes. One bandwagon stood out. Sparkling with gold mermaids and swans, it was like something from a fairy tale. *Tone*

The cage wagons displayed exotic animals, including a pygmy hippo, a buffalo, and a giraffe. I even saw a liger (a cross between a lion and a tiger).

Most splendid were the tableau wagons. Filled with carved and painted wooden figures, they are historical scenes on wheels. A woman dressed as Cleopatra rode a tableau pulled by camels. A two-headed green dragon roared from the top of a tableau that celebrated the age of knights and castles.

At the end of the parade were lumbering elephants and a steam calliope. Belching out plumes of smoke and hooting old-time melodies, the calliope bid farewell to the satisfied crowd. I smiled all the way home, thinking about those sunburst wheels. I'm still smiling. Maybe I should run off to join the circus parade.

Writing Traits
(Student pages 10–11)

Eyewitness Account

Tell students you are going to tell them about something you witnessed. Choose something interesting or exciting, such as a big sporting event, a rescue, or a newsworthy local event. Be sure to include the 5 W's in your account.

Afterward, ask students to identify the who, what, when, where, and why in your story. Tell or remind the students that eyewitness accounts should include the 5 W's. Ask them to think about how many of the 5 W's were used early on in your account to draw them into your story. Point out that in an eyewitness account, interesting details should be included in the beginning to draw readers in.

Tell students they will be studying strategies for writing eyewitness accounts. They will also use these strategies to write their own eyewitness accounts. A good eyewitness account has the traits listed on Student page 10. Have one or more volunteers read aloud the traits and their descriptions.

Ask students to listen for these traits as you read aloud "The Great Circus Parade" on Student page 11.

Differentiating Instruction

English-Language Learners Preteach key words such as *knickers, tableau,* and *calliope*. After reading "The Great Circus Parade," help English-Language Learners understand the story by reviewing additional vocabulary and idioms with them. For example, tell students that a *drum troop* is "a group of people playing the drums." Continue reading the sentence and ask students to guess what *stirred up the crowd* means.

Using context clues is important for ELLs. On the board, write the sentence, *Magnificent bandwagons carried musicians playing grand old tunes.* Then have students guess the meaning of the sentence based on the context clues. Have students identify the words they are familiar with in order to figure out what the sentence means. Then have them guess what the meanings of the other words might be. Over time, ELLs will become more tolerant of not knowing every word in a story, and their confidence in interpreting text will increase.

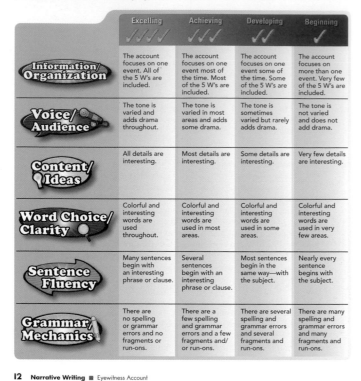

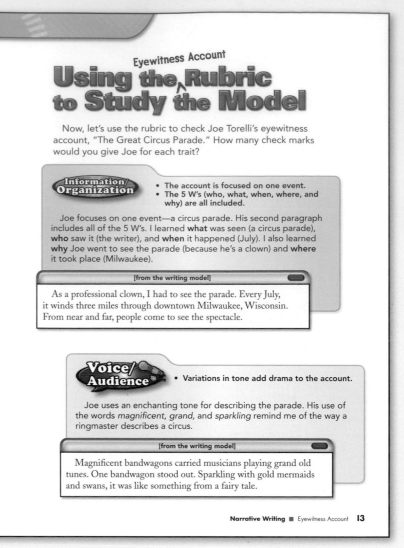

Using the Rubric
(Student page 12)

Explain that a rubric is a tool that helps you evaluate a piece of writing. It also helps you write because it tells what is expected in a piece of writing. The rubric on Student page 12 can be used to evaluate an eyewitness account. It is based on the traits for an eyewitness account on Student page 10.

Draw students' attention to the terms above each column: Excelling, Achieving, Developing, and Beginning. Briefly review the four descriptors that follow each trait. Note how strong writing skills are listed under the *Excelling* column, while weaknesses in writing are listed under the *Beginning* column.

Study the Model
(Student pages 13–15)

Explain that Student pages 13–15 show how the writing model on Student page 11 meets all six traits of the rubric. Read each section with the students. Have students look for other examples of each trait in the writing model.

Ask students how many check marks they would assign the writing model for each trait. Then, as a class, decide how you would rate the writing model overall.

Remind students to use the rubric as they write their own eyewitness account to be sure they are meeting all six writing traits.

Eyewitness Account

Content/Ideas
- The account contains many interesting details.

There are tons of details in Joe's writing. The exciting words in the first sentence make me want to read further to find out what happened. The descriptive details in the next sentence make me want to hear more about the parade itself.

[from the writing model]

Last week I was amazed, astounded, flabbergasted, and stupefied! I saw wild animals, dozens of circus wagons and bands, hundreds of horses, and thousands of people in costumes. I, Bongo the Clown, fell under the spell of the Great Circus Parade.

Word Choice/Clarity
- Colorful and interesting words make the meaning clear.

Interesting and colorful words help me picture what's happening. For example, the elephants don't just walk, they lumber. And the smoke doesn't just come out of the calliope, it belches out in plumes. I think Joe's use of description is great!

[from the writing model]

At the end of the parade were lumbering elephants and a steam calliope. Belching out plumes of smoke and hooting old-time melodies, the calliope bid farewell to the satisfied crowd.

Sentence Fluency
- Different sentence beginnings make the account lively.

Joe uses many different sentence patterns to make the writing flow. I think the changes give the writing energy.

[from the writing model]

Most splendid were the tableau wagons. Filled with carved and painted wooden figures, they are historical scenes on wheels. A woman dressed as Cleopatra rode a tableau pulled by camels. A two-headed green dragon roared from the top of a tableau that celebrated the age of knights and castles.

Notice how Joe uses a vivid phrase to begin the first sentence and an interesting clause to begin the second. See how the next two sentences start with the subject? I like the change in sentence patterns because I don't feel bored by the writing.

Grammar/Mechanics
- Spelling, punctuation, and capitalization are correct. There are no sentence fragments or run-on sentences.

I went back and checked Joe's account to see if there were any mistakes. There aren't any sentence fragments or run-ons because every sentence has a subject and a verb. None of the words are misspelled, and all of the sentences are capitalized and punctuated correctly.

[from the writing model]

The clowns were funny, but I was more impressed by the historic circus wagons. Each one showed off a dazzling color scheme. As the wheels turned, yellow and orange webbing between the spokes swirled like sunbursts.

My Turn!

I'm going to write an eyewitness account of something that I have seen. I'll follow the rubric and use good writing strategies. Read on to see how I do it!

Differentiating Instruction

Support To help students understand tone, ask them to listen as you describe the same event using two different tones. For example, talk about hearing the stairs creak in your home using a frightened, fearful tone, and then again in a humorous tone that conveys how you feel about your quirky stairs. Help students identify words that indicate different tones in stories about the same thing.

Writing an Eyewitness Account

Prewriting Gather Information

Information/Organization The account is focused on one event.

Writing Strategy Choose an incident and make notes on what I saw and heard.

I've been thinking about my topic ever since my teacher said we were going to write an eyewitness account. I live on a ranch in Arizona, so there's always a lot going on. I could write about the first time I saw a calf being born, or maybe the time the ranch flooded. But I think I'll write about the rodeo I saw last summer in Cody, Wyoming. It was so exciting that I know my readers will love hearing about it!

My Notes on the Cody Stampede Rodeo
- ✔ every year during July 1–4, in Cody, Wyoming
- ✔ smells like animal sweat and dust
- ✔ noisy: announcer, crowd cheering, buzzers, animals banging against fences
- ✔ Grand Entry parade: flag colors, 4th of July
- ✔ timed events: calf roping, barrel racing—fast cowgirl event
- ✔ bulldogging (steer wrestling): invented in early 1900s by Will Pickett, an African American cowboy
- ✔ rough stock events: bareback, saddle bronc, bull riding— 8 seconds and one hand
- ✔ rodeo clowns: protect bull riders from bulls
- ✔ pickup men: protect bronc riders from broncs
- ✔ winners get prize money and rodeo buckle

Practice!

Now it's your turn. Choose an event that you witnessed. Gather information by making notes on what you saw.

Prewriting Organize Ideas

Information/Organization The 5 W's (who, what, when, where, and why) are all included.

Writing Strategy Make a 5 W's Chart to organize my notes.

Writer's Term
5 W's Chart
A **5 W's Chart** organizes information according to what happened, who was there, why it happened, when it happened, and where it happened.

The rubric says that for a good eyewitness account, it's important to include the 5 W's. A 5 W's Chart will help me organize my notes and keep me from forgetting important information.

 Chart

What happened? Buffalo Bill Cody Stampede Rodeo, bronc rider bucked high, bull rider thrown over horns, sharpshooter act

Who was there? my dad and I, cowboys and cowgirls, crowd, rodeo announcers and judges, clowns, animals, sharpshooter

Why did it happen? so cowboys and cowgirls can show off their skills and entertain people

When did it happen? July 1–4 last summer (and annually)

Where did it happen? Cody, Wyoming

Practice!

Now it's your turn. Organize your ideas by using your notes to make a 5 W's Chart.

Reflect
How did I do? Did I include each one of the 5 W's on my chart?

Prewriting

(Student pages 16–17)

Ask if any of the students have gone to a public event lately, such as a festival or parade. If so, they might choose to write about that experience, just as Marco has chosen to write about the excitement of witnessing a rodeo.

Have the students go through each item in Marco's notes and identify whether it relates to the who, what, when, where, or why of his story.

Point out that writing can be organized in many ways, and one way is organizing the information into a 5 W's Chart. Using a 5 W's Chart will ensure that students get all the important information in their stories.

Differentiating Instruction

Enrichment Challenge students to take a newspaper article and put the information from the article into a 5 W's Chart. Point out that news stories typically include the 5 W's in them.

Enrichment Have your students create a lead paragraph for an eyewitness account by using information from a 5 W's Chart. First, create a 5 W's Chart on the board with information about a fictional event. Have student volunteers provide the information for each of the 5 W's. Once the 5 W's Chart is complete, have each of the students write an introductory paragraph to an eyewitness account using the information on the board. Choose volunteers to read their paragraphs aloud.

WORK with a PARTNER
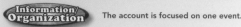
Have students select an event that they have witnessed to share. Then ask them to gather information by jotting down their own notes about it, just as Marco did. Have students read their notes to a writing partner.

More Practice!

For more practice with these writing strategies, you may wish to have students use the Strategy Practice Book. See the appendix for annotated Strategy Practice Book pages.

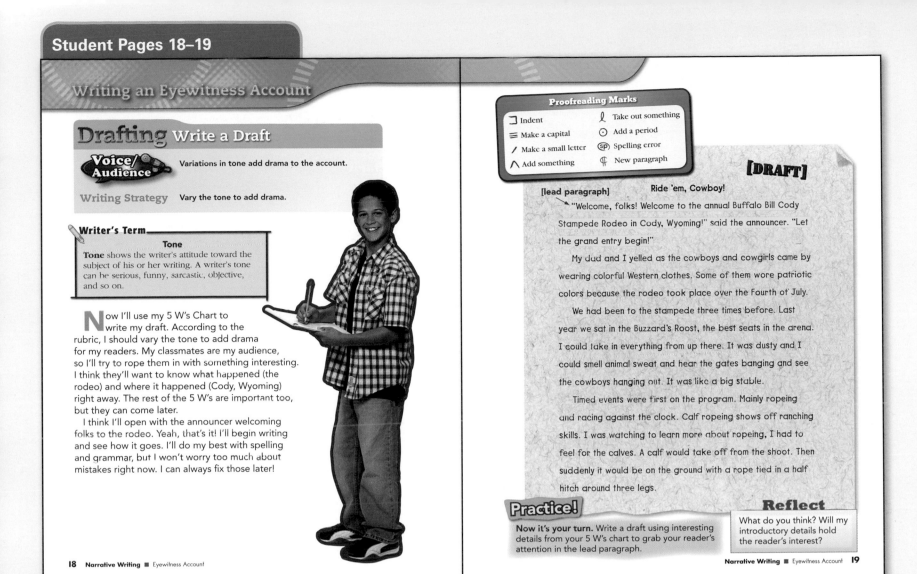

Drafting
(Student pages 18–19)

Explain that writing a draft allows writers to get their ideas on paper without having to worry about making mistakes.

Read the information about tone in the "Writer's Term" on Student page 18 with the students. Then read Marco's draft on Student page 19 together. Ask how he uses tone to add drama to his writing. Have students explain why they felt the beginning was interesting or not. Have students identify which details from the 5 W's Chart Marco chose to use in his beginning and how they helped him set the tone.

Point out that Marco refers to the rubric as he writes. Encourage students to get in the habit of using the rubrics to help guide their own writing.

Have students use the information from their 5 W's Chart to write a draft for their eyewitness accounts. Remind them to select interesting details from their 5 W's Chart to use in their beginnings.

Writing Across the Curriculum

Social Studies Marco writes about going to the rodeo. Explain that the rodeo has been a popular sport in America for many years and that the term *rodeo* is actually a form of a Spanish term that means "to surround or round up." Encourage students to learn more about the history of the rodeo and about the history of Buffalo Bill Cody. Divide the class into two groups, and have one group look into the history of the rodeo. Have the other group study the history of Buffalo Bill Cody. Provide time for student volunteers from each group to share what they learned with the class.

Writing an Eyewitness Account

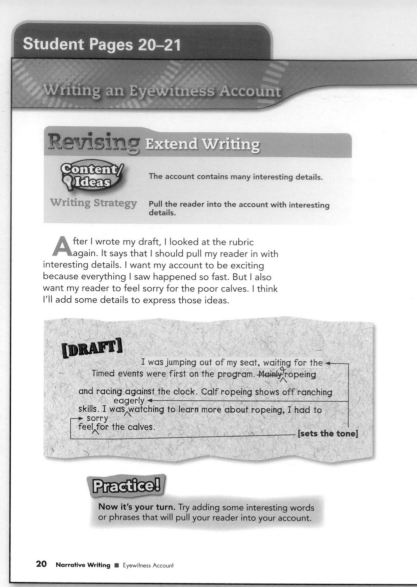

Revising Extend Writing

Content/Ideas The account contains many interesting details.

Writing Strategy Pull the reader into the account with interesting details.

After I wrote my draft, I looked at the rubric again. It says that I should pull my reader in with interesting details. I want my account to be exciting because everything I saw happened so fast. But I also want my reader to feel sorry for the poor calves. I think I'll add some details to express those ideas.

[DRAFT]

I was jumping out of my seat, waiting for the
Timed events were first on the program. ~~Mainly~~ roping
eagerly
and racing against the clock. Calf roping shows off ranching
sorry
skills. I was watching to learn more about roping, I had to
feel for the calves.
[sets the tone]

Practice!

Now it's your turn. Try adding some interesting words or phrases that will pull your reader into your account.

20 **Narrative Writing** ■ Eyewitness Account

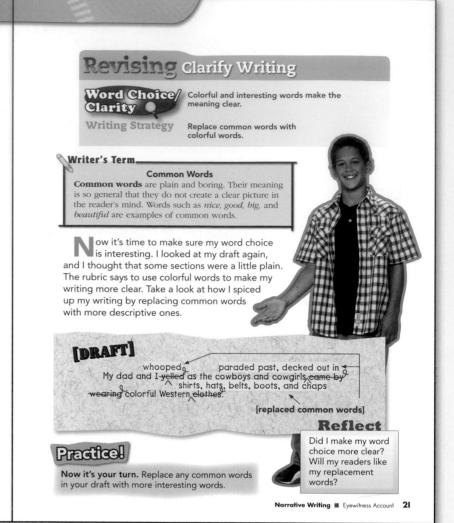

Revising Clarify Writing

Word Choice/Clarity Colorful and interesting words make the meaning clear.

Writing Strategy Replace common words with colorful words.

Writer's Term

Common Words
Common words are plain and boring. Their meaning is so general that they do not create a clear picture in the reader's mind. Words such as *nice, good, big,* and *beautiful* are examples of common words.

Now it's time to make sure my word choice is interesting. I looked at my draft again, and I thought that some sections were a little plain. The rubric says to use colorful words to make my writing more clear. Take a look at how I spiced up my writing by replacing common words with more descriptive ones.

[DRAFT]

whooped   paraded past, decked out in
My dad and I ~~yelled~~ as the cowboys and cowgirls ~~came by~~
shirts, hats, belts, boots, and chaps
~~wearing~~ colorful Western ~~clothes.~~
[replaced common words]

Reflect
Did I make my word choice more clear? Will my readers like my replacement words?

Practice!

Now it's your turn. Replace any common words in your draft with more interesting words.

Narrative Writing ■ Eyewitness Account 21

Revising

(Student pages 20–21)

Write the sentence *I waited for the bus* on the board. To show students how interesting details can pull the reader into their writing, write below that sentence, *Pacing back and forth, I waited eagerly for the bus to round the corner.* Ask students to determine how the added words in the second sentence made the writing more interesting. Invite students to suggest a variety of ways to rewrite the first sentence to grab a reader's attention. Review with students the ways Marco revised his draft to make his writing more interesting. Have students look for places in their eyewitness accounts where they can add words or phrases to create more drama.

Review the "Writer's Term" box on Student page 21 with the students. Have students study the draft paragraph on Student page 21 and identify the words that Marco added to make his writing more colorful. Review the use of proofreading marks with the students.

Have students check their drafts to see where they can make their word choices more colorful.

Differentiating Instruction

Enrichment To further understand tone, have students select a paragraph from a book, magazine, or newspaper and identify the tone used in the writing. Have them identify words or phrases in the paragraph that create the tone. Have student volunteers read their paragraphs aloud and encourage other students to determine the tone of the paragraph.

Support To help students identify common words in their writing that should be replaced with more colorful terms, have them underline the verbs in their draft. If they notice that many of the verbs they used are common verbs such as *went, came, saw, spoke, told,* etc., ask them to come up with verbs or phrases that are less common and more exciting. Ask students to reflect on how the change affected the sentence. Did it make things more clear?

Writing an Eyewitness Account

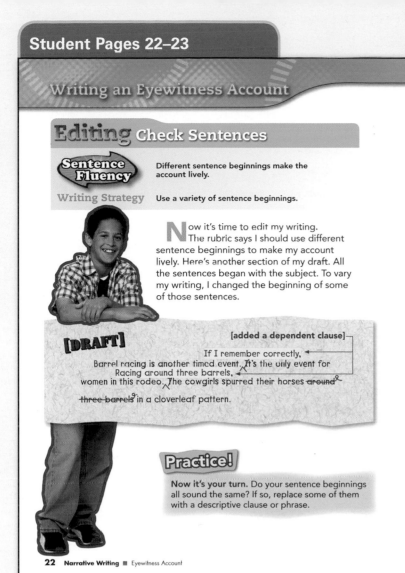

Editing Check Sentences

Sentence Fluency

Different sentence beginnings make the account lively.

Writing Strategy Use a variety of sentence beginnings.

Now it's time to edit my writing. The rubric says I should use different sentence beginnings to make my account lively. Here's another section of my draft. All the sentences began with the subject. To vary my writing, I changed the beginning of some of those sentences.

[DRAFT]

[added a dependent clause]

If I remember correctly,
Barrel racing is another timed event. It's the only event for
Racing around three barrels,
women in this rodeo. The cowgirls spurred their horses ~~around~~

~~three barrels~~ in a cloverleaf pattern.

Practice!

Now it's your turn. Do your sentence beginnings all sound the same? If so, replace some of them with a descriptive clause or phrase.

22 **Narrative Writing** ■ Eyewitness Account

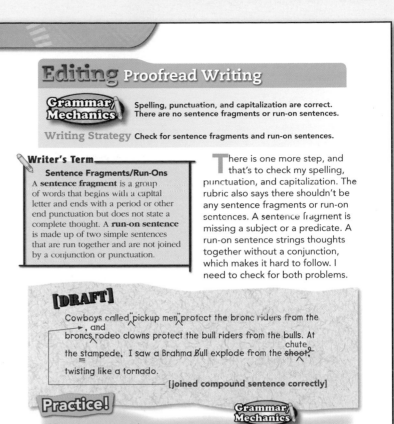

Editing Proofread Writing

Grammar Mechanics Spelling, punctuation, and capitalization are correct. There are no sentence fragments or run-on sentences.

Writing Strategy Check for sentence fragments and run-on sentences.

Writer's Term

Sentence Fragments/Run-Ons
A **sentence fragment** is a group of words that begins with a capital letter and ends with a period or other end punctuation but does not state a complete thought. A **run-on sentence** is made up of two simple sentences that are run together and are not joined by a conjunction or punctuation.

There is one more step, and that's to check my spelling, punctuation, and capitalization. The rubric also says there shouldn't be any sentence fragments or run-on sentences. A sentence fragment is missing a subject or a predicate. A run-on sentence strings thoughts together without a conjunction, which makes it hard to follow. I need to check for both problems.

[DRAFT]

Cowboys called "pickup men" protect the bronc riders from the
, and
broncs, rodeo clowns protect the bull riders from the bulls. At
chute
the stampede, I saw a Brahma Bull explode from the ~~shoot~~,

twisting like a tornado.

[joined compound sentence correctly]

Practice!

Now it's your turn. Edit your draft for spelling, punctuation, and capitalization. Be sure to fix sentence fragments and run-ons.

Grammar Mechanics

For more practice fixing fragments and run-ons, use the exercises on the next two pages.

Reflect

I worked hard to replace plain sentence beginnings with interesting phrases. I also tried to avoid any fragments or run-ons. Did it make my writing more lively?

Narrative Writing ■ Eyewitness Account 23

Editing

(Student pages 22–23)

Write the following sentences on the board: *The rain stopped. The dog barked. He drove the car.* Ask students what makes the structure of these sentences similar. **They all start with the subject.** Explain to students that a story that contained similar sentence beginnings throughout would be dull. Especially with an eyewitness account, where students are asked to explain events as they happened, it's easy to fall into this trap.

Have students come up with ways to change the structure of the sentences on the board by beginning them with dependent clauses. **Possible reponses: All at once, the rain stopped. With one hand on the wheel and the other on his cell phone, he drove the car.**

Have students begin checking the sentences in their eyewitness accounts to ensure that they have included a variety of sentence beginnings.

If some of your students are having trouble identifying sentence fragments or run-on sentences, you may wish to teach the Mini-Lesson on page 34 of this Teacher Edition. Then, have students complete the exercises on

pages 24–25 of their books. Review the answers and possible rewrites with them.

Have students begin checking their eyewitness accounts for sentence fragments and run-on sentences. Remind them of the importance of checking to be sure their spelling, punctuation, and capitalization are correct.

WORK with a PARTNER Have students swap their drafts with another student. Each student should read the other's eyewitness account to check for mistakes in sentence construction, spelling, punctuation, and capitalization.

Sentence Fragments and Run-ons

KNOW the RULE

A sentence that is missing a subject or a predicate is called a **fragment**.

Fragment: Looked forward to the rodeo.
(subject missing)

Fragment: A clown on the fence.
(predicate missing)

When you join two sentences as a **compound sentence**, put a comma followed by a conjunction between them. You can also join them with a semicolon. Sentences that are not joined correctly are called **run-ons**.

Run-on: Rodeo clowns look funny they take their work seriously.

Correct: Rodeo clowns look funny, but they take their work seriously.

Correct: Rodeo clowns look funny; they take their work seriously.

Practice the Rule

Correct each sentence fragment and run-on below. Then write the complete sentences on a separate piece of paper.

1. Gripping the reins tightly.
2. Bulls with names like Turbo and Jackhammer.
3. Streaked from the chute like a shot from a cannon.
4. The announcer named the winners the crowd cheered for each one.
5. Some people protest the use of animals in rodeos rodeo animals are treated well.

Apply the Rule

Read the following paragraphs. Correct any sentence fragments or run-ons, and rewrite the paragraphs on a separate sheet of paper.

"Buffalo Bill" Cody's Wild West Show spread the myth of the West for more than 30 years. The show began in 1882. Reenactments of stagecoach robberies and buffalo hunts. Cody died in 1917, his last words were said to be, "Let my show go on!"

In true cowboy spirit, Montie Montana Jr. did just that! Montana brought Buffalo Bill's Wild West Show back to life and I'm sure Buffalo Bill would have approved. In fact, has been to twenty-six different countries because of his skill at trick roping, he has starred in the Wild West Show, along with many other TV shows, radio programs, and movies.

Has spent his whole life working in rodeos, has always helped to promote and preserve Western culture. By the age of three, Montana was in his first show and he still does them today. Even wants to have a reunion in Buffalo Bill Cody's hometown of LeClaire, Iowa. Born in 1935, he is still alive today. It's just too bad never met Montana. I bet they would have made a great team!

Grammar Mechanics Mini-Lesson

(Student pages 24–25)

Sentence Fragments and Run-Ons

Remind students that every sentence must contain a subject and a predicate and express a complete thought.

Write the following on the board: *Painting walls messy chore.*

Ask students if this is a complete sentence or a sentence fragment. **a sentence fragment** What is the fragment missing? **a predicate** Ask volunteers for suggestions on how to make the fragment a complete sentence. **Possible response: Painting walls can be a messy chore.**

Explain to students that run-on sentences are two simple sentences that run together and are not joined by a conjunction or punctuation.

Write the following on the board: Hybrid cars are more fuel efficient engines rely on both gasoline and electric power.

Ask students if this is a compound sentence or a run-on sentence. **a run-on sentence** What is the sentence missing? **a conjunction or semicolon** Ask volunteers for sug-gestions on how to make the run-on a complete sentence. **Possible response: Hybrid cars are more fuel efficient; their engines rely on both gasoline and electric power.**

Answers for Practice the Rule

1. **The nervous rider was gripping the reins tightly.**
2. **At the rodeo, there were bulls with names like Turbo and Jackhammer.**
3. **The bull streaked from the chute like a shot from a cannon.**
4. **The announcer named the winners, and the crowd cheered for each one.**
5. **Some people protest the use of animals in rodeos, but rodeo animals are treated well.**

Answers for Apply the Rule

"Buffalo Bill" Cody's Wild West Show spread the myth of the West for more than 30 years. The show began in 1882, and it featured reenactments of stagecoach robberies and buffalo hunts. When Cody died in 1917, his last words were said to be, "Let my show go on!"

In true cowboy spirit, Montie Montana Jr. did just that!

(Answers continue on page 35.)

Writing an Eyewitness Account

Publishing Share Writing

Add my account to a class journal.

My eyewitness account is done! Now it's time to publish it. There are a lot of ways to publish my work. I could share it with my writing partner or submit it for publication to a newspaper or a Web site, but I think I'll add mine to our class journal. Before publishing my work, I want to read through it one last time to make sure it includes all of the items on this checklist.

My Checklist

✓ The 5 W's are all included.

✓ There are lots of interesting and accurate details.

✓ The tone adds to the drama.

✓ Common words are replaced with descriptive words.

✓ Sentences are varied.

✓ Capitalization, punctuation, and spelling are all correct. There are no fragments or run-ons.

Practice!

Now it's your turn. Check your eyewitness account against your own checklist. Then make a final draft to publish.

26 Narrative Writing ■ Eyewitness Account

RIDE 'EM, COWBOY!

by Marco

"Welcome, folks! Welcome to the annual Buffalo Bill Cody Stampede Rodeo in Cody, Wyoming!" the announcer's voice blared from the loudspeakers. "Let the Grand Entry begin!"

My dad and I whooped as the cowboys and cowgirls paraded past, decked out in colorful Western shirts, hats, belts, boots, and chaps. Some wore red, white, and blue because the rodeo took place over the Fourth of July.

We had been to the Stampede three times before, but this time we sat in the Buzzard's Roost, the best seats in the arena. From up there, I could take in the entire scene. I could smell animal sweat, hear the gates banging, and see the cowboys hanging out. It was like a big, dusty stable.

Timed events were first on the program. I was jumping out of my seat, waiting for the roping and racing against the clock. Calf roping shows off ranching skills. I was eagerly watching to learn more about roping, but I had to feel sorry for the calves. One second a calf was running from the chute, and less than 30 seconds later it was on the ground bawling, with a rope tied in a half hitch around three legs.

Narrative Writing ■ Eyewitness Account 27

(Answers continued from page 34.)

Montana brought Buffalo Bill's Wild West Show back to life, and I'm sure Buffalo Bill would have approved. In fact, Montana has been to twenty-six different countries because of his skill at trick roping. He has also starred in the Wild West Show, along with many other TV shows, radio programs, and movies.

Montana has spent his whole life working in rodeos and has always helped to promote and preserve Western culture. By the age of three, Montana was in his first show, and he still does them today. He even wants to have a reunion in Buffalo Bill's hometown of LeClaire, Iowa. Born in 1935, he is still alive today. It's just too bad Buffalo Bill never met Montana. I bet they would have made a great team!

✓ For more practice with grammar/mechanics skills, see Zaner-Bloser's *G.U.M.* materials.

Publishing

(Student pages 26–27)

Have students review the ways Marco thought about publishing his work. Ask them what they think of Marco's choice to include his eyewitness account in the class journal. Remind the class that even though Marco has edited his draft, he still takes one more opportunity to read through it again before he publishes it.

Have students make a checklist to check their own eyewitness accounts. Aside from including their stories in the class journal, ask students who else might enjoy reading their eyewitness accounts. Encourage them to give or send copies to friends and relatives who would enjoy reading about their experiences.

Barrel racing is another timed event. If I remember correctly, it's the only event for women in this rodeo. Racing around three barrels, the cowgirls spurred their horses in a cloverleaf pattern. Skillfully, they avoided knocking down any barrels.

Almost 100 years ago, an African American cowboy named Will Pickett invented steer wrestling—my favorite timed event. Leaning off the side of his horse, he seized a steer by its horns and slid to the ground. Then he dug in his boot heels and twisted the steer over onto its side. Pickett called it "bulldogging." At the Stampede, the steers were dropping like flies.

Rough stock is the tough stuff: bareback riding, saddle bronc riding, and bull riding. To qualify for the next round in rough stock events, a cowboy has to hang on to a bucking beast with one hand and hold out for at least eight seconds. The first bareback rider flew so high you could see daylight between him and the horse. Yee haw! If the rider's free hand touches anything, the judges disqualify him. Then the announcer always remarks, "Let's give him a hand, folks. It may be all he's taking home tonight."

Rodeo is downright dangerous. Broken bones, cuts and bruises, pulled muscles, and concussions are common. Riders are sometimes trampled. Cowboys called pickup men protect the bronc riders from the broncs, and rodeo clowns protect the bull riders from the bulls. At the Stampede, I saw a Brahma bull explode from the chute, twisting like a tornado. The rider flipped over the bull's horns and flopped at its feet. In a flash, a red-nosed rodeo clown distracted the bull, and the cowboy sprang up and scrambled over the fence to safety.

The Stampede always has a famous specialty act. One year, it was a trained buffalo. Last summer, it was a sharpshooter who also did tricks with a bullwhip and a lasso. He snapped a target from his own mouth with the whip! Crrrrack!

On the last night, the winners got to take home prize money and a rodeo trophy: a belt buckle. I took home a new rodeo poster and a saddlebag of memories.

Reflect

What do you think? Did I use all the traits of a good eyewitness account in my writing? Check it against the rubric. Don't forget to use the rubric to check your own eyewitness account.

Establishing a Cooperative Atmosphere
by Ken Stewart, *Master Teacher*

An important component of the cooperative classroom is cooperative learning groups. Follow these simple steps to give students experiences in becoming cooperative learners.

1. Post five easy-to-follow classroom rules:

   Rule 1: Always do your best work.

   Rule 2: When you think you have done your best, challenge yourself to make it better.

   Rule 3: Stay on task and be responsible for your own actions.

   Rule 4: When working in a group, use a 12-inch voice. (Speak softly.)

   Rule 5: Share all information, and respect others' ideas. If one member of your group understands the lesson, all the members should understand.

2. Create mini-lessons that give your students lots of opportunities to use cooperative learning in a variety of ways.

3. When introducing a cooperative learning style, allow at least five minutes for the whole class to process the positives and negatives of the experience. Offer encouragement for positive behaviors; allow students to suggest improvements.

4. Create a fun activity to allow students to process why working on a team is often better than working individually.

Ways to Publish an Eyewitness Account

As you decide how to publish your work, make sure you think about who will be reading it. Then pick the best way to share it. Here are some ideas for publishing your eyewitness account.

✓ **Read your account to your writing partner. Then discuss his or her reaction.**

✓ **Submit your account to a local newspaper or magazine that publishes student work.**

✓ Research and find a Web site suitable to your topic. Then submit your work.

✓ Take your account home and share it with family and friends.

✓ Include your eyewitness account as part of a multimedia presentation to the class.

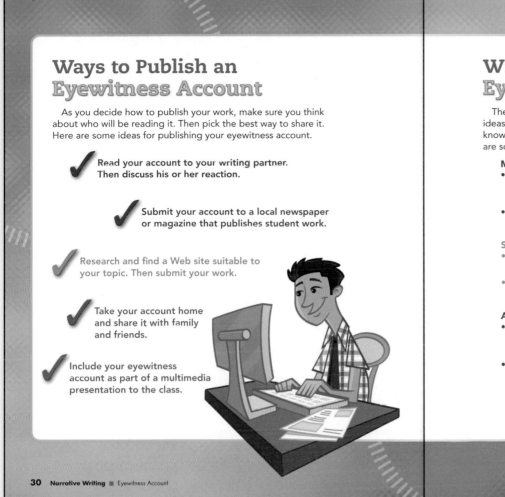

30 **Narrative Writing** ■ Eyewitness Account

Writing Across the Content Areas Eyewitness Account

The subjects you study in school can give you many ideas for writing. Just pick a subject, and before you know it, you'll think of a topic that relates to it. Here are some examples.

Math
• Write about a time when you saw something you wanted to buy and had to figure out how you could purchase it.
• Report on a sporting event in which the final score was the end-of-game tiebreaker.

Social Studies
• Write about the first time you saw a historical place or monument.
• Report on a time you saw people working together for a good cause.

Art and/or Music
• Describe a show or event you've seen in which music and/or dance was the main focus.
• Report on a visit to an art or historical museum near where you live.

Narrative Writing ■ Eyewitness Account **31**

Ways to Publish
(Student page 30)

Read and discuss with students the different publishing options on Student page 30. Encourage students to explore these options further and possibly to submit their eyewitness accounts using one of these suggestions. Ask for student volunteers to provide a description of their eyewitness accounts and to suggest appropriate Web sites that might want to feature their stories.

Writing Across the Content Areas
(Student page 31)

Remind your students that writing is not just for English or language arts class. There are many other subjects that contain ideas, characters, and events that students may want to write about. Have students consider using one of the content areas on Student page 31 to write another eyewitness account. Students may wish to consult with other teachers for more ideas on writing in their content areas.

Historical Episode Overview

Students will learn how to write a historical episode in this chapter. They will learn the different elements of a historical episode—setting, characters, accuracy, and interest—and some reasons for writing a historical episode. Then, students will compare a model writing sample against a historical episode rubric.

After that, students will again join the student guide as he goes through the writing stages for a historical episode, including prewriting, drafting, revising, editing, and publishing. Throughout the chapter, students will be directed to practice the strategies in their own writing. First, they will choose an interesting historical event and gather information about the event. Students will use a Story Map to organize their ideas, and then write a draft using their Story Map as a guide. They will revise their drafts by explaining difficult words in their stories and then reordering events in a logical fashion. Next, students will edit their stories by varying the length and structure of sentences. They will also edit their drafts to be sure they have used the correct spelling, punctuation, and capitalization and that they have punctuated their quotations correctly. Once they have completed their final drafts, they will think about how to publish their work.

You may wish to send to families the School-Home Connection Letter for this chapter, located at the end of this unit in the Teacher Edition.

Historical Episode Writing Traits

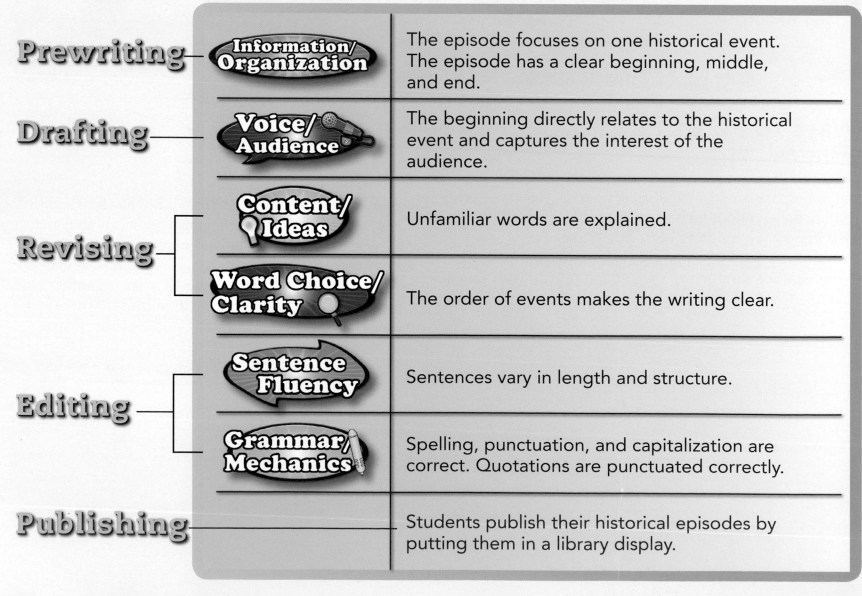

Prewriting	Information/Organization	The episode focuses on one historical event. The episode has a clear beginning, middle, and end.
Drafting	Voice/Audience	The beginning directly relates to the historical event and captures the interest of the audience.
Revising	Content/Ideas	Unfamiliar words are explained.
	Word Choice/Clarity	The order of events makes the writing clear.
Editing	Sentence Fluency	Sentences vary in length and structure.
	Grammar/Mechanics	Spelling, punctuation, and capitalization are correct. Quotations are punctuated correctly.
Publishing		Students publish their historical episodes by putting them in a library display.

Historical Episode Time Management

WEEK 1

	Day 1	Day 2	Day 3	Day 4	Day 5
Learning Objectives	Students will: • learn the components of a historical episode.	Students will: • learn how to gather information for a historical episode.	Students will: • practice gathering information for their own historical episodes.	Students will: • learn how to make a Story Map to organize their notes.	Students will: • practice organizing their own notes to make a Story Map.
Activities	• Discuss the elements and traits of a historical episode (Student pages 32–34). • Use the rubric to study the model (Student pages 35–41).	• Read and discuss **Prewriting: Gather Information** (Student page 42).	• Brainstorm ideas and choose a historical episode to share. • Gather information and take notes on historical episodes.	• Read and discuss **Prewriting: Organize Ideas** (Student page 43).	• Use notes to fill in the Story Map.

WEEK 2

	Day 1	Day 2	Day 3	Day 4	Day 5
Learning Objectives	Students will: • learn how to introduce the historical event to the reader in a clear and interesting way.	Students will: • practice writing their own drafts.	Students will: • learn how to explain unfamiliar words to their readers.	Students will: • practice adding words or phrases that will explain any difficult vocabulary.	Students will: • learn how to reorder events so that they are logically placed.
Activities	• Read and discuss **Drafting: Write a Draft** (Student page 44).	• Use their Story Map to write a draft. • Make the beginning clear so that readers are placed in the historical period.	• Read and discuss **Revising: Extend Writing** (Student page 46).	• Add words or phrases that will explain any difficult vocabulary.	• Read and discuss **Revising: Clarify Writing** (Student page 47).

WEEK 3

	Day 1	Day 2	Day 3	Day 4	Day 5
Learning Objectives	Students will: • practice reordering events to make their writing clearer.	Students will: • learn that varying the length and structure of sentences can make the writing interesting.	Students will: • learn how to correctly punctuate quotations.	Students will: • practice editing their drafts for spelling, punctuation, and capitalization.	Students will: • learn different ways to publish their historical episodes.
Activities	• Reread drafts to see if sentences are in logical order. • Rearrange any sentences that are not in logical order.	• Read and discuss **Editing: Check Sentences** (Student page 48). • Add descriptive clauses and new sentence patterns for variety.	• Read and discuss **Editing: Proofread Writing** (Student page 49). • Make sure quotations are punctuated correctly.	• Fix any spelling, punctuation, or capitalization errors in drafts. • Fix any quotation punctuation mistakes.	• Read and discuss **Publishing: Share Writing** (Student page 52).

* To complete the chapter in fewer days, teach the learning objectives and activities for two days in one day.

This planning chart, correlated to your state's writing standards, is available on-line at http://www.zaner-bloser.com/sfw.

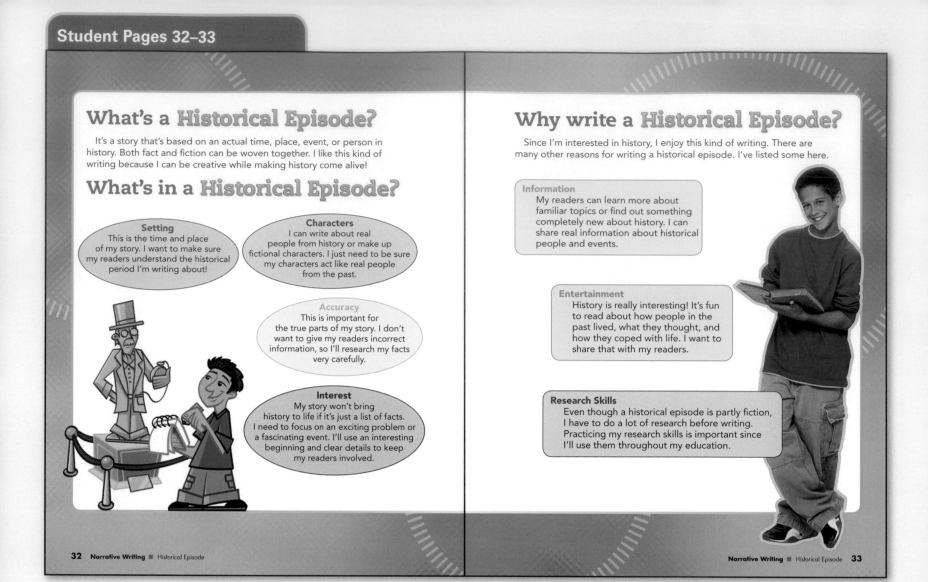

What's a Historical Episode?

It's a story that's based on an actual time, place, event, or person in history. Both fact and fiction can be woven together. I like this kind of writing because I can be creative while making history come alive!

What's in a Historical Episode?

Setting
This is the time and place of my story. I want to make sure my readers understand the historical period I'm writing about!

Characters
I can write about real people from history or make up fictional characters. I just need to be sure my characters act like real people from the past.

Accuracy
This is important for the true parts of my story. I don't want to give my readers incorrect information, so I'll research my facts very carefully.

Interest
My story won't bring history to life if it's just a list of facts. I need to focus on an exciting problem or a fascinating event. I'll use an interesting beginning and clear details to keep my readers involved.

Why write a Historical Episode?

Since I'm interested in history, I enjoy this kind of writing. There are many other reasons for writing a historical episode. I've listed some here.

Information
My readers can learn more about familiar topics or find out something completely new about history. I can share real information about historical people and events.

Entertainment
History is really interesting! It's fun to read about how people in the past lived, what they thought, and how they coped with life. I want to share that with my readers.

Research Skills
Even though a historical episode is partly fiction, I have to do a lot of research before writing. Practicing my research skills is important since I'll use them throughout my education.

32 **Narrative Writing** ■ Historical Episode

Narrative Writing ■ Historical Episode 33

Define the Genre
(Student page 32)
Historical Episode

Discuss what comprises a historical episode with students. Ask a student volunteer to name an important historical event. Have him or her share what he or she knows about what happened and who was involved. Explain that the student is describing a historical episode. In this type of narrative writing, the writer tells the story of an actual historical event, weaving together fact and fiction.

Elements of the Genre
Historical Episode

Read and discuss each of the elements of a historical episode with the students. Refer back to the historical episode shared by the student volunteer, and have the students determine how that story relates to each of these elements.

Authentic Writing
(Student page 33)
Historical Episode

Ask students what reasons they can think of for writing a historical account. Read and discuss with students the reasons on Student page 33. Explain that the tone and focus of their writing will be shaped by their reasons for writing a historical episode. A writer who would like to share information about the past with his or her readers will get details and information about the past that will educate the readers. A writer who wishes to entertain will look for the most interesting details and focus on how characters lived in the past. Point out, too, that one reason for writing a historical account—practicing research skills—enables students to practice a skill that they will be using throughout their education. Ask students to think about reasons they would write a historical episode. Remind them that these reasons will help set the tone of their stories.

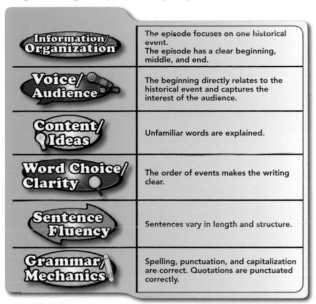

Historical Episode Writing Traits

What makes a good historical episode? How can I write about history in a way my readers will find interesting? I'll use the six traits of good writing to help me write my story.

Information/ Organization	The episode focuses on one historical event. The episode has a clear beginning, middle, and end.
Voice/ Audience	The beginning directly relates to the historical event and captures the interest of the audience.
Content/ Ideas	Unfamiliar words are explained.
Word Choice/ Clarity	The order of events makes the writing clear.
Sentence Fluency	Sentences vary in length and structure.
Grammar/ Mechanics	Spelling, punctuation, and capitalization are correct. Quotations are punctuated correctly.

I can use Kim Lee's historical episode on the next page as a model for my own writing. Let's see how Kim used these traits to help her write.

Historical Episode Model

Conquest of the Stratosphere

by Kim Lee

Setting and characters

Two men sat across from each other on a train chugging through the Swiss Alps. They had met only an hour earlier, but they were enjoying each other's company. Auguste Piccard, the elder one, was a long-limbed professor. A wreath of wild hair encircled his balding crown. Small round glasses perched on his long slender nose. His mustache wiggled as he talked. Paul Kipfer, the younger man, had sandy hair and soft blue eyes. He didn't talk much. Instead, he listened intently as Auguste described his research on cosmic rays in the atmosphere.

After a pause in the conversation, Auguste asked Paul, "Are you married?"

"No," Paul replied.   *Interesting beginning →*

"Good," Auguste said eagerly. "Are you engaged?"

"No," said Paul, puzzled by Auguste's questions.

"Ah, wonderful!" Auguste exclaimed. "Would you like to go up into the stratosphere in a balloon with me? We could study the cosmic rays!"

In 1930, this was a dangerous proposal. The stratosphere begins 6 to 8 miles above Earth's surface. It is deadly cold and lacks enough oxygen for survival. Paul knew that no one had ever been up there and returned alive. Balloons had only open-air baskets. Even airplanes did not yet have pressurized cabins to hold in oxygen.   *Illustrates historical period*

Auguste knew it was risky, too. That was why he wanted an assistant without a wife and family. Auguste's family accepted his determination to make the hazardous trip. Paul also felt the force of that determination. He listened to Auguste's plan. By the time the train arrived in Brussels, Belgium, where Auguste lived, Paul had agreed to be his assistant. *Setting*

Writing Traits

(Student pages 34–35)

Historical Episode

Ask students if any of them have seen the movie *Pocahontas*. Point out that the movie is a historical account of the life of the Native American Pocahontas. Explain that though the story is fictionalized, it is also based on history. This is the same approach students will take when they write their historical episode.

Review with students the writing traits of a historical episode. Ask student volunteers to name historical events that might be used for a historical episode. Then explain that in a historical episode, the writing should be a complete story with a beginning, middle, and end.

Explain to students that they will be studying strategies for writing historical episodes. They will also be using these strategies to write their own historical episodes. Point out that a good historical episode will have the traits listed on Student page 34. Have one or more volunteers read aloud the traits and their descriptions.

Have students identify these traits as you read aloud "Conquest of the Stratosphere" on Student pages 35–37.

Auguste took care of every detail. The giant balloon was made of rubberized cotton. Attached to it was a pressurized cabin. It consisted of an airtight aluminum sphere with portholes as windows. It included a system that recycled oxygen so it would last longer. No lightweight crash helmets ← were available in those days, so Auguste created some out of upside-down sewing baskets. He added seat cushions for padding. Illustrates historical period

Accurate historical facts On the morning of May 27, 1931, Paul and Auguste prepared for take-off in Augsburg, Germany. As the balloon was being inflated, Auguste imagined all he would learn on this scientific adventure. Suddenly, a gust of wind rolled the cabin off its platform, and it crashed to the ground. It had only slight damage, so the launch continued as scheduled.

A few minutes later, however, the men heard a hissing sound. The cabin was leaking air. Auguste patched the leak with petroleum jelly and waited with his fingers crossed.

Communication with the ground crew would be impossible. Radio was only in its infancy, and satellite technology was decades in the future. Like the early explorers, the scientists sailed alone into an uncharted world.

By afternoon, the balloon had safely risen nearly 10 miles, well into the stratosphere. Auguste and Paul made some observations and measurements. Then they prepared for their descent, but something went wrong. The ropes that release the gas from the balloon had become tangled. The two men were stuck in the stratosphere!

Hours passed. The sun's heat raised the temperature inside the cabin to ← over 90 degrees. Sweating, the men eyed the gauges on the oxygen tanks in their silver bubble. **Accurate historical facts**

Auguste was certain that at nightfall the air in the balloon would cool, and they would start to descend. Yet even after the sun went down, the balloon did not. Around 6:00 AM, Auguste wrote in his log, "We have oxygen left for only four hours."

In the meantime, people around the world waited for each day's newspaper to learn about the fate of the scientists. Readers were troubled by headlines that the balloon was out of control. In the midst of a worldwide economic depression, people craved hope and heroes.

Finally, the balloon started to float slowly down. Auguste and Paul landed the next night on top of a glacier—but where? They crawled from the cramped cabin. Unprepared for a freezing climate, they wrapped themselves in the balloon fabric to stay warm. At dawn, they picked their way down the ice slope. A rescue party soon caught up with them.

Shivering, Auguste asked a round man with a pointed wool hat, "Wh—wh—what country are we in?"

"Austria," the man answered. "We're near a village called Obergurgl."

Auguste Piccard and Paul Kipfer had spent 16 hours inside the sphere. They had ascended 51,775 feet, a height no one had reached before. Not only did they gather valuable scientific data, but they also proved that people could survive in pressurized cabins high above Earth. Their conquest of the stratosphere paved the way for future air and space travel. The publicity also established Obergurgl as a famous ski resort!

Differentiating Instruction

English-Language Learners To help students understand how context clues can provide explanations and definitions of unfamiliar words, work with them to identify other words in the writing model with which they are unfamiliar. Have them look for context clues within the sentence or in the surrounding text to try to come up with the meaning of the word. If they cannot determine the meaning, look up its definition with them. Make sure they understand the definition.

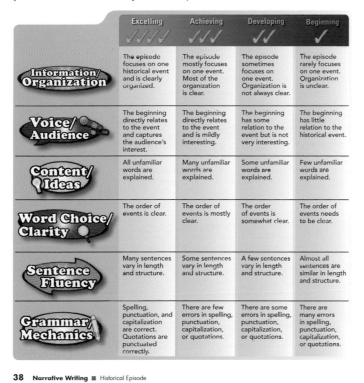

Historical Episode
Rubric

The traits of a good historical episode from page 34 have been used to make the rubric below. By using 1, 2, 3, or 4 check marks to judge each trait, you can decide how well any historical episode was written.

	Excelling ✓✓✓✓	Achieving ✓✓✓	Developing ✓✓	Beginning ✓
Information/Organization	The episode focuses on one historical event and is clearly organized.	The episode mostly focuses on one event. Most of the organization is clear.	The episode sometimes focuses on one event. Organization is not always clear.	The episode rarely focuses on one event. Organization is unclear.
Voice/Audience	The beginning directly relates to the event and captures the audience's interest.	The beginning directly relates to the event and is mildly interesting.	The beginning has some relation to the event but is not very interesting.	The beginning has little relation to the historical event.
Content/Ideas	All unfamiliar words are explained.	Many unfamiliar words are explained.	Some unfamiliar words are explained.	Few unfamiliar words are explained.
Word Choice/Clarity	The order of events is clear.	The order of events is mostly clear.	The order of events is somewhat clear.	The order of events needs to be clear.
Sentence Fluency	Many sentences vary in length and structure.	Some sentences vary in length and structure.	A few sentences vary in length and structure.	Almost all sentences are similar in length and structure.
Grammar/Mechanics	Spelling, punctuation, and capitalization are correct. Quotations are punctuated correctly.	There are few errors in spelling, punctuation, capitalization, or quotations.	There are some errors in spelling, punctuation, capitalization, or quotations.	There are many errors in spelling, punctuation, capitalization, or quotations.

38   **Narrative Writing** ■ Historical Episode

Historical Episode
Using the Rubric to Study the Model

Let's use the rubric to check Kim's historical episode, "Conquest of the Stratosphere." How many check marks would you give Kim for each trait?

Information/Organization
- The episode focuses on one historical event.
- The episode has a clear beginning, middle, and end.

Kim focuses on the historical event throughout the episode. The beginning, middle, and end of the story are all clearly written. Here's the part in the middle where Kim describes a problem during the launch.

[from the writing model]

As the balloon was being inflated, Auguste imagined all he would learn on this scientific adventure. Suddenly, a gust of wind rolled the cabin off its platform, and it crashed to the ground.

Voice/Audience
- The beginning directly relates to the historical event and captures the interest of the audience.

The writer uses an interesting and puzzling conversation to introduce the historical event and the characters involved. Remember this part?

[from the writing model]

After a pause in the conversation, Auguste asked Paul, "Are you married?"

"No," Paul replied.

"Good," Auguste said eagerly. "Are you engaged?"

"No," said Paul, puzzled by Auguste's questions.

"Ah, wonderful!" Auguste exclaimed. "Would you like to go up into the stratosphere in a balloon with me? We could study the cosmic rays!"

Narrative Writing ■ Historical Episode   39

Using the Rubric
(Student page 38)

Remind students that rubrics are helpful tools for evaluating writing. The rubric on Student page 38 shows the same traits that are outlined on Student page 34. Point out that a writer who included all of the writing traits found on Student page 34 would receive Excelling marks.

As an example, review with students the traits under each of the categories for Voice/Audience. Note that an Excelling score of four checks has a beginning that relates to the historical event and captures the audience's interest. Ask students if they felt that the "Conquest of the Stratosphere" should receive an Excelling mark for Voice/Audience based on this rubric.

Study the Model
(Student pages 39–41)

Read Student pages 39–41 with your students to compare the writing model to the rubric. As you review each of the traits, ask students as a group to determine how many check marks they would give the writer. Encourage students to explain their responses.

Ask students if they can find other examples for each trait in the writing model.

Finally, stress to students the importance of using the rubric when they write their own historical episodes.

Historical Episode

Content/Ideas
• Unfamiliar words are explained.

The writer does a good job explaining words such as *stratosphere* and *pressurized cabin*. That really helps me understand the story.

[from the writing model]

The stratosphere begins 6 to 8 miles above Earth's surface. It is deadly cold and lacks enough oxygen for survival.

[from the writing model]

The giant balloon was made of rubberized cotton. Attached to it was a pressurized cabin. It consisted of an airtight aluminum sphere with portholes as windows. It included a system that recycled oxygen so it would last longer.

Word Choice/Clarity
• The order of events makes the writing clear.

It is easy for me to understand a story when the events are in a logical order. Kim uses mostly chronological order—the time order of the events. See how each sentence tells what happened next?

[from the writing model]

By afternoon, the balloon had safely risen nearly 10 miles, well into the stratosphere. Auguste and Paul made some observations and measurements. Then they prepared for their descent, but something went wrong. The ropes that release the gas from the balloon had become tangled. The two men were stuck in the stratosphere!

Hours passed. The sun's heat raised the temperature inside the cabin to over 90 degrees. Sweating, the men eyed the gauges on the oxygen tanks in their silver bubble.

Sentence Fluency
• Sentences vary in length and structure.

Kim varies her sentences to make her writing flow and to keep it lively. Read the following paragraph. Do you see how Kim uses sentences of different lengths? Some of her sentences start with a subject, and others start with a clause. She even ends one sentence with a question!

[from the writing model]

Finally, the balloon started to float slowly down. Auguste and Paul landed the next night on top of a glacier—but where? They crawled from the cramped cabin. Unprepared for a freezing climate, they wrapped themselves in the balloon fabric to stay warm. At dawn, they picked their way down the ice slope. A rescue party soon caught up with them.

Grammar/Mechanics
• Spelling, punctuation, and capitalization are correct. Quotations are punctuated correctly.

I checked Kim's story for mistakes. None of the words are misspelled, and all of the sentences are capitalized and punctuated correctly. And Kim really knows how to use quotes. Every time a character speaks in this story, his exact words have quotation marks around them. The rest of the punctuation for each quotation is correct, too. Check it out!

[from the writing model]

Shivering, Auguste asked a round man with a pointed wool hat, "Wh—wh—what country are we in?"

"Austria," the man answered. "We're near a village called Obergurgl."

Now I'm going to use the rubric to help me write a historical episode. Read along and see how I do it.

Differentiating Instruction

Support To help your students understand the basic structure of the sample historical episode, organize the class into small groups. Have each group try to summarize the story "Conquest of the Stratosphere." Ask them to identify the story's beginning, middle, and end, as well as the historical event on which the story is centered.

Writing a Historical Episode

Prewriting Gather Information

Information/Organization The episode focuses on one historical event.

Writing Strategy Use several sources to take notes on a historical event.

I found out about the Cardiff Giant hoax online. I was fascinated! When my teacher asked us to write a historical episode, I decided to write about the Giant. First, I read an overview of the event in an encyclopedia. Then I looked at a library book and some reliable Web sites on the topic. Here are some of the notes I took.

My Notes on the Cardiff Giant

✔ 1866: George Hull heard some people talk about giants on Earth—he got an idea

✔ 1868: Hull sent a chunk of gypsum from Ft. Dodge to Chicago

✔ stonecutters made 10-foot man, twisted body, calm face—acid to make it look old

✔ Hull buried statue near Cardiff, NY, on farm of William Newell, his relative who was in on hoax

✔ Oct. 16, 1869: well diggers found giant, Newell put up tent, charged 300–500 people daily to see statue

✔ people say they saw Hull and wagon with box the year before—Hull admits hoax on Dec. 10

✔ "We'll make a fortune off the fools."—Hull's partner

✔ giant stored, exhibited at fairs, bought by Farmers' Museum in Cooperstown, NY, in 1947

✔ period: after Civil War, mid-Victorian Age—growth in business, science, and technology (no cars or phone)

Practice!

Now it's your turn. Choose an interesting historical event. Gather information from several sources, and take notes on the event.

42 Narrative Writing ■ Historical Episode

Prewriting Organize Ideas

Information/Organization The episode has a clear beginning, middle, and end.

Writing Strategy Make a Story Map to organize my notes.

Writer's Term
Story Map
A **Story Map** organizes the setting, characters, problem, plot, and ending of a story.

The rubric stresses organization. I'm going to use a Story Map to organize the information in my notes. The Story Map will help me think about the information I've gathered and find a way to present this episode so my audience can easily follow along.

STORY MAP

Setting: Time: 1866–1869   Place: farm near Cardiff, NY

Characters: George Hull, William Newell, well diggers, scientist

Problem: Hull has to convince people that a stone sculpture is a giant fossilized prehistoric man and get them to pay to see it.

Plot/Events: Hull learns about the giant story, comes up with a hoax, has a stone sculpture made, and has it buried on a relative's farm. It's discovered, people pay to see it, and Hull sells part ownership of it. People start to doubt Hull's claims and check into them.

Ending (Resolution): Hull admits the hoax. The giant is moved around for years. It finally ends up in a NY museum.

Reflect
How did I do? Did I organize my story in a clear and logical way?

Practice!

Now it's your turn. Organize your ideas by using your notes to make a Story Map.

Narrative Writing ■ Historical Episode 43

Prewriting

(Student pages 42–43)

Ask if any of the students enjoy reading about history, as Marco does. Point out that Marco's interest in reading about history may have helped him decide on a topic. Explain to students that their interests and hobbies can help them choose a topic to write about. For instance, if any of the students are equestrians, or interested in horses, they might research famous race horses or racing history to select a topic.

Once students have selected a topic, they should begin researching their topics using encyclopedias, library books, or Web sites.

Remind students of the importance of using a graphic organizer. Tell them that a Story Map will help them organize their notes and make writing a draft easier.

More Practice!

For more practice with these writing strategies, you may wish to have students use the Strategy Practice Book. See the appendix for reduced Strategy Practice Book pages.

Differentiating Instruction

English-Language Learners English-language learners may choose to focus on a historical event in their culture's history. Encourage them to use events that interest them, regardless of where they took place. Point out that they may need to add details and explanations to help their readers understand an unfamiliar place as well as the time period.

Enrichment Help students hone their research skills by providing a historical topic for them to research and take notes on. For instance, have them research the *Titanic* disaster and develop a list of notes about that event. As a class, try to come up with a historical episode about the *Titanic* and create a story map using details from their notes.

WORK with a PARTNER

Explain that there is a vast amount of research available on most topics and that working with a partner can help narrow down the information. Once students have selected a historical event to write about, have them work with a partner to research their topics together.

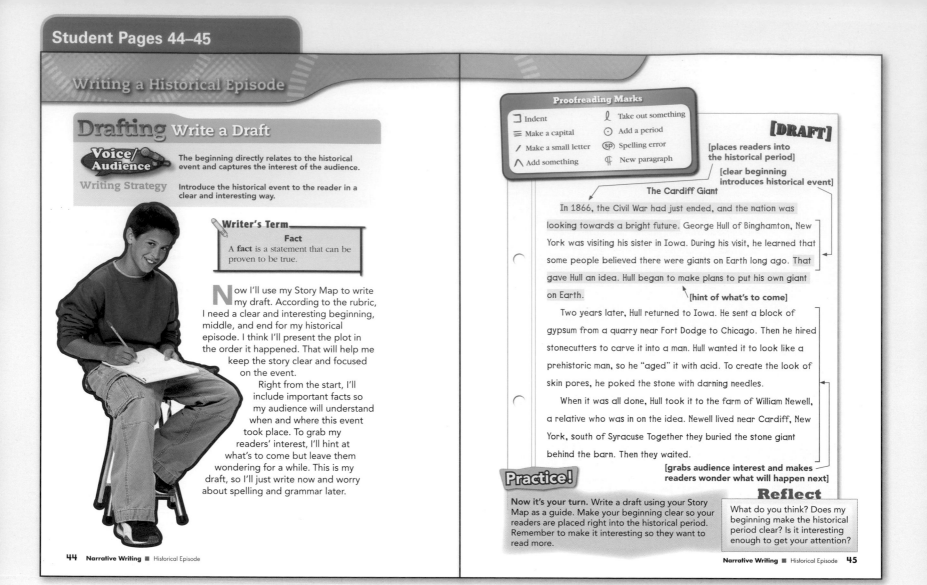

Writing a Historical Episode

Drafting Write a Draft

Voice/Audience The beginning directly relates to the historical event and captures the interest of the audience.

Writing Strategy Introduce the historical event to the reader in a clear and interesting way.

Writer's Term

Fact
A **fact** is a statement that can be proven to be true.

Now I'll use my Story Map to write my draft. According to the rubric, I need a clear and interesting beginning, middle, and end for my historical episode. I think I'll present the plot in the order it happened. That will help me keep the story clear and focused on the event.

Right from the start, I'll include important facts so my audience will understand when and where this event took place. To grab my readers' interest, I'll hint at what's to come but leave them wondering for a while. This is my draft, so I'll just write now and worry about spelling and grammar later.

Proofreading Marks

⌐ Indent
≡ Make a capital
/ Make a small letter
∧ Add something
ℓ Take out something
⊙ Add a period
SP Spelling error
¶ New paragraph

[DRAFT]

[places readers into the historical period]

[clear beginning introduces historical event]

The Cardiff Giant

In 1866, the Civil War had just ended, and the nation was looking towards a bright future. George Hull of Binghamton, New York was visiting his sister in Iowa. During his visit, he learned that some people believed there were giants on Earth long ago. That gave Hull an idea. Hull began to make plans to put his own giant on Earth.

[hint of what's to come]

Two years later, Hull returned to Iowa. He sent a block of gypsum from a quarry near Fort Dodge to Chicago. Then he hired stonecutters to carve it into a man. Hull wanted it to look like a prehistoric man, so he "aged" it with acid. To create the look of skin pores, he poked the stone with darning needles.

When it was all done, Hull took it to the farm of William Newell, a relative who was in on the idea. Newell lived near Cardiff, New York, south of Syracuse Together they buried the stone giant behind the barn. Then they waited.

[grabs audience interest and makes readers wonder what will happen next]

Practice!

Now it's your turn. Write a draft using your Story Map as a guide. Make your beginning clear so your readers are placed right into the historical period. Remember to make it interesting so they want to read more.

Reflect

What do you think? Does my beginning make the historical period clear? Is it interesting enough to get your attention?

Drafting

(Student pages 44–45)

Ask students if they understand why Marco is not worried about spelling and grammar when he writes his draft. **Possible response: It's just a first, or rough, draft.** Remind students that when they write their drafts, they should not be concerned about making mistakes either; they will have opportunities to correct them in the revision and editing processes. Their drafts may be changed and corrected several times before they are finished. It's more important to get their ideas down on paper.

Note, though, that Marco does keep the rubric in mind as he writes his draft. He wants to be sure to have a clear and interesting beginning, middle, and end to his story. He also wants to include historical facts right away and grab his readers' interest. Read the draft aloud, and ask the class whether they think Marco has used facts and captured their interest.

Have students use the information from their Story Map to write a draft of their historical episodes. Remind them to have a clear beginning and to grab their readers' attention from the start.

Writing Across the Curriculum

Social Studies Researching and writing a historical episode enables students to study history. Ask students to discuss what life might be like if we knew nothing about our past—nothing about the important people who have helped shape our world or about how previous generations lived. Have students list reasons that studying the past is important.

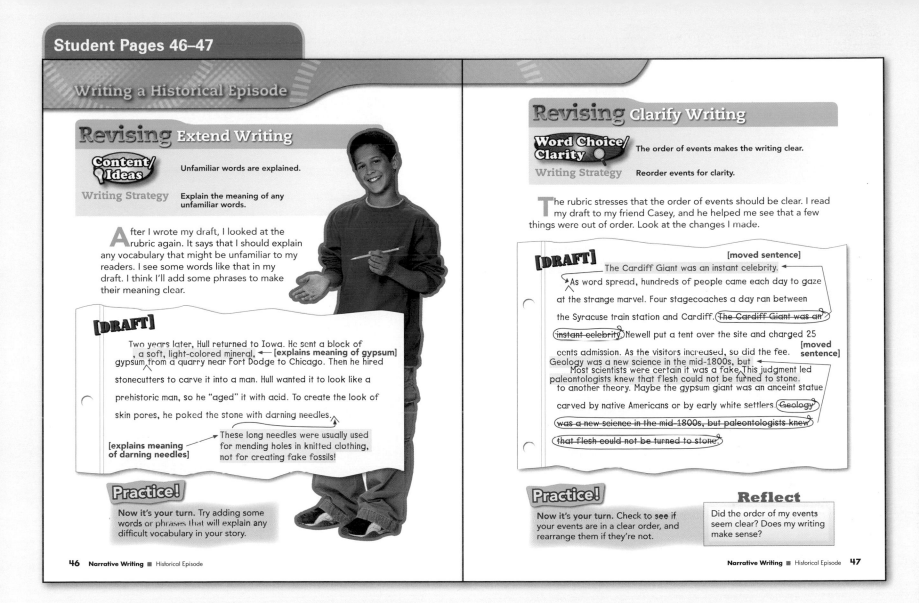

Writing a Historical Episode

Revising Extend Writing

Content/Ideas

Unfamiliar words are explained.

Writing Strategy

Explain the meaning of any unfamiliar words.

After I wrote my draft, I looked at the rubric again. It says that I should explain any vocabulary that might be unfamiliar to my readers. I see some words like that in my draft. I think I'll add some phrases to make their meaning clear.

[DRAFT]

Two years later, Hull returned to Iowa. He sent a block of , a soft, light-colored mineral, ← [explains meaning of gypsum] gypsum from a quarry near Fort Dodge to Chicago. Then he hired stonecutters to carve it into a man. Hull wanted it to look like a prehistoric man, so he "aged" it with acid. To create the look of skin pores, he poked the stone with darning needles.

[explains meaning of darning needles] → These long needles were usually used for mending holes in knitted clothing, not for creating fake fossils!

Practice!

Now it's your turn. Try adding some words or phrases that will explain any difficult vocabulary in your story.

46 Narrative Writing ■ Historical Episode

Revising Clarify Writing

Word Choice/Clarity

The order of events makes the writing clear.

Writing Strategy

Reorder events for clarity.

The rubric stresses that the order of events should be clear. I read my draft to my friend Casey, and he helped me see that a few things were out of order. Look at the changes I made.

[DRAFT]

[moved sentence] The Cardiff Giant was an instant celebrity. ←

As word spread, hundreds of people came each day to gaze at the strange marvel. Four stagecoaches a day ran between the Syracuse train station and Cardiff. The Cardiff Giant was an instant celebrity. Newell put a tent over the site and charged 25 cents admission. As the visitors increased, so did the fee.

[moved sentence] Geology was a new science in the mid-1800s, but

Most scientists were certain it was a fake. This judgment led paleontologists knew that flesh could not be turned to stone. to another theory. Maybe the gypsum giant was an ancient statue carved by native Americans or by early white settlers. Geology was a new science in the mid-1800s, but paleontologists knew that flesh could not be turned to stone.

Practice!

Now it's your turn. Check to see if your events are in a clear order, and rearrange them if they're not.

Reflect

Did the order of my events seem clear? Does my writing make sense?

Narrative Writing ■ Historical Episode 47

Revising

(Student pages 46–47)

Write the sentence *They feasted on fish maw* on the board. Ask if any of the students know what the sentence means, and point out that no, it does not mean that they were feasting on the fish's mom. Explain to students that it is important to explain the meanings of unfamiliar words to their readers. Tell students that fish maw is the dried stomach lining of a fish and is considered an Asian delicacy. Ask students to rewrite the sentence in order to explain the term. **Possible response: They feasted on an Asian delicacy, fish maw, which is the dried stomach lining of a fish.**

Ask students to review their drafts for unfamiliar words. Have them add words or phrases to explain difficult vocabulary.

Remind students that the rubric also states that sentences should be placed in logical order. Explain that the events in their story should make sense and be easy to read. Read through the first paragraph of Marco's draft on Student page 47. Ask students why they think Marco decided to move the sentence "The Cardiff Giant was an instant celebrity" to the top. **Possible responses: It seems out of place in the middle of the paragraph; it should be first because it explains what the paragraph is about.**

Have students read through their drafts to be sure they flow easily and clearly. Instruct them to rearrange sentences if needed.

Differentiating Instruction

Support To help students identify areas in their drafts that are not clear, have them swap their drafts with another student. Ask each student to read through the draft and point out words that are unclear and sentences that do not seem to be placed in logical order. Have them review what they found with the writer.

Enrichment Have students rewrite the following sentences by adding words or phrases that explain the underlined word:

1. Some climbers on Mount Everest experience hypothermia.

2. The building cantilevered over the harbor.

3. In knitting class, she learned how to purl.

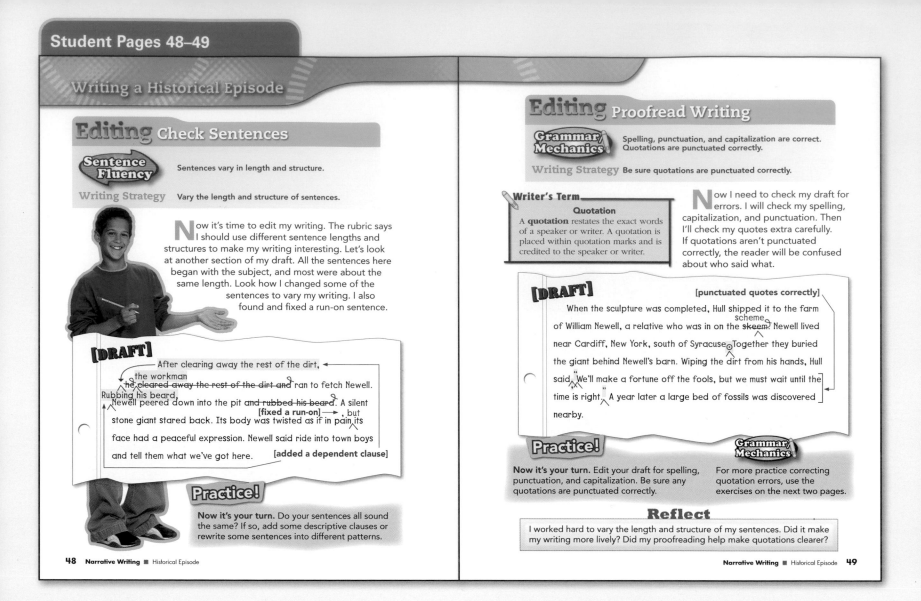

Writing a Historical Episode

Editing Check Sentences

Sentence Fluency
Sentences vary in length and structure.

Writing Strategy Vary the length and structure of sentences.

Now it's time to edit my writing. The rubric says I should use different sentence lengths and structures to make my writing interesting. Let's look at another section of my draft. All the sentences here began with the subject, and most were about the same length. Look how I changed some of the sentences to vary my writing. I also found and fixed a run-on sentence.

[DRAFT]

After clearing away the rest of the dirt,
the workman
~~he cleared away the rest of the dirt and~~ ran to fetch Newell.
Rubbing his beard,
Newell peered down into the pit ~~and rubbed his beard.~~ A silent
[fixed a run-on] → , but
stone giant stared back. Its body was twisted as if in pain its
face had a peaceful expression. Newell said ride into town boys
and tell them what we've got here. **[added a dependent clause]**

Practice!

Now it's your turn. Do your sentences all sound the same? If so, add some descriptive clauses or rewrite some sentences into different patterns.

Editing Proofread Writing

Grammar Mechanics Spelling, punctuation, and capitalization are correct. Quotations are punctuated correctly.

Writing Strategy Be sure quotations are punctuated correctly.

Writer's Term___
Quotation
A **quotation** restates the exact words of a speaker or writer. A quotation is placed within quotation marks and is credited to the speaker or writer.

Now I need to check my draft for errors. I will check my spelling, capitalization, and punctuation. Then I'll check my quotes extra carefully. If quotations aren't punctuated correctly, the reader will be confused about who said what.

[DRAFT] **[punctuated quotes correctly]**

When the sculpture was completed, Hull shipped it to the farm
of William Newell, a relative who was in on the ~~skeem?~~ scheme. Newell lived
near Cardiff, New York, south of Syracuse. Together they buried
the giant behind Newell's barn. Wiping the dirt from his hands, Hull
said, "We'll make a fortune off the fools, but we must wait until the
time is right." A year later a large bed of fossils was discovered
nearby.

Practice!

Now it's your turn. Edit your draft for spelling, punctuation, and capitalization. Be sure any quotations are punctuated correctly.

Grammar Mechanics
For more practice correcting quotation errors, use the exercises on the next two pages.

Reflect

I worked hard to vary the length and structure of my sentences. Did it make my writing more lively? Did my proofreading help make quotations clearer?

Editing

(Student pages 48–49)

Write the following paragraph on the board: *I went to the car. I got in. I put my key in. I turned the key. The car did not start.* Ask students if the paragraph is interesting and well-written. Have them explain why. **Possible responses: It's boring; the sentences are all the same.** Remind students that when they write, they should try to use a variety of sentence types and lengths.

Ask student volunteers to revise the sentences in the paragraph on the board by changing the length and structure of the sentences. Write their responses on the board.

Have students read through their drafts and identify sentences that can be changed. Tell them to change the sentence patterns or add descriptive clauses to improve their drafts.

Then write the following sentence on the board: That is great he said. Ask for student volunteers to correct the punctuation in the sentence. **"That is great," he said.** Remind them that a direct quotation should be contained in quotation marks.

If some or many of your students are having trouble punctuating quotations, you may wish to teach the Mini-Lesson on page 49 of this Teacher Edition. Then have students complete the exercises on Student pages 50–51. Review the answers and possible rewrites with them.

Have students read their historical episode drafts to be sure that they have punctuated quotations correctly. Have them check for correct spelling, punctuation, and capitalization.

WORK with a **PARTNER** Tell students that nearly every piece of published information, such as newspapers, books, or magazines, has been proofread by someone other than the writer. Explain that oftentimes it is easier for another person to identify mistakes in grammar and mechanics. Have students swap their papers with a partner to check for grammar and mechanics errors.

Quotations

KNOW the RULE

A **quotation** is the exact words of a speaker or a writer. Quotations can add interest to nearly every piece of writing. Quotations must be punctuated correctly.

Use **quotation marks** at the beginning and end of a quote. Use a comma to separate the speaker's words from the rest of the sentence. If a quotation is a complete sentence, begin it with a capital letter. Add the correct end punctuation before the last quotation mark.

Examples: "Will people believe us?" asked Newell.
Hull said, "Of course they will!"

Practice the Rule

Correct each quotation below. Then write the correct sentences on a separate piece of paper.

1. To the people at the quarry, Hull said The stone is for a patriotic statue.
2. One article said, Hull was the model for the giant's face.
3. Newell asked "Should I dig up the giant myself or have it dug up by others."
4. What is it? Who carved it? How old is it? Why was it buried? everyone asked.
5. People began telling each other, The giant is a Goliath"!

Apply the Rule

The Cardiff Giant hoax occurred during the Victorian Age. On your paper, rewrite this article about the Victorian Age. Correct any mistakes in the punctuation of the quotations.

The Victorian Age might have been called the Alexandrina Age. Queen Victoria was christened Alexandrina Victoria, but she was always called Victoria. People preferred the name Victoria, historians wrote.

Victoria was a lively and stubborn child who liked drawing, horseback-riding, and writing in her diary. She sometimes rated her behavior in the diary. Once she wrote VERY VERY VERY VERY HORRIBLY NAUGHTY!!!!!"

The governess who educated Victoria at home said "Victoria first learned of her future role as the British ruler during a history lesson when she was about 10 years old.

In response to this news, Victoria said I will be good

Queen Victoria ascended to the throne in 1837 and moved into Buckingham Palace. She said "I never had a room all to myself before"!

Victoria married her cousin, Albert, who was a prince in Germany. He helped her rule the British Empire. When he died in 1861, Victoria remarked that a new reign was beginning. She grieved his loss for the rest of her life.

Grammar/Mechanics Mini-Lesson

(Student pages 50–51)

Quotations

Remind students that quotation marks are used at the beginning and end of a quote. A comma should be used to separate the speaker's words from the rest of the sentence.

Write the following on the board: *I'll be home around five o'clock she said.*

Ask students if the sentence is punctuated correctly. **no** Ask volunteers to punctuate the sentence correctly. **"I'll be home around five o'clock," she said.**

Explain to the students that the end punctuation should be within the last quotation mark.

Write the following on the board: *He yelled, "Stay away from that door"!*

Ask students if this quotation is punctuated correctly. **no** Ask them how to revise the quotation so that it is correct. **Exclamation mark should be within quote: He yelled, "Stay away from that door!"**

Answers for Practice the Rule

1. To the people at the quarry, Hull said, "The stone is for a patriotic statue."
2. One article said, "Hull was the model for the giant's face."
3. Newell asked, "Should I dig up the giant myself or have it dug up by others?"
4. "What is it? Who carved it? How old is it? Why was it buried?" everyone asked.
5. People began telling each other, "The giant is a Goliath!"

Answers for Apply the Rule

The Victorian Age might have been called the Alexandrian Age. Queen Victoria was christened Alexandria Victoria, but she was always called Victoria. "People preferred the name Victoria," historians wrote.

Victoria was a lively and stubborn child who liked drawing, horseback riding, and writing in her diary. She sometimes rated her behavior in the diary. Once she wrote, "VERY VERY VERY VERY VERY HORRIBLY NAUGHTY!!!!!"

(Answers continue on page 50.)

Writing a Historical Episode

Publishing Share Writing

Put my historical episode in a library display.

My historical episode is finished! Now it's time to publish it. There are all kinds of ways to publish my work, but I think I'll put my story in our library. Our librarians are putting together displays on historical periods, and they asked my class to help. My historical episode will be part of the display for the nineteenth century. Before putting my work on display, I'll read it through one last time to make sure it includes all of the items on my checklist.

My Checklist

✔ There's a clear beginning, middle, and end.

✔ The beginning brings my readers right into the historical period and gets them interested.

✔ Unfamiliar words are explained.

✔ The sentences are placed in a logical order.

✔ Sentences are varied.

✔ Spelling, capitalization, and punctuation are all correct. Quotations are punctuated correctly.

Practice!

Now it's your turn. Check your historical episode against your checklist. Then make a final draft to publish.

The Cardiff Giant
by Marco

It was 1866. The Civil War had just ended, and the nation was looking toward a brighter future. George Hull of Binghamton, New York, was visiting his sister in Iowa. During his visit, he learned that some people believed there were giants on Earth long ago. That gave Hull an idea for a new business venture. On the long trip home by steamboat and train, Hull began to hatch a plan to put a giant on Earth.

Two years later, Hull returned to Iowa. He shipped a 3,000-pound block of gypsum, a soft, light-colored mineral, from a quarry near Fort Dodge to Chicago. Then he hired stonecutters to secretly carve the hunk of rock into the shape of a man more than 10 feet tall.

Hull wanted the statue to look like a petrified prehistoric man, so he "aged" it with acid. To create the appearance of skin pores, he pounded the stone with darning needles. These long needles were usually used for mending holes in knitted clothing, not for creating fake fossils!

When the sculpture was completed, Hull shipped it to the farm of William Newell, a relative who was in on the scheme. Newell lived near Cardiff, New York, south of Syracuse. Together they buried the giant

---

(Answers continued from page 49.)

The governess who educated Victoria at home said, "Victoria first learned of her future role as the British ruler during a history lesson when she was about 10 years old."

In response to this news, Victoria said, "I will be good."

Queen Victoria ascended to the throne in 1837 and moved into Buckingham Palace. She said, "I never had a room all to myself before!"

Victoria married her cousin, Albert, who was a prince in Germany. He helped her rule the British Empire. When he died in 1861, Victoria remarked that a new reign was beginning. She grieved his loss for the rest of her life.

 For more practice with grammar/mechanics skills, see Zaner-Bloser's *G.U.M.* materials.

Publishing
(Student pages 52–53)

Tell students that before Marco publishes his work in the school library, he goes through a final checklist to be sure that he has followed the instructions from the rubric. Remind students that they should check their work one last time before they submit a final draft for publication.

Ask students what other ways Marco might have chosen for publishing his story, "The Cardiff Giant." Have students look for ideas within Marco's story to determine a good audience for his story. Who else might be interested in reading about the giant? **Possible response: people visiting the Farmers' Museum** Suggest that students think about who else might be interested in reading their stories.

Writing a Historical Episode

behind Newell's barn. Wiping the dirt from his hands, Hull said, "We'll make a fortune off the fools, but we must wait until the time is right."

A year later, a large bed of fossils was discovered nearby. Hull sent a mysterious telegram to Newell. It read, "Strike while the iron is hot."

On October 16, 1869, Newell hired two men to dig a well at a certain spot near the barn. A few feet down, their shovels clanked against something. "I declare, someone has been buried here!" said one of the workmen as he uncovered a stone foot.

After clearing away the rest of the dirt, the workman ran to fetch Newell. Rubbing his beard, Newell peered down into the pit. A silent stone giant stared back. Its body was twisted as if in pain, but its face had a peaceful expression. Newell said, "Ride into town, boys, and tell them what we've got here."

The Cardiff Giant was an instant celebrity. As word spread, hundreds of people came each day to gaze at the strange marvel. Four stagecoaches a day ran between the Syracuse train station and Cardiff. Newell put a tent over the site and charged 25 cents admission. As the number of visitors increased, so did the fee.

At first, many thought the sculpture really was a petrified man from an earlier time. After all, the region was known for its fossils. Recent advances in science and technology made the public believe that almost anything was possible.

Most scientists were certain it was a fake. Geology was a new science in the mid-1800s, but paleontologists knew that flesh could not be turned to stone. This judgment led to another theory: Maybe the gypsum giant was an ancient statue carved by Native Americans or by early white settlers.

Hull suspected his hoax would soon be revealed. He sold part ownership of the giant to a group of local business people. It was moved to Syracuse and then toured other cities in New York.

In the meantime, an investigation was started. Local people remembered they had seen Hull traveling with a large wooden crate on a wagon the year before. On December 10, Hull admitted the hoax. One of Hull's partners commented, "What a bunch of fools!"

The Cardiff Giant toured for a while and then went into storage. Later it appeared at fairs in Iowa and New York. It was even stored in a child's playroom for a while. In 1947, the Farmers' Museum in Cooperstown, New York, bought the giant.

Today, visitors to the museum stand under a tent just like the first visitors did in 1869. There, they ponder the Cardiff Giant, America's greatest hoax.

Reflect

What do you think? Did I use all the traits of a good historical episode in my writing? Check it against the rubric. Don't forget to use the rubric to check your own historical episode.

Differentiating Instruction

Support To help students understand sentence variety, read this passage to them:

When the sculpture was completed, Hull shipped it to the farm of William Newell, a relative who was in on the scheme. Newell lived near Cardiff, New York, south of Syracuse. Together they buried the giant behind Newell's barn. Wiping the dirt from his hands, Hull said, "We'll make a fortune off the fools, but we must wait until the time is right."

Then ask them to rewrite the passage using subject-verb-predicate pattern. Discuss how sentence variety adds interest to a passage.

Ways to Publish a
Historical Episode

When I think about publishing what I write, I first think about who will be reading it. Then I ask myself, "What's the best way to get my writing to my readers?" Here are some ideas for publishing your historical episode.

✓ Read your account to a younger class, and show them photos or illustrations related to the historical event.

✓ Combine your episode with your classmates' episodes to make a book. Give it a title, such as "Fascinating Moments in History."

✓ Research and find a Web site suitable for your topic. Then submit your work.

✓ Take your account home and share it with your family.

✓ Submit your story to your school newspaper.

Writing Across the Content Areas
Historical Episode

Sometimes it's hard to come up with ideas on what to write about. Looking at the subjects you study in school is a great way to get an idea. Take a look at these subjects for some ideas on different ways you can write a historical episode.

Language Arts
• Think of a novel you like that has a historical setting. Write a new scene for the book.
• Write a historical episode in which you travel back in time and meet an author or person from the past.

Social Studies
• Pick a time from your history book. Make up a character, and write about what happens to that person in your chosen time.
• Write about something that happened to a historical person as if you were that person.

Science
• Research an important scientific discovery, and write about the process that led to it.
• Study the life of a scientist, and write about a time in his/her life.

Ways to Publish
(Student page 56)

Student page 56 contains a list of places students might want to publish their historical accounts. Go through the suggestions with students. Ask for suggestions for other places to publish historical episodes. Ask for student volunteers to share the title and subjects of their historical episodes. Write responses on the board. Have students come up with suggestions for a title and subtitle of a book containing the different titles you have written on the board. Encourage students to share their stories with others or publish them using one of the suggestions on Student page 56.

Writing Across the Content Areas
(Student page 57)

Explain to students that writing a historical episode can apply to other subjects as well. Read the ideas and subjects on Student page 57 with the class. Ask student volunteers to come up with a story suggestion based on one of the ideas on the page. Encourage them to talk to teachers of other subjects to get more ideas on writing a historical episode for that content area.

Books for Professional Development

Allen, Camille Ann. *The Multigenre Research Paper: Voice, Passion and Discovery in Grades 4–6.* **Portsmouth: Heinemann, 2001.**

This book helps teachers guide students as they write historical episodes and other kinds of research reports. It offers tips on how to work with students in selecting genres, choosing topics, and planning multigenre presentations.

Morgan, Bruce with Deb Odom. *Writing Through the Tween Years.* **Portland: Stenhouse, 2004.**

No longer little children, but not yet teenagers, tweens are beginning to see themselves as autonomous while still struggling to understand where they fit in. The authors teach together at a school where formula writing led to stagnant writing scores, student boredom, and teacher discouragement. They worked with their colleagues in grades 3–6 to collectively make some dramatic changes in their writing instruction. This book documents how teachers can get back to the job of teaching writing in a literature-rich, thoughtful environment.

Gallagher, Kelly. *Teaching Adolescent Writers.* **Portland: Stenhouse, 2006.**

Infused with humor and illuminating anecdotes, Gallagher's book draws on his classroom experiences and his work as co-director of a regional writing project to offer teachers practical ways of incorporating writing instruction into their everyday lessons.

Clark, Roy Peter. *Free to Write: A Journalist Teaches Young Writers.* **Portsmouth: Heinemann, 1995.**

The author is a professional writer who follows the model of journalism and uses the real world as the source of all writing. He has students write every day, gathering and sifting information, seeking a focus, building momentum, rethinking and correcting their work to better reach their audience. Strategies are applicable at grade six. The presentation is primarily anecdotal but is loaded with tips and strategies. Genres include news stories, letters to the editor, and narrative.

Short Story Overview

In this chapter, students will learn how to write a short story. They will learn the different elements of a short story—protagonist, point of view, plot, and realism—and some reasons for writing a short story, including for personal enjoyment, to improve their writing skills, to entertain, and to gain better understanding of other stories and writers. By comparing the writing model to the rubric, students will learn how to assess the qualities of a short story.

As the student guide goes through the writing stages for a short story, including prewriting, drafting, revising, editing, and publishing, students will follow along. They will be directed to practice the strategies in their own writing and will have the opportunity to write a short story of their own. Like the student guide, they will put their ideas in a Storyboard and use the Storyboard to create a draft. Then they will revise their drafts by adding sensory details and replacing overused words. When they edit their stories, they will be strengthening sentences by using active voice and ensuring that indefinite pronouns are used correctly. They will also correct any spelling and grammatical errors. Finally, they will explore ways to publish their short stories.

You may wish to send to families the School-Home Connection Letter for this chapter, located at the end of this unit in the Teacher Edition.

Short Story Writing Traits

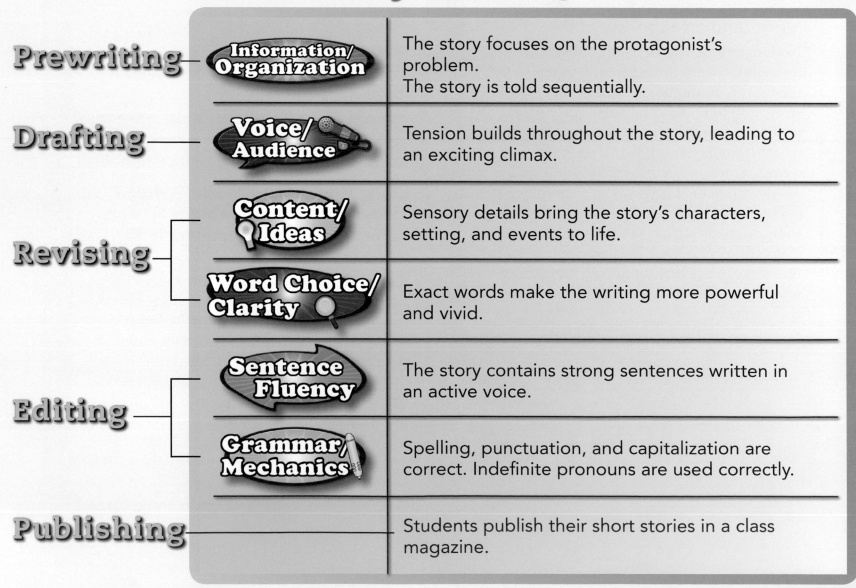

Prewriting	Information/Organization	The story focuses on the protagonist's problem. The story is told sequentially.
Drafting	Voice/Audience	Tension builds throughout the story, leading to an exciting climax.
Revising	Content/Ideas	Sensory details bring the story's characters, setting, and events to life.
	Word Choice/Clarity	Exact words make the writing more powerful and vivid.
Editing	Sentence Fluency	The story contains strong sentences written in an active voice.
	Grammar/Mechanics	Spelling, punctuation, and capitalization are correct. Indefinite pronouns are used correctly.
Publishing		Students publish their short stories in a class magazine.

Short Story Time Management

WEEK 1

	Day 1	Day 2	Day 3	Day 4	Day 5
Learning Objectives	Students will: • learn the components of a short story.	Students will: • learn how to gather information for a short story.	Students will: • practice gathering information for their own short stories.	Students will: • learn how to make a Storyboard to organize their notes.	Students will: • practice organizing their own notes to make a Storyboard.
Activities	• Discuss the elements and traits of a short story (Student pages 58–60). • Use the rubric to study the model (Student pages 61–65).	• Read and discuss **Prewriting: Gather Information** (Student page 66).	• Brainstorm ideas and choose a short story. • Gather information and take notes on short stories.	• Read and discuss **Prewriting: Organize Ideas** (Student page 67).	• Use notes to fill in the Storyboard.

WEEK 2

	Day 1	Day 2	Day 3	Day 4	Day 5
Learning Objectives	Students will: • learn how to build tension throughout the story to lead to an exciting climax.	Students will: • practice writing their own drafts.	Students will: • learn how to add sensory details to make the story come alive.	Students will: • practice adding sensory details to their own drafts.	Students will: • learn how exact words can make their writing powerful and vivid.
Activities	• Read and discuss **Drafting: Write a Draft** (Student page 68)	• Use Storyboard to write a draft. • Build tension throughout stories leading up to an exciting climax.	• Read and discuss **Revising: Extend Writing** (Student page 70).	• Add sensory details to make stories come alive.	• Read and discuss **Revising: Clarify Writing** (Student page 71).

WEEK 3

	Day 1	Day 2	Day 3	Day 4	Day 5
Learning Objectives	Students will: • practice replacing overused words with more exact words.	Students will: • learn about using active voice instead of passive in their sentences.	Students will: • learn how to correctly punctuate indefinite pronouns.	Students will: • practice editing their drafts for spelling, punctuation, and capitalization.	Students will: • learn different ways to publish their short stories.
Activities	• Reread drafts for word choice to avoid overused words. • Replace overused words with more exact and vivid words.	• Read and discuss **Editing: Check Sentences** (Student page 72). • Change sentences written in passive voice to active voice.	• Read and discuss **Editing: Proofread Writing** (Student page 73). • Make sure any indefinite pronouns are punctuated correctly.	• Fix any spelling, punctuation, or capitalization errors in their drafts. • Fix any indefinite pronoun errors.	• Read and discuss **Publishing: Share Writing** (Student page 76).

* To complete the chapter in fewer days, teach the learning objectives and activities for two days in one day.

This planning chart, correlated to your state's writing standards, is available on-line at http://www.zaner-bloser.com/sfw.

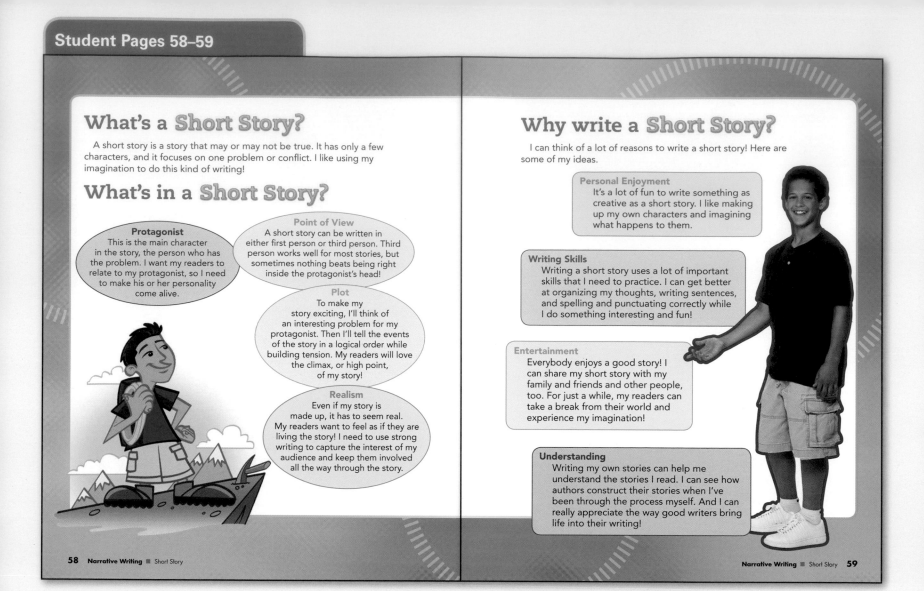

What's a Short Story?

A short story is a story that may or may not be true. It has only a few characters, and it focuses on one problem or conflict. I like using my imagination to do this kind of writing!

What's in a Short Story?

Protagonist
This is the main character in the story, the person who has the problem. I want my readers to relate to my protagonist, so I need to make his or her personality come alive.

Point of View
A short story can be written in either first person or third person. Third person works well for most stories, but sometimes nothing beats being right inside the protagonist's head!

Plot
To make my story exciting, I'll think of an interesting problem for my protagonist. Then I'll tell the events of the story in a logical order while building tension. My readers will love the climax, or high point, of my story!

Realism
Even if my story is made up, it has to seem real. My readers want to feel as if they are living the story! I need to use strong writing to capture the interest of my audience and keep them involved all the way through the story.

Why write a Short Story?

I can think of a lot of reasons to write a short story! Here are some of my ideas.

Personal Enjoyment
It's a lot of fun to write something as creative as a short story. I like making up my own characters and imagining what happens to them.

Writing Skills
Writing a short story uses a lot of important skills that I need to practice. I can get better at organizing my thoughts, writing sentences, and spelling and punctuating correctly while I do something interesting and fun!

Entertainment
Everybody enjoys a good story! I can share my short story with my family and friends and other people, too. For just a while, my readers can take a break from their world and experience my imagination!

Understanding
Writing my own stories can help me understand the stories I read. I can see how authors construct their stories when I've been through the process myself. And I can really appreciate the way good writers bring life into their writing!

58 **Narrative Writing** ■ Short Story

Narrative Writing ■ Short Story 59

Define the Genre

(Student page 58)

Short Story

Discuss what comprises a short story with students. Point out that short stories will give students the opportunity to use their imaginations and create a story and characters that will come to life for their readers.

Elements of the Genre

Short Story

Read and discuss each of the elements of a short story with the students. Ask a student volunteer to tell the class about his or her favorite story. Have him or her provide a short summary of what happens in the story. Tell them that short stories contain many of the same elements as a novel, including a protagonist, point of view, plot, and realism. Ask students to try and identify these elements in the student's favorite story.

Authentic Writing

(Student page 59)

Short Story

Ask students to suggest reasons that a person might want to become a fiction writer. **Possible responses: because it's fun; for the money; for the fame.** Point out that all writing has a purpose and that there are many different reasons that fiction writers choose to write. Some do it for the potential fame or money, while others do it for the pure enjoyment of it. Still others have a strong desire to entertain other people through their stories. Read and discuss with students the reasons for writing a short story on Student page 59. Remind students that their writing, too, has a purpose. In the case of a short story, writers are being given an opportunity to have fun and exercise their imaginations. Writing a short story can give students a chance to improve their writing skills. And remind them that the writing process will enable them to gain a better understanding of the thought and work that goes into writing stories.

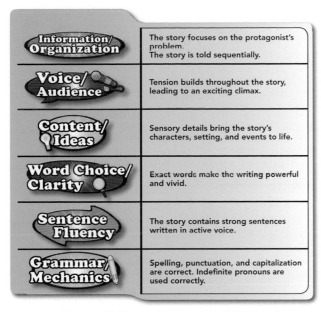

Short Story Writing Traits

There are six traits of good writing. To write a good short story, I'll use the traits that are listed below.

Information/Organization	The story focuses on the protagonist's problem. The story is told sequentially.
Voice/Audience	Tension builds throughout the story, leading to an exciting climax.
Content/Ideas	Sensory details bring the story's characters, setting, and events to life.
Word Choice/Clarity	Exact words make the writing powerful and vivid.
Sentence Fluency	The story contains strong sentences written in active voice.
Grammar/Mechanics	Spelling, punctuation, and capitalization are correct. Indefinite pronouns are used correctly.

Let's see how Ivan Phillips used these traits to help him write the short story on the next page.

60   **Narrative Writing** ■ Short Story

Short Story Model

Loser!
By Ivan Phillips

Protagonist — "What are you doing here?" demanded David. *Third person point of view*

Stephanie hopped off her bike and looked at the other club members. Everyone stood beside a sleek, high-tech bicycle that made her rusty clunker look prehistoric. "I . . . I came for the marathon," she replied.

"But you just joined the club two days ago!" cried Jenna. ← *Realism*
"Everybody else has trained for months," added Miller.

They were saying she couldn't handle such a long ride. But Stephanie liked challenges. "I really want to try this," she said quietly.

David snorted. "Well, we really want to win. So don't expect us to hold back for you."   *Plot—protagonist's problem*

As the marathon began, Stephanie kept up with the others in her club. But soon everybody else shot ahead. "See you later, loser!" someone called back.

She tried to catch up, pumping hard until her legs ached, but the others quickly became colorful blobs in the heat waves far down the road. Then they disappeared.   *Plot—building tension* →

Realism — After that, Stephanie slowed to a steady pace. For a while, other bikers zoomed by, their wheels whizzing smoothly on the pavement. Then she biked on alone with just the rumbling of the support van's engine behind her. She must be the very last biker!

When the enormous hill appeared ahead, Stephanie was already exhausted from riding so long. Her lungs burned with every breath, and her rubbery legs quivered. She wouldn't give up now. She couldn't!   *Plot—building tension*

The bike crept upwards, rocking side-to-side as Stephanie strained against the pedals. The higher she rose, the harder she struggled. Grunting out the last of her breath, she finally felt the pedals ease beneath her. She had reached the top!

Realism → Below her stretched a golden valley of corn waving in the breeze. The flags of the finish line flapped beside a barn less than a mile away!   *Plot—climax*

Stephanie coasted downhill and then pedaled with new energy. Only a few people waited at the finish line, so she knew she was terribly late. Still, she lifted her arms in victory as she sailed under the flags. So what if she came in last? Completing the marathon made her feel like a real winner.

Narrative Writing ■ Short Story   **61**

Writing Traits
Short Story

(Student pages 60–61)

Ask students to think about the story of Cinderella. Who is the protagonist in the story? **Cinderella.** What problem does she face? **Possible answer: Her evil stepmother and stepsisters keep her captive in their home.** Ask them if they feel there is tension in the story, and have them explain. **Possible answer: She meets a prince but leaves before he can learn her identity.** Finally, ask a student volunteer to guess what the exciting climax of the story is. **Possible answer: The prince finally discovers her when her foot fits into the glass slipper.**

Explain to students that the elements you discussed in "Cinderella"—protagonist, problem, tension, and climax—should be elements of their short stories. Review the writing traits of a short story on Student page 60. Explain to students that they will be studying strategies for writing short stories. They will also be using these strategies to write their own short stories. Point out that a good short story contains the traits listed on Student

page 60. Have one or more volunteers read aloud the traits and their descriptions.

Encourage students to identify these traits in the story "Loser!" on Student page 61 as you read it aloud.

Differentiating Instruction

English-Language Learners Explain to students that some of the phrases that they will read in English are specialized terms that may be hard to understand or translate. Ask students if they know the meaning of the phrase *out of breath*. Explain that literally, it would mean that a person is no longer able to breathe, but that it is a phrase that means a person is tired or winded. Explain that the phrase *Grunting out the last of her breath* in the story means that Stephanie is too tired to continue. Have students look for other phrases in the story that, translated literally, have a different meaning than what is intended in the story. Ask them to come up with phrases in their own language that a person unfamiliar with the language would have a hard time translating. Point out that as they get more familiar with the English language, they will have a better understanding of these phrases and will be able to incorporate them into their own writing.

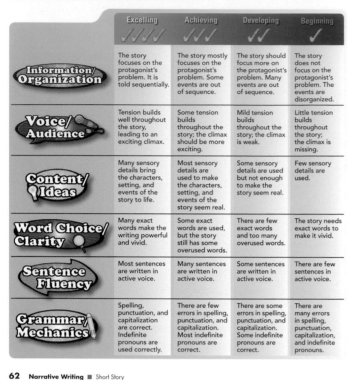

Short Story Rubric

The traits of a good short story from page 60 have been used to make the rubric below. By using 1, 2, 3, or 4 check marks to judge each trait, you can decide how well any short story was written.

	Excelling ✓✓✓✓	Achieving ✓✓✓	Developing ✓✓	Beginning ✓
Information/Organization	The story focuses on the protagonist's problem. It is told sequentially.	The story mostly focuses on the protagonist's problem. Some events are out of sequence.	The story should focus more on the protagonist's problem. Many events are out of sequence.	The story does not focus on the protagonist's problem. The events are disorganized.
Voice/Audience	Tension builds well throughout the story, leading to an exciting climax.	Some tension builds throughout the story; the climax should be more exciting.	Mild tension builds throughout the story; the climax is weak.	Little tension builds throughout the story; the climax is missing.
Content/Ideas	Many sensory details bring the characters, setting, and events of the story to life.	Most sensory details are used to make the characters, setting, and events of the story seem real.	Some sensory details are used but not enough to make the story seem real.	Few sensory details are used.
Word Choice/Clarity	Many exact words make the writing powerful and vivid.	Some exact words are used, but the story still has some overused words.	There are few exact words and too many overused words.	The story needs exact words to make it vivid.
Sentence Fluency	Most sentences are written in active voice.	Many sentences are written in active voice.	Some sentences are written in active voice.	There are few sentences in active voice.
Grammar/Mechanics	Spelling, punctuation, and capitalization are correct. Indefinite pronouns are used correctly.	There are few errors in spelling, punctuation, and capitalization. Most indefinite pronouns are correct.	There are some errors in spelling, punctuation, and capitalization. Some indefinite pronouns are correct.	There are many errors in spelling, punctuation, capitalization, and indefinite pronouns.

62   **Narrative Writing** ■ Short Story

Using the Short Story Rubric to Study the Model

Let's use the rubric to check Ivan's short story, "Loser!" How many check marks would you give Ivan for each trait?

Information/Organization
- The story focuses on the protagonist's problem.
- The story is told sequentially.

There are several characters in the story and plenty of things going on, but Ivan keeps his story focused on the protagonist. Look at how he gets our interest and makes the problem clear.

[from the writing model]

> Stephanie hopped off her bike and looked at the other club members. Everyone stood beside a sleek, high-tech bicycle that made her rusty clunker look prehistoric. "I . . . I came for the marathon," she replied.
> "But you just joined the club two days ago!" cried Jenna.
> "Everybody else has trained for months," added Miller.

Voice/Audience
- Tension builds throughout the story, leading to an exciting climax.

Things seem to get worse and worse for Stephanie! First, the club members leave her behind. Then the other bikers pass her by. She bikes until she's exhausted. You really wonder if she's going to make it! Finally she crosses the finish line in the exciting climax below.

[from the writing model]

> Stephanie coasted downhill and then pedaled with new energy. Only a few people waited at the finish line, so she knew she was terribly late. Still, she lifted her arms in victory as she sailed under the flags.

Narrative Writing ■ Short Story   63

Using the Rubric
(Student page 62)

Remind students that rubrics enable you to assess writing. The rubric on Student page 62 includes the same traits found on Student page 60—the traits students will be keeping in mind as they write their short stories.

Ask a student volunteer to read aloud how a paper receiving four checks under organization would be organized. **The story focuses on the protagonist's problem; it is told sequentially.** Now ask the student to read how a story receiving one check under organization would be organized. **The story does not focus on the protagonist's problem; the events are disorganized.**

Tell students that they should strive to follow the guidelines in the rubric under the Excelling category.

Study the Model
(Student pages 63–65)

Ask students if they felt that the story "Loser!" was well written. Have them explain why they feel that way. Then read Student pages 63–65 with your students to compare the writing model to the rubric.

As you compare each of the writing traits in the rubric against the story, ask students to try to identify other examples within the writing model that show how the writer followed each trait in the rubric.

Tell students that as they write, edit, and revise their stories, they will continually refer to the rubric to be sure that they do not forget to include any of the traits listed.

Short Story

Content/Ideas

• Sensory details bring the story's characters, setting, and events to life.

Ivan uses a lot of sensory details to make this story seem real. We really see, feel, and hear what Stephanie is experiencing! Don't you feel as if you're really there in the following paragraphs?

[from the writing model]

She tried to catch up, pumping hard until her legs ached, but the others quickly became colorful blobs in the heat waves far down the road. Then they disappeared.

After that, Stephanie slowed to a steady pace. For a while, other bikers zoomed by, their wheels whizzing smoothly on the pavement. Then she biked on alone with just the rumbling of the support van's engine behind her. She must be the very last biker!

Word Choice/Clarity

• Exact words make the writing powerful and vivid.

Ivan chooses his words carefully. Instead of writing with overused words, he uses exact words that make the story come alive. He could have written something like this: "The bike *went* upwards, *moving* side-to-side as Stephanie *pushed* against the pedals. The higher she *went*, the harder she *worked*." Instead, look at how the author uses vivid words instead of overused words as he writes.

[from the writing model]

The bike *crept* upwards, *rocking* side-to-side as Stephanie *strained* against the pedals. The higher she *rose*, the harder she *struggled*.

Sentence Fluency

• The story contains strong sentences written in active voice.

A verb is in active voice if the subject of the sentence is doing the action. A verb is in passive voice if the subject of the sentence is not doing the action. Sometimes passive voice works well, but usually sentences are stronger if they're written in active voice.

Obviously, Ivan knew that! He could have written sentences such as "Stephanie had been exhausted by the long ride" or "Her lungs were burned by every breath." But look how he used active voice to make the following paragraph strong.

[from the writing model]

When the enormous hill appeared ahead, Stephanie was already exhausted from riding so long. Her lungs burned with every breath, and her rubbery legs quivered. She wouldn't give up now. She couldn't!

Grammar/Mechanics

• Spelling, punctuation, and capitalization are correct. Indefinite pronouns are used correctly.

I checked Ivan's story for mistakes, but I don't see any, do you? He has spelled, capitalized, and punctuated everything correctly. And he knows how to use indefinite pronouns correctly, too. You can tell that from the paragraph below.

[from the writing model]

As the marathon began, Stephanie kept up with the *others* in her club. But soon *everybody* else shot ahead. "See you later, loser!" *someone* called back.

My Turn!

I'm going to write my own short story! I'll follow the rubric and use good writing strategies. You can read along and see how I do it.

Differentiating Instruction

Enrichment To help students further understand how to use tension and conflict to lead to an exciting climax, write the following on the board: *The mouse saw the cheese on the counter and knew he had to have it.* Have the students write a paragraph that begins with that sentence and uses tension and conflict to lead to an exciting climax. Have them underline the areas in the paragraph that help build tension and circle the climax. Ask for volunteers to read their paragraphs to the class; then ask the class to try to identify the tension within the story.

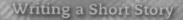

Writing a Short Story

Prewriting Gather Information

Information Organization The story focuses on the protagonist's problem.

Writing Strategy Brainstorm characters and events to use in my story.

Ever since our teacher asked us to write a short story, I've been kicking around some ideas. Here are the notes I jotted down about possible characters and events for my story.

Notes

Characters:	Events:
• brave firefighter	• mountain-climbing expedition
• boy my age who's afraid of something	• school play
• spunky lady who likes adventure	• skydiving lesson
• cowboy	• a rescue
• girl my age who likes sports	• sleepover
	• big game
	• camping trip

I decided I'd like to write a story about a boy my age, so I chose the boy who's afraid of something as my protagonist. I don't want him to be afraid of something obvious such as skydiving or seeing an alien, so I think I'll make him afraid of something at a sleepover. Maybe the sleepover can be held at a scary, creepy, old house. He will have to pretend he's not scared in front of his friends. Hey, I think I have a good idea for my story!

Practice!

Now it's your turn. Brainstorm some ideas for characters and events for your story. Jot down your ideas and put your imagination to work!

Prewriting Organize Ideas

Information Organization The story is told sequentially.

Writing Strategy Make a Storyboard to organize my ideas.

Writer's Term

Storyboard
A **Storyboard** can help you plot the main parts of a story in chronological order. Each frame in the Storyboard represents a part of the story. Words and/or pictures can be used in a Storyboard.

Now that I've decided on my protagonist and his problem, I have to plan my story. I want to be sure to tell the story in a logical sequence so my readers can easily follow what's happening. I used a Storyboard to organize my ideas below.

STORYBOARD

EVENT 1 Chris and his best friend arrive at a creepy house for a sleepover. Chris is scared and has to hide his fear.

EVENT 2 Chris and his friend go in and find that the party is normal. Chris has a good time.

EVENT 3 At bedtime, Chris gets scared again and can't go to sleep.

EVENT 4 Chris hears footsteps and thinks someone is hurting his best friend!

EVENT 5—CLIMAX Even though he's scared, Chris tries to save his friend. He jumps on the figure and knocks him down!

EVENT 6 It was just the host of the party sleepwalking, but Chris feels good that he handled his fear.

Practice!

Now it's your turn. Use a Storyboard to organize your story.

Reflect

How did I do? Did I plan out an exciting story?

Prewriting

(Student pages 66–67)

Review Student page 66 with the students. Take a look at the notes Marco wrote. Explain to students that he used this opportunity to brainstorm ideas so that he could come up with a story. Ask them why they think Marco decided to write about a boy his age. Explain to students that a good writer needs to know and understand his protagonist, either through personal experience or research.

Point out that before they start writing their drafts, they should have a good idea of not only what they are going to write about but how it will be organized. Remind them that a graphic organizer enables them to gather and organize their ideas.

More Practice!

For more practice with these writing strategies, you may wish to have students use the Strategy Practice Book. See the appendix for reduced Strategy Practice Book pages.

Differentiating Instruction

Support If any of your students are having a hard time coming up with ideas, remind them that many great fiction stories are inspired by real life. Encourage them to read a newspaper or magazine to see if any of the stories spark their interest. Have them create a fictional story based on one of those stories.

Enrichment Encourage students to incorporate several blocks of dialogue into their short stories. Point out that good dialogue should sound realistic and that if it is a quote, it does not necessarily need to be grammatically correct. Instead, it should reflect how the character would really speak. Suggest that they look through other novels and short stories to see how experienced writers use dialogue.

WORK with a PARTNER

Once students have come up with a protagonist and an idea for their plot, encourage them to work with a partner to further develop their stories. A partner can help provide creative input and perhaps give suggestions on what would make the story even better.

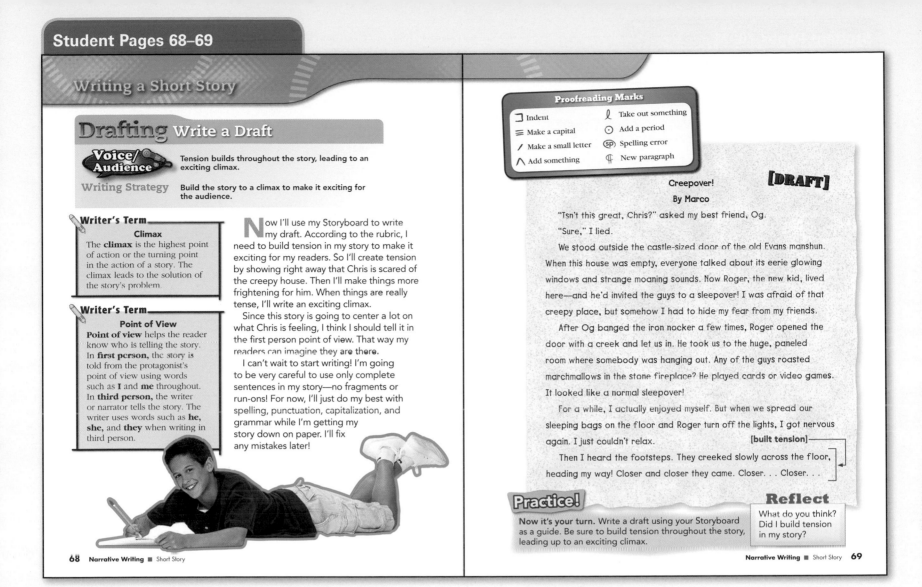

Drafting

(Student pages 68–69)

Read aloud the description of point of view from the Writer's Term box. Recite the line "Call me Ishmael" from *Moby Dick*. Ask students what point of view Melville uses in this story. **first person** Have a student volunteer rewrite the sentence in the third person. **Possible response: His name was Ishmael.**

Point out that Marco chooses to use the first person point of view in his story because he wants to focus on how the character Chris is feeling. Marco writes as if he himself were Chris. That way, he can express Chris's own thoughts and feelings. If Marco wanted to say that Chris was really a big 'fraidy cat but didn't know it, he might have chosen instead to use third person point of view. Then instead of saying "I was afraid of that creepy place," he might say, "Chris cringed when he heard the sleepover was going to be at the Evans mansion."

Remind students to decide on the point of view for their story and then stick with that point of view throughout the story.

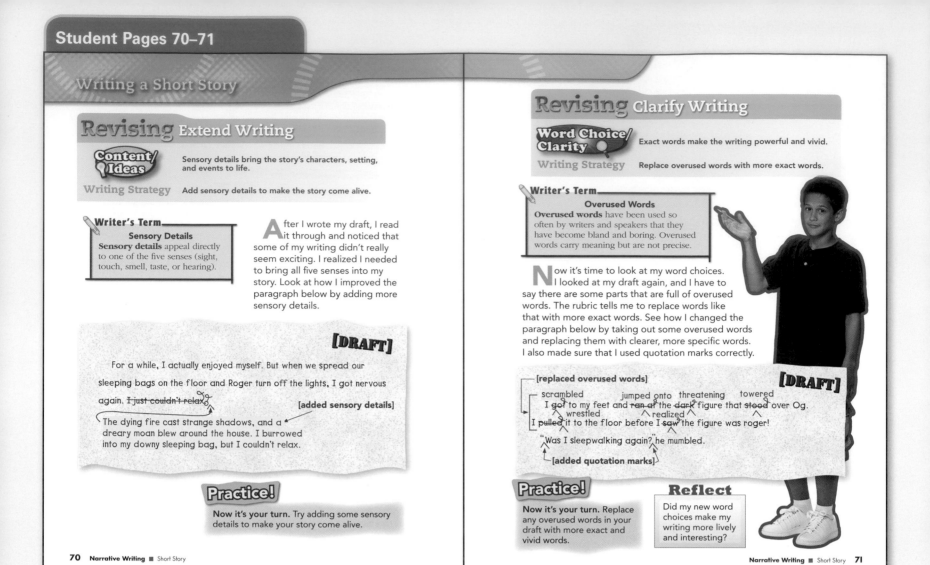

Revising

(Student pages 70–71)

Write each of the following senses on the board: *sight, touch, smell, taste, hearing.* Under the word *sight* on the board, write this sentence: *Through the fog, I spotted a large figure, bigger than any person I'd ever seen before.* Tell students that writing about what they see appeals to the reader's sense of sight. Have student volunteers come up with sentences for each of the additional words on the board. Write down their responses.

Have students read through their drafts to identify places they can add sensory details.

Next, review with students the information on Student page 71. Read the draft paragraph on the page before the words were changed. Then read it again with the changes Marco made. Write these words on the board: got, ran at, dark, stood, pulled, saw. Tell students that while the words are correct and work in the places that Marco used them, he was creative in changing these words to make his writing more vivid. Ask students to come up with other words or phrases that could be used as replacements for the words on the board. Write down their responses.

Instruct students to go through their own stories to find words that can be replaced with more exact and vivid words.

Differentiating Instruction

Enrichment To help students practice including sensory details in their writing, have them refer back to the paragraph from above that they have corrected by replacing overused words. Now ask them to make the paragraph come to life even more by adding sensory details. Encourage them to write more about how the food looked, smelled, tasted, or even sounded.

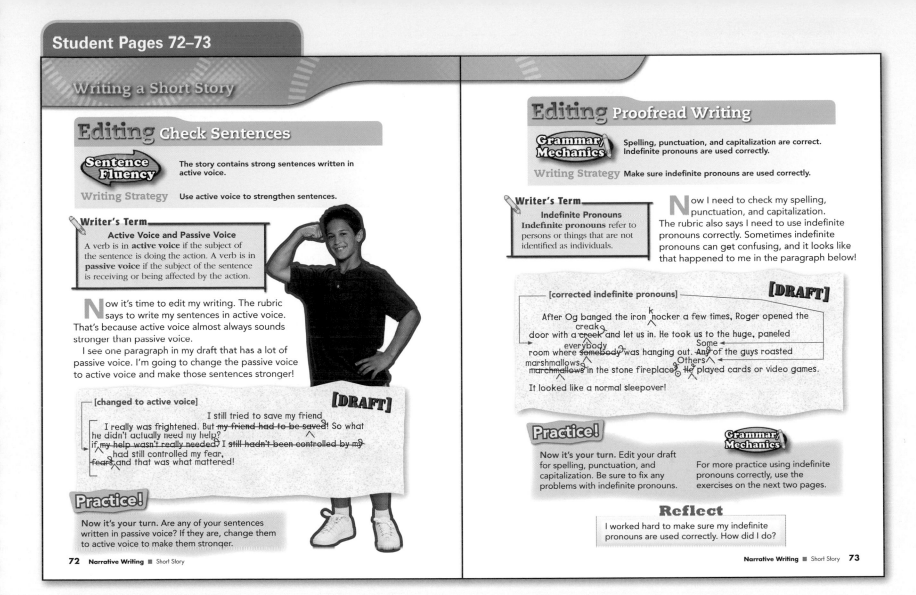

Editing

(Student pages 72–73)

Write the following sentence on the board: *The customer was thanked by the cashier.* Ask students if the sentence is active or passive. **passive** Ask a student volunteer to change the sentence from passive to active. **Possible answer: The cashier thanked the customer.** Tell students that oftentimes the word "by" is a good clue that the sentence is written in the passive voice. Instead of having something happen to the subject in the sentence, point out that students should have the subject in the sentence do the action.

Have students read through their drafts and identify any sentences that have been written using a passive voice. Have them rewrite the sentences in active voice.

Next, read aloud the definition of an indefinite pronoun from the Writer's Term box on Student page 73. Go through the draft paragraph on this page to see how Marco corrected misused pronouns in his draft. Ask the students to look through their drafts to be sure they have used indefinite pronouns correctly.

If students are having trouble with indefinite pronouns, you may wish to teach the Mini-Lesson on page 64 of this Teacher Edition. Then, have students complete the exercises on Student pages 74–75. Review the answers and possible rewrites with them.

At this point, students should also read through their short stories to be sure that there are no grammatical mistakes. Have them check for correct spelling, punctuation, and capitalization. Remind students that they should always proofread their stories.

WORK with a PARTNER Have students exchange their papers with a partner to check for grammar and mechanics errors.

 Practice!

Indefinite Pronouns

 KNOW the RULE

An **indefinite pronoun** refers to persons or things that are not identified as individuals. Indefinite pronouns include *all, any, anybody, anything, both, each, either, everybody, everyone, everything, few, many, most, nobody, no one, nothing, one, several, some,* and *someone.*

Practice the Rule

Rewrite each sentence by writing an indefinite pronoun from the Word Bank. Remember to capitalize any words that begin a sentence. Some sentences could have more than one correct answer. Some words may be used more than once.

Word Bank

one	many	everyone	some
no one	somebody	most	all
someone	anybody	something	several

1. ___ has lived in the Evans mansion for years.
2. Maybe that's why so ___ of us find the old house mysterious.
3. I don't believe ___ of the stories about the Evans mansion.
4. Still, ___ about that old house creeps me out.
5. ___ say they have seen strange lights glowing in its windows.
6. ___ of my friends claims to have heard eerie noises around there.
7. I think ___ of the weirdest things about the house is its enormous front door.
8. ___ houses today don't have doors that look like they belong on a castle!
9. People say that ___ once robbed a bank and hid the loot in the house.
10. ___ around here has heard the story.

Apply the Rule

Read this article about crop circles. Rewrite the story on a separate sheet of paper, correcting any errors in the use of indefinite pronouns.

Hardly nobody got excited when crop circles appeared in the grain fields of England in the late 1970s. Simple circles of flattened grain had been discovered now and then in the past. Few people worried about what caused them.

Each changed in the 1980s when the media began to run stories about crop circles. As television and newspapers drew attention to the mysterious phenomena, people found more of them. Everyone seemed to form overnight, but anybody knew how.

Many of the theories about crop circles was that aliens caused them by landing spacecraft in the fields. However, nothing could offer proof of alien visitors.

Another explanation was that spiraling winds created the circles. But then more complicated patterns began to appear. Both included circles within circles and straight lines that could not have been caused by the wind.

In 1991, two friends, Doug Bower and Dave Chorley, finally confessed. They had been making the circles and patterns for years. Either appeared on television and showed how they did it. Other hoaxers came forward, too. But even today, many people still believe crop circles cannot be made by humans.

 Mini-Lesson

(Student pages 74–75)

Indefinite Pronouns

Explain to students that indefinite pronouns refer to persons or things not identified as individuals. These are different from pronouns such as *him, her, she,* and *he,* which do refer to individuals.

Write the following on the board: *The whole team went out for pizza.*

Ask students to change the phrase "the whole team" into an indefinite pronoun. **Possible response: All of them went out for pizza.**

Answers for Practice the Rule

1. **No one**
2. **many**
3. **all**
4. **something**
5. **Many**
6. **One**
7. **one**
8. **Many/Most**
9. **someone/somebody**
10. **Everyone**

Answers for Apply the Rule

Hardly anybody got excited when crop circles appeared in the grain fields of England in the late 1970s. Simple circles of flattened grain had been discovered now and then in the past. Few people worried about what caused them.

Everything changed in the 1980s when the media began to write stories about crop circles. As television and newspapers drew attention to the mysterious phenomena, people found more of them. Many seemed to form overnight, but nobody knew how.

One of the theories about crop circles was that aliens caused them by landing spacecraft in the fields. However, no one could offer proof of alien visitors.

Another explanation was that spiraling winds created the circles. But then more complicated patterns began to appear. Many included circles within circles and straight lines that could not have been caused by the wind.

In 1991, two friends, Doug Bower and Dave Chorley, finally confessed. They had been making circles and patterns for years. Both appeared on television and showed how they did it. Other hoaxers came forward, too. But even today, many people still believe crop circles cannot be made by humans.

Writing a Short Story

Publishing Share Writing

Publish my short story in a class magazine.

Now it's time to publish my short story! I could submit my story to a creative writing contest for kids, read it to my friends, or make it into a picture book using my own illustrations. I think I'll publish my story in our class magazine. Everyone in our class is contributing something to the magazine. I can't wait to see my story in print! Before I submit the story, I want to read it through one last time to make sure it includes all of the items on my checklist.

My Checklist

✔ My story has a lively protagonist with an interesting problem.

✔ The story moves along in a logical way, building tension until it reaches an exciting climax.

✔ Sensory details and vivid language make my story come to life.

✔ I used strong sentences written in active voice.

✔ Spelling, capitalization, and punctuation are all correct. I used indefinite pronouns correctly.

Practice!

Now it's your turn. Check your short story against your own checklist. Then make a final draft to publish.

76 **Narrative Writing** ■ Short Story

Creepover!

By Marco Guerrero

"This is going to be so great, Chris," said my best friend, Og. "Don't you think?"

"Sure," I lied.

We stood outside the castle-sized front door of the old Evans mansion. When the house stood empty, everyone talked about its eerie glowing windows and the strange moaning that couldn't be just the wind. Now Roger, the new kid, lived here—and Og and I were invited to a sleepover in the creepiest house around. I was afraid of that place, but somehow I had to hide my fear for the whole night!

After Og banged the heavy iron knocker a few times, Roger opened the door with a creak and let us in. He took us to the huge, paneled room where everybody was hanging out. Some of the guys roasted marshmallows in the stone fireplace. Others played cards or video games. It looked like a normal sleepover!

For a while, I forgot where I was and just enjoyed myself. But when we spread our sleeping bags on the floor and Roger turned off the lights, I got nervous again. The dying fire cast strange shadows, and a dreary moan blew around the house. I burrowed into my downy sleeping bag, but I couldn't relax.

Then I heard the footsteps. They creaked slowly across the floor, heading my way! Closer and closer they came. Closer. . . Closer. . .

Someone groaned in pain. Then a muffled voice choked out, "Get away from me!"

It was Og! And he needed help!

I scrambled to my feet and jumped onto the threatening figure that towered over Og. I wrestled it to the floor before I realized the figure was Roger!

"Was I sleepwalking again?" he mumbled.

"Yeah," said Og. "You stepped right on me!"

"Sorry." Roger crawled back to his spot, closed his eyes, and started snoring.

"He scared me to death," said Og, settling back down.

"Yeah, me, too." As I slid into my sleeping bag, I realized something. Even though I was frightened, I still tried to save my friend. So what if he didn't actually need my help? The important thing was that I had controlled my fear instead of letting it control me!

Finally, I nestled into my bag and took a deep breath. Something was scratching against the windowpane, but I closed my eyes anyway.

"It's just a branch," I told myself right before I fell asleep.

Reflect

What do you think? Did I use all the traits of a good short story in my writing? Check it against the rubric. Then use the rubric to check your own story.

Narrative Writing ■ Short Story 77

Publishing

(Student pages 76–77)

Review Student page 76 with students. Point out that before Marco submits his final draft for the class magazine, he takes another look at his checklist to be sure he hasn't missed anything. Encourage students to use their checklists to review their final drafts. Have students read Marco's final draft of "Creepover!" using his checklist to assess his short story. Did Marco include all of the items on his checklist?

You might suggest that the class develop a magazine featuring all of their short stories. Have each of them design a title page for their stories that includes the title, their byline, and an illustration that represents their story. Ask students who they think might like to receive or read such a magazine.

Tips for the Writing Classroom

Using Student/Teacher Writing Models
by Ken Stewart, *Master Teacher*

Help students understand the criteria you are looking for in a piece of writing by modeling the revision process with student input. Follow these simple steps:

1. Choose a student's piece of writing. Ask for permission before sharing it with the class.
2. Make copies for each student to correct.
3. Display an overhead transparency of the piece of writing.
4. Read the writing aloud. Then go back and read it sentence by sentence, asking for specific changes. Use the proofreading marks in the Student Edition.
5. After you and the class have made your changes, reread the piece and analyze why the revised version is better.

Ways to Publish a
Short Story

As you decide how to publish your writing, think about your audience. What's the best way to share your story so your readers will enjoy it and get the most out of it? Here are some ideas for publishing your short story.

 Submit your story to a creative writing contest for kids. If you don't know about a contest, ask your teacher for help. Maybe you can have a contest in your own school!

 Turn your story into a picture book. Break the story into small parts, and write or print each part at the bottom of a page with your own illustration in the space above.

 Set up a story time with a younger class. You and your classmates can take turns reading your stories aloud.

 Publish your story on your blog. Break it into parts, and publish one part at a time to keep your audience guessing!

Writing Across the Content Areas
Short Story

You can write a short story about all kinds of things! Look at the subjects you study in school. Many of them can give you ideas for writing. Read below for some subject-related ideas for short stories.

Language Arts
- Write a story in which a character from one book is dealing with a situation from another book.
- Take a short story and rewrite it with one of the secondary characters as the protagonist.

Social Studies
- Pretend you are at a historical event. Write a story about it in first person point of view.
- Write a short story about someone who is in a situation that tests his/her character.

Art or Music
- Listen to a piece of classical music or a favorite song, and then write a story inspired by what you heard or about why the music was written.
- Find an interesting painting or illustration, and write a story about what happened just before or just after the event in the picture.

Ways to Publish
(Student page 78)

Point out that there are many more ways students can publish their short stories. Go through the suggestions listed on Student page 78. Ask students if they have any other ideas to add to the list. Suggest that students pursue outlets in which to publish their stories. Try to have available a list of contests in which students may submit their short stories, and encourage them to enter.

Writing Across the Content Areas
(Student page 79)

Remind students that writing is not just for English or language arts class. Tell them that ideas for short stories can come from many places, including other school subjects. Encourage students to continue writing short stories, using the ideas on Student page 79 as inspiration. Review the ideas on Student page 79 with the students and ask for additional input on where students think they can find ideas and inspiration.

Books for Professional Development

Brusko, Mike. *Writing Rules: Teaching Kids to Write for Life, Grades 4–8.* Portsmouth: Heinemann, 1999.

The author focuses on the writing skills that students need in everyday life. He pays special attention to clarifying the purpose for writing and getting the reader's attention.

Wood, Karen D and Maryann Mraz. *Teaching Literacy in Sixth Grade (Tools for Teaching Literacy).* San Francisco: Guilford, 2005.

Sixth grade marks the transition to middle school and, for many students, the transition to early adolescence. The sixth-grade classroom is a place where problem solving and abstract thinking skills can flourish as teachers devise creative ways to integrate language arts with effective content-area instruction. This book takes the reader through everyday life in a successful sixth-grade language arts/social studies classroom and provides foundational knowledge and hands-on strategies for working with diverse learners.

Stewig, John Warren. *Read to Write: Using Children's Literature as a Springboard for Teaching Writing.* 3rd ed. Katonah: Richard C. Owen, 1990.

This source for teachers of grades 3–8 offers strategies for using characterization, point of view, setting, plot, and conflict to help build a story. The author also focuses on editing strategies that students can use to improve their stories.

Soven, Margot Iris. *Teaching Writing in Middle and Secondary Schools: Theory, Research and Practice.* Boston: Allyn & Bacon, 1998.

This book uses practical explanations of teaching strategies, many examples of assignments and student writing, and original methods for teaching the writing process, including new techniques to effectively evaluate and respond to student writers.

Narrative Test Writing

Students will learn about narrative test writing in this chapter. They will learn about the parts of a writing prompt—setup, task, and scoring guide—and see how the writing prompt relates to the writing traits they have been studying throughout the chapter. Students will use the scoring guide to assess a model writing sample.

Then, students will follow the student guide as he goes through the writing stages for a narrative writing test, including planning one's time, prewriting, drafting, revising, and editing.

As you review this chapter with your students, emphasize that there is no reason to be concerned about writing tests. You may wish to relate each of the steps in the test writing process to steps they have used in other chapters in this unit. Stress to them that many of the steps and strategies that they have learned in earlier chapters can be applied to writing tests as well.

You may wish to send to families the School-Home Connection Letter for this chapter, located at the end of this unit in the Teacher Edition.

Writing Traits in the Scoring Guide

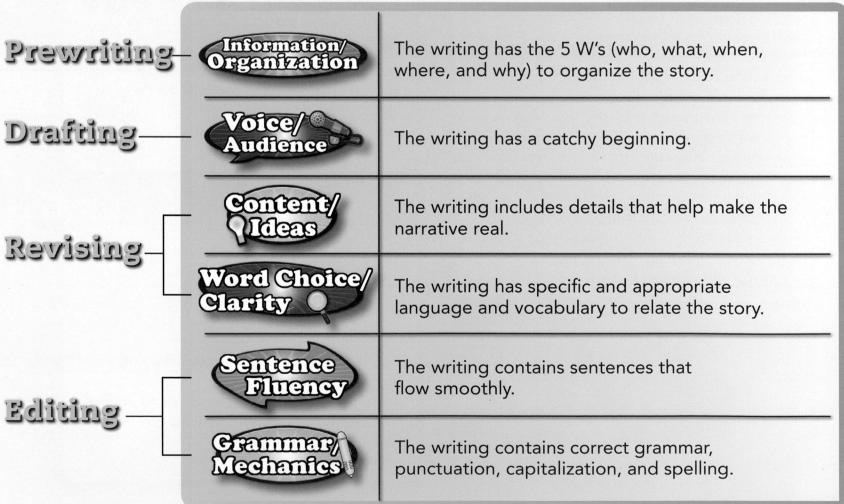

Prewriting	**Information/ Organization**	The writing has the 5 W's (who, what, when, where, and why) to organize the story.
Drafting	**Voice/ Audience**	The writing has a catchy beginning.
Revising	**Content/ Ideas**	The writing includes details that help make the narrative real.
	Word Choice/ Clarity	The writing has specific and appropriate language and vocabulary to relate the story.
Editing	**Sentence Fluency**	The writing contains sentences that flow smoothly.
	Grammar/ Mechanics	The writing contains correct grammar, punctuation, capitalization, and spelling.

Narrative Test Writing Time Management

WEEK 1

	Day 1	Day 2	Day 3	Day 4	Day 5
Learning Objectives	Students will: • learn the components of the writing prompt.	Students will: • recognize the relationship of the scoring guide to the rubric and the six traits of writing. • read a model writing test response.	Students will: • apply the scoring guide to a model test response.	Students will: • apply the scoring guide to a model test response.	Students will: • learn how to budget their time during a writing test.
Activities	• Discuss the components of the writing prompt. (Student pages 80–81)	• Read and discuss the scoring guide chart. (Student page 82) • Read the model. (Student page 83)	• Read and discuss **Using the Scoring Guide to Study the Model.** (Student pages 84–85)	• Read and discuss **Using the Scoring Guide to Study the Model.** (Student page 86)	• Read and discuss **Planning My Time.** (Student page 87)

WEEK 2

	Day 1	Day 2	Day 3	Day 4	Day 5
Learning Objectives	Students will: • learn to read and understand a writing test prompt for test writing. • apply the six traits of writing to the writing prompt.	Students will: • learn how to respond to the task in the writing prompt.	Students will: • learn how to choose a graphic organizer for the writing prompt.	Students will: • learn how to check the graphic organizer against the scoring guide.	Students will: • use the graphic organizer to begin a writing test response story.
Activities	• Read and discuss **Prewriting: Study the Writing Prompt.** (Student pages 88–89)	• Read and discuss **Prewriting: Gather Information.** (Student page 90)	Read and discuss **Prewriting: Organize Ideas.** (Student page 91)	• Read and discuss **Prewriting: Check the Scoring Guide.** (Student pages 92–93)	• Read and discuss **Drafting: Write a Draft.** (Student pages 94–95)

WEEK 3

	Day 1	Day 2	Day 3	Day 4	Day 5
Learning Objectives	Students will: • add details to their writing test response story.	Students will: • use clear and specific language in their writing test response story.	Students will: • make sentences flow smoothly to clarify their writing test response story.	Students will: • edit their writing test response story for grammar and mechanics.	Students will: • review tips for writing for a test
Activities	• Read and discuss **Revising: Extend Writing.** (Student Page 96)	• Read and discuss **Revising: Clarify Writing.** (Student Page 97)	• Read and discuss **Editing: Check Sentences.** (Student page 98)	• Read and discuss **Editing: Proofread Writing.** (Student pages 99–100)	• Read and discuss **Test Tips** (Student page 101)

To complete the chapter in fewer days, teach the learning objectives and activities for two days in one day.
This planning chart, correlated to your state's writing standards, is available on-line at http://www.zaner-bloser.com/sfw.

NARRATiVE test writing

Read the Writing Prompt

When you take a writing test, you'll get a writing prompt. Most writing prompts have three parts:

Setup This part of the writing prompt gives you the background information you need to get ready to write.

Task This part of the writing prompt tells you exactly what you are supposed to write: an eyewitness account about a newsworthy event that you observed.

Scoring Guide This section tells how your writing will be scored. To do well on the test, you should make sure you do everything on the list.

Remember the rubrics you used earlier in the unit? When you take a writing test, you don't always have all of the information that's on a rubric. But the scoring guide is a lot like a rubric. It lists everything you need to think about to write a good paper. Like the rubrics you've used in this unit, many scoring guides are based on these important traits of writing:

- Information/Organization
- Content/Ideas
- Sentence Fluency
- Voice/Audience
- Word Choice/Clarity
- Grammar/Mechanics

Writing MODEL Prompt

Think about a newsworthy event, one that might make the local news. It can be something you saw or heard about or something you made up yourself.

Then write an eyewitness account telling about the event.

Be sure your writing

- has the 5 W's (who, what, when, where, and why) to organize the story.
- has a catchy beginning.
- includes details that help make the narrative real.
- has specific and appropriate language and vocabulary to relate the story.
- contains sentences that flow smoothly.
- contains correct grammar, punctuation, capitalization, and spelling.

Introduce the Writing Prompt
(Student pages 80–81)

Narrative Writing

Write the word *prompt* on the board. Ask students if they know what it means to be prompt. **Possible response: on time** Then ask if anyone knows other meanings for prompt. Explain that one meaning for *prompt* is "to cause." Ask a student volunteer to explain why an assigned writing topic is called a writing prompt. **Possible response: It causes someone to write on a particular subject.**

Read through the three parts of a writing prompt with your students. Explain that within the scoring guide part of the writing prompt, they will find traits similar to those they have seen in the rubrics throughout this chapter. Point out that just as a rubric includes the qualities that comprise a good paper, the scoring guide includes the qualities that comprise a good test response.

Read the model writing prompt aloud, being sure to point out the setup, task, and scoring guide sections of the prompt.

Differentiating Instruction

Support To help students better understand the writing prompt, write the following on the board:

Setup: Background

Task: Assignment

Scoring Guide: Rubric

Explain that the setup provides background information that they need to know in order to write their essay. Tell them the task is really the assignment and will often include the type of writing they will be doing, such as a historical episode or a short story. Remind them that the scoring guide is much like a rubric and gives them the information they need to know and follow in order to do well on the test.

Writing Traits
in the Scoring Guide

Now let's look back at the scoring guide in the writing prompt on page 81. Even though not every test prompt will include each of the writing traits, we can see that this one does. Take a look at the following chart. It will help you better understand the connection between the scoring guide and the writing traits in the rubrics you've been using.

 **Information/Organization**
- Be sure your writing has the 5 W's (who, what, when, where, and why) to organize the story.

 **Voice/Audience**
- Be sure your writing has a catchy beginning.

 Content/Ideas
- Be sure your writing includes details that help make the narrative real.

 **Word Choice/Clarity**
- Be sure your writing has specific and appropriate language and vocabulary to relate the story.

 Sentence Fluency
- Be sure your writing contains sentences that flow smoothly.

 Grammar/Mechanics
- Be sure your writing contains correct grammar, punctuation, capitalization, and spelling.

Look at Olivia Mayes's story on the next page. Did she follow the scoring guide?

82 **Narrative Writing** ■ Narrative Test

Bucky's Big Break
by Olivia Mayes

I knew something was wrong the moment my mom turned onto our street Monday afternoon. Several of our neighbors were standing outside and so, I noticed, was another resident of Shelton Lane. Bucky, the 1,000-pound longhorn who lived in a field across the street from us, had escaped once again. The neighbors were banding together to bring him back home.

My mom rolled down her window. "Looks like Bucky is up to his old tricks again," she told Mr. Thatcher, Bucky's owner. Bucky had been known in the past to break through the fence of the Thatchers' yard in order to take a stroll through the neighborhood. Mr. Thatcher just shook his head.

Slowly, we drove by Bucky, who was standing in the Garcias' front yard, happily chomping on Mrs. Garcia's flowers, or what was left of her flowers! Bucky gazed up at us, oblivious to what was about to happen.

After we parked in our driveway, mom and I walked back to the front yard to witness the action. Kenny, Mr. Thatcher's teenage son, was hammering away at the fence, repairing the break that Bucky had used for his escape. "Okay, ready!" he called to his dad and the other neighbors. Lassoing this wandering longhorn and guiding him back to the field was a four-person effort!

Although Bucky was a gentle animal who mainly stayed in the yard, lazily eating and observing the neighborly goings-on, he was still a big animal. The men approached him cautiously.

"Okay, boy," Mr. Thatcher said, "time to come home."

Pausing from his afternoon snack, Bucky turned his head toward the men and seemed to realize the party was about to end. Quickly, he started to move away. The men trailed him, ready with the lasso. Bucky picked up his pace.

Then the men tossed the lasso over his head and tugged. Bucky stopped, appearing quite annoyed that his play time was ending. The men led him back to the open gate. Without missing a beat, Bucky resumed his eating, and the neighbors returned home knowing this wouldn't be the last time they'd have to bring Mr. Thatcher's wayward longhorn home again.

Narrative Writing ■ Narrative Test 83

Writing Traits in the Scoring Guide
(Student pages 82–83)

Ask students to recall the traits of writing they have been studying throughout the chapter. If they are having trouble providing a response, remind them that the first trait is Information/Organization. Write this trait down on the board. Then write their correct responses on the board, including Voice/Audience, Content/Ideas, Word Choice/Clarity, Sentence Fluency, and Grammar/Mechanics. Tell them that when they read their scoring guide, they should try to identify the traits within it. This will help them to think about the purpose of each item in the scoring guide. It will also help them relate to what they have learned in these writing lessons.

Ask a student volunteer to read the traits in the scoring guide on Student page 82.

Read the Model
Writing Prompt Response

Point out that a good test contains the traits listed in the scoring guide. As students read the model writing prompt response, ask them to look for the traits in the scoring guide.

Differentiating Instruction

English-Language Learners Preteach the terms *longhorn* and *lasso*. After reading "Bucky's Big Break," ask the students if there were other terms they were unfamiliar with. Point out context clues to help students identify words and phrases they do not understand. For instance, if students are unfamiliar with the term *oblivious*, ask them to note that Bucky was eating and not bothered by anything. He was oblivious to what was going on, or unaware. Even though students may not determine the precise definition of every word, they will get the general idea of what the story is about. Later, they can go back and look up words in the dictionary to determine their actual meanings.

Using the Scoring Guide to Study the Model

Now let's use the scoring guide to check Olivia's writing test, "Bucky's Big Break." We'll see how well her essay meets each of the six writing traits.

Information/Organization
- The writing has the 5 W's (who, what, when, where, and why) to organize the story.

From the start, Olivia tells you all about what happened. She explains who (her neighbors), what (banding together to get the longhorn home), when (Monday afternoon), where (on her street), and why (because Bucky had escaped again). Then as you read further, you get even more details about what happened. Can you identify the 5 W's in her opening paragraph?

I knew something was wrong the moment my mom turned onto our street Monday afternoon. Several of our neighbors were standing outside and so, I noticed, was another resident of Shelton Lane. Bucky, the 1,000-pound longhorn who lived in a field across the street from us, had escaped once again. The neighbors were banding together to bring him back home.

Voice/Audience
- The writing has a catchy beginning.

Olivia begins her story by stating that something was wrong. It makes you want to read further to see what happened, and as you do, you get even more hooked. After all, I've never read about a 1,000-pound longhorn escaping! How were they going to get that big animal back to his field?

Bucky, the 1,000-pound longhorn who lived in a field across the street from us, had escaped once again. The neighbors were banding together to bring him back home.

Content/Ideas
- The writing includes details that help make the narrative real.

The use of interesting details in Olivia's account makes the story seem real. She talks about what happens as Bucky is approached by the men with the lasso. She gives us a good picture of what happened.

Pausing from his afternoon snack, Bucky turned his head toward the men and seemed to realize the party was about to end. Quickly, he started to move away. The men trailed him, ready with the lasso. Bucky picked up his pace.

Word Choice/Clarity
- The writing has specific and appropriate language and vocabulary to relate the story.

I can tell by reading the story that the writer has chosen the appropriate language to describe what happened. Olivia could have said the longhorn was "eating" flowers, but instead she used the word "chomping." I think that's a much better way to describe how a 1,000-pound animal eats. She also says he "gazed up" at the men, instead of "looked up." I'd say she definitely made the right word choices!

Slowly, we drove by Bucky, who was standing in the Garcias' front yard, happily chomping on Mrs. Garcia's flowers, or what was left of her flowers! Bucky gazed up at us, oblivious to what was about to happen.

Using the Scoring Guide to Study the Model

(Student pages 84–85)

Review and discuss the meaning and function of a scoring guide. You may want to have students look at a rubric from an earlier chapter. Point out the similarities and differences between a rubric and the scoring guide. Students should understand that although scoring guides in writing prompts do not include the criteria for various levels of accomplishment, they do provide guidance in the six key areas of assessment: Information/Organization, Voice/Audience, Content/Ideas, Sentence Fluency, and Grammar/Mechanics.

Explain that in the same way rubrics are used to assess writing, the criteria in the scoring guides are used to assess test writing. It is important for them to use the scoring guide when they are writing for a test to ensure that they meet all of the writing traits.

Read through Student pages 84–86 with students, and discuss the ways "Bucky's Big Break" meets the traits set forth in the scoring guide. Ask students to look for other examples, when appropriate, that show how Olivia's essay meets the scoring guide traits.

Differentiating Instruction

Enrichment Have the students design a rubric based on the traits in the scoring guide. Have them write the four different levels of assessment for each of the six writing categories. Point out that a well-written test will follow the traits listed in the scoring guide and would receive Excelling marks based on the rubric they create. Have them think about what would constitute a writing test that would receive Beginning marks. Have them fill in their scoring guides appropriately.

Using the Scoring Guide to Study the Model

Sentence Fluency
- The writing contains sentences that flow smoothly.

The story really flowed naturally as I read it. I think it helps that Olivia uses a variety of sentences and starts sentences in different ways. For instance, look at the last paragraph. She starts off with a signal word, "Then." She also starts sentences with clauses and adverbs.

Then the men tossed the lasso over his head and tugged. Bucky stopped, appearing quite annoyed that his play time was ending. The men led him back to the open gate. Without missing a beat, Bucky resumed his eating, and the neighbors returned home knowing this wouldn't be the last time they'd have to bring Mr. Thatcher's wayward longhorn home again.

Grammar/Mechanics
- The writing contains correct grammar, punctuation, capitalization, and spelling.

It looks as though Olivia didn't make any grammar or spelling mistakes. I know that's really important when you take a test. That's why it's a good idea to check for mistakes in your own work. Throughout the writing process, you should edit for correct grammar, punctuation, capitalization, and spelling. That way, you won't have any errors on your final test.

Planning My Time

Before giving us a writing test prompt, my teacher tells us how much time we'll have to complete the test. Since I'm already familiar with the writing process, I can think about how much total time I need and then divide it up into the different parts of the writing process. If the test takes an hour, here's how I can organize my time. Planning your time will help you, too!

Step 4: Editing 10 minutes

Step 1: Prewriting 25 minutes

Step 3: Revising 10 minutes

Step 2: Drafting 15 minutes

Planning My Time
(Student pages 86–87)

Explain to students the importance of organizing their time when they are planning for a test. Point out that when they take a writing test, they will have a limited amount of time. Tell them it's important to set aside blocks of time for each of the steps in the writing process.

Ask a student volunteer to tell the class what stage Marco plans to spend the most time on. **prewriting** Point out that many students do poorly on writing tests because they begin writing before they have a plan and continue writing until they run out of time. Stress to students the importance of including time to prewrite, revise, and edit.

Writing a Narrative Test

Prewriting Study the Writing Prompt

Writing Strategy Study the writing prompt to be sure I know what to do.

I study the writing prompt as soon as I get it so that I know exactly what I'm supposed to do. The writing prompt usually has three parts. Since the parts aren't always labeled, you'll have to find and label them on your own, just like I did below. Then circle key words in the setup and the task that tell what kind of writing you need to do and who your audience will be. I circled the words *newsworthy event* in the setup in red. I circled the words *eyewitness account telling about the event* in the task in blue. Since my writing prompt doesn't say who the audience is, I'm going to write for my teacher.

My Writing Test Prompt

Setup — Think about a newsworthy event, one that might make the local news. It can be something you saw or heard about or something you made up yourself.

Task — Then write an eyewitness account telling about the event.

Be sure your writing

Scoring Guide
- has the 5 W's (who, what, when, where, and why) to organize the story.
- has a catchy beginning.
- includes details that help make the narrative real.
- has specific and appropriate language and vocabulary to relate the story.
- contains sentences that flow smoothly.
- contains correct grammar, punctuation, capitalization, and spelling.

You'll want to think about how the scoring guide relates to the writing traits you've studied in the rubrics. All of the traits might not be included in every scoring guide, but you need to remember them all to write a good essay.

Information/Organization
- Be sure your writing has the 5 W's (who, what, when, where, and why) to organize the story.

I want to be sure the 5 W's are included and are in the right place.

Voice/Audience
- Be sure your writing has a catchy beginning.

To get my readers interested from the very beginning, I'll start my story with a fun and interesting beginning.

Content/Ideas
- Be sure your writing includes details that help make the narrative real.

I have to remember to include plenty of details when I write my story.

Word Choice/Clarity
- Be sure your writing has specific and appropriate language and vocabulary to relate the story.

My writing will be much more interesting if I replace vague language with specific language.

Sentence Fluency
- Be sure your writing contains sentences that flow smoothly.

I'll pay close attention to the sentences I use, and I'll make sure that the story flows well.

Grammar/Mechanics
- Be sure your writing contains correct grammar, punctuation, capitalization, and spelling.

It's really important to edit my story for correct grammar and mechanics!

Study the Writing Prompt
(Student pages 88–89)

Read Marco's words on Student page 88 aloud. Emphasize the importance of reading and understanding the writing prompt. Point out that even if they write a great paper, they won't receive a great score unless they have followed the instructions set forth in the scoring guide.

Ask a student volunteer to tell the class what type of essay Marco is supposed to write. **an eyewitness account** Explain that Marco needs to come up with a newsworthy event and write an eyewitness account on that event.

Read through the scoring guide portion of the writing prompt. Then review Student page 89 with the students. Read how each of the traits relates to the six key areas of assessment. Remind students that these traits would be traits seen under the Excelling category if they were in a rubric. Point out that even before Marco begins to pre-write, he thinks about each of the traits he will need to include in his writing test.

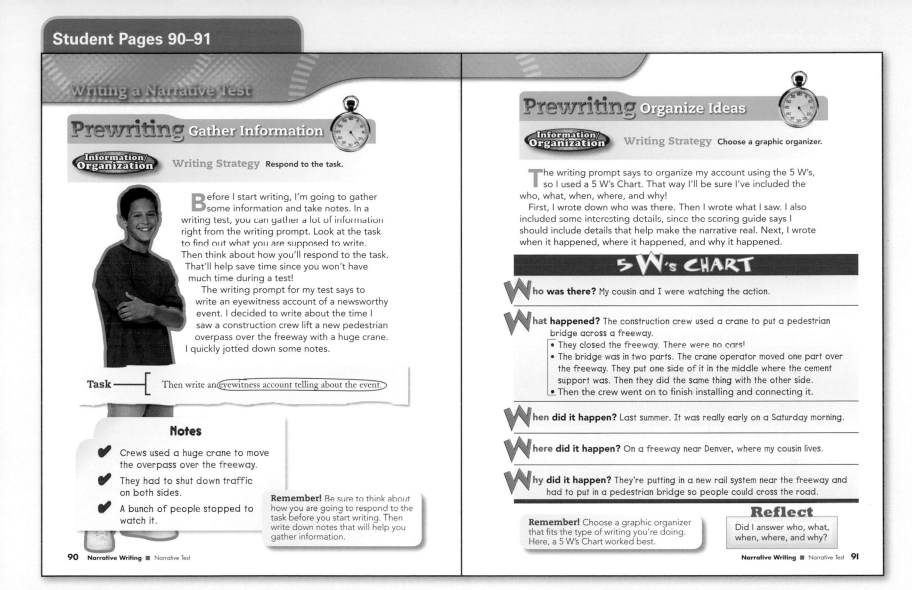

Gather Information and Organize Ideas

(Student pages 90–91)

Ask students to recall what they learned about prewriting in other chapters in this unit. Remind them that during the prewriting stage, they thought about what it is they were supposed to write and then jotted notes down to help them get started. Point out that during a writing test, students will also think about what they are supposed to write and will gather notes on what they will be writing. In a writing test, though, they will get the information about what they are supposed to write from the writing prompt. Read Marco's words on Student page 90 aloud.

Explain to students that they should use a graphic organizer to organize their ideas when they are writing for a test. Remind them that prewriting should take up the biggest chunk of their time and that using a graphic organizer can help them save time when they write their drafts because they will have all of their ideas organized on paper.

Tell students that during a writing test, they will not be told what kind of graphic organizer to use. They should think about how they have used graphic organizers in the

past in order to come up with a useful graphic organizer for that particular type of writing.

Read through Marco's 5 W's Chart. Point out that even before he starts writing his test paper, he already has written down much of the information that will appear in his essay.

Differentiating Instruction

Support To help students recall how graphic organizers can be used to help them organize their notes, ask for volunteers to name the different types of graphic organizers that they are familiar with. Have them think about the graphic organizers they have used throughout the unit. **Possible responses: 5 W's Chart, Story Map, Storyboard.** Ask them to suggest when they might use each of the types of graphic organizers they mentioned. **Possible responses: 5 W's Chart for eyewitness account; Story Map for historical episode; Storyboard for short story** Remind them to look for clues in the test writing prompt to help them figure out what graphic organizer they should use. In Marco's case, the part of the scoring guide in the writing prompt that dealt with Information/Organization said he should include the 5 W's. That's why he chose to use a 5 W's Chart to organize his ideas.

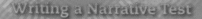

Writing a Narrative Test

Prewriting Check the Scoring Guide

Information/Organization Writing Strategy Check my graphic organizer against the scoring guide.

You won't have much time, if any, to revise when you take some tests. That's why prewriting is important! Before I start to write, I'll check my 5 W's Chart against the scoring guide in the writing prompt.

Who **was there?** My cousin and I were watching the action.

What **happened?** The construction crew used a crane to put a pedestrian bridge across a freeway.
- They closed the freeway. There were no cars!
- The bridge was in two parts. The crane operator moved one part over the freeway. They put one side of it in the middle where the cement support was. Then they did the same thing with the other side.
- Then the crew went on to finish installing and connecting it.

When **did it happen?** Last summer. It was really early on a Saturday morning.

Where **did it happen?** On a freeway near Denver, where my cousin lives.

Why **did it happen?** They're putting in a new rail system near the freeway and had to put in a pedestrian bridge so people could cross the road.

92 **Narrative Writing** ■ Narrative Test

Information/Organization
- Be sure your writing has the 5 W's (who, what, when, where, and why) to organize the story.

Since I used a 5 W's Chart for my graphic organizer, I think I've got this covered!

Voice/Audience
- Be sure your writing has a catchy beginning.

I'll need to grab the reader's attention from the start by pulling the most interesting details from the "What happened?" box on my 5 W's Chart.

Content/Ideas
- Be sure your writing includes details that help make the narrative real.

In my 5 W's Chart, I included lots of details about what happened. I'll be sure to use them in my narrative.

Word Choice/Clarity
- Be sure your writing has specific and appropriate language and vocabulary to relate the story.

Even though I have the details written down, I'll need to use the right language and vocabulary as I write.

Sentence Fluency
- Be sure your writing contains sentences that flow smoothly.

As I write my draft, I'll pay attention to how my sentences are flowing.

Grammar/Mechanics
- Be sure your writing contains correct grammar, punctuation, capitalization, and spelling.

I'll check my writing closely for errors when I go back and edit my draft.

Remember! You'll want to go back and reread the writing prompt one more time so you know just what to do when you start writing your draft.

Reflect

My 5 W's Chart covers a lot of the points from the scoring guide. Still, I want to be sure I don't miss anything.

Narrative Writing ■ Narrative Test 93

Check the Scoring Guide
(Student pages 92–93)

Ask students why they think Marco is not yet ready to write even though he has organized his notes in a graphic organizer. **Possible response: He needs to be sure he checks his notes against the scoring guide.** Emphasize the importance of paying attention to the scoring guide throughout the test writing process. Note that Marco once again refers back to each of the points in the scoring guide to be sure he has met all of them. Explain that during this step of the test writing process, students may need to add information or change information in their graphic organizers to meet the criteria set forth in the scoring guide portion of the writing prompt.

Point out that while the graphic organizer helped Marco get his notes organized and meet some of the criteria in the scoring guide, Marco will still need to think about other parts of the scoring guide as he writes, including Word Choice/Clarity and Sentence Fluency. During the editing process, he will address Grammar/Mechanics.

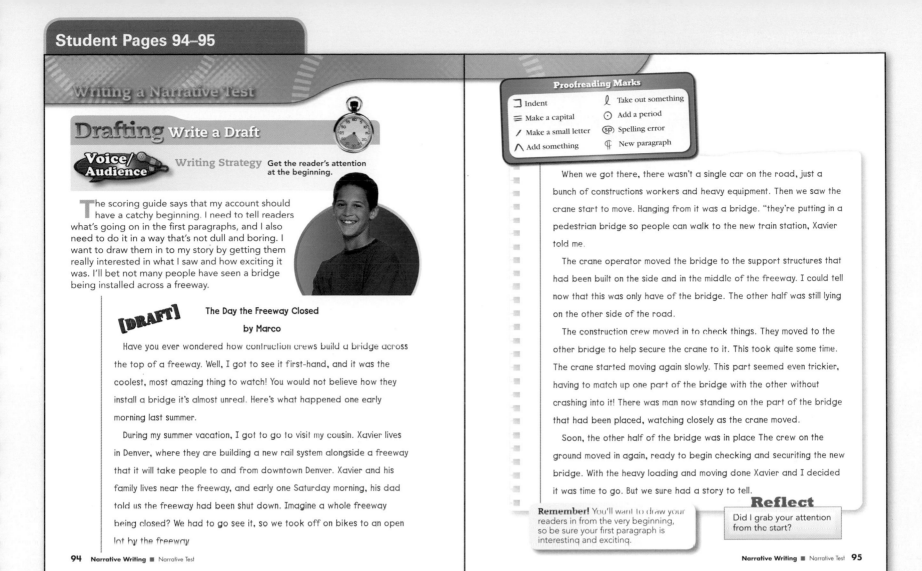

Drafting

(Student pages 94–95)

Read Marco's words on Student page 94. Point out that once again, Marco refers back to the scoring guide as he writes his draft. Tell students that when they write for a test, they should use their graphic organizers to guide them during the draft writing process. Explain that since they have allotted time for editing, they will want to leave space between the lines of their essays so that they will have room to make changes and additions. Remind them, too, that it is important to write neatly, since the edited draft will likely be their final version for scoring. After all, the test evaluator needs to be able to read what they have written.

Discuss Marco's draft. Have students refer back to his graphic organizer to see how Marco included the information that he outlined in his 5 W's Chart. Ask students what they think of Marco's draft. Point out that there are mistakes in the draft, but that Marco has remembered to

leave time to edit his draft. He will be able to go through and change any errors he has made in spelling and grammar during the editing stage.

Review the proofreading checklist with students. Tell them that these marks will be helpful as they revise and edit and their drafts.

Differentiating Instruction

English-Language Learners Remind students to use the drafting time during a test to get the ideas from their graphic organizer down on paper. Tell them that if they are having trouble coming up with words or phrases to use, they can leave blank spots in their writing and come back to them. Tell them, too, that they should not be overly concerned with their spelling and grammar at this stage. Instead, they should leave time to edit their drafts after they have completed them.

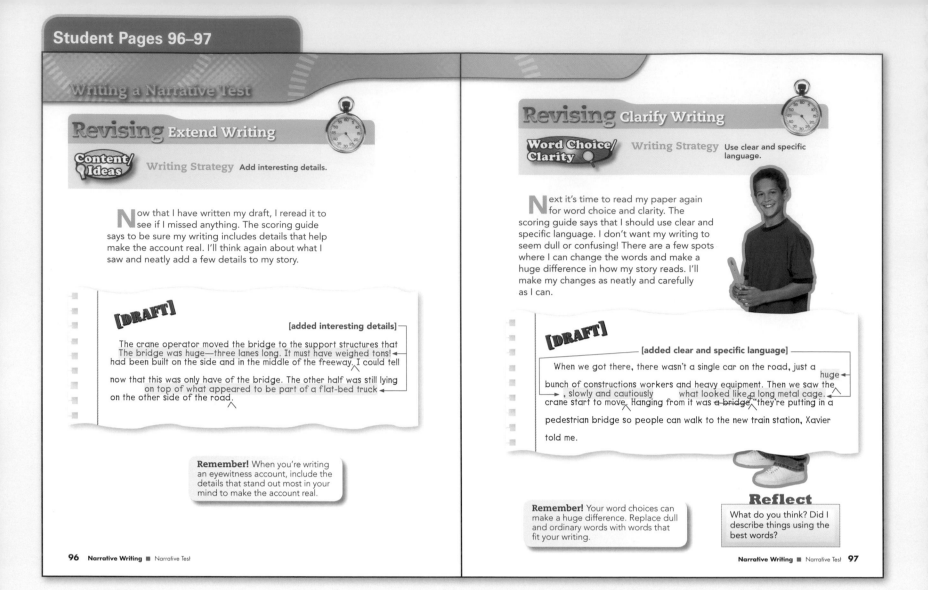

Revising

(Student pages 96-97)

Discuss the ways Marco has revised his test: adding interesting details and using clear and specific language. Point out Marco once again reviewed his scoring guide in order to determine what he should focus on. Encourage students to refer back to the scoring guide section of the test writing prompt even after they have completed their drafts.

Look at the ways Marco added interesting details to his writing. Ask students whether they feel the additions Marco added helped make the account more real. Ask them if there are any other places in Marco's draft where they feel he could also add interesting details.

Next, review with students the ways Marco changed the language in his draft so that it was more clear and specific. Have students explain why they feel Marco added each block of text to his draft. Ask them if they feel Marco's changes improved his draft.

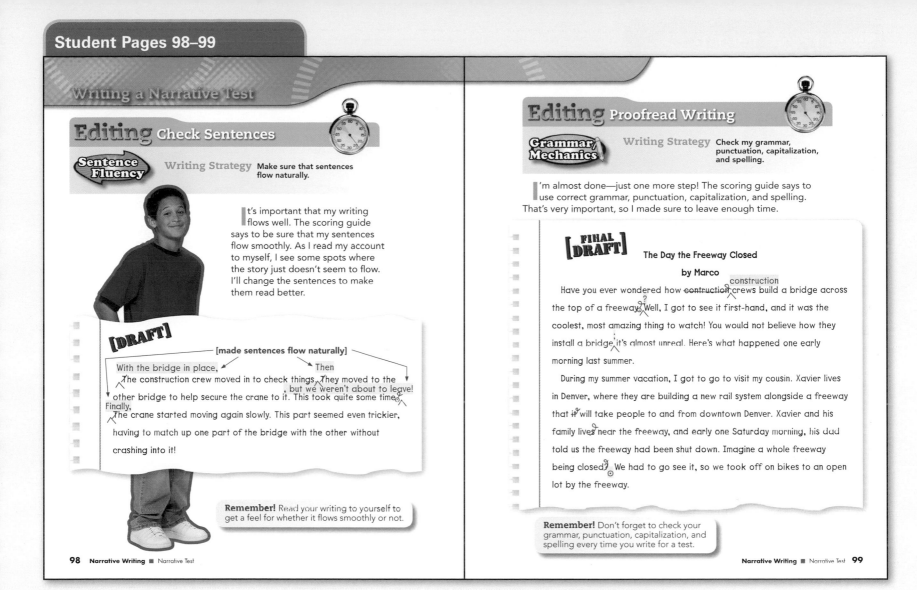

Editing

(Student pages 98–99)

Read the section of Marco's unedited draft shown on Student page 98. Ask students if they think the first sentences in the draft flow smoothly. Have them recall how they changed sentences to improve them during earlier lessons in this unit. Remind them of how they were asked to change the structure of sentences to help them flow more smoothly. Point out that many of Marco's sentences in this draft paragraph were similar: they contained a subject first and then a predicate. Point out that one way to help Marco's sentences flow naturally is to change the structure. Now read aloud Marco's edited paragraph on the same page. Ask students whether they feel his changes have helped make the sentences flow better.

Urge students to allow time to edit and proofread their writing. Instruct them to look for errors as they proofread their drafts. Stress, though, that basic errors in sentence completeness, punctuation, and spelling will likely affect their scores more than minor errors will.

Differentiating Instruction

Support To help students better understand how to edit their drafts so that they are clear to read, write the following on the board:

1. *Where is the cat.*

2. *The cat is chazing the mouse.*

3. *The cat and the mouse has become friends.*

Ask a student volunteer to point out what is wrong with the first sentence. **It should have a question mark instead of a period.** Then have the volunteer come to the board and edit the sentence using the proper editing marks. **delete mark to indicate delete period; caret under an added question mark** Have student volunteers provide the correct edits for sentences two and three. Have them once again review the proofreading marks on Student page 95. Explain that as they use these editing marks more frequently, they will become more familiar with them.

[FINAL DRAFT]

When we got there, there wasn't a single car on the road, just a

bunch of constructions workers and heavy equipment. Then we saw the huge

, slowly and cautiously what looked like a long metal cage.

crane start to move. Hanging from it was a bridge "they're putting in a

pedestrian bridge so people can walk to the new train station, Xavier

told me."

cement

The crane operator moved the bridge to the support structures that
        The bridge was huge—three lanes long. It must have weighed tons!
had been built on the side and in the middle of the freeway. I could tell
                    half
now that this was only have of the bridge. The other half was still lying
                on top of what appeared to be part of a flat-bed truck
on the other side of the road.
        With the bridge in place,   Then
                The construction crew moved in to check things. They moved to the
        other bridge to help secure the crane to it. This took quite some time.
                    , but we weren't about to leave!
Finally,
        The crane started moving again slowly. This part seemed even trickier,

having to match up one part of the bridge with the other without
                        a
crashing into it! There was man now standing on the part of the bridge

that had been placed, watching closely as the crane moved.

    Soon, the other half of the bridge was in place. The crew on the
                                                securing
ground moved in again, ready to begin checking and securiting the new

bridge. With the heavy loading and moving done, Xavier and I decided

to leave. But we sure had a story to tell.

Reflect

Did I miss anything? I'll check it against the scoring guide one last time. It's important to use your writing prompt's scoring guide to check your writing any time you take a test!

Well, we're done. And it wasn't so bad, was it? Here are some helpful tips for when you write for a test.

TEST TiPS

1. **Study the writing prompt before you start to write.** Most writing prompts have three parts: the setup, the task, and the scoring guide. The parts probably won't be labeled. You'll have to figure them out for yourself!

2. **Make sure you understand the task before you start to write.**
   • Read all three parts of the writing prompt carefully.
   • Circle key words in the task part of the writing prompt that tell what kind of writing you need to do. The task might also identify your audience.
   • Make sure you know how you'll be graded.
   • Say the assignment in your own words to yourself.

3. **Keep an eye on the clock.** Decide how much time you will spend on each part of the writing process and try to stick to your schedule. Don't spend so much time on prewriting that you don't have enough time left to write.

4. **Reread your writing. Compare it to the scoring guide at least twice.** Remember the rubrics you have used all year? A scoring guide on a writing test is like a rubric. It can help you keep what's important in mind.

5. **Plan, plan, plan!** You don't get much time to revise during a test, so planning is more important than ever.

6. **Write neatly.** Remember, if the people who score your test can't read your writing, it doesn't matter how good your essay is!

Differentiating Instruction

Enrichment Have students write a narrative test using the writing prompt on Student page 88. Give them one hour to complete the test, and instruct them to structure their time according to the chart on Student page 87. Stress to them the importance of prewriting, revising, and editing their drafts before submitting them. Be sure that they refer to the writing prompt throughout the test writing process. After they have completed their writing tests, ask them to check their papers against the writing traits in the scoring guide. Ask if they followed the traits and why they believe their papers would receive good grades.

Test Tips

Help students recall the lessons they learned in this chapter. Encourage them to describe the important steps to take when writing for a test. **Possible responses: follow the writing prompt, plan their time, save time for editing and revising.** Read the test tips on Student page 101 aloud. Have them think about the ways Marco followed each of these tips during the test writing process.

Remind students that test writing is similar to writing for a class assignment. The big difference is that they will have a limited amount of time when they write for a test. Tell them that is why the test tips to "Keep an eye on the clock," and "Plan, plan, plan," are so important. Point out that they should keep each of these six tips in mind when they write for a test.

Books for Professional Development

Atwell, Nancie, ed. *Coming to Know: Writing to Learn in the Intermediate Grades*. Portsmouth: Heinemann, 1990.

This book focuses on content-area writing, especially the research report. Providing narratives, it shows how to make good use of learning logs. The appendix lists 30 genres for report writing.

Graves, Donald H. *Build a Literate Classroom (The Reading/Writing Teacher's Companion)*. Canada: Stoddard Publishing, 1998.

The reading and writing processes have historically been kept apart, but with this book students can enjoy their interconnectedness in ways that unite the processes meaningfully and productively. It helps teachers learn how to uncover students' potential so that they can be lifelong readers and writers.

Harris, Karen R., and Steven Graham. *Making the Writing Process Work: Strategies for Composition and Self-Regulation*. Cambridge: Brookline, 1996.

Emphasizing "strategy instruction," the authors offer teachers of grades 4–8 clear instruction in the areas of generating content, planning, writing, and revising. The focus is on the narrative genre, but the approach applies to other areas as well, including report writing.

Harvey, Stephanie. *Nonfiction Matters: Reading, Writing, and Research in Grades 3–8*. Portland: Stenhouse, 1998.

The author discusses the nature of nonfiction writing, describing the selection of topics and the use of primary and secondary sources, including those on the Internet. The author also covers organizing information, revising drafts, creating oral presentations to accompany written reports, and designing rubrics.

School-Home Connection

Dear Family,

In *Strategies for Writers,* your child is gaining writing skills that he or she will use throughout life. In this chapter, your child will be learning about how to write an eyewitness account. He or she will get to don a newspaper-reporter's cap and write about something he or she witnessed in real life.

As your student will learn, writing is a process made up of these five basic steps:

1. **Prewriting:** First, the writer gathers and organizes information. For eyewitness accounts, he or she will organize this information into a 5 W's Chart.

2. **Drafting:** Next, the writer writes the first version of a document—the draft. It might be messy and full of mistakes, but that's okay.

3. **Revising:** The writer then elaborates by adding missing information and clarifies his or her writing by ensuring the writing is clear and concise.

4. **Editing:** This is the time when the writer fixes the spelling and other mistakes.

5. **Publishing:** Finally, the writer makes a final copy of the work and shares it with others—including you!

As your child chooses a topic to report on and finds ways to improve his or her draft, please look over his or her work. I encourage you to write down any questions we might discuss. With our guidance and encouragement, we can help these young writers do their best.

Thanks for your help in the writing process!

School-Home Connection

Dear Family,

In this chapter of *Strategies for Writers,* your child will be learning about how to write a historical episode. He or she will be asked to think about a historic event and write a story based on that event. It will give him or her an opportunity to hone research skills and to share the information that he or she has discovered.

As with all of the writing lessons, your child will be instructed to include a set of writing traits in his or her story. For a historical episode, the writing should

1. focus on one historical event and have a clear beginning, middle, and end.

2. have a beginning that directly relates to the historical event and captures the interest of the audience.

3. explain any unfamiliar words.

4. include events that are placed in logical order.

5. contain sentences that vary in length and structure.

6. contain correct spelling, punctuation, and capitalization, and include quotations that are punctuated correctly.

As your child chooses and researches a topic and begins writing a draft, I hope that you have the opportunity to review his or her work. Please let me know if you have any questions about the lessons in this chapter.

Thanks for your help in the writing process!

School-Home Connection

Dear Family,

In this chapter of *Strategies for Writers,* your child will get to use his or her imagination to create a short story. He or she will be asked to brainstorm ideas for a short story and to use the guidelines in this chapter to create their stories. In the process, he or she will learn the traits of a good short story.

The guidelines that we will be using to assess short stories are

1. **Information/Organization:** The story focuses on the protagonist's problem and is told sequentially.

2. **Voice/Audience:** Tension builds throughout the story, leading to an exciting climax.

3. **Content/Ideas:** Sensory details bring the story's characters, setting, and events to life.

4. **Word Choice/Clarity:** Exact words make the writing powerful and vivid.

5. **Sentence Fluency:** The story contains strong sentences in an active voice.

6. **Grammar/Mechanics:** Spelling, punctuation, and capitalization are correct. Indefinite pronouns are used correctly.

This is a great opportunity for your child to flex his or her creative muscles, so we encourage you to take an interest in his or her story. As you review his or her work, please write down any questions I can answer for you.

Thanks for your help in the writing process!

School-Home Connection

Dear Family,

In this chapter of *Strategies for Writers,* your child will learn how to take a narrative writing test. He or she will follow a child guide in the book as he prepares for and writes a narrative writing test. It will give your student an opportunity to learn how to follow the writing instructions and to plan his or her time to complete a test.

One of the things we will be discussing in this chapter is the writing prompt. A writing prompt provides your child with the setup, task, and scoring guide information for a writing test. I'll stress how important it is to pay attention to the details in the writing prompt in order to do well on a writing test!

We've been using rubrics to analyze writing throughout this unit; in a writing test, however, the scoring guide provides the details on how a test will be scored. Just as with a rubric, most scoring guides contain some or all of the writing traits we have been studying throughout this chapter, including

1. Information/Organization

2. Voice/Audience

3. Content/Ideas

4. Word Choice/Clarity

5. Sentence Fluency

6. Grammar/Mechanics

One of the goals of this chapter is to make test writing less intimidating for students by showing students that they already possess the knowledge and ability to do well on a test. I encourage you to review your child's work throughout this chapter. Please be sure to share your thoughts or questions with me.

Thanks for your help in the writing process!

DESCRIPTiVE writing strategies

IN THIS UNIT

1 Descriptive Essay

- Choose a picture and make notes about its sensory details.
- Use a Spider Map to organize my notes.
- Use vivid imagery to help the reader visualize the picture.
- Add effective metaphors.
- Replace dull words with interesting words.
- Make sure all the detail sentences relate to the topic sentence in every paragraph.
- Check that I have used appositives correctly.

2 Observation Report

- Observe and take notes.
- Make a Sequence Chain of the steps in the experiment.
- Clearly describe the experiment so the reader can imagine each step.
- Add diagrams or charts.
- Add time-order words to clarify the process.
- Use questions and exclamations to make my report flow.
- Be sure apostrophes are used correctly in possessive nouns and contractions.

3 Descriptive Article

- Jot down some notes on my favorite spot in my neighborhood.
- Use a Five-Senses Chart to organize my notes.
- Include word pictures to help the reader "see" my topic.
- Add sensory details.
- Replace clichés with interesting phrases.
- Repeat a sentence pattern to emphasize a point.
- Make sure all the verbs are in the proper tense.

4 Writing for a Test

- Study the writing prompt to be sure I know what to do.
- Respond to the task.
- Choose a graphic organizer.
- Check my graphic organizer against the scoring guide.
- Remember my audience and my purpose as I write.
- Add specific details.
- Replace boring language with more personal language.
- Delete sentences that are off topic.
- Check my grammar, punctuation, capitalization, and spelling.

DESCRIPTIVE writing describes something to the reader.

Hi! I'm Denise. I'm learning about descriptive writing in school. I like this kind of writing because it's so real. When you read a good description, you feel as if you're actually experiencing something right at that moment. I want to learn how to write like that!

IN THIS UNIT

1. Descriptive Essay
2. Observation Report
3. Descriptive Article
4. Writing for a Test

Name: Denise
Home: Minnesota
Hobbies: modeling, cooking, and photography

102 Descriptive Writing

Descriptive Writing 103

IN THIS UNIT

Descriptive Essay This genre enables students to write an essay that gives a clear, detailed picture of a person, place, thing, or event.

Observation Report In this genre, students describe the details of an object, person, event, or process.

Descriptive Article This genre gives students a chance to describe a person, place, thing, or event to inform the readers of a newspaper, magazine, brochure, or other publication.

Narrative Test Students will learn and practice how to read a descriptive test prompt and plan their time when taking a test. They will also learn and practice writing strategies for successful test writing in the descriptive mode.

Meet Denise

Denise, a girl from Minnesota, is the student guide for this chapter. Read aloud Denise's hobbies and remind students that Denise will rely on her interests, background, and hobbies to come up with story ideas and make her writing more real. Explain to students that when they have knowledge about a subject or an interest in a subject on which they are writing, their writing will likely be more genuine. Encourage them to think about their own interests as they come up with ideas for their descriptive writing examples. Descriptive writing should bring details and information alive for the reader—and when students can make a connection with their subjects, it will be reflected positively in their writing.

Internet TIPS for the Writing Classroom

by Julie Coiro, Ph.D.
University of Connecticut

Locating Resources: Generating Keyword Searches

There are different keyword strategies you can use to quickly locate the Internet materials you need. If you are using a search engine designed for children, you should get relatively good results by just inserting the topic into the search bar and clicking "search." However, if you or your students are using a more advanced search engine like **Google** or **Yahoo**, you may wish to try the following.

- **Choose your keywords wisely.** Indicate in the search bar a subject area or a specific topic. Use quotations to group two or more words together as a phrase. For example, if you are looking for a lesson on descriptive writing, you would enclose the phrase in quotation marks: "descriptive writing."

- **Narrow your search with a "topic+focus" keyword strategy.** If you preface both topic and focus words/phrases with a plus sign (+lesson+"descriptive writing"), the search engine will only look for hits that have both topic and focus words/phrases on the same Web page.

- **Specify an appropriate grade level, if desired.** If you find your search results are not appropriate for students at your grade level, include the grade level or grade range in quotes before or after your search ("third grade"+"writing lesson").

- **Think of a synonym or skim the search result annotations for more appropriate keywords.** Sometimes reading within the search results or on a few related Web sites creates more familiarity with the language around that topic. This will help you generate more appropriate search terms for your needs.

Here are some examples of the keyword strategies listed above:

"lesson plans" + "descriptive writing"
"fifth grade" + "biography project"
webquest + poetry
quiz + biography
cyberhunt + "Ancient Egypt"

Critical Evaluation: Evaluating Bias

One aspect of reading critically involves the ability to detect bias, or the stance with which an author shapes information for different purposes. Information on the Internet is widely available from people who have strong political, economic, or religious stances, so we must assist students in becoming critical consumers of such information.

One strategy for helping students understand the concept of biased information involves helping them distinguish between facts, opinions, and points of view. A classroom discussion about descriptive writing techniques can provide an excellent context within which to introduce these ideas. Your students are bound to have different opinions about various topics, so you may wish to highlight these differences by selecting a topic that some students really like and others really don't. Ask students to write three factual non-opinionated descriptive statements that describe the topic. Then, ask them to write three opinionated descriptive sentences. Encourage students to share their sentences while others try to guess whether

they're facts or opinions. Categorize the sentences that reflect one point of view (e.g., *I like broccoli*) versus another (e.g., *I don't like broccoli*), and explain that both are valid but come from different perspectives. Thus, the descriptions are biased toward one perspective or another. Explain that a complete description of this topic would include sentences that represent both perspectives.

Point out to students that many Web sites are written from only one perspective. This is important to know so that students do not base their whole thinking about an issue on one person's point of view. For example, take some time to explore **Kids Web Japan** at **http://web-japan.org/kidsweb** and ask why students would not find negative information about Japan at this site. Similarly, visit **The National Wildlife Federation** Web site at **http://www.nwf.org** and ask why students would not find information about hunting at this site. If students feel they are not getting "the whole story" from one Web site, they should look for another that offers a different perspective.

Communicating Globally: Publishing Descriptive Writing

There are a number of interesting on-line projects that can prompt descriptive writing ideas as well as provide space for students to publish their final work. Here are two examples.

- **Art Tales** at **http://www.wildlifeart.org/ArtTales** is sponsored by the National Museum of Wildlife Art. Students are invited, via a unique interactive interface, to explore a wide range of stunning wildlife drawings and paintings while playing the role of a frontier explorer, field guide writer, or museum curator. They select the paintings most relevant for their needs and compile them, with support, into a descriptive journal, informational field guide, or an art exhibition. When they finish, their work is published at the Web site.

- **New Moon Blog** at **http://newmoonnews.blogspot.com** is an exciting new publishing opportunity designed for girls to talk and write about things from their perspective. Created by the publishers of *New Moon:*

The Magazine for Girls and Their Dreams at **http://www.newmoon.org**, it provides screened and safe opportunities for girls ages 10 and up to publish their descriptive stories, book reviews, reactions to current events, and other news about girls. Their companion Web site, **For Girls and their Dreams** at **http://www.forgirlsandtheirdreams.org**, hosts additional opportunities for girls to share their dreams and life goals, discuss hot topics, explore others' countries, and e-mail their opinions. This site is an example of the new social networking experiences that are quickly becoming part of daily life for adolescents.

Supporting and Extending Writing: Sparking Writing Ideas

As part of this descriptive writing unit, you may wish to spend a few minutes of class time to highlight the following on-line science experiment collections from which your students can select an experiment, try it out at home, and then formally write up their procedures and observations in their scientific observations.

- **PBS Science Activities** at **http://pbskids.org/zoom/activities/sci** includes experiments especially designed for exploring concepts such as chemistry, engineering, the five senses, and life science.

- **Energy Quest Science** at **Projects** **http://www.energyquest.ca.gov/projects/index.html** offers fun experiments for exploring chemical, geothermal, and nuclear energy.

- **Exploratorium Science Snacks** at **http://www.exploratorium.edu/snacks/snackintro.html** are mini-versions of the most popular exhibits at the Exploratorium Museum of Science, Art, and Human Perception in San Francisco, California. Each features ideas about what to do after setting up an experiment.

- **Steve Spangler's Easy Science Experiment Projects** at **http://www.stevespanglerscience.com/experiments** features a list of top ten science experiments. Don't miss the videos, too, at **http://www.stevespanglerscience.com/video**.

- **Little Shop of Physics** at **http://littleshop.physics.colostate.edu/onlineexperiments.htm** is part of Colorado State University's hands-on science outreach program, featuring experiments about the physics of objects using household items or a computer.

- **Science Experiments at Home** at **http://members.ozemail.com.au/~macinnis/scifun/miniexp.htm** is a collection of short experiments sure to prompt writing ideas.

- **Wondernet: Science That Matters** at **http://www.chemistry.org/portal/a/c/s/1/wondernetdisplay.html?DOC=wondernet\topics_list\index.html** is sponsored by the American Chemical Society. It combines chemical reactions with graphing activities that can easily be converted into scientific observations.

Descriptive Essay Overview

Students will learn how to write a descriptive essay in this chapter. They will learn the different elements of a descriptive essay—vivid imagery, lively language, point of view, and organization—and why one might write a descriptive essay. Students will look at a model writing sample and assess it using a descriptive essay rubric.

Students will follow Denise as she goes through the writing stages of a descriptive essay—prewriting, drafting, revising, editing, and publishing. They will have the opportunity to practice each step in the process as they write their own descriptive essays. Students will find an interesting subject to describe, make notes about its sensory details, and use a Spider Map to organize their notes. They will use the notes from their Spider Maps to write a draft. Then they will revise the draft by adding effective metaphors and replacing dull words with interesting words. In the editing stage, students will make sure all the detail sentences relate to the topic sentence in every paragraph. They will then edit their drafts for spelling, punctuation, and capitalization errors and check to be sure they have used appositives correctly. With their final drafts completed, students will learn ways to publish their essays. You may wish to send to families the School-Home Connection Letter for this chapter, located at the end of this unit in the Teacher Edition.

Descriptive Essay Writing Traits

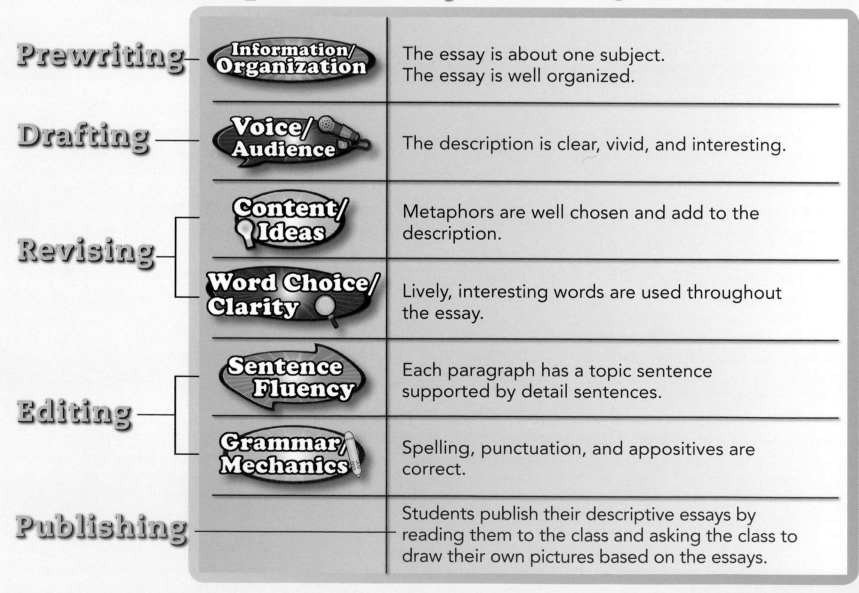

Prewriting	Information/ Organization	The essay is about one subject. The essay is well organized.
Drafting	Voice/ Audience	The description is clear, vivid, and interesting.
Revising	Content/ Ideas	Metaphors are well chosen and add to the description.
	Word Choice/ Clarity	Lively, interesting words are used throughout the essay.
Editing	Sentence Fluency	Each paragraph has a topic sentence supported by detail sentences.
	Grammar/ Mechanics	Spelling, punctuation, and appositives are correct.
Publishing		Students publish their descriptive essays by reading them to the class and asking the class to draw their own pictures based on the essays.

Descriptive Essay Time Management

WEEK 1

	Day 1	Day 2	Day 3	Day 4	Day 5
Learning Objectives					
	Students will: • study the components of a descriptive essay.	Students will: • learn how to gather information for a descriptive essay.	Students will: • practice gathering information for their own descriptive essays.	Students will: • learn how to make a Spider Map to organize their notes.	Students will: • practice organizing their notes into a Spider Map.
Activities					
	• Discuss the elements and traits of a descriptive essay (Student pages 104–106). • Use the rubric to study the model (Student pages 107–111).	• Read and discuss **Prewriting: Gather Information** (Student pages 112–113).	• Brainstorm ideas and choose an interesting subject to share. • Work with a partner to gather information for descriptive essays.	• Read and discuss **Prewriting: Organize Ideas** (Student pages 114–115).	• Look at notes for a descriptive essay. • Make a Spider Map to organize the notes.

WEEK 2

	Day 1	Day 2	Day 3	Day 4	Day 5
Learning Objectives					
	Students will: • learn how to use vivid imagery to help the reader visualize the picture.	Students will: • practice writing their drafts.	Students will: • learn how to add effective metaphors that add to the description.	Students will: • practice adding effective metaphors.	Students will: • learn how to replace dull words with interesting words.
Activities					
	• Read and discuss **Drafting: Write a Draft** (Student pages 116–117).	• Use a Spider Map to write a draft.	• Read and discuss **Revising: Extend Writing** (Student page 118).	• Add metaphors to help the readers visualize the subject.	• Read and discuss **Revising: Clarify Writing** (Student page 119).

WEEK 3

	Day 1	Day 2	Day 3	Day 4	Day 5
Learning Objectives					
	Students will: • practice replacing dull words with more interesting words.	Students will: • learn how topic sentences should be supported by detail sentences.	Students will: • learn how to use appositives correctly.	Students will: • practice editing their drafts for spelling, punctuation, and capitalization.	Students will: • learn different ways to publish their descriptive essays.
Activities					
	• Reread draft, looking for dull words. • Replace dull words with lively, interesting words.	• Read and discuss **Editing: Check Sentences** (Student page 120). • Make sure draft includes detail sentences that relate to the topic sentence in every paragraph.	• Read and discuss **Editing: Proofread Writing** (Student page 121). • Make sure appositives are used correctly.	• Fix any spelling, punctuation, or capitalization errors in draft. • Fix any misused appositives.	• Read and discuss **Publishing: Share Writing** (Student page 124).

* To complete the chapter in fewer days, teach the learning objectives and activities for two days in one day.
This planning chart, correlated to your state's writing standards, is available on-line at http://www.zaner-bloser.com/sfw.

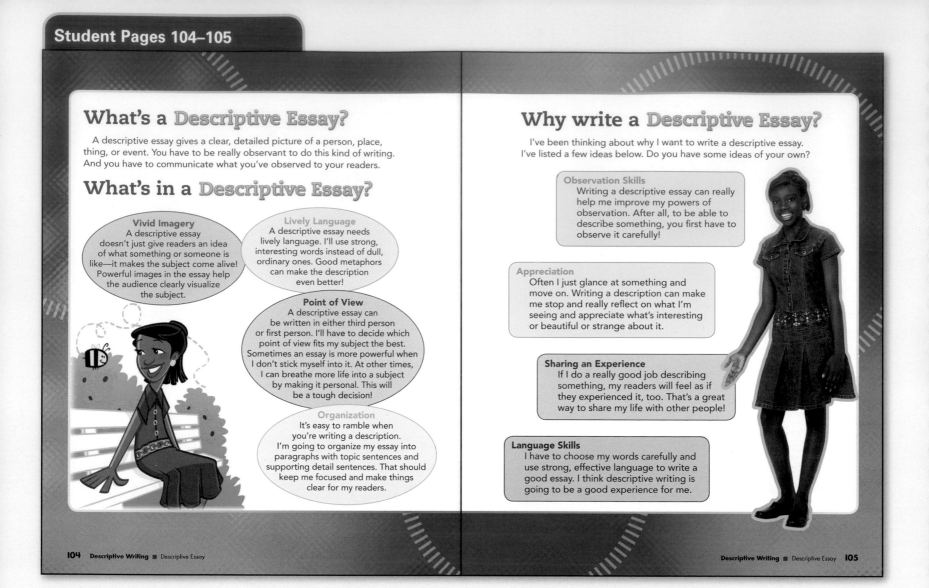

What's a Descriptive Essay?

A descriptive essay gives a clear, detailed picture of a person, place, thing, or event. You have to be really observant to do this kind of writing. And you have to communicate what you've observed to your readers.

What's in a Descriptive Essay?

Vivid Imagery
A descriptive essay doesn't just give readers an idea of what something or someone is like—it makes the subject come alive! Powerful images in the essay help the audience clearly visualize the subject.

Lively Language
A descriptive essay needs lively language. I'll use strong, interesting words instead of dull, ordinary ones. Good metaphors can make the description even better!

Point of View
A descriptive essay can be written in either third person or first person. I'll have to decide which point of view fits my subject the best. Sometimes an essay is more powerful when I don't stick myself into it. At other times, I can breathe more life into a subject by making it personal. This will be a tough decision!

Organization
It's easy to ramble when you're writing a description. I'm going to organize my essay into paragraphs with topic sentences and supporting detail sentences. That should keep me focused and make things clear for my readers.

Why write a Descriptive Essay?

I've been thinking about why I want to write a descriptive essay. I've listed a few ideas below. Do you have some ideas of your own?

Observation Skills
Writing a descriptive essay can really help me improve my powers of observation. After all, to be able to describe something, you first have to observe it carefully!

Appreciation
Often I just glance at something and move on. Writing a description can make me stop and really reflect on what I'm seeing and appreciate what's interesting or beautiful or strange about it.

Sharing an Experience
If I do a really good job describing something, my readers will feel as if they experienced it, too. That's a great way to share my life with other people!

Language Skills
I have to choose my words carefully and use strong, effective language to write a good essay. I think descriptive writing is going to be a good experience for me.

Define the Genre
(Student page 104)

Descriptive Essay

Have a student read the definition of a descriptive essay on Student page 104. Ask a student to describe a favorite place or thing. Prompt him or her to provide details that will help the rest of the class get a vivid picture of this place or thing. Explain that the way the student is describing the place or thing is how students will be describing something or someone for their own descriptive essays. Note that a descriptive essay should provide a "clear, detailed picture," so students will need to keep in mind the elements of a descriptive essay.

Elements of the Genre
Descriptive Essay

Read and discuss the elements of a descriptive essay with the students. Explain that vivid imagery and lively language help give the reader a clear, detailed picture of a person, place, thing, or event. Point out that in a descriptive essay, it's not enough to write, for example, *He was wearing a hat,* but instead to describe the hat in detail by writing, *He was wearing a purple and gold baseball cap that was pulled low over his forehead, making his eyes barely visible.* Explain, too, that a descriptive essay needs to have a point of view and be well organized.

Authentic Writing
(Student page 105)

Descriptive Essay

As students go through the various writing chapters and practice their own writing, it is helpful to remind them that all writing has a purpose and that learning the different genres of writing will help them become better writers. These authentic purposes also help to shape their writing. Read and discuss with students the reason for writing a descriptive essay on Student page 105. Tell them that they will be improving their observation skills by learning to write a descriptive essay and that this is something that they will use as they recount information and stories to other people. Encourage students to think about their reasons for writing a descriptive essay and how these reasons will affect the tone and focus of their writing.

Descriptive Essay
Writing Traits

What makes a good descriptive essay? My teacher says that good writing has the six traits below. I'll try to include them all in my essay.

Information/ Organization	The essay is about one subject. The essay is well organized.
Voice/ Audience	The description is clear, vivid, and interesting.
Content/ Ideas	Metaphors are well chosen and add to the description.
Word Choice/ Clarity	Lively, interesting words are used throughout the essay.
Sentence Fluency	Each paragraph has a topic sentence supported by detail sentences.
Grammar/ Mechanics	Spelling, punctuation, and appositives are correct.

I wonder how well Anna Yuishmal used these traits in her descriptive essay. Let's read and find out on the next page.

Descriptive Essay Model

A STRIKING IMAGE
by Anna Yuishmal

Point of view—first person

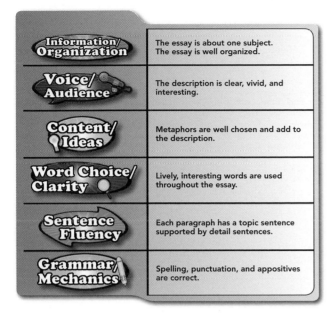

Vivid imagery

I was leisurely thumbing through a book about weather recently when I was suddenly struck by lightning—in a photograph. Filling the page was a lightning storm, a monstrous fire in the sky. Against an inky black sky, mounds of angry clouds piled on top of each other. A charred, smoky-gray mass smoldered near the bottom of the photo. A raging orange cloud exploded like lava. Looming above was a brilliant yellow cloudburst, singed red at its edges. The lightning bolts were a tangle of glowing white wires that sliced the night into jagged pieces.

Lightning is a split-second show, a glimpse of nature's awesome energy. Zing! Steely fingers reach out to snatch a piece of the sky. Poof! They are gone. The photographer captured the brief moment. As the lightning flashed, the shutter snapped.   Lively language

The image reminded me of what comes after a lightning strike. The metallic odor of burnt oxygen, or ozone, follows the flash. Then comes thunder, a distant rolling rumble or a sudden echoing boom. To me, thunder is the delicious dessert after the lightning.

As I closed the book, I could still feel the high-voltage force of the fleeting event caught in the photo. A shiver like a lightning bolt ran down my spine and stayed there.   Organization—supporting details

Organization—topic sentence

Writing Traits
(Student pages 106–107)

Descriptive Essay

Explain to your students what a metaphor is. You may wish to use an example such as *The swimmer's hair had turned a shade of green that reminded me of the skin of a Granny Smith apple.* Explain that a good descriptive essay will include metaphors to help the audience get a clearer picture. Point out that if you wanted to make the sentence even more lively, you could add more interesting words, such as *The swimmer's pale blonde hair had turned a shade of green that reminded me of the skin of a Granny Smith apple.* Point out that using metaphors and lively, interesting words are ways to make a descriptive essay come to life for the reader.

Next, review with students the traits of a descriptive essay on Student page 106. As students study the strategies for writing descriptive essays in this chapter, they will refer to these writing traits. Note that a good descriptive essay will include all of the traits listed on this page.

Tell the students that you will be looking at a model writing sample that includes these traits. Ask them to pay attention to the traits as they read the essay "A Striking Image."

Differentiating Instruction

Support To help students understand metaphors, write the name of a familiar object on the board, such as *skyscraper.* Ask them for words that describe a skyscraper. **tall, glass, huge, imposing, dominating** Then help students think of other objects with similar features, such as *a giant.* Guide them to write a metaphor that compares the two. **The skyscraper was a glass giant.** Point out that students should not use the words *like* or *as.* They might want to use this template sentence: *The [blank] was a [blank].* Have the students practice using metaphors by completing sentences using this template.

Descriptive Essay

Rubric

The traits of a good descriptive essay from page 106 have been used to make the rubric below. By using 1, 2, 3, or 4 check marks to judge each trait, you can decide how well any descriptive essay was written.

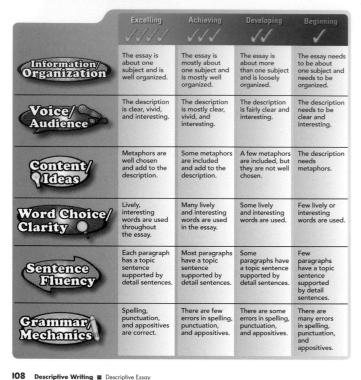

	Excelling ✓✓✓✓	Achieving ✓✓✓	Developing ✓✓	Beginning ✓
Information/ Organization	The essay is about one subject and is well organized.	The essay is mostly about one subject and is mostly well organized.	The essay is about more than one subject and is loosely organized.	The essay needs to be about one subject and needs to be organized.
Voice/ Audience	The description is clear, vivid, and interesting.	The description is mostly clear, vivid, and interesting.	The description is fairly clear and interesting.	The description needs to be clear and interesting.
Content/ Ideas	Metaphors are well chosen and add to the description.	Some metaphors are included and add to the description.	A few metaphors are included, but they are not well chosen.	The description needs metaphors.
Word Choice/ Clarity	Lively, interesting words are used throughout the essay.	Many lively and interesting words are used in the essay.	Some lively and interesting words are used.	Few lively or interesting words are used.
Sentence Fluency	Each paragraph has a topic sentence supported by detail sentences.	Most paragraphs have a topic sentence supported by detail sentences.	Some paragraphs have a topic sentence supported by detail sentences.	Few paragraphs have a topic sentence supported by detail sentences.
Grammar/ Mechanics	Spelling, punctuation, and appositives are correct.	There are few errors in spelling, punctuation, and appositives.	There are some errors in spelling, punctuation, and appositives.	There are many errors in spelling, punctuation, and appositives.

Using the Rubric to Study the Model

Descriptive Essay

Let's use the rubric to check Anna's descriptive essay, "A Striking Image." How many check marks would you give Anna for each trait?

Information/ Organization
- The essay is about one subject.
- The essay is well organized.

The writer chose an exciting photograph of a lightning storm as the subject of her essay. She does a great job of describing the picture in a logical, organized way. She grabs my attention with her very first sentence, shown below. Then she describes the appearance of the storm and the lightning. It's a logical order that flows just right.

[from the writing model]

I was leisurely thumbing through a book about weather recently when I was suddenly struck by lightning—in a photograph.

Voice/ Audience
- The description is clear, vivid, and interesting.

The writer describes the photograph with vivid and exciting details. Her description is so powerful, you clearly visualize the picture even when you're not looking at it!

[from the writing model]

the page was a lightning storm, a monstrous fire in the sky. Against an inky black sky, mounds of angry clouds piled on top of each other. A charred, smoky-gray mass smoldered near the bottom of the photo. A raging orange cloud exploded like lava. Looming above was a brilliant yellow cloudburst, singed red at its edges. The lightning bolts were a tangle of glowing white wires that sliced the night into jagged pieces.

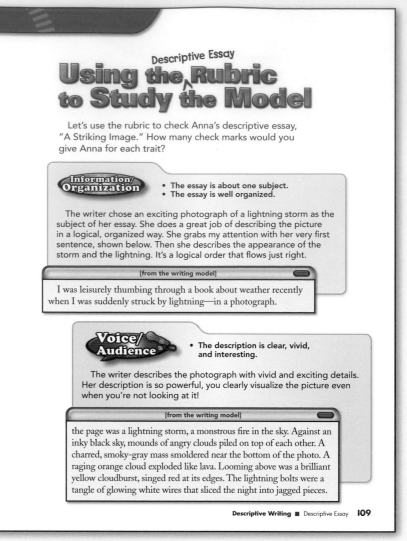

Using the Rubric

(Student page 108)

Remind students that the purpose of a rubric is to help the reader evaluate a piece of writing. The rubric on Student page 108 can be used to evaluate a descriptive essay. It is based on the same traits for a descriptive essay that students read on Student page 106.

Make sure that students have a good grasp of the qualities featured in the descriptive essay rubric. Note that the rubric can also help students identify and correct weaknesses in a descriptive essay. For example, if few lively or interesting words are used (a beginning mark under Word Choice/Clarity in the rubric), the writer will want to revise his or her draft to be sure that lively, interesting words are used throughout the essay.

Study the Model

(Student pages 109–111)

Explain that Student pages 109–111 show how the writing model on Student page 107 meets all six traits of the rubric. Read each section on these pages. Discuss whether students agree or disagree with how Denise assessed the model. For example, could they think of how the organization of the essay could be improved?

Remind students to use the rubric as they write their descriptive essays, to be sure they are meeting all six writing traits.

Descriptive Essay

Content/Ideas
• Metaphors are well chosen and add to the description.

This essay is loaded with metaphors! By using metaphors, the writer compares two unlike things to help us "see" what is in the photograph. Here are two of my favorite metaphors from Anna's essay. One metaphor compares lightning to fingers. Another compares thunder to dessert because thunder comes after lightning, which is like dessert coming after the main course.

> [from the writing model]
> Zing! Steely fingers reach out to snatch a piece of the sky.

> [from the writing model]
> To me, thunder is the delicious dessert after the lightning.

Word Choice/Clarity
• Lively, interesting words are used throughout the essay.

Talk about lively language! Anna used exciting words all through her essay, but I especially like the language in the following paragraph. Instead of simply telling us that lightning doesn't last long, she made us feel its speed and power!

> [from the writing model]
> Lightning is a split-second show, a glimpse of nature's awesome energy. Zing! Steely fingers reach out to snatch a piece of the sky. Poof! They are gone. The photographer captured the brief moment. As the lightning flashed, the shutter snapped.

Sentence Fluency
• Each paragraph has a topic sentence supported by detail sentences.

In every paragraph, the writer has a strong topic sentence that tells you what the paragraph is about. For example, you know from the first sentence that this paragraph is about what happens after lightning strikes. The following sentences provide details about that topic.

> [from the writing model]
> The image reminded me of what comes after a lightning strike. The metallic odor of burnt oxygen, or ozone, follows the flash. Then comes thunder, a distant rolling rumble or a sudden echoing boom.

Grammar/Mechanics
• Spelling, punctuation, and appositives are correct.

I checked over Anna's essay, and I didn't find any mistakes. She even used appositives correctly to add more information about nouns in her sentences. In the sentence below, for example, "ozone" is an appositive that provides more information about the burnt oxygen. She also punctuates appositives correctly by setting them off with commas.

> [from the writing model]
> The metallic odor of burnt oxygen, or ozone, follows the flash.

My Turn!
Now I'm ready to write my own descriptive essay. I already have some ideas. Read along and see how I do it. I'm going to use what I learned from the rubric and good writing strategies.

Differentiating Instruction

Support To help students understand topic sentences, ask them to identify the topic sentence in another paragraph from the model writing sample. Then have them identify how the other sentences in the paragraph support the topic sentence by providing details. As students write their essays, they should remember to include a topic sentence that states what the paragraph is about. They should also be sure that the topic sentence is supported with detail sentences throughout the paragraph. If a sentence does not provide details about the topic sentence, it does not belong in that paragraph.

Writing a Descriptive Essay

Prewriting Gather Information

Information/Organization The essay is about one subject.

Writing Strategy Choose a picture and make notes about its sensory details.

While I was looking for a subject for my descriptive essay assignment, I found this photograph of a cat and a fish. It was in a magazine ad, and I couldn't stop looking at it.

I took these notes on the sensory details in the photograph so I could use them in my essay. I have to use my imagination for the see, feel, hear, taste, and smell of things in the picture. I didn't take any notes on smells or tastes, though. I don't think there are any—unless the cat catches the fish!

My Notes on the Picture of the Cat and Fish

✔ **see:** cat looking into fishbowl; looks like cat's face is inside bowl; cat's ears—small pink shark fins; eyes—big baby-blue and black marbles in pink ovals; nose—pale pink; whiskers—white; goldfish—on cat's nose, plump, shiny yellow with bright orange at front, black ink dot for eye, 2 tiny bubbles from open mouth; bowl—open on top, curved edges, water line below cat's ears, white gravel

✔ **feel:** cat's nose—velvety; ears—fluffy inside; whiskers—sharp; fish's tail—gauzy, delicate

✔ **hear:** cat saying, "Mmmm!"; fish saying, "Uh-oh!"

Practice!

Now it's your turn. Choose an interesting subject to describe, and take notes about as many sensory details as possible.

112 **Descriptive Writing** ■ Descriptive Essay

Descriptive Writing ■ Descriptive Essay 113

Prewriting

(Student pages 112–113)

Remind students that one of Denise's hobbies is photography. Note that for her descriptive essay, she has chosen to write about a particular photo she found striking. Then she wrote down notes about the photo that provided descriptions of sensory details in the photo.

Ask students to think about a person, place, thing, or event that really made an impression on them. Next, they should jot down notes about their subjects, being sure to provide detailed information that can be used in their descriptive essays.

More Practice!

For more practice with these writing strategies, you may wish to have students use the Strategy Practice Book. See the appendix for annotated Strategy Practice Book pages.

Differentiating Instruction

English-Language Learners Students may need extra help with descriptive adverbs and adjectives. Suggest that they choose simple descriptive words when jotting down notes about their subjects and then look the words up in a thesaurus to find other English words with similar meanings.

Enrichment Have your students look through books and magazines to find a sample descriptive essay or paragraph. Ask them to highlight any descriptive words, metaphors, or details that help make the writing lively and engage the reader. Ask student volunteers to read the descriptive paragraphs or essays they found, and have the class decide whether they think the writing examples are effective.

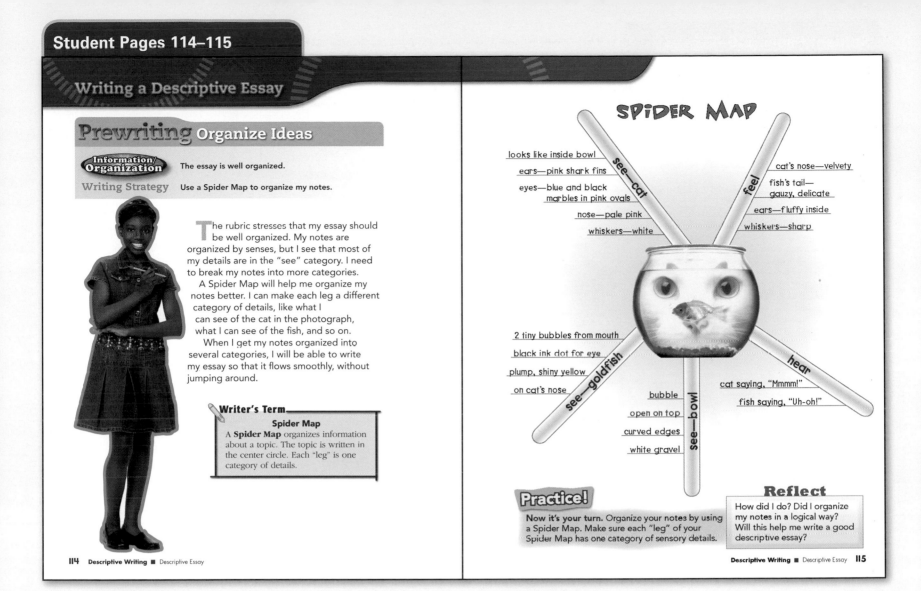

Writing a Descriptive Essay

Prewriting Organize Ideas

Information/Organization   The essay is well organized.

Writing Strategy   Use a Spider Map to organize my notes.

The rubric stresses that my essay should be well organized. My notes are organized by senses, but I see that most of my details are in the "see" category. I need to break my notes into more categories.

A Spider Map will help me organize my notes better. I can make each leg a different category of details, like what I can see of the cat in the photograph, what I can see of the fish, and so on.

When I get my notes organized into several categories, I will be able to write my essay so that it flows smoothly, without jumping around.

Writer's Term
Spider Map
A **Spider Map** organizes information about a topic. The topic is written in the center circle. Each "leg" is one category of details.

114   **Descriptive Writing** ■ Descriptive Essay

SPIDER MAP

see—cat
looks like inside bowl
ears—pink shark fins
eyes—blue and black marbles in pink ovals
nose—pale pink
whiskers—white

feel
cat's nose—velvety
fish's tail—gauzy, delicate
ears—fluffy inside
whiskers—sharp

see—goldfish
2 tiny bubbles from mouth
black ink dot for eye
plump, shiny yellow
on cat's nose

hear
cat saying, "Mmmm!"
fish saying, "Uh-oh!"

see—bowl
bubble
open on top
curved edges
white gravel

Practice!
Now it's your turn. Organize your notes by using a Spider Map. Make sure each "leg" of your Spider Map has one category of sensory details.

Reflect
How did I do? Did I organize my notes in a logical way? Will this help me write a good descriptive essay?

Descriptive Writing ■ Descriptive Essay   115

Prewriting
(Student pages 114–115)

Read Denise's words on Student page 114. Then look at the Spider Map she developed on Student page 115, using her notes about the photograph. Point out that each leg of the spider includes one category of sensory details. This will help ensure that she does not focus too much on one aspect of the photo and neglect details about the other aspects. Note, too, that she provides details about the feel and sound of the photo—or what she thinks the elements of the photos might feel like or sound like.

WORK with a PARTNER
Once students have come up with a topic, have them work with a partner to organize notes about their subjects on a Spider Map. By working together, students can be sure that they have gathered enough details and have not focused too much on one aspect of their subject.

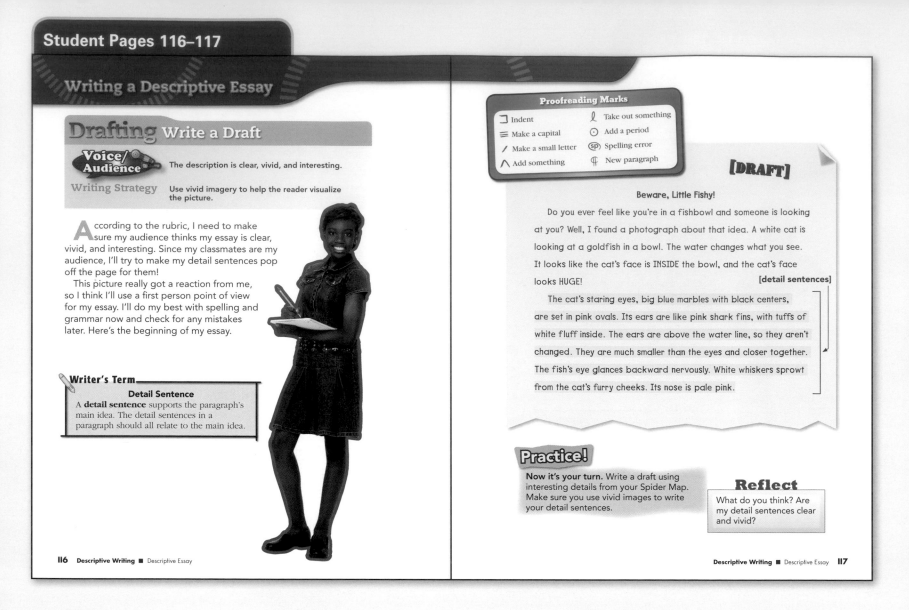

Drafting

(Student pages 116–117)

Remind students that a draft is a temporary or "rough" form of a piece of writing. A draft will be changed and corrected several times before it is finished. That's why it's more important to get the information on paper and not worry too much about such things as mistakes in spelling and grammar.

Point out that Denise refers to the rubric as she writes—that's how she focuses on making sure her audience thinks her essay is clear, vivid, and interesting. Encourage students to get in the habit of using a rubric to help guide their own writing.

Have a student read the definition of a detail sentence. Discuss whether they think Denise's sentences did a good job of describing the photo.

Have students use the information from their Spider Maps to write the drafts for their descriptive essays. Remind them to think about their audience and to be sure their descriptions are clear, vivid, and interesting.

Writing Across the Curriculum

Science In Denise's draft, she describes how the water changes what you see, making the cat's face look huge and as if it is inside the fishbowl. Ask students to think about lessons that they have had in science in order to figure out why the cat's face looks so big on the other side of the glass. They may wish to research this on their own or ask a science teacher about it. Have each student write an explanation of why the cat's face appears as it does in the photo. Then ask for student volunteers to read aloud their explanations. You may even wish to have students try to replicate the effect by using a glass or bowl of water.

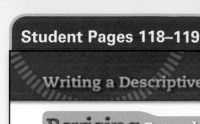

Writing a Descriptive Essay

Revising Extend Writing

Content/Ideas Metaphors are well chosen and add to the description.

Writing Strategy Add effective metaphors.

Writer's Term

Metaphor
A **metaphor** compares two different things. For example, in "Its ears are the fins of prowling pink sharks," the writer is comparing a cat's ears with shark fins. A metaphor is like a simile, but it does not use the word *like* or *as*.

As I read my draft, I wondered if my reader would be able to picture the cat in the fishbowl. Then I remembered that the rubric recommends using metaphors to help describe things. I added a metaphor about the fish's eye. I really think it will help my reader picture it. I thought of a metaphor for the cat's nose, so I added it, too.

[DRAFT]

, an inky black dot,
The fish's eye glances backward nervously. White whiskers sprout
a velvety cushion for the goldfish
from the cat's furry cheeks. Its nose is pale pink.

[added metaphor—compares nose to a cushion]

Practice!
Now it's your turn. Add some metaphors to your essay to help your readers visualize your subject.

Revising Clarify Writing

Word Choice/Clarity Lively, interesting words are used throughout the essay.

Writing Strategy Replace dull words with interesting words.

The rubric says I should use lively words in my essay, but I see some places where I didn't do that. I'm going to take out the dull words I see and replace them with more interesting words. See how I improved the paragraph below?

[DRAFT]

watching
Do you ever feel like you're in a fishbowl and someone is looking
peering intently   distorts
at you? Well, I found a photograph about that idea. A white cat is looking at a goldfish in a bowl. The water changes what you see.

It looks like the cat's face is INSIDE the bowl, and the cat's face looks HUGE!

[replaced dull words]

Practice!
Now it's your turn. Replace any dull words in your essay with lively, interesting words.

Reflect
Did I make my writing more lively? Are there any other dull words in my essay that I need to replace?

Revising

(Student pages 118–119)

Ask a student to read Denise's words on Student page 118 to the class.

Explain that one good way to help readers visualize a picture is to extend the writing by using metaphors. Metaphors show readers that what is being described is similar to something they are already familiar with. Metaphors help make the description clearer.

Have students study the definition in the box. Encourage them to offer metaphors of their own.

Next, have a student read Denise's words on Student page 119. Explain that a descriptive essay needs lively language. Remind them that they want to make the subject come alive for their readers, and dull language won't do that. Ask students why they think Denise changed the sentence to say "someone is watching you" instead of "someone is looking at you." **Possible response: "Someone is watching you" sounds more threatening or creepy; it helps set the tone.**

Have students check their drafts to see if they can replace any dull words in their essay with lively, interesting words.

Differentiating Instruction

Enrichment Challenge gifted students to use submerged metaphors, which are implied comparisons such as *She dove into her work.* Students may want to try extended metaphors, which involve several sentences. For example, several sentences might compare a busy playground with a circus.

English-Language Learners Students who are learning English may have trouble identifying dull words in their essays and replacing them with more lively words. Encourage them to review their drafts sentence-by-sentence. Encourage them to ask themselves if each sentence provides good, engaging details about their subjects. Can they think of other words that might provide a better description of their subject? They should think about the senses—sight, smell, touch, taste, and sound—and come up with words that help convey sensory details.

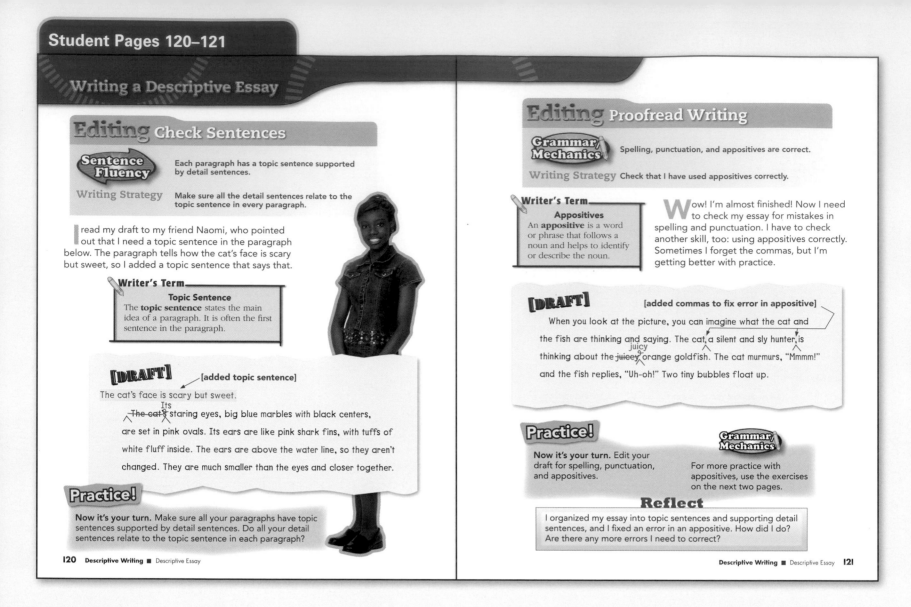

Editing

(Student pages 120–121)

Ask a student to read Denise's words on Student page 120 to the class. Explain that one way to improve sentence fluency is to make sure that every paragraph has a topic sentence and that all the detail sentences relate to that topic. Have students read the definition in the Writer's Term box. Ask why some topic sentences are not placed first in a paragraph. **Possible response: Sometimes writers want to lead up to the topic sentence, so they place it at the end of the paragraph.**

Next, have a student read Denise's words on Student page 121. Then read the definition of appositives from the Writer's Term box. Point out that an appositive can also be a metaphor. Have students reread this sentence from the essay on Student page 107: *Filling the page was a lightning storm, a monstrous fire in the sky.* The word *fire* is both a part of an appositive and a metaphor.

If some of your students are having trouble understanding appositives, you may wish to teach the Mini-Lesson on page 101 of this Teacher Edition. Then have students complete the exercises on Student pages 122–123 of their books. Review the answers and possible rewrites with them.

Remind students that in the editing step, they look for errors in grammar, spelling, punctuation, and sentence structure. Have students look through their drafts to check for and correct errors.

WORK with a PARTNER Have students swap their drafts with another student. Each student should read the other's descriptive essay to check for mistakes in sentence construction, spelling, punctuation, capitalization, and appositive use.

Appositives

An appositive is a word or phrase that follows a noun and helps identify or describe it. Appositives are usually separated from the rest of the sentence by commas.

Examples: Dolly, **my cat**, came to our house as a stray.
My neighbor's dogs, **two boxers**, bark at night.

Practice the Rule

Number your paper 1–10. For the first group of sentences below, write the noun and the appositive that follows.

1. Here are some tips, or guidelines, for getting good photographs of your pets.
2. The first tip, and the most important one, is to study your pet.
3. Find your pet's favorite spot, the place where it likes to spend most of its time.
4. For example, Bubba, my shaggy sheepdog, likes to hang out on the braided rug in the den.
5. Observe your pet's typical behavior, what he or she does every day.

In this group of sentences, notice the underlined nouns or pronouns. On your paper, write an appositive that you could use for each underlined word.

6. Our neighbor, ___, likes to take pictures of his dog.
7. His best picture, ___, won a prize last year.
8. Our neighbor's daughter, ___, takes the dog for walks.
9. They usually head for their favorite spot, ___.
10. Our neighbor has many pictures of the two of them, ___, at the park.

Apply the Rule

Read this descriptive essay about two cats. Write the essay on your paper, correcting any errors in appositives.

My Tigers

Tigers don't make good pets, but tiger cats or tabbies, do. A tabby is a striped shorthair or breed of cat. I have two tabbies, and I love them!

Hansel, the male cat is a butterscotch tabby with lemon-drop eyes. He loves to watch the world from his favorite spot our picture window. His long, white whiskers twitch when he sees birds outside, and his tail is a snake that can't keep still. When Thunder our neighbor's Chihuahua, wanders into our yard, Hansel bats at the window with one soft paw. I don't think Hansel the king of the beasts likes Thunder trespassing in his domain!

Hansel's sister, Gretel, is a chocolate-cinnamon tabby. She likes to lie beside me her favorite person and be petted. As I stroke the silk of her fur, she purrs loudly. Sometimes her tongue, a piece of pink sandpaper darts out and licks my hand. Gretel loves to take it easy, but she gets a burst of energy when she sees a toy filled with catnip a kind of mint that cats like.

Hansel and Gretel are named for the storybook characters the ones who are abandoned in the woods. My cats look like they live in the candy house because they are so chubby and sweet.

(Student pages 122–123)

Appositives

Explain to the students that appositives are words or phrases that follow a noun and help describe it.

Write the following on the board: *Jack and Sam, the twins who lived next door, were known for causing havoc in the neighborhood.*

Ask students to identify the appositive in the sentence. **the twins who lived next door**

Explain to the students that appositives are usually separated from the rest of the sentence by commas.

Write the following on the board: *Once they covered Sage our neighbor's Labrador Retriever in mud.*

Ask students to correct the sentence. **Once they covered Sage, our neighbor's Labrador Retriever, in mud.**

Answers for Practice the Rule

1. tips, or guidelines
2. tip, and the most important one
3. spot, the place where it likes to spend most of its time
4. Bubba, my shabby sheepdog
5. behavior, what he or she does every day

Answers for 6 through 10 will vary.

Answers for Apply the Rule

Tigers don't make good pets, but tiger cats, or tabbies, do. A tabby is a striped shorthair, or breed of cat. I have two tabbies, and I love them!

Hansel, the male cat, is a butterscotch tabby with lemon-drop eyes. He loves to watch the world from his favorite spot, our picture window. His long, white whiskers twitch when he sees birds outside, and his tail is a snake that can't keep still. When Thunder, our neighbor's Chihuahua, wanders into our yard, Hansel bats at the window with one soft paw. I don't think Hansel, the king of the beasts, likes Thunder trespassing in his domain!

(Answers continue on page 102.)

Publishing Share Writing

Read my essay to my classmates. Ask them to draw their own pictures based on my essay.

Our class likes to do art projects and discuss them. I think reading my essay to my classmates would be a good publishing option. It would help us explore how written descriptions can help us understand pictures. It can also help us improve our abilities to observe, describe, and even listen! Before I read my essay, I want to check it over one more time. I'll use the checklist below.

My Checklist

✔ The essay is well organized and paints a clear, vivid picture of the photograph.

✔ Well chosen metaphors bring the description to life.

✔ I've replaced dull words with lively, interesting words throughout the essay.

✔ Each paragraph has a topic sentence and supporting sentences that relate to the topic sentence.

✔ Spelling, capitalization, and appositives are all correct.

Practice!

Now it's your turn. Make a checklist to check your descriptive essay. Then make a final draft to publish.

Beware, Little Fishy!

By Denise

Do you ever feel like you're in a fishbowl and someone is watching you? Well, I found a photograph about that idea. A white cat is peering intently at a goldfish in a bowl. The water distorts what you see, so it looks like the cat's face is INSIDE the bowl, and it's HUGE!

The cat's face is scary but sweet. Its staring eyes, big blue marbles with black centers, are set in pink ovals. Its ears are like pink shark fins, with tufts of white fluff inside. The ears are above the water line, so they aren't distorted. They are much smaller than the eyes and set closer together. Spears of white whiskers sprout from the cat's furry cheeks. Its nose is a velvety cushion for the goldfish.

Shimmering in the center of the glass bubble, the goldfish is particularly appealing. Its plump little body is shiny yellow, with a bright orange face and shoulders. Its gauzy, delicate tail is a waving fan that casts a shadow on the cat's cheek.

When you look at the picture, you can imagine what the cat and the fish are thinking and saying. The cat, a silent and sly hunter, is thinking about the juicy orange goldfish. The cat murmurs, "Mmmm!" and the fish replies, "Uh-oh!" Two tiny bubbles float up.

Normally carefree, the goldfish seems to sense the possible danger. Its eye, an inky black dot, glances backward nervously. The curving sides of the bowl frame the tense situation. Beware, little fishy! You may feel safe behind your glass wall, but remember this: the bowl is open on top!

Reflect

What did you think? Did I use all the traits of a good descriptive essay in my writing? Check it against the rubric. Then use the rubric to check your own descriptive essay.

(Answers continued from page 101.)

Hansel's sister, Gretel, is a chocolate-cinnamon tabby. She likes to lie beside me, her favorite person, and be petted. As I stroke the silk of her fur, she purrs loudly. Sometimes her tongue, a piece of pink sandpaper, darts out and licks my hand. Gretel loves to take it easy, but she gets a burst of energy when she sees a toy filled with catnip, a kind of mint that cats like.

Hansel and Gretel are named for the storybook characters, the ones who are abandoned in the woods. My cats look like they live in a candy house because they are so chubby and sweet.

 For more practice with grammar/mechanics skills, see Zaner-Bloser's *G.U.M.* materials.

Publishing

(Student pages 124–125)

Have a student read Denise's words on Student page 124. Explain that one of the definitions of publish is "to make publicly known." So even though Denise is not reprinting her essay, she is still publishing it by making it known to the class by reading it aloud.

Point out that before Denise publishes her essay, she takes a final look to be sure everything is correct. Ask a student to read the checklist on Student page 124. Ask students how they think Denise came up with this checklist.

Possible response: using the rubric

Have students make a checklist to check their own descriptive essays before writing their final drafts.

Ways to Publish a
Descriptive Essay

I can think of several ways to share a descriptive essay. Here are some of my ideas, and maybe you have some of your own.

✓ Read your essay to a friend or family member without showing the picture. Then let the person see the picture and tell you how the picture compares with what he or she visualized.

✓ Combine all your classmates' photos and descriptive essays with your own, and bind them into a book. Donate the book to your school library.

✓ Display a photograph of your subject, along with your essay, on a bulletin board at school.

✓ Ask a friend to write a descriptive essay about your subject. Then discuss your essays.

✓ Set up a contest using your descriptive essay along with some of your classmates' essays. Who can most closely re-create the described pictures?

Writing Across the Content Areas
Descriptive Essay

Look through your textbooks and find pictures you might like to describe. Here are some other ideas, too.

Art and/or Music
- Write a descriptive essay about a painting by a famous artist.
- Take a photograph of something interesting. Then describe the photograph in an essay.

Language Arts
- Using the author's descriptions and your own imagination, visualize a character from a book. Then write a descriptive essay about the character.
- Write a descriptive essay about a character from a story or book, leaving out identifying details. Can your classmates guess who the essay is about?

Math
- Study a mathematical device such as an abacus, calculator, ruler, or compass. Describe the device in a short essay.
- Choose a picture from a coin or bill and examine it carefully. Then write an essay describing the picture.

Ways to Publish
(Student page 126)

Read and discuss with students the different publishing options on Student page 126. Challenge students to think of other ways Denise could share her essay. Then have students think about ways to publish their essays.

Writing Across the Content Areas
(Student page 127)

Remind your students that writing is not just for English or language arts class. There are many other subjects that contain persons, places, things, or events they may want to describe. Ask students if they can think about other subjects that offer opportunities for writing descriptive essays. For example, have them think about social studies. They could visit a historical site, for example, and write about it. Or they could observe a painting of a famous person from history and write a description of that person. Encourage them to think about descriptive essays as they study other subjects in school.

Observation Report Overview

Students will learn how to write an observation report in this chapter. Point of view, details, organization, and clarity are all elements of an observation report. Students will learn about these elements and explore some of the reasons they might write such a report. The chapter includes an observation report model that students will study using an observation report rubric.

Then the student model will go through the process of writing an observation report. As she goes through each step, including prewriting, drafting, revising, editing, and publishing, students will have a chance to follow along and practice these strategies in their own writing. They will observe an experiment and take notes, which they will then organize into a Sequence Chain. They will use their Sequence Chains to write their drafts, describing each step of the experiment. To revise their drafts, they will add diagrams or charts and time-order words to clarify the process. Next, they will edit their drafts by using questions and exclamations to make the report flow naturally, and they will check that apostrophes are used correctly. They will also check for correct spelling and punctuation. Once they have completed their observation reports, they will publish their reports. You may wish to send to families the School-Home Connection Letter for this chapter, located at the end of this unit in the Teacher Edition.

Observation Report Writing Traits

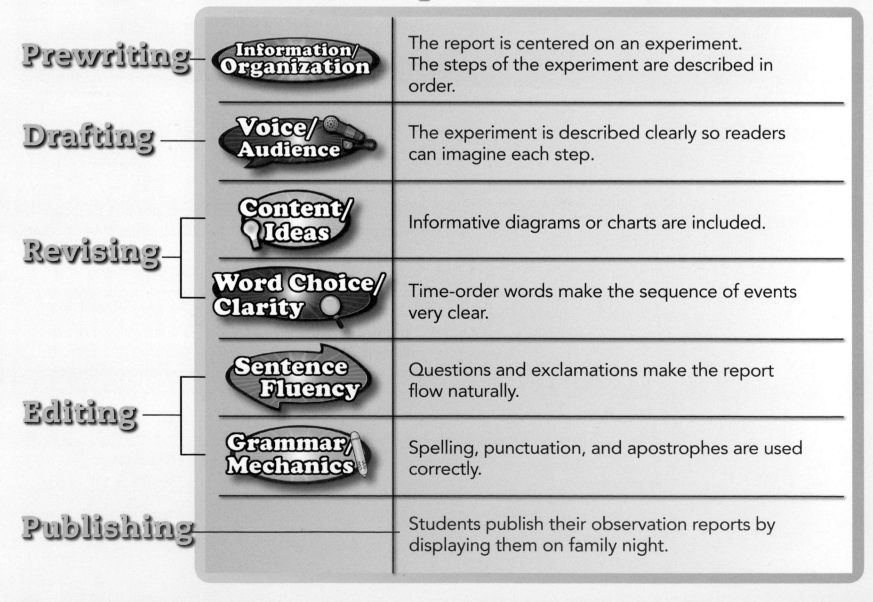

Prewriting — Information/Organization
The report is centered on an experiment. The steps of the experiment are described in order.

Drafting — Voice/Audience
The experiment is described clearly so readers can imagine each step.

Revising — Content/Ideas
Informative diagrams or charts are included.

Word Choice/Clarity
Time-order words make the sequence of events very clear.

Editing — Sentence Fluency
Questions and exclamations make the report flow naturally.

Grammar/Mechanics
Spelling, punctuation, and apostrophes are used correctly.

Publishing
Students publish their observation reports by displaying them on family night.

Observation Report Time Management

WEEK 1

	Day 1	Day 2	Day 3	Day 4	Day 5
Learning Objectives					
	Students will: • learn the components of an observation report.	Students will: • learn how to observe an experiment and take notes.	Students will: • practice observing an experiment and taking notes.	Students will: • learn how to make a Sequence Chain to describe the steps in the experiment.	Students will: • practice organizing their notes to make a Sequence Chain.
Activities					
	• Discuss the elements and traits of an observation report (Student pages 128–130). • Use the rubric to study the model (Student pages 131–135).	• Read and discuss **Prewriting: Gather Information** (Student page 136).	• Conduct an experiment while a partner observes and takes notes. • Take notes on the experiment for the observation report.	• Read and discuss **Prewriting: Organize Ideas** (Student page 137).	• Look at notes on the experiment. • Use notes to fill in the Sequence Chain.

WEEK 2

	Day 1	Day 2	Day 3	Day 4	Day 5
Learning Objectives					
	Students will: • learn how to describe the experiment so readers can imagine each step.	Students will: • practice writing their drafts.	Students will: • learn how to add diagrams or charts to their observation reports.	Students will: • practice adding diagrams or charts to their observation reports.	Students will: • learn how to add time-order words to make the sequence of events very clear.
Activities					
	• Read and discuss **Drafting: Write a Draft** (Student pages 138–139).	• Use a Sequence Chain to write a draft. • Describe the experiment clearly so readers can imagine each step.	• Read and discuss **Revising: Extend Writing** (Student page 140).	• Add diagrams or charts on the experiment to their observation reports.	• Read and discuss **Revising: Clarify Writing** (Student page 141).

WEEK 3

	Day 1	Day 2	Day 3	Day 4	Day 5
Learning Objectives					
	Students will: • practice adding time-order words to their drafts.	Students will: • learn how to use questions and exclamations to make the report flow naturally.	Students will: • learn how to correctly use apostrophes.	Students will: • practice editing their drafts for spelling, punctuation, and apostrophe use.	Students will: • learn different ways to publish their observation reports.
Activities					
	• Reread drafts to see where time-order words will help clarify the process. • Add time-order words where appropriate.	• Read and discuss **Editing: Check Sentences** (Student page 142). • Reread drafts and add questions and exclamations to make the report flow.	• Read and discuss **Editing: Proofread Writing** (Student page 143). • Make sure apostrophes are used correctly in possessive nouns and contractions.	• Fix any spelling and punctuation errors in drafts. • Fix any incorrectly used apostrophes.	• Read and discuss **Publishing: Share Writing** (Student pages 146–150).

To complete the chapter in fewer days, teach the learning objectives and activities for two days in one day.
This planning chart, correlated to your state's writing standards, is available on-line at http://www.zaner-bloser.com/sfw.

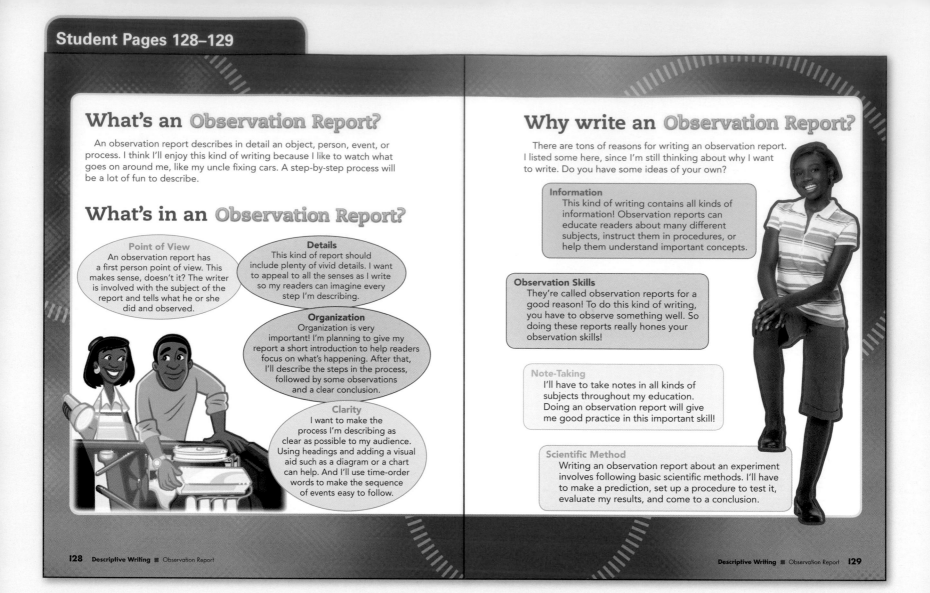

Define the Genre

(Student page 128)

Observation Report

Ask students to describe formal or informal science experiments they have conducted. Did they record the results? How? What are the advantages of recording what they did and what happened as a result of their actions? **Possible response: A record of the experiment allows others to learn from it. That's how scientists build their knowledge.** Many science projects require students to write observation reports. What parts of an experiment should be recorded? **Possible responses: the setup; the materials and equipment needed; the steps of the experiment; what happened; conclusions**

Explain that a written description of a science experiment is an observation report.

Elements of the Genre

Observation Report

Read and discuss each of the elements of an observation report. Note that first person point of view is necessary, since the writer is writing what he or she has observed. Ask students why they think organization is important in an observation report. **Possible response: It's important to describe the steps as they happen so the reader can understand the process.** Point out that in this form of writing, writers may need to include visual aids such as diagrams or charts.

Authentic Writing

(Student page 129)

Observation Report

Review the purposes for writing an observation report on Student page 129. Ask students why they think note-taking is helpful when writing an observation report. **Possible responses: Because they will be describing all the details of an experiment, they will need to know how to take good notes; they may not have a chance to observe the experiment a second time, so it's important they take good notes the first time.** After reviewing the reasons to write an observation report, ask students what they feel the tone of an observation report should be—informal and breezy or matter-of-fact? **Possible response: matter-of-fact**

Observation Report
Writing Traits

A good observation report has the traits listed below, so I need to include them all in my report.

Information/ Organization	The report is centered on an experiment. The steps of the experiment are described in order.
Voice/ Audience	The experiment is described clearly so readers can imagine each step.
Content/ Ideas	Informative diagrams or charts are included.
Word Choice/ Clarity	Time-order words make the sequence of the events very clear.
Sentence Fluency	Questions and exclamations make the report flow naturally.
Grammar/ Mechanics	Spelling, punctuation, and apostrophes are used correctly.

An observation report by Mark Volk is on the next page. Let's see how Mark used the traits in his writing.

Observation Report Model

Growing Paintbrush Mold
by Mark Volk

First person point of view

Penicillium notatum is a green mold that grows on cheese, bread, and fruit. This disgusting mold is the source of penicillin, an antibiotic! I already knew that mold grows better in a moist environment. How would temperature affect this mold's growth? My prediction was that the mold would grow better in a warm, moist environment than in a cold, moist environment.

PROCEDURE — Heading

Step 1: First, I rubbed two lemons on the floor to roughen up their skin. Then I left them on the kitchen table overnight. This way, penicillin mold spores, which are in soil and air, would be more likely to stick to the fruit.

Step 2: The next day, I put one of the lemons and one moist cotton ball in a paper bag and closed the bag. I put the bag in the refrigerator. Then I repeated this process with the other lemon and put that paper bag in a warm corner of the kitchen.

Step 3: For the next two weeks, I checked the lemons every day, took notes in my observation log, and made several color sketches.

Step 4: At the end of the two weeks, one lemon was covered with green mold. I scraped a little of this mold into a drop of water on a microscope slide and looked at it. I didn't get too close to the mold or breathe in any of it. Then I sketched the slide for my observation log.

Organization →

Details

OBSERVATIONS

During the whole experiment, the lemon in the refrigerator didn't change much. By the end of the experiment, it was a little drier but still firm and bright yellow. However, on the third day the lemon in the warm corner began to show spots of green powder. By the end of the two weeks, it had turned into a spongy, aqua-colored fuzz ball. It also had a strong smell because it had started to rot. ← Vivid details

What did the mold look like under the microscope? It resembled a cluster of stems with feathery ends—something like a paintbrush. That makes sense because penicillin is named for the Latin word penicillus, which means "brush."

Visual aid for clarity

CONCLUSION

Penicillin grew on the lemon kept warm and moist, but not on the one in the refrigerator. A warm, moist environment is better than a cold, moist one for growing penicillin mold.

Writing Traits

(Student pages 130–131)

Observation Report

Read through each of the steps in the procedure for the observation report "Growing Paintbrush Mold" on Student page 131. Ask students to identify the point of view that the writer is using in describing these steps. **first person point of view** Note that in the first step, the writer uses the time-order word *first* to indicate what he did first. Ask students to identify time-order words in the other steps that help indicate the order of events. **Possible responses: The next day; For the next two weeks; At the end of two weeks** Explain that using time-order words helps to describe the process of the experiment and clarify the order of events.

Tell students that they are going to be studying strategies for writing observation reports. They will also be using these strategies to write their own observation reports.

A good observation report will have the traits listed on Student page 130. Review with students the writing traits and their descriptions.

Have students listen and try to identify these traits as you read aloud "Growing Paintbrush Mold" on Student page 131.

Differentiating Instruction

English-Language Learners In order to help students understand and identify time-order words, provide them with a word bank of time-order words. Ask them to translate them into their native languages. Then have them list, in order, the actions they performed since getting up this morning. Ask them to use their lists to write a paragraph, drawing from the word bank as needed.

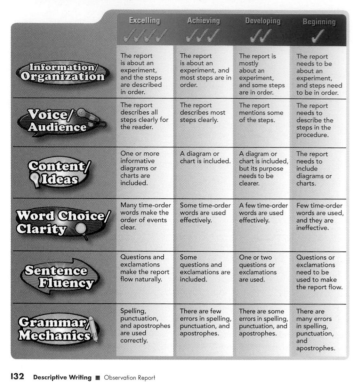

Observation Report

Rubric

The traits of a good observation report from page 130 have been used to make the rubric below. By using 1, 2, 3, or 4 check marks to judge each trait, you can decide how well any observation report was written.

	Excelling ✓✓✓✓	Achieving ✓✓✓	Developing ✓✓	Beginning ✓
Information/ Organization	The report is about an experiment, and the steps are described in order.	The report is about an experiment, and most steps are in order.	The report is mostly about an experiment, and some steps are in order.	The report needs to be about an experiment, and steps need to be in order.
Voice/ Audience	The report describes all steps clearly for the reader.	The report describes most steps clearly.	The report mentions some of the steps.	The report needs to describe the steps in the procedure.
Content/ Ideas	One or more informative diagrams or charts are included.	A diagram or chart is included.	A diagram or chart is included, but its purpose needs to be clearer.	The report needs to include diagrams or charts.
Word Choice/ Clarity	Many time-order words make the order of events clear.	Some time-order words are used effectively.	A few time-order words are used effectively.	Few time-order words are used, and they are ineffective.
Sentence Fluency	Questions and exclamations make the report flow naturally.	Some questions and exclamations are included.	One or two questions or exclamations are used.	Questions or exclamations need to be used to make the report flow.
Grammar/ Mechanics	Spelling, punctuation, and apostrophes are used correctly.	There are few errors in spelling, punctuation, and apostrophes.	There are some errors in spelling, punctuation, and apostrophes.	There are many errors in spelling, punctuation, and apostrophes.

Observation Report

Using the Rubric to Study the Model

Now we can use the rubric to check Mark's observation report, "Growing Paintbrush Mold." How many check marks should Mark receive for each trait?

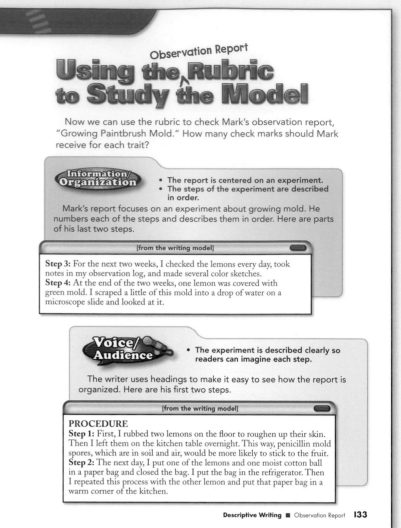

Information/ Organization
- The report is centered on an experiment.
- The steps of the experiment are described in order.

Mark's report focuses on an experiment about growing mold. He numbers each of the steps and describes them in order. Here are parts of his last two steps.

[from the writing model]

Step 3: For the next two weeks, I checked the lemons every day, took notes in my observation log, and made several color sketches.
Step 4: At the end of the two weeks, one lemon was covered with green mold. I scraped a little of this mold into a drop of water on a microscope slide and looked at it.

Voice/ Audience
- The experiment is described clearly so readers can imagine each step.

The writer uses headings to make it easy to see how the report is organized. Here are his first two steps.

[from the writing model]

PROCEDURE
Step 1: First, I rubbed two lemons on the floor to roughen up their skin. Then I left them on the kitchen table overnight. This way, penicillin mold spores, which are in soil and air, would be more likely to stick to the fruit.
Step 2: The next day, I put one of the lemons and one moist cotton ball in a paper bag and closed the bag. I put the bag in the refrigerator. Then I repeated this process with the other lemon and put that paper bag in a warm corner of the kitchen.

Using the Rubric
(Student page 132)

Remind students that rubrics are tools that help the reader evaluate a piece of writing. The rubric on Student page 132 can be used to evaluate an observation report. Ask students to refer back to the traits for an observation report on Student page 130. Note that the rubric is based on the same traits.

Read through the traits for Content/Ideas for Excelling, Achieving, Developing, and Beginning. Note that it is not enough for students to just include a diagram or chart in their observation report; they must include one, or more, that is informative. Point out that if the student model had included a diagram of which shelf in his refrigerator contained the experimental lemons, it would not have helped his reader understand the experiment any better. Ask students if they can think of other charts or diagrams that the writer of the observation report model might have included that would have been helpful and informative. **Possible responses: a chart showing what was happening with the lemons each day; one of his color sketches of the lemons**

Study the Model
(Student pages 133–135)

Explain that Student pages 133–135 show how the writing model on Student page 131 meets all six traits of the rubric. Ask student volunteers to read each section. Then have students identify other examples of each trait in the writing model.

Ask students if they agree with Denise's assessment of the model. If not, how would they have rated each of the traits from the rubric in the writing model? How would they rate the report overall?

Remind students that they should use the rubric as they write their own observation report so that they can be sure to meet all six writing traits.

Observation Report

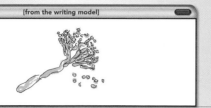
Content/Ideas
• Informative diagrams or charts are included.

I like the drawing of the penicillin mold that he included. I can see what this mold looks like under a microscope—and why its name means "brush." I would also like to see the writer's observation log that he mentioned in Step 3. I think that would have been interesting, too.

[from the writing model]

Word Choice/Clarity
• Time-order words made the sequence of the events very clear.

The report uses time-order words and phrases to let the reader know when each step or each change occurs. *During the whole experiment, By the end of the experiment, on the third day,* and other phrases tell us exactly when he observed changes—or no changes.

[from the writing model]

OBSERVATIONS
During the whole experiment, the lemon in the refrigerator didn't change much. By the end of the experiment, it was a little drier but still firm and bright yellow. However, on the third day the lemon in the warm corner began to show spots of green powder. By the end of the two weeks, it had turned into a spongy, aqua-colored fuzz ball. It also had a strong smell because it had started to rot.

Sentence Fluency
• Questions and exclamations make the report flow naturally.

Mark's description of his experiment could have sounded dull, but he made sure that didn't happen! He included interesting questions and exclamations to make the writing flow. See how he did that in his opening paragraph?

[from the writing model]

Penicillium notatum is a green mold that grows on cheese, bread, and fruit. This disgusting mold is the source of penicillin, an antibiotic! I already knew that mold grows better in a moist environment. How would temperature affect this mold's growth? My prediction was that the mold would grow better in a warm, moist environment than in a cold, moist environment.

Grammar/Mechanics
• Spelling, punctuation, and apostrophes are used correctly.

This writer always uses apostrophes correctly. Read the two sentences below. One shows how he correctly punctuated a contraction. The second sentence includes a possessive noun, with the apostrophe placed correctly.

[from the writing model]

During the whole experiment, the lemon in the refrigerator didn't change much.

[from the writing model]

mold grows better in a moist environment. How would temperature affect this mold's growth?

My Turn!

Now it's my turn! I'm going to write an observation report that follows the rubric and good writing strategies. Read along and see how I do it!

Differentiating Instruction

Enrichment Challenge students to read and analyze observation reports of experiments from scientific magazines, journals, or textbooks. Make a photocopy of several for students to analyze. Ask them to look for and number the steps in the process, explain how charts and diagrams add to the report, and underline any time-order words. Then have students assess the observation reports using the observation report rubric.

Prewriting Gather Information

Information/Organization The report is centered on an experiment.

Writing Strategy Observe and take notes.

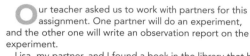

Our teacher asked us to work with partners for this assignment. One partner will do an experiment, and the other one will write an observation report on the experiment.

Lisa, my partner, and I found a book in the library that has experiments in speed. One experiment shows how gravity affects acceleration (how fast an object starts to move).

We decided that Lisa would do the experiment, and I would write the report.

My Notes on the Acceleration Experiment

- **Our question:** How would attaching weights to a car affect its acceleration?
- **Our prediction:** Each additional weight would increase the car's acceleration.
- **What we did:** attached paper clip hook to car with string; put one weight (washer) on hook and hung it over edge; held car 2.5 ft from edge; let car go and started timing with stopwatch; stopped timing when car hit cardboard bumper; recorded time in log; averaged time over 3 runs; repeated with more weights.
- **The results (averages):** 1 weight: car hit bumper in 2.6 seconds; 2 weights: car hit in 1.8 seconds; 3 weights: 1.4 seconds; 4 weights: 1.1 seconds; 5 weights: .7 seconds
- **Conclusion:** Our prediction is correct. More weights mean a faster acceleration rate.

Practice!

Now it's your turn. Conduct or observe an experiment. Take notes on what you observed.

136 **Descriptive Writing** ■ Observation Report

Prewriting Organize Ideas

Information/Organization The steps of the experiment are described in order.

Writing Strategy Make a Sequence Chain of the steps in the experiment.

Writer's Term
Sequence Chain
A **Sequence Chain** shows steps or events in the order they happen.

According to the rubric, I need to explain the steps in our experiment in the order we did them. A Sequence Chain is a good way to do that.

Sequence Chain

Step 1: To set up the experiment, we
a) made a paper clip into a hook.
b) used tape to mark a starting line 2.5 ft from the edge of a table.
c) taped a cardboard bumper to the edge of the table to stop the car; made a hole at the bottom of the bumper for the string.
d) cut 2.5 ft of string; tied one end to the car's axle and the other end to the hook.
e) pushed the hook through the hole in the bumper.

Step 2: Lisa put one weight on the hook.

Step 3: Next, she held the weight over the edge of the table.

Step 4: With her other hand, she put the car at the starting line.

Step 5: She let the weight fall, and I started the stopwatch.

Step 6: I stopped timing when the car hit the bumper. I recorded the time.

Step 7: We repeated Steps 2–6 two more times. Then we averaged the times.

Step 8: We repeated Steps 2–7 with 2, 3, 4, and 5 weights. We recorded and averaged the times.

Practice!

Now it's your turn. Organize your notes by using a Sequence Chain.

Reflect
How did I do? Is my Sequence Chain organized and complete? Will it help me write a well-organized report?

Descriptive Writing ■ Observation Report 137

Prewriting

(Student pages 136–137)

Read Denise's words on Student page 136 aloud. Discuss her reasons for choosing this experiment for her report. Ask students what they notice about her notes. **Possible responses: Denise's notes include the question she and her partner are trying to answer and their prediction of the answer. The notes are brief but very specific. They are divided into categories.**

Next, review the purpose of a graphic organizer. Explain that a graphic organizer, such as a Sequence Chain, is one way to organize information in preparation for writing. Read the definition of a Sequence Chain from the Writer's Term box on Student page 137. Then have students review Denise's Sequence Chain.

More Practice!

For more practice with these writing strategies, you may wish to have students use the Strategy Practice Book. See the appendix for annotated Strategy Practice Book pages.

Differentiating Instruction

Support Some students may have trouble organizing the steps in a Sequence Chain. In order to help them describe steps in order, conduct the following experiment in front of the class. Instruct the students to observe and take notes about each of the steps you are taking. First, take a sheet of white paper and fold it lengthwise and then widthwise. Next, cut the edges around the paper into an arc, so that the remaining paper will be a circle. Unfold the paper to reveal the circle. Ask students to organize the steps that you took into a Sequence Chain. You may wish to draw a blank Sequence Chain on the board with space for each of the three steps. Once they have correctly organized the steps in the Sequence Chain, ask the students to insert time-order words that will help others understand in what order each step was taken.

WORK with a PARTNER

Students should work with a partner on their observation reports. One partner should conduct the experiment while the other partner takes notes. Then they should work together to organize the notes into a Sequence Chain that both can use to write their observation reports.

Writing an Observation Report

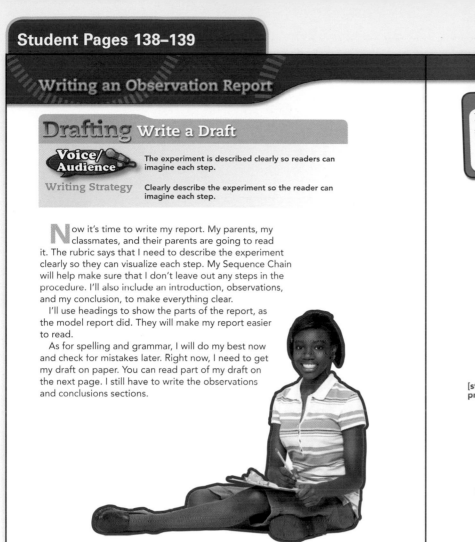

Drafting — Write a Draft

Voice/Audience The experiment is described clearly so readers can imagine each step.

Writing Strategy Clearly describe the experiment so the reader can imagine each step.

Now it's time to write my report. My parents, my classmates, and their parents are going to read it. The rubric says that I need to describe the experiment clearly so they can visualize each step. My Sequence Chain will help make sure that I don't leave out any steps in the procedure. I'll also include an introduction, observations, and my conclusion, to make everything clear.

I'll use headings to show the parts of the report, as the model report did. They will make my report easier to read.

As for spelling and grammar, I will do my best now and check for mistakes later. Right now, I need to get my draft on paper. You can read part of my draft on the next page. I still have to write the observations and conclusions sections.

138 **Descriptive Writing** ■ Observation Report

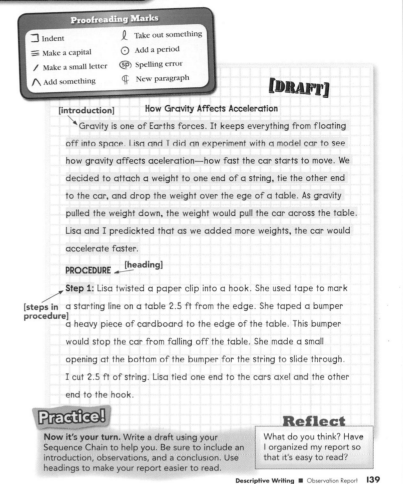

Proofreading Marks

⊐ Indent
≡ Make a capital
/ Make a small letter
∧ Add something

ℓ Take out something
⊙ Add a period
SP Spelling error
¶ New paragraph

[DRAFT]

[introduction] **How Gravity Affects Acceleration**

Gravity is one of Earths forces. It keeps everything from floating off into space. Lisa and I did an experiment with a model car to see how gravity affects aceleration—how fast the car starts to move. We decided to attach a weight to one end of a string, tie the other end to the car, and drop the weight over the ege of a table. As gravity pulled the weight down, the weight would pull the car across the table. Lisa and I predickted that as we added more weights, the car would accelerate faster.

PROCEDURE [heading]

[steps in procedure] **Step 1:** Lisa twisted a paper clip into a hook. She used tape to mark a starting line on a table 2.5 ft from the edge. She taped a bumper a heavy piece of cardboard to the edge of the table. This bumper would stop the car from falling off the table. She made a small opening at the bottom of the bumper for the string to slide through. I cut 2.5 ft of string. Lisa tied one end to the cars axel and the other end to the hook.

Practice!

Now it's your turn. Write a draft using your Sequence Chain to help you. Be sure to include an introduction, observations, and a conclusion. Use headings to make your report easier to read.

Reflect

What do you think? Have I organized my report so that it's easy to read?

Descriptive Writing ■ Observation Report 139

Drafting

(Student pages 138–139)

Review the purpose of a draft. Note that the draft is a temporary form of a piece of writing that should be changed and corrected several times before it is finished. Next have a student read Denise's words on Student page 138.

Point out that Denise refers to the rubric as she completes this step in the writing process. Remind students to get into the habit of referring to the rubric so they fully understand its use as a tool for shaping their writing.

Have students read Denise's draft on Student page 139. Discuss how the headings help her organize her draft and how they will make it easier for readers to skim it to find the sections they most want to read. Ask students which trait on the rubric they use when they are organizing. **Information/Organization**

Writing Across the Curriculum

Science Writing an observation report helps students understand the scientific process. When they conduct science experiments, they will need to make a prediction, set up a procedure to test it, evaluate their results, and come to a conclusion. Remind students that scientists do this so that others can learn from their work. Have the students form small groups. Ask them to follow the steps from Denise's experiment in order to come up with the same results. Have students compare their results with the results in Denise's observation log. Did they have the same results? Ask them why their results may have differed. **Possible responses: The size and weight of the car they used were different. The size and weight of the string and paper clips were different.**

Writing an Observation Report

Revising Extend Writing

Content/Ideas Informative diagrams or charts are included.

Writing Strategy Add diagrams or charts.

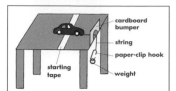

Diagram labels: cardboard bumper, string, paper-clip hook, starting tape, weight

After I read my report to Lisa, she wondered if our classmates would understand what we had done. It sounded kind of confusing. Then I remembered what the rubric said about adding diagrams or charts. That would help! I also drew a diagram to show how we set up the experiment.

[DRAFT]

Observation Log

Time in Seconds to Reach Table's Edge

Number of Weights	Run #1	Run #2	Run #3	Average
1	2.7	2.6	2.6	2.6
2	1.7	1.9	1.8	1.8
3	1.4	1.2	1.6	1.4
4	1.2	1.1	1.0	1.1
5	0.8	0.5	0.9	0.7

Practice!

Now it's your turn. Add a diagram or chart to clarify what happened in your experiment.

Revising Clarify Writing

Word Choice/Clarity Time-order words make the sequence of the events very clear.

Writing Strategy Add time-order words to clarify the process.

Writer's Term

Time-Order Words
Time-order words show when different steps or events take place. They include words such as *after, during, first, second, third, until, meanwhile, next, soon, later, finally, then,* and *as soon as.*

Writing the report in steps showed the order in which Lisa and I did things. However, I knew I could add more time-order words, and Lisa agreed. She also agreed I should check the report for appositives. I found one mistake in punctuating appositives and corrected it.

[DRAFT]   [added time-order words]

To begin setting up the experiment, Next,
Step 1: Lisa twisted a paper clip into a hook. She used tape to mark
                                                                    Then
a starting line on a table 2.5 ft from the edge. She taped a bumper

a piece of heavy cardboard to the edge of the table. This bumper
                                       ← [added commas to set off appositive]
would stop the car from falling off the table. She made a small

opening at the bottom of the bumper for the string to slide through.

Practice!

Now it's your turn. Add time-order words to your report to make the sequence of events crystal clear.

Reflect
Did I make the sequence clearer by adding time-order words?

Revising

(Student pages 140–141)

Ask students to read Denise's words on Student page 140. Explain that one good way to make sure an observation report is complete is to add diagrams or charts, as many as are necessary. Ask students how these additions are helpful. **Possible responses: Diagrams can show the setup and actions that are hard to describe in words. Charts present data in an organized way.**

Next, have students read Denise's words on Student page 141. Point out that time-order words can help make a report clearer. Ask a student to read the definition and examples from the Writer's Term box. Ask students how using time-order words improves a report. **Possible response: The words help make clear the order in which steps were completed or events occurred.**

Differentiating Instruction

Support To help students understand the importance of time-order words, have them do the following experiment. On separate strips of paper, have them write down the steps they need to take in order to eat a bowl of cereal. Write the following steps:

Set out a bowl	*Insert spoon*
Pour the cereal	*Lift spoon to mouth*
Pour the milk	*Take a bite*

Have them put each of the strips into a bowl or basket. Then have a student pull out one strip at a time and read the step aloud. Write that step on the board next to the following time-order words, in this order:

First,	*Then,*
Second,	*After that,*
Next,	*Finally,*

Students will see that, out of order, the steps do not make sense and can even cause a mess. Point out that it's important to use time-order words to help indicate how steps have taken place or should take place.

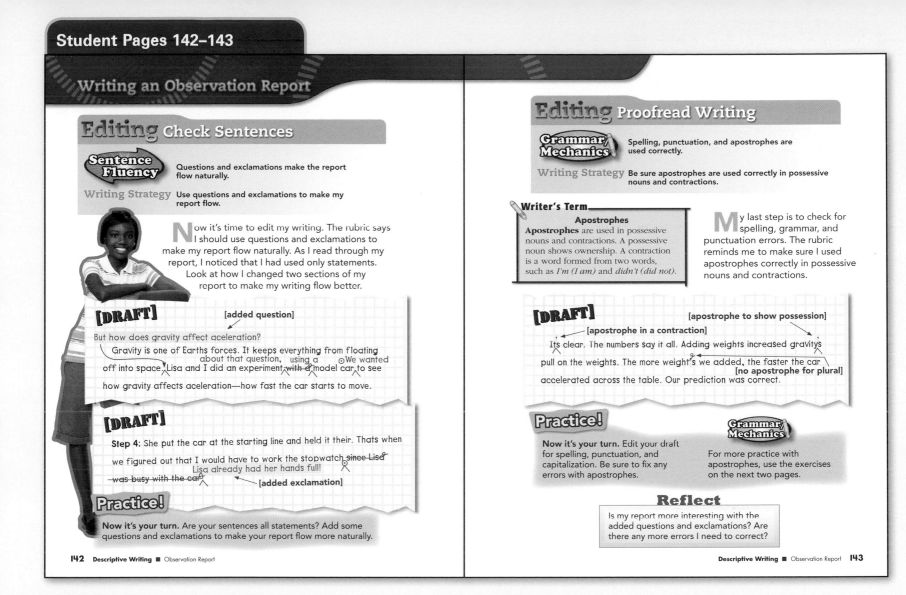

Editing

(Student pages 142–143)

Ask a student to read Denise's words on Student page 142 to the class. Explain that using questions and exclamations can help make the report flow. Ask students why they think questions and exclamations help in an observation report. **Possible responses: If the report has only statements, it won't read well; an observation report might be boring if it is just full of scientific statements.**

Next, have a student read Denise's words on Student page 143 to the class. Remind students that good writers search for all kinds of spelling, punctuation, and grammar errors when they proofread. They also focus on the kinds of skills they have had problems with in the past. Have a student read the definition of an apostrophe from the Writer's Term box. Note that it's not uncommon for apostrophes to be used incorrectly, especially in possessive nouns and contractions. Students will want to review their drafts to be sure they have used them correctly.

If students are having trouble with apostrophes, you may wish to teach the Mini-Lesson on page 114 of this Teacher Edition. Then have students complete the exercises on Student pages 144–145. Review the answers and possible rewrites with them.

Differentiating Instruction

English-Language Learners Students may need help with *who* and *whom*. Suggest that whenever they use *whom*, they should check to see that something is being done to the person replaced by that pronoun. If *whom* is doing something—and is not the object of someone else's action—then students should use *who*. To help them remember the rule, tell them, "Who can do. Whom is done to."

WORK with a PARTNER

Students should work with the partner with whom they conducted the experiment to share their drafts with each other. This will be a good chance for both to ensure that they have organized their reports well and included all of the steps in the order in which they were taken. Partners can also look for errors in spelling, punctuation, and apostrophe use.

Grammar/Mechanics Practice!

Apostrophes

KNOW the RULE

To form the **possessive** of a singular noun, add an apostrophe and *s*.
  Example: My brother**'s** hobby is racing slot cars.

To form the **possessive** of a plural noun that ends in *s*, just add an apostrophe.
  Example: He joined a slot car racer**s'** club.

To form the **possessive** of a plural noun that does not end in *s*, add an apostrophe and *s*.
  Example: The club has a large men**'s** group and a small women**'s** group.

To form a **contraction**, use an apostrophe to replace dropped letters.
  Example: They're crazy about this hobby.

Practice the Rule

Number a sheet of paper 1–5. Read each sentence, choose the correct form in parentheses, and write it on your paper.

1. One (dictionary's/dictionarys') definition says a slot car is "an electric toy racing car with a pin underneath that fits into a groove on a track."
2. The (car's/cars') bodies are made of plastic or metal.
3. A slot (car's/cars') power is transmitted through steel rails in the track.
4. My (dad's/dads') oldest track layout is from the 1960s.
5. (It's/Its') a two-lane plastic track that snaps together.

Apply the Rule

Read the following paragraphs from an observation report. Correct any mistakes in apostrophes, and rewrite the paragraphs on another sheet of paper.

The Effect's of Parachute Size

After seeing skydiver's at the air show, I wondered about parachutes. What effect did a parachutes' size have on the impact of a skydivers' landing? I decided an experiment on this question would be a good science project for me and my friend's.

Taylor, LaShawn, and I could'nt find an appropriate experiment in a book, so we made up our own. We decided to use eggs' as skydivers and piece's of cloth as parachutes. We varied the parachute's sizes, but we tried to keep the eggs weight's approximately equal. After attaching a parachute to each egg, we climbed to the top of the baseball fields bleacher's.

At that moment, we realized we hadnt made any predictions' about what would happen. Our teacher says thats' an important part of the scientific method! We discussed thing's and agreed a larger parachute would be better than a smaller parachute.

Once w'ed decided that, I asked, "Is everybody ready?"

"Were ready," answered my fellow scientist's.

At the count of three, we dropped our skydivers. Taylors 5-inch parachute hit the ground first. Splat! The eggs' yellow innards oozed through a big break in it's shell. My 10-inch parachute hit next, followed by LaShawns' 15-inch parachute. My egg suffered injurie's, but they werent serious. LaShawn's skydiver did'nt have a crack!

Grammar/Mechanics Mini-Lesson

(Student pages 144–145)

Apostrophes

Explain to the students that to form the possessive of a singular noun, add an apostrophe and an *s*.

Write the following on the board: *My friends cat likes to sleep next to the heater.*

Ask students to correct the sentence by adding an apostrophe where needed. **friend's**

Explain to the students that you form the possessive of a plural noun that ends in an *s* by adding an apostrophe at the end; if the noun does not end in an *s*, add an apostrophe and an *s*.

Write the following on the board: *The photographers club was meeting to discuss how to take childrens portraits.*

Ask students to correct the sentence by adding apostrophes in the correct places. **The photographers' club was meeting to discuss how to take children's portraits.**

Explain to the students that to form a contraction, use an apostrophe to replace dropped letters.

Write the following on the board: *We are thrilled with our new car.*

Ask students to form a contraction by combining the words *we* and *are* and placing an apostrophe where needed. **we're**

Answers for Practice the Rule

1. **dictionary's**   3. **car's**   5. **It's**
2. **cars'**   4. **dad's**

Answers for Apply the Rule

The Effects of Parachute Size

After seeing skydivers at the air show, I wondered about parachutes. What effect did a parachute's size have on the impact of a skydiver's landing? I decided an experiment on this question would be a good science project for me and my friends.

Taylor, LaShawn, and I couldn't find an appropriate experiment in a book, so we made up our own. We

(Answers continue on page 115.)

Writing an Observation Report

Publishing Share Writing

Display my report on family night.

When you carry out science experiments, you have to observe carefully and record your observations in writing. Our class decided to display our observation reports on science experiments during Family Night because our reports were so good. Before Lisa and I turned in our report for the display, we checked it one last time using this checklist.

My Checklist

✔ The report focuses on our experiment, and all the steps are described in order.

✔ We described our experiment very clearly, using a diagram, a chart, and time-order words.

✔ Our readers can visualize all the steps in our experiment, and they could repeat the experiment themselves following our report.

✔ We used questions and exclamations to make the report flow.

✔ Spelling, capitalization, and apostrophes are all correct.

Practice!

Now it's your turn. Check your observation report against your checklist. Then make a final draft to publish.

146 Descriptive Writing ■ Observation Report

How Gravity Affects Acceleration
by Lisa and Denise

Gravity is one of Earth's forces. It keeps everything from floating off into space. But how does gravity affect acceleration? Lisa and I did an experiment about that question, using a model car. We wanted to see how gravity affects acceleration—how fast the car starts to move. We decided to attach a weight to one end of a string, tie the other end to the car, and drop the weight over the edge of a table. As gravity pulled the weight down, the weight would pull the car across the table. Lisa and I predicted that as we added more weight, the car would accelerate faster.

PROCEDURE

Step 1: To begin setting up the experiment, Lisa twisted a paper clip into a hook. Next, she used tape to mark a starting line on a table 2.5 feet from the edge of the table. Then she taped a bumper, a heavy piece of cardboard, to the edge of the table. This bumper would stop the car from falling off the table. She made a small opening at the bottom of the bumper for the string to slide through. Meanwhile, I cut 2.5 feet of string. Lisa tied one end to the car's axle and the other end to the hook. To finish setting up, she pushed the hook through the opening at the bottom of the bumper.

Step 2: Lisa slipped one weight on the hook.

Step 3: Then she held the weight over the edge of the table.

Step 4: She put the car at the starting line and held it there. That's when we figured out that I would have to work the stopwatch. Lisa already had her hands full!

Step 5: Lisa let the weight fall, and I started the stopwatch.

Descriptive Writing ■ Observation Report 147

(Answers continued from page 114.)

decided to use eggs as skydivers and pieces of cloth as parachutes. We varied the parachutes' sizes, but we tried to keep the eggs' weight approximately equal. After attaching a parachute to each egg, we climbed to the top of the baseball field's bleachers.

At that moment, we realized we hadn't made any predictions about what would happen. Our teacher says that's an important part of the scientific method! We discussed things and agreed a larger parachute would be better than a smaller parachute.

Once we'd decided that, I asked, "Is everybody ready?"

"We're ready," answered my fellow scientists.

At the count of three, we dropped our skydivers. Taylor's 5-inch parachute hit the ground first. Splat! The egg's yellow innards oozed through a big break in its shell. My 10-inch parachute hit next, followed by LaShawn's 15-inch parachute. My egg suffered injuries, but they weren't serious. LaShawn's skydiver didn't have a crack!

Publishing
(Student pages 146–147)

Ask a student to read Denise's words on Student page 146. Note that Denise and her partner are using a checklist based on the writing traits for an observation report to review their reports one last time. Remind students to review their drafts against their own checklists to be sure that they have included everything they need to include.

Have students suggest other ways Denise could share her report. Discuss what they feel are the benefits of publishing an observation report on Family Night.

 For more practice with grammar/mechanics skills, see Zaner-Bloser's *G.U.M.* materials.

Step 6: I stopped the stopwatch when the car hit the bumper. Actually, I had to practice this several times before I could do it right. That car moved fast!

Step 7: Lisa and I timed the car with one weight on it two more times. Then I added the times and divided by 3 to get the average. I wrote that in our observation log.

Step 8: Then we repeated the whole process with 2, 3, 4, and 5 weights hanging on the hook. We did each number of weights 3 times and averaged the speed.

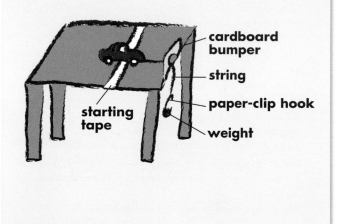

cardboard bumper

string

paper-clip hook

starting tape

weight

148 **Descriptive Writing** ■ Observation Report

OBSERVATIONS

When I looked at our observation log, I didn't see a pattern at first, but Lisa pointed it out. As the number of weights increased, the time decreased.

Observation Log
Time in Seconds to Reach Table's Edge

Number of Weights	Run #1	Run #2	Run #3	Average
1	2.7	2.6	2.6	2.6
2	1.7	1.9	1.8	1.8
3	1.4	1.2	1.6	1.4
4	1.2	1.1	1.0	1.1
5	0.8	0.5	0.9	0.7

CONCLUSION

It's clear. The numbers say it all. Adding weights increased gravity's pull on the weights. The more weights we added, the faster the car accelerated across the table. Our prediction was correct.

Reflect

What did you think? Did I use all the traits of a good observation report in my writing? Check it against the rubric. Then check your own observation report with the rubric.

Descriptive Writing ■ Observation Report 149

TIPS for the Writing Classroom

Flexibility and Student Input

by Ken Stewart, *Master Teacher*

The words *writing process* convey to our students that writing (no matter which genre) is a process. We want our students to follow the logical, orderly steps of prewriting, drafting, revising, editing, and publishing. Since writing is a process, we must allow for individual differences and build flexibility and choice into our learning structure.

Too often, we give writing assignments and expect everyone to finish them at the same time. Many times, we should be engaging students in discussions as to what they think are fair time estimates to complete the task at a high level. If we allow ourselves to "think outside of the box" (a concept that may be difficult due to our own experiences in school), we will begin to see that expecting everyone to finish a process assignment at the same time is unrealistic and could be harmful to real learning.

Try the following suggestions and see how your students react.

1. Establish clear and concise criteria for the writing assignment, and share these criteria with your class.
2. Let your students know how long you think the assignment should take to complete. (Include time for peer tutorials.)
3. Ask your students how long they think the assignment will take to complete.
4. Come to a consensus. (Discuss what the term *consensus* means.)
5. After the class decides on a due date, make the assignment due over the course of that week. (For example, if the due date is on Tuesday, October 2, make the due date the week of October 1 through October 5.)
6. Have your students record the due dates; then follow your established policy on handling late assignments.
7. Encourage your students to turn in their revised "final" paper at the beginning of the week (Monday/Tuesday) in order to get it back within a day or two with your comments so they may make corrections if they choose to do so.

Although this process will not eliminate late work, it will greatly reduce the number of late papers. You have given students input and ownership in the decision-making process. You have made a significant choice in sharing some of your power with your students. This is just one of the small steps that will eventually lead to a classroom structure in which your students will, with your guidance, plan their own lessons and evaluate the quality of their own work.

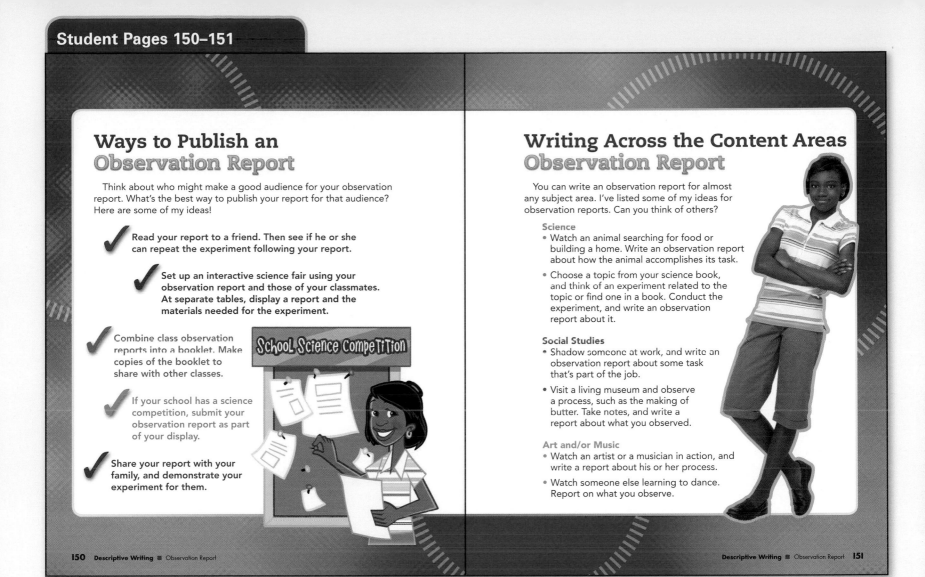

Ways to Publish an
Observation Report

Think about who might make a good audience for your observation report. What's the best way to publish your report for that audience? Here are some of my ideas!

✔ Read your report to a friend. Then see if he or she can repeat the experiment following your report.

✔ Set up an interactive science fair using your observation report and those of your classmates. At separate tables, display a report and the materials needed for the experiment.

✔ Combine class observation reports into a booklet. Make copies of the booklet to share with other classes.

✔ If your school has a science competition, submit your observation report as part of your display.

✔ Share your report with your family, and demonstrate your experiment for them.

School Science Competition

Writing Across the Content Areas
Observation Report

You can write an observation report for almost any subject area. I've listed some of my ideas for observation reports. Can you think of others?

Science
• Watch an animal searching for food or building a home. Write an observation report about how the animal accomplishes its task.

• Choose a topic from your science book, and think of an experiment related to the topic or find one in a book. Conduct the experiment, and write an observation report about it.

Social Studies
• Shadow someone at work, and write an observation report about some task that's part of the job.

• Visit a living museum and observe a process, such as the making of butter. Take notes, and write a report about what you observed.

Art and/or Music
• Watch an artist or a musician in action, and write a report about his or her process.

• Watch someone else learning to dance. Report on what you observe.

Ways to Publish
(Student page 150)

Have students read the different publishing options on Student page 150. Ask students if any of the options sound like good ways for them to publish their observation reports. You may wish to follow the second example and create an interactive science fair in your class so that students can display their reports and conduct their experiments for others to see. Explain to students that each time they write a report, they should think about the many ways that the report can be published. Encourage them to look outside of the classroom when considering ways to publish what they have written.

Writing Across the Content Areas
(Student page 151)

Observation reports are not just for English or for science class. As Student page 151 shows, students can write an observation report for many subject areas. Ask a volunteer to read the different content areas for which an observation report can be written. Ask students if they have other examples to add to the list.

Descriptive Article Overview

This chapter introduces students to descriptive articles. The first step is to learn about the elements of a descriptive article—vivid imagery, point of view, lively language, and audience appeal. They will learn some of the reasons to write a descriptive article, including informing others, reflecting on a subject, entertaining others, and sharing information. Students will review the traits of a good descriptive article and then study the student model using these traits.

Students will have the opportunity to follow the student model as she writes a descriptive article. They will practice each step of the writing process in writing their own descriptive articles. They will come up with a subject for their articles and then organize their notes into

a Five-Senses Chart. Using their Five-Senses Chart, they will write a draft that includes word pictures to help readers "see" the topic. Then they will revise their drafts by adding sensory details and replacing clichés with interesting phrases. Students will check their sentences and add repetitive sentence patterns to emphasize a point. They will also check for spelling and punctuation errors and make sure their verbs are in the proper tense. After their drafts have been edited, they will explore ways to publish their articles. You may wish to send to families the School-Home Connection Letter for this chapter, located at the end of this unit in the Teacher Edition.

Descriptive Article Writing Traits

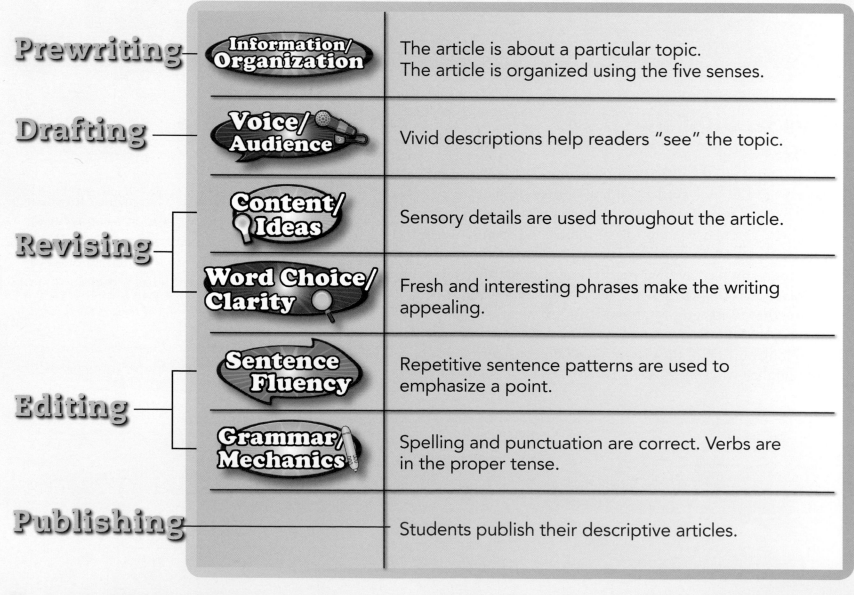

Prewriting — Information/Organization
The article is about a particular topic.
The article is organized using the five senses.

Drafting — Voice/Audience
Vivid descriptions help readers "see" the topic.

Revising — Content/Ideas
Sensory details are used throughout the article.

Word Choice/Clarity
Fresh and interesting phrases make the writing appealing.

Editing — Sentence Fluency
Repetitive sentence patterns are used to emphasize a point.

Grammar/Mechanics
Spelling and punctuation are correct. Verbs are in the proper tense.

Publishing — Students publish their descriptive articles.

Descriptive Article Time Management

Day 1	Day 2	Day 3	Day 4	Day 5
Learning Objectives				
Students will: • study the components of a descriptive article.	Students will: • learn how to gather information for a descriptive article.	Students will: • practice gathering information for their own descriptive articles.	Students will: • learn how to make a Five-Senses Chart to organize their notes.	Students will: • practice organizing their notes into a Five-Senses Chart.
Activities				
• Discuss the elements and traits of a descriptive article (Student pages 152–154). • Use the rubric to study the model (Student pages 155–159).	• Read and discuss **Prewriting: Gather Information** (Student page 160).	• Brainstorm ideas and choose a descriptive article. • Gather information and take notes on a descriptive article.	• Read and discuss **Prewriting: Organize Ideas** (Student page 161).	• Look at the notes made on a descriptive article. • Use notes to fill in the Five-Senses Chart.

WEEK 2

Day 1	Day 2	Day 3	Day 4	Day 5
Learning Objectives				
Students will: • learn how to include vivid descriptions to help readers "see" the topic.	Students will: • practice writing their own drafts.	Students will: • learn how to add sensory details.	Students will: • practice adding sensory details to their drafts.	Students will: • learn how to replace clichés with interesting phrases.
Activities				
• Read and discuss **Drafting: Write a Draft** (Student pages 162–163).	• Use Five-Senses Charts to write a draft. • Include vivid descriptions to help the reader "see" their topics.	• Read and discuss **Revising: Extend Writing** (Student page 164).	• Look for areas where more sensory details can be added. • Add sensory details to make the subject come alive.	• Read and discuss **Revising: Clarify Writing** (Student page 165).

WEEK 3

Day 1	Day 2	Day 3	Day 4	Day 5
Learning Objectives				
Students will: • practice replacing clichés with interesting phrases.	Students will: • learn about repeating sentence patterns to emphasize a point.	Students will: • learn how to use verbs in their proper tenses.	Students will: • practice editing their drafts for spelling, punctuation, and verb tense errors.	Students will: • learn different ways to publish their descriptive articles.
Activities				
• Reread drafts to find clichés that can be replaced. • Replace clichés with interesting phrases.	• Read and discuss **Editing: Check Sentences** (Student page 166). • Add repetitive sentence patterns to emphasize a point.	• Read and discuss **Editing: Proofread Writing** (Student page 167). • Make sure all verbs are in the proper tense.	• Fix any spelling, punctuation, or verb tense errors in drafts.	• Read and discuss **Publishing: Share Writing** (Student page 170).

To complete the chapter in fewer days, teach the learning objectives and activities for two days in one day.

This planning chart, correlated to your state's writing standards, is available on-line at http://www.zaner-bloser.com/sfw.

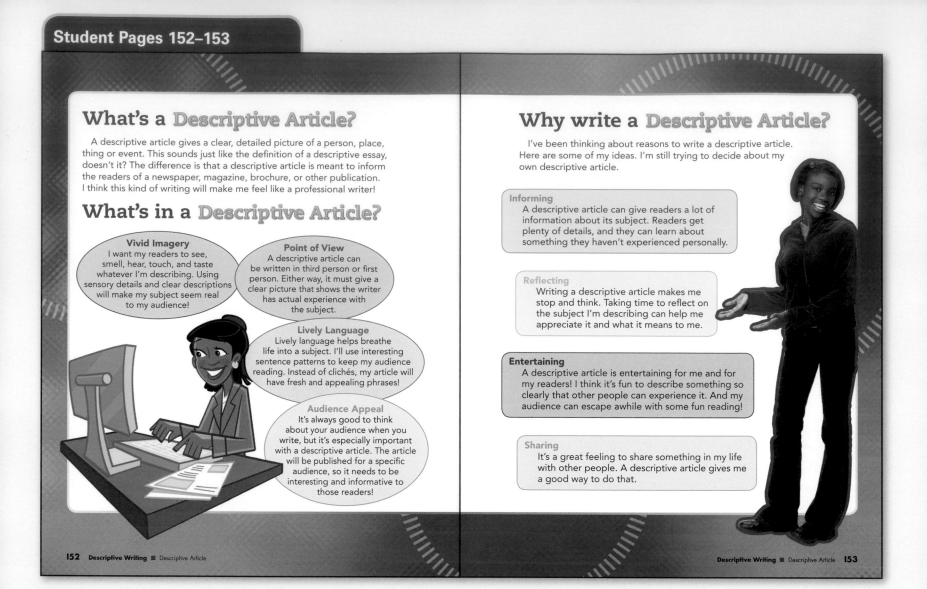

Define the Genre

(Student page 152)

Descriptive Article

Ask students to name a place near where they live. Then ask them to identify the five senses so you can write them on the board as headings. **see, hear, taste, touch, smell** Next, have them contribute sensory details about the place they chose. Have them choose the appropriate column for each detail so you can list it there. Point out that students could write a paragraph about the place using this information. Now, tell them to think about how they would write the paragraph about this place for the local paper or for an article in the town's visitor guide. Explain that such a paragraph would be an example of a descriptive article.

Tell students that this chapter will help them learn how to write an effective descriptive article.

Elements of the Genre
Descriptive Article

Read and discuss each of the elements of a descriptive article with the students. Point out that these are similar to the elements of a descriptive essay, but that one element—audience appeal—is unique to descriptive articles, which are meant to be published for others to read.

Authentic Writing

(Student page 153)

Descriptive Article

Have student volunteers read each of the reasons for writing a descriptive article listed on Student page 153. Ask them which of the reasons listed benefit the reader. **Informing, entertaining, and sharing benefit the reader.** Remind students that as they write their descriptive articles, they will want to think about their audience. Descriptive articles are meant to inform readers, and this will affect the tone of their writing. Read Denise's words at the top of Student page 153. Point out that Denise mentions she is still trying to decide about her own article. That means she does not yet know her reasons for writing a descriptive article. Once she does decide what to write about and why, she will be better able to set the tone for her article.

Descriptive Article
Writing Traits

A good descriptive article has the traits in this chart. I'll use the traits to help me write my article.

Information/ Organization	The article is about a particular topic. The article is organized using the five senses.
Voice/ Audience	Vivid descriptions help readers "see" the topic.
Content/ Ideas	Sensory details are used throughout the article.
Word Choice/ Clarity	Fresh and interesting phrases make the writing appealing.
Sentence Fluency	Repetitive sentence patterns are used to emphasize a point.
Grammar/ Mechanics	Spelling and punctuation are correct. Verbs are in the proper tense.

Let's see how Adam Riley used the traits to help him write his descriptive article on the next page.

Descriptive Article Model

Neighborhood Notes
by Adam Riley

Lively language

Growling cars crawl down Main Street. Happy customers swarm the stores. Luscious aromas float out of restaurants. Our little town is bustling as usual. This is a wonderful place to live, but do you ever wish you could slip away to someplace quiet? *Audience appeal*

I do! Luckily, I found the perfect location for a little escape just steps away from Main Street. My family and I love it so much, you'll find us picnicking there almost every weekend.

First person point of view

To get to our almost-secret spot, we walk behind the town hall and towards the dense patch of woods that borders the lawn. There's a secluded path back there that few people have discovered. As soon as we step onto the path, the sounds of town begin to fade. The leaves above us whisper hushed hellos, and unseen birds warble a friendly welcome. After a short walk, we hear a gurgling noise, like a cheerful baby is playing somewhere nearby. That's Buck Creek, of course! *Lively language*

Suddenly the flickering shadows of the woods give way to the bright sunshine of a large, grassy clearing. The path winds past an old fire pit and down a slope. We see sun sparks dancing on the flowing waters of the creek.

We plop down on the soft grass under the old tree but only for a moment. In no time, we've stripped off our shoes and socks and raced down to the creek to wade in the cool water. *Vivid imagery*

After playing in the water awhile, we relax under the big oak. Even though we're actually still in town, the air smells fresher here. Sometimes the sharp scent of an evergreen blows our way on a gentle breeze.

There's nothing like the first bite of homemade fried chicken, crisp and warm and juicy! Add the creamy tang of coleslaw and the salty crunch of chips, and you're in picnic heaven! Cold, sweet iced tea washes it all down.

We pack up and head back home feeling like new people. We're relaxed. We're refreshed. We're ready to face our busy lives. Won't you join us sometime, neighbor? *Audience appeal*

Writing Traits
(Student pages 154–155)

Descriptive Article

Have students read the writing traits for a descriptive article on Student page 154. Explain to students that they will be studying strategies for writing descriptive articles. Note that they are going to be using these same strategies to write their own descriptive articles. A good descriptive article contains the traits listed on Student page 154, so students should be sure their articles contain these traits.

Have students read the descriptive article model on Student page 155. Ask them to look at how the writer used the traits to write his article.

Descriptive Article

Rubric

The traits of a good descriptive article from page 154 have been used to make the rubric below. By using 1, 2, 3, or 4 check marks to judge each trait, you can decide how well any descriptive article was written.

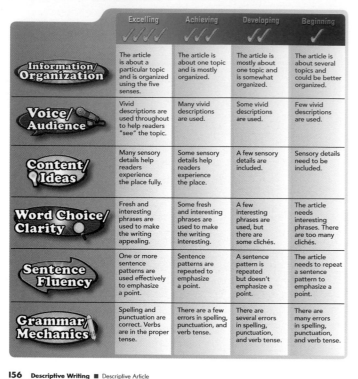

	Excelling ✓✓✓✓	Achieving ✓✓✓	Developing ✓✓	Beginning ✓
Information/ Organization	The article is about a particular topic and is organized using the five senses.	The article is about one topic and is mostly organized.	The article is mostly about one topic and is somewhat organized.	The article is about several topics and could be better organized.
Voice/ Audience	Vivid descriptions are used throughout to help readers "see" the topic.	Many vivid descriptions are used.	Some vivid descriptions are used.	Few vivid descriptions are used.
Content/ Ideas	Many sensory details help readers experience the place fully.	Some sensory details help readers experience the place.	A few sensory details are included.	Sensory details need to be included.
Word Choice/ Clarity	Fresh and interesting phrases are used to make the writing appealing.	Some fresh and interesting phrases are used to make the writing interesting.	A few interesting phrases are used, but there are some clichés.	The article needs interesting phrases. There are too many clichés.
Sentence Fluency	One or more sentence patterns are used effectively to emphasize a point.	Sentence patterns are repeated to emphasize a point.	A sentence pattern is repeated but doesn't emphasize a point.	The article needs to repeat a sentence pattern to emphasize a point.
Grammar/ Mechanics	Spelling and punctuation are correct. Verbs are in the proper tense.	There are a few errors in spelling, punctuation, and verb tense.	There are several errors in spelling, punctuation, and verb tense.	There are many errors in spelling, punctuation, and verb tense.

Using the Rubric to Study the Model
Descriptive Article

Let's use the rubric to check Adam Riley's descriptive article from his "Neighborhood Notes" column. How many check marks would you give him for each trait?

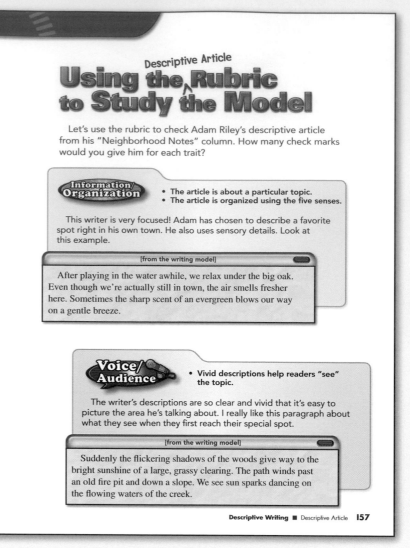

Information/ Organization
- The article is about a particular topic.
- The article is organized using the five senses.

This writer is very focused! Adam has chosen to describe a favorite spot right in his own town. He also uses sensory details. Look at this example.

[from the writing model]

After playing in the water awhile, we relax under the big oak. Even though we're actually still in town, the air smells fresher here. Sometimes the sharp scent of an evergreen blows our way on a gentle breeze.

Voice/ Audience
- Vivid descriptions help readers "see" the topic.

The writer's descriptions are so clear and vivid that it's easy to picture the area he's talking about. I really like this paragraph about what they see when they first reach their special spot.

[from the writing model]

Suddenly the flickering shadows of the woods give way to the bright sunshine of a large, grassy clearing. The path winds past an old fire pit and down a slope. We see sun sparks dancing on the flowing waters of the creek.

Using the Rubric
(Student page 156)

Have students review the qualities of a good descriptive article shown in the rubric on Student page 156. Tell them that they will be using the rubric to determine whether or not the model was well written. Note that they should also use the rubric as they write their own articles to be sure that they have included all the traits of a good descriptive article.

Ask students to refer to the model descriptive article as they go through each of the traits in the rubric.

Study the Model
(Student pages 157–159)

Ask for student volunteers to read the bulleted points on Student pages 157–159. As you read through each of the traits, discuss whether students feel that the writing sample has followed the traits. Ask them to look for other examples in the descriptive article for each trait. Finally, have them decide as a class how many check marks they would give the writer for each trait.

This is a good time to remind students that as they write, edit, and revise their stories, they should continually refer to the rubric to be sure that they do not forget to include any of the traits listed.

Descriptive Article

Content/Ideas
- Sensory details are used throughout the article.

This article is full of sensory details that bring the whole experience to life. I got hungry just reading this tasty paragraph!

[from the writing model]

There's nothing like the first bite of homemade fried chicken, crisp and warm and juicy! Add the creamy tang of coleslaw and the salty crunch of chips, and you're in picnic heaven! Cold, sweet iced tea washes it all down.

Word Choice/Clarity
- Fresh and interesting phrases make the writing appealing.

Adam could have used worn-out phrases and old clichés in his descriptive article, but he kept his writing fresh. For example, in the sentences below, he could have said that the leaves rustled, the birds sang, and the creek babbled. Instead, he tried to think of new ways to describe these things.

[from the writing model]

The leaves above us whisper hushed hellos, and unseen birds warble a friendly welcome. After a short walk, we hear a gurgling noise, like a cheerful baby is playing somewhere nearby.

Sentence Fluency
- Repetitive sentence patterns are used to emphasize a point.

It's usually a good idea to vary sentence patterns to keep your writing interesting, but repetition has its place, too. This writer sometimes repeated sentence patterns to make a point. For example, he started his article with repetitive sentences that felt as busy as his little town.

[from the writing model]

Growling cars crawl down Main Street. Happy customers swarm the stores. Luscious aromas float out of restaurants.

Grammar/Mechanics
- Spelling and punctuation are correct.
- Verbs are in proper tense.

I couldn't find any mistakes in Mr. Riley's article. His spelling and punctuation were perfect! And he did a great job putting each verb in the correct tense. In this paragraph, he correctly used verbs in present, past, and future tense!

[from the writing model]

I do! Luckily, I found the perfect location for a little escape just steps away from Main Street. My family and I love it so much, you'll find us picnicking there almost every weekend.

My Turn!
I'm going to write a descriptive article about one of my favorite places. I'll follow the rubric and use good writing strategies. Read on to see how I do it!

Differentiating Instruction

English-Language Learners English-language learners may not be able to identify when clichés are used. Come up with a list of common clichés and write them on the board for students to see. Note that clichés are unoriginal, commonly used descriptions of things. Students may want to search the Internet for databases of the most commonly used clichés. Explain that as they write their own drafts, students will want to be sure to come up with fresh and original descriptions.

Writing a Descriptive Article

Prewriting Gather Information

Information Organization The article is about a particular topic.

Writing Strategy Jot down some notes on my favorite spot in my neighborhood.

When I got my assignment, I decided to write about one of my favorite places—my grandmother's kitchen. To get started, I jotted down sights, sounds, feelings, smells, and tastes of Grandma's kitchen. Here are my notes.

My Notes on Grandma's Kitchen

Family uses back door, goes right into kitchen.
African violets in crusty pots on windowsill
Good smells on back porch, something baking, meat
Kitchen is tiny.
She always fixes me something to eat!
Stuff bubbling on stove
White cabinets, green walls like kiwi
We can sit and be quiet or sit and talk.
Mmmm . . . fresh cookies, melted chocolate chips
Volcano chili—hot as fire!
Grandma tells about old times in low husky voice.
House creaks.
Grandma—big smile, twinkling eyes, strong hands, busy
What she makes is always special.
Refrigerator hums.
Wash dishes in warm, soapy water.
Dry hands on crisp towel.
Can still feel hug after she lets go

Practice!
Now it's your turn. Choose your favorite spot, and jot down some notes about it.

160 Descriptive Writing ■ Descriptive Article

Prewriting Organize Ideas

Information Organization The article is organized using the five senses.

Writing Strategy Use a Five-Senses Chart to organize my notes.

Writer's Term
Five-Senses Chart
A Five-Senses Chart organizes descriptive words according to the five senses.

It looks like I have some good ideas for my article, but I have to get things organized! I can use a Five-Senses Chart to do that. I'll divide a sheet of paper into five parts, one for each sense. Then I'll rewrite my notes in the right spaces. This will help me organize my thoughts and keep me from forgetting anything important.

Five-Senses Chart

Smell: on back porch
something baking
meat
delicious!

Sight:
Kitchen—back door leads to kitchen
tiny, cheery, bright
kiwi green walls
fresh white cabinets
square wooden table in corner
two purple chairs
deep purple African violets in crusty pots on windowsill
Grandma—wide smile
twinkling eyes
strong, busy hands

Taste: fresh, home-made cookies, melted chocolate chips
volcano chili—hot as fire
everything she makes is special

Sound: stuff bubbling on stove
house creaks
refrigerator hums
Grandma's low, husky voice
Grandma's sympathetic sounds

Touch: warm, soapy dishwater
dry hands on crisp, cotton towel
Grandma's arms, soft, warm, strong
can still feel hug when she lets go

Practice!
Now it's your turn. Organize your notes with a Five-Senses Chart.

Reflect
How did I do? Are my notes well organized?

Descriptive Writing ■ Descriptive Article **161**

Prewriting
(Student pages 160–161)

Ask a student to read Denise's words on Student page 160. Remind students that when you first met Denise, you learned that one of her interests was cooking. It's not surprising, then, that Denise chooses her grandmother's kitchen to write about for this assignment. Ask students why they think she will write an article on this subject and what her interest in cooking will bring to the article. **Possible responses: She likes to cook, so she will be able to talk about cooking in the kitchen or the smells and tastes of her grandmother's cooking. She is very familiar with her grandmother's kitchen and will be able to describe it in detail.** Remind students that they should choose a topic that interests them and in which they have knowledge.

Explain that a graphic organizer, such as a Five-Senses Chart, is one way to organize information in preparation for writing. Ask a student to read the definition of a Five-Senses Chart from the Writer's Term box on Student page 161. Point out that this type of graphic organizer will help writers organize information about how a subject affects all five of the senses. Look at Denise's Five-Senses Chart. Discuss how she organized her notes from Student page 160 into each of the five categories before she began writing.

More Practice!

For more practice with these writing strategies, you may wish to have students use the Strategy Practice Book. See the appendix for annotated Strategy Practice Book pages.

WORK with a PARTNER
Encourage students to work with partners to come up with ideas for their descriptive articles. Once the student has decided on a subject, he or she should work with his or her partner to fill in information in their Five-Senses Chart.

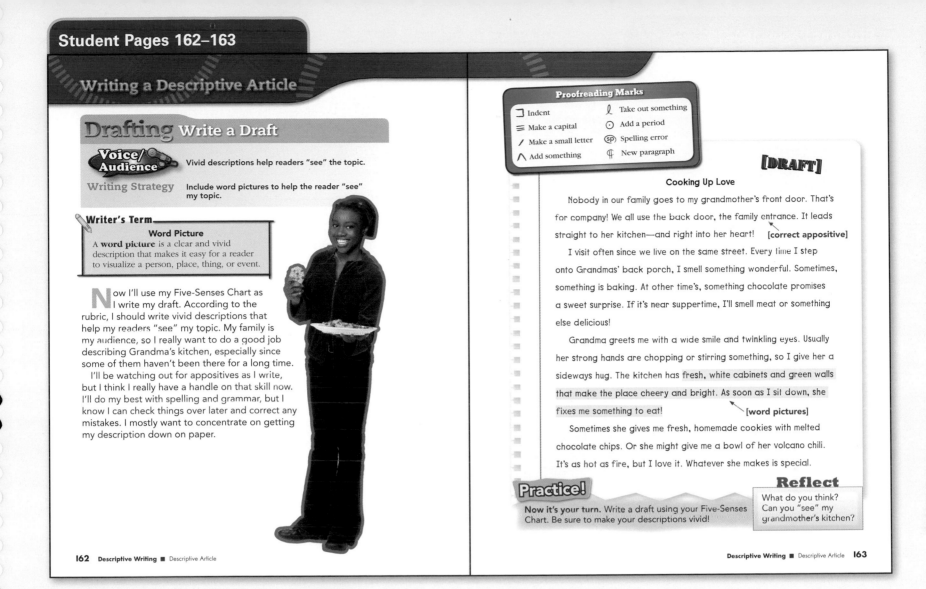

Writing a Descriptive Article

Drafting — Write a Draft

Voice/Audience — Vivid descriptions help readers "see" the topic.

Writing Strategy — Include word pictures to help the reader "see" my topic.

Writer's Term

Word Picture
A **word picture** is a clear and vivid description that makes it easy for a reader to visualize a person, place, thing, or event.

Now I'll use my Five-Senses Chart as I write my draft. According to the rubric, I should write vivid descriptions that help my readers "see" my topic. My family is my audience, so I really want to do a good job describing Grandma's kitchen, especially since some of them haven't been there for a long time.

I'll be watching out for appositives as I write, but I think I really have a handle on that skill now. I'll do my best with spelling and grammar, but I know I can check things over later and correct any mistakes. I mostly want to concentrate on getting my description down on paper.

Proofreading Marks

⸥ Indent	ℓ Take out something
≡ Make a capital	⊙ Add a period
/ Make a small letter	(SP) Spelling error
∧ Add something	¶ New paragraph

[DRAFT]

Cooking Up Love

Nobody in our family goes to my grandmother's front door. That's for company! We all use the back door, the family entrance. It leads straight to her kitchen—and right into her heart! **[correct appositive]**

I visit often since we live on the same street. Every time I step onto Grandmas' back porch, I smell something wonderful. Sometimes, something is baking. At other time's, something chocolate promises a sweet surprise. If it's near suppertime, I'll smell meat or something else delicious!

Grandma greets me with a wide smile and twinkling eyes. Usually her strong hands are chopping or stirring something, so I give her a sideways hug. The kitchen has fresh, white cabinets and green walls that make the place cheery and bright. As soon as I sit down, she fixes me something to eat! **[word pictures]**

Sometimes she gives me fresh, homemade cookies with melted chocolate chips. Or she might give me a bowl of her volcano chili. It's as hot as fire, but I love it. Whatever she makes is special.

Practice!
Now it's your turn. Write a draft using your Five-Senses Chart. Be sure to make your descriptions vivid!

Reflect
What do you think? Can you "see" my grandmother's kitchen?

162 Descriptive Writing ■ Descriptive Article

Descriptive Writing ■ Descriptive Article 163

Drafting

(Student pages 162–163)

Review what it means to write a draft. Remind students that a draft is a temporary form of writing that should be corrected later. Have a student read aloud Denise's words on Student page 162. Note that Denise is concentrating on getting her description down on paper and not worrying at this point about spelling and grammar.

Ask a student to read the definition of *word picture* from the Writer's Term box. Have students look for examples of word pictures as they read Denise's draft on Student page 163. Ask students if they feel Denise has done a good job of helping the reader "see" her grandmother's kitchen.

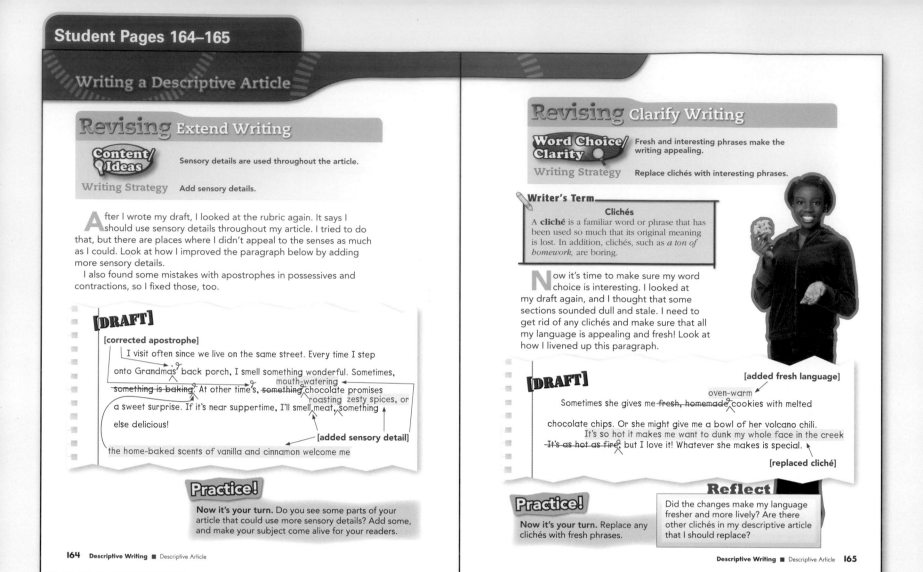

Revising

(Student pages 164–165)

Ask a student to read Denise's words on Student page 164. Remind students of the meaning of sensory details. Look at the changes Denise made to her draft. Ask students why they think she added the word *roasting* to describe the meat? **Possible response: It appeals to the readers' sense of smell.** Ask students if they feel that Denise's changes have made her draft more appealing for readers.

Note, too, that Denise has found and corrected some grammatical errors in her draft. As students go through their drafts, they will want to fix mistakes they find in each step of the revising and editing process.

Next, have a student read Denise's words on Student page 165. Then read the definition of *cliché* in the Writer's Term box. In this step of the revising process, Denise is looking for ways to make her writing more appealing. One of the ways writers can make their writing more appealing is by replacing clichés and uninteresting language with fresh and interesting phrases. Ask students why fresh and interesting language is important in a

descriptive article. **Possible response: Readers won't be bored by the descriptions.** Encourage students to look through their drafts and replace clichés and uninteresting descriptions with fresh, original descriptions.

Differentiating Instruction

Enrichment Write the following on the board:

The sky was blue, and the air was icy cold. I trudged through the snow to get to the bus stop. By the time I got there, my fingers were like icicles. Boy, was I happy as a clam when I saw the bus roll around!

Now ask the students to identify tired descriptions and clichés in the paragraph. **Possible responses: sky was blue; air was icy cold; trudged through the snow; fingers were like icicles; happy as a clam; bus roll around** Have them rewrite the paragraph by replacing the clichés and uninteresting phrases with fresh and interesting language. Encourage them to share their writing with a partner.

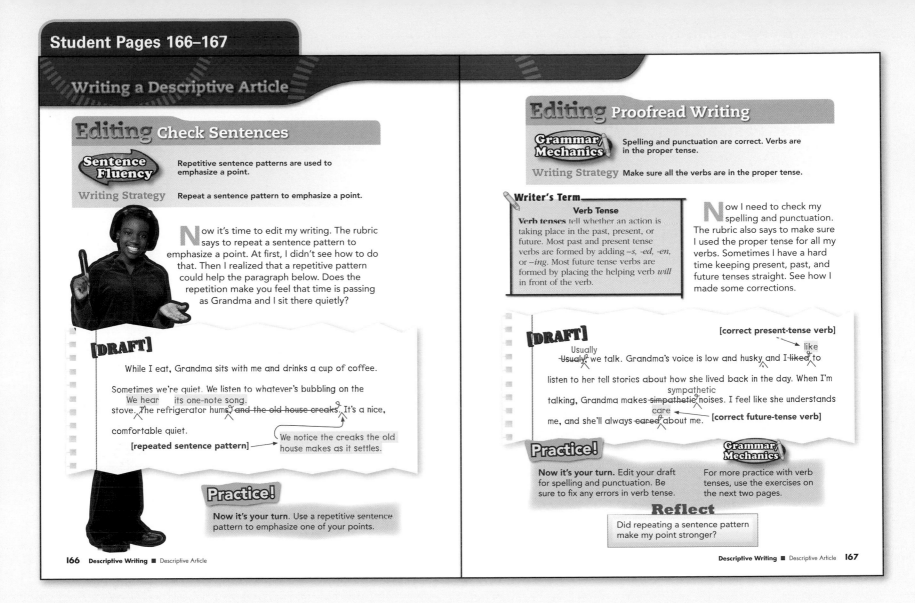

Editing
(Student pages 166–167)

Ask a student to read Denise's words on Student page 166. Point out that one way writers can emphasize a point is by repeating a sentence pattern. Read aloud the two sentences that Denise has revised in her draft. Ask students why they think Denise has decided to repeat the sentence pattern for that part of her article. **Possible response: She wants readers to feel as though time is passing as she and her grandmother notice what's going on around them.**

Next, have a student read Denise's words on Student page 167. Then have a student read the definition of *verb tense* from the Writer's Term box on Student page 167. Ask students why they think Denise needed to change the word *liked* to *like*. **Her story is written in present tense and *liked* is past tense.** Remind students to pay attention to verb tense in their own drafts. If they

have chosen to write something in the present tense, they should be sure they did not slip into using the past tense in their drafts. If students are having trouble with verb tense, you may wish to teach the Mini-Lesson on page 128 of this Teacher Edition. Then have students complete the exercises on Student pages 168–169. Review the answers and possible rewrites with them.

In addition to checking for correct verb tense, students should also read their drafts thoroughly to be sure there are no spelling or punctuation mistakes. Remind students that they should always proofread their reports.

WORK with a PARTNER
Students may find it helpful to swap their drafts with a partner. Have students use the writing traits for a descriptive article as they review their partner's draft to be sure that the writing includes all of the traits for a good descriptive article.

Grammar/Mechanics Practice!

Present, Past, and Future Tenses

KNOW the RULE

A **present-tense verb** is used to indicate that something happens regularly or is true now.
Example: Our family **holds** a reunion every summer.

A **past-tense verb** tells about something that has already happened. Regular verbs form the past tense by adding –ed.
Example: Mom and I **created** a scrapbook to take to this year's reunion.
Irregular verbs change their spelling in the past tense.
Example: The scrapbook **took** hours and hours of work.

A **future-tense verb** tells what is going to happen. Add the helping verb *will* to the present-tense form of a verb to form the future tense.
Example: Everyone **will enjoy** looking at the family scrapbook.

Practice the Rule

Copy the sentences onto a sheet of paper. Underline each past-tense verb, circle each present-tense verb, and draw a box around each future-tense verb.

1. We started the scrapbook six months before the reunion.
2. Mom and I like to take our time with projects.
3. First, we looked through all our boxes of old photos.
4. An old family photo really brings back memories!
5. Someone labeled most of the photos, but we will never know all the people in the really old pictures.
6. From now on, we will label all our photos for future generations.

Apply the Rule

Read the following paragraphs taken from a descriptive article. Correct any errors in verb tense as you write the article on a sheet of paper.

Family Matters

My summer always ends with a Labor Day family reunion. I enjoyed that event more than anything else I will do during vacation. My family really makes it special!

Mom, Dad, my brother, and I always get up early the morning of the reunion. We packed everything in the van and will hit the road before the sun rises. The drive will taken hours, and we'll got tired and sleepy. But when we arrived at the park, we get a burst of energy. We explodes out of the car and dashed to the shelter we always reserved for the reunion.

Most of our family will arrived earlier, and they shouted when they see us. I usually ran right to Grandpa George. I will know he wanted to be the first to hug me. I wrapped my arms around his pillowy waist and bury my face in the softness of his favorite sweatshirt. One rough hand strokes my hair while the other held me close. Sometimes surprise tears will sting my eyes, but I know they won't lasted long. I felt so happy to be with my family again!

After that, everyone will hug everybody and caught up on all the news. We all talked at once, so things get pretty loud. Last year we will sound as noisy as a whole zoo under the roof of the shelter. Every so often, someone roar with laughter or shrieked or even will burst into song. I'm sure we be just as rowdy this year!

Grammar/Mechanics Mini-Lesson

(Student pages 168–169)

Present, Past, and Future Tenses

Read the Know the Rule box on Student page 168. Explain that a present-tense verb indicates something that is true now, while a past-tense verb recalls something that has already happened. Note that regular verbs form the past tense by adding *-ed*.

Write the following on the board: *She lifts her arms up in the air to stretch.*

Ask students whether the sentence uses a present- or a past-tense verb. **present** Have students rewrite the sentence so that it is in the past tense. **She lifted her arms up in the air to stretch.**

Explain that future-tense verbs tell what is going to happen. By adding the helping verb *will* to the present-tense form of a verb, you can form the future tense.

Ask students to rewrite the sentence from above into the future tense. **She will lift her arms up in the air to stretch.**

Answers for Practice the Rule

1. underline *started*
2. circle *like*
3. underline *looked*
4. circle *brings*
5. underline *labeled*; box *will never know*
6. box *will label*

Answers for Apply the Rule

Family Matters

My summer always ends with a Labor Day family reunion. I enjoy that event more than anything else I do during vacation. My family really makes it special!

Mom, Dad, my brother, and I always get up early the morning of the reunion. We pack everything in the van and hit the road before the sun rises. The drive will take hours, and we'll get tired and sleepy. But when we arrive at the park, we get a burst of energy. We explode out of the car and dash to the shelter we always reserve for the reunion.

(Answers continue on page 129.)

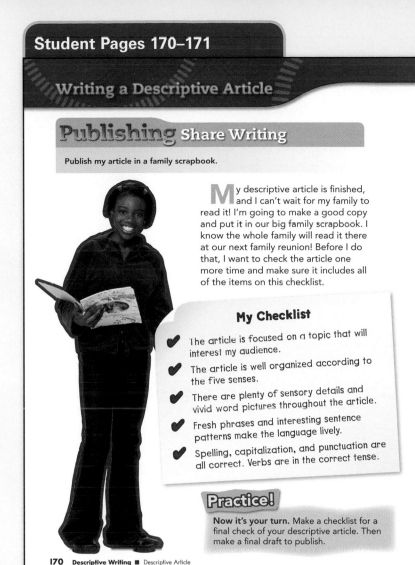

Writing a Descriptive Article

Publishing Share Writing

Publish my article in a family scrapbook.

My descriptive article is finished, and I can't wait for my family to read it! I'm going to make a good copy and put it in our big family scrapbook. I know the whole family will read it there at our next family reunion! Before I do that, I want to check the article one more time and make sure it includes all of the items on this checklist.

My Checklist

✓ The article is focused on a topic that will interest my audience.

✓ The article is well organized according to the five senses.

✓ There are plenty of sensory details and vivid word pictures throughout the article.

✓ Fresh phrases and interesting sentence patterns make the language lively.

✓ Spelling, capitalization, and punctuation are all correct. Verbs are in the correct tense.

Practice!

Now it's your turn. Make a checklist for a final check of your descriptive article. Then make a final draft to publish.

170 Descriptive Writing ■ Descriptive Article

Cooking Up Love
By Denise

Nobody in our family goes to my grandmother's front door. That's for company! We all use the back door, the family entrance. It leads straight to her kitchen—and right into her heart!

I visit often since we live on the same street. Every time I step onto Grandma's back porch, I smell something wonderful. Sometimes, the home-baked scents of vanilla and cinnamon welcome me. At other times, mouth-watering chocolate promises a sweet surprise. If it's near suppertime, I'll smell roasting meat, zesty spices, or something else I can only identify as delicious!

Grandma greets me with a wide smile and twinkling eyes. Usually her strong hands are chopping or stirring something, so I give her a sideways hug. The kitchen has fresh, white cabinets and green walls that make the place cheery and bright. As soon as I sit down, she fixes me something to eat!

Sometimes she gives me oven-warm cookies with melted chocolate chips. Or she might give me a bowl of her volcano chili. It's so hot it makes me want to dunk my whole face in the creek, but I love it! Whatever she makes is special.

While I eat, Grandma sits with me and drinks a cup of coffee. Sometimes we're quiet. We listen to whatever's bubbling on the stove. We hear the refrigerator hum its one-note song. We notice the creaks the old house makes as it settles. It's a nice, comfortable quiet.

Usually, we talk. Grandma's voice is low and husky, and I like to listen to her tell stories about how she lived back in the day. When I'm talking, Grandma makes sympathetic noises. I feel like she understands me, and she'll always care about me.

When it's time to go, I wash my dishes in warm, soapy water and dry my hands on a crisp, cotton towel. Then Grandma wraps me tightly in her arms, soft and warm and strong. After she lets go, it feels like she's still holding me. I hurry home, full of good food and Grandma's love!

Reflect

What did you think? Did I use all the traits of a good descriptive article in my writing? Check it against the rubric. Don't forget to use the rubric to check your own descriptive article.

Descriptive Writing ■ Descriptive Article **171**

(Answers continued from page 128.)

Most of our family will have arrived earlier, and they shout when they see us. I usually run right to Grandpa George. I know he wants to be the first to hug me. I wrap my arms around his pillowy waist and bury my face in the softness of his favorite sweatshirt. One rough hand strokes my hair while the other holds me close. Sometimes surprise tears will sting my eyes, but I know they won't last long. I feel so happy to be with my family again!

After that, everyone hugs everybody and catches up on all the news. We all talk at once, so things get pretty loud. Last year we sounded as noisy as a whole zoo under the roof of the shelter. Every so often, someone will roar with laughter or shriek or even will burst into song. I'm sure we will be just as rowdy this year!

Publishing
(Student pages 170–171)

Review Student page 170 with students. Ask students why they think Denise has chosen to publish her paper in a family scrapbook. **Possible response: It's a subject her family would be interested in reading about.** Have students brainstorm other ideas for publishing Denise's article.

Point out that Denise is going over the writing traits for a descriptive article one last time as she compares her article against the checklist. Suggest that students also read their papers to be sure they have not missed anything before they publish them.

 For more practice with grammar/mechanics skills, see Zaner-Bloser's *G.U.M.* materials.

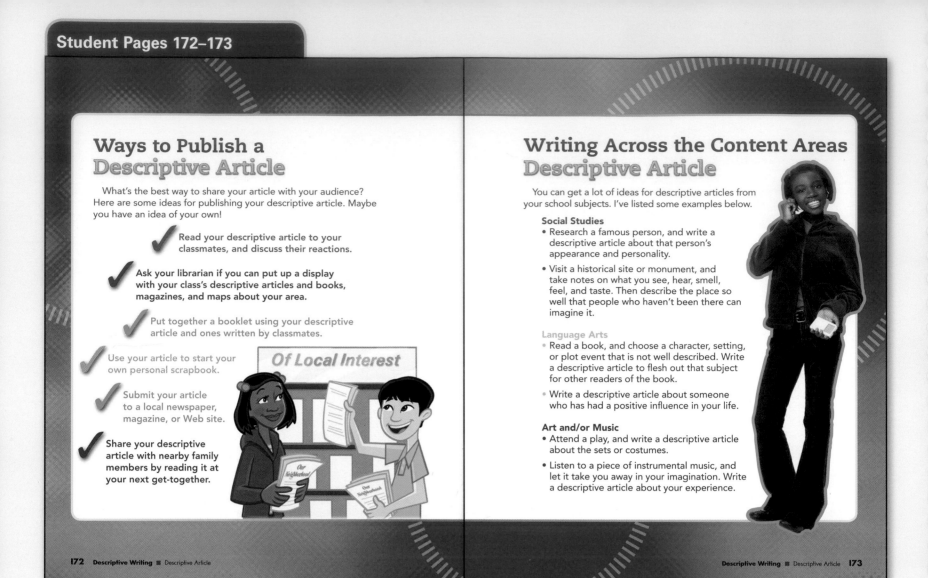

Ways to Publish
(Student page 172)

Ask students to read the suggestions for publishing a descriptive article shown on Student page 172. As a class, you may wish to use one or more of these suggestions to publish the students' reports. For instance, you can create a booklet that contains all of your students' descriptive articles. Ask students to think about other ways they could publish their descriptive articles. Suggest also that students try to publish their reports in one of the ways listed on this page, or another way they feel would be a good choice for their descriptive articles.

Writing Across the Content Areas
(Student page 173)

Point out that ideas for writing descriptive articles can come from other subjects as well as English or language arts. Remind them, though, that descriptive articles are meant to inform readers of a newspaper, magazine, brochure, or other publication. As you read the ideas on Student page 173 aloud, challenge the students to think about ways to publish a descriptive article based on each idea. For example, where might they publish a descriptive article about a famous person's appearance and personality? Note that these are just a few examples of the possibilities for writing descriptive articles based on school subjects. Students may wish to speak with other teachers for more ideas on writing in their content areas.

Books for Professional Development

Peterson, Art. *The Writer's Workout Book: 113 Stretches Toward Better Prose*. Berkeley: National Writing Project, 1996.

This book provides succinct and engaging activities on topics as varied as developing concrete details, writing for an audience, sequencing paragraphs, varying sentences, and choosing detailed words. The book also features a number of short, humorous essays about life as a writing teacher.

Fountas, Irene C, and Gay Su Pinnell. *Guiding Readers and Writers (Grades 3–6): Teaching Comprehension, Genre, and Content Literacy*. Portsmouth: Heinemann, 2002.

This book contains a wealth of ideas that will inspire students to become more literate. It is a valuable resource that helps teachers create classrooms where children are valued and encouraged to express themselves, take risks, and celebrate their unique perspective on the world.

Calkins, Lucy McCormick. *The Art of Teaching Writing*. 2nd ed. Portsmouth: Heinemann, 1994.

This source offers valuable insights on teaching writing, conferring with students, and working with different forms of writing. The author explains how children change as writers as they progress through the grades. One technique she explains is having students start with something they have noticed or wondered about and develop a story or idea from there.

Graves, Donald H. *A Fresh Look at Writing*. Portsmouth: Heinemann, 1994.

This book is an informative and useful guide for helping teachers implement worthy strategies in the classroom to help children strengthen their writing skills. It explains how strategies such as the "author's chair" and port-folios can help children practice and take pride in their writing. This book focuses on kinder-garten through sixth grade, but its methods can be modified to fit any grade level.

Descriptive Test Writing

This chapter is intended to give students an overview of descriptive test writing. First, they will review the parts of a writing prompt—the setup, task, and scoring guide—and relate the writing prompt to the writing traits they have been studying throughout the chapter. They will review a descriptive test scoring guide and then use it to study a model writing prompt response.

Students will follow Denise, the student guide, as she goes through each of the steps involved in completing a writing test, including planning one's time, prewriting, drafting, revising, and editing. You may wish to send to families the School-Home Connection Letter for this chapter, located at the end of this unit in the Teacher Edition.

Writing Traits in the Scoring Guide

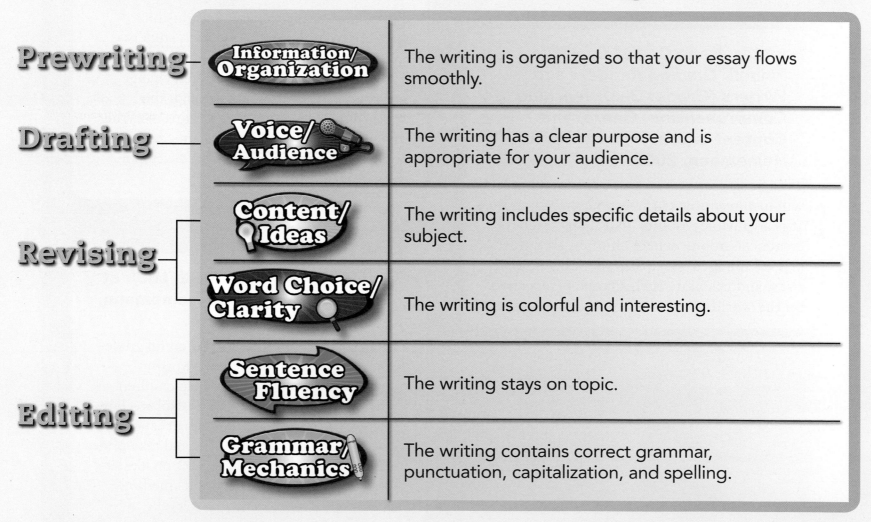

Prewriting — **Information/ Organization**	The writing is organized so that your essay flows smoothly.
Drafting — **Voice/ Audience**	The writing has a clear purpose and is appropriate for your audience.
Revising — **Content/ Ideas**	The writing includes specific details about your subject.
Word Choice/ Clarity	The writing is colorful and interesting.
Editing — **Sentence Fluency**	The writing stays on topic.
Grammar/ Mechanics	The writing contains correct grammar, punctuation, capitalization, and spelling.

Descriptive Test Writing Time Management

WEEK 1

Day 1	Day 2	Day 3	Day 4	Day 5
Learning Objectives				
Students will: • study the components of a writing prompt.	Students will: • recognize the relationship of the scoring guide to the rubric and the six traits of writing. • read a writing prompt response model.	Students will: • apply the scoring guide to a model test response.	Students will: • apply the scoring guide to a model test response.	Students will: • learn how to budget their time during a writing test.
Activities				
• Discuss the components of a writing prompt (Student pages 174–175).	• Read and discuss the scoring guide (Student page 176). • Read the model (Student page 177).	• Read and discuss **Using the Scoring Guide to Study the Model** (Student pages 178–179).	• Read and discuss **Using the Scoring Guide to Study the Model** (Student page 180).	• Read and discuss **Planning My Time** (Student page 181).

WEEK 2

Day 1	Day 2	Day 3	Day 4	Day 5
Learning Objectives				
Students will: • learn to read and understand a writing test prompt for test writing. • apply the six traits of writing to the writing prompt.	Students will: • learn how to respond to the task in the writing prompt.	Students will: • learn how to choose a graphic organizer for the writing prompt.	Students will: • learn how to check the graphic organizer against the scoring guide.	Students will: • use the graphic organizer to begin a writing test response.
Activities				
• Read and discuss **Prewriting: Study the Writing Prompt** (Student pages 182–183).	• Read and discuss **Prewriting: Gather Information** (Student page 184).	• Read and discuss **Prewriting: Organize Ideas** (Student page 185).	• Read and discuss **Prewriting: Check the Scoring Guide** (Student pages 186–187).	• Read and discuss **Drafting: Write a Draft** (Student pages 188–189).

WEEK 3

Day 1	Day 2	Day 3	Day 4	Day 5
Learning Objectives				
Students will: • add specific details to their writing test response.	Students will: • replace boring language with more personal language.	Students will: • delete sentences that are off-topic in their writing test response.	Students will: • edit their writing test response for grammar and mechanics.	Students will: • review tips for writing for a test.
Activities				
• Read and discuss **Revising: Extend Writing** (Student page 190).	• Read and discuss **Revising: Clarify Writing** (Student page 191).	• Read and discuss **Editing: Check Sentences** (Student page 192).	• Read and discuss **Editing: Proofread Writing** (Student pages 193–194).	• Read and discuss **Test Tips** (Student page 195).

* To complete the chapter in fewer days, teach the learning objectives and activities for two days in one day.

This planning chart, correlated to your state's writing standards, is available on-line at http://www.zaner-bloser.com/sfw.

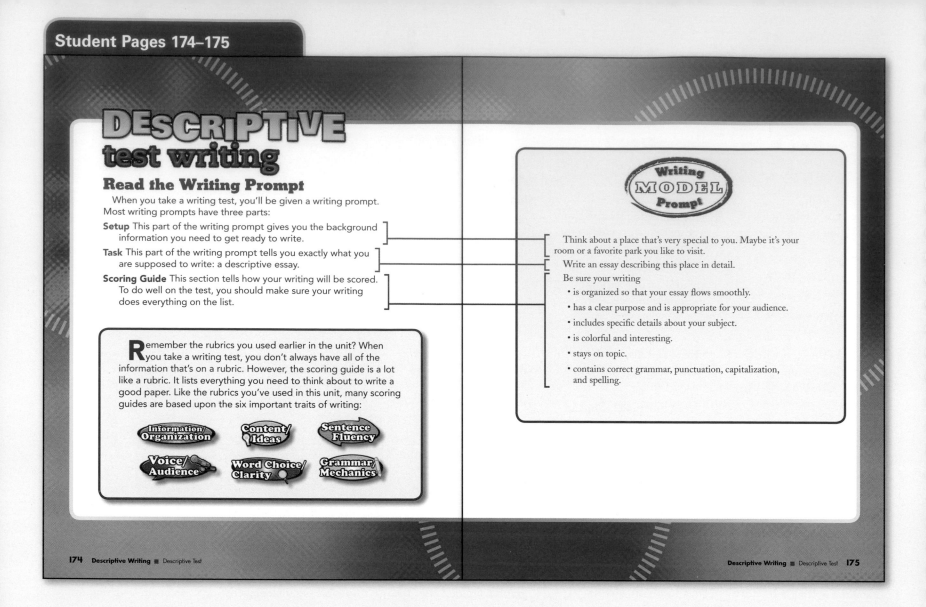

Introduce the Writing Prompt
Descriptive Writing

(Student pages 174–175)

Read aloud the information in the writing prompt on Student page 175. Point out that the setup, task, and scoring guide are probably not going to be labeled for them when they take a test, but they will be able to identify these parts on their own by analyzing the writing prompt.

Ask students to look at the writing prompt on Student page 175. Ask them what the writing prompt is instructing the writer to do. **Write an essay describing a place that is special to him or her.** Explain that they have just listed the task, or what the writer is being asked to do. Ask students why they feel that the setup part of the writing prompt is important. **Possible response: It gives background information that the writer needs to know in order to complete the task.** Next, ask students what the writer needs to do in order to get a good grade on this test.

Students should respond by listing the items in the scoring guide section of the writing prompt. Point out that these instructions form the scoring guide section of the writing prompt. Before a student can begin writing for a test, he or she needs to know this information.

Differentiating Instruction

Support Help students understand that the setup part of the writing prompt provides background information. It describes the situation they will write about or pretend to be experiencing. The task is the actual assignment, what they will write. The task often includes a word that tells the kind of writing they should do, such as *explain*, *describe*, *convince*, or *persuade*.

Writing Traits
in the Scoring Guide

Let's take a look back at the scoring guide in the writing prompt on page 175. Not every test prompt will include each of the six writing traits, but we can see that this one does. Take a look at the following chart. It will help you better understand the connection between the scoring guide and the writing traits in the rubrics you've been using.

 **Information/Organization**
- Be sure your writing is organized so that your essay flows smoothly.

 Voice/Audience
- Be sure your writing has a clear purpose and is appropriate for your audience.

 **Content/Ideas**
- Be sure your writing includes specific details about your subject.

 Word Choice/Clarity
- Be sure your writing is colorful and interesting.

 Sentence Fluency
- Be sure your writing stays on topic.

Grammar/Mechanics
- Be sure your writing contains correct grammar, punctuation, capitalization, and spelling.

Look at Daniel Maloney's story on the next page. Did he follow the scoring guide?

Writing Prompt MODEL Response

Sitting on the Dock

by Daniel Maloney

I really didn't want to spend my summer vacation with my family at Bass Lake—I wanted to stay home with my friends. But by the end of our vacation, my parents practically had to drag me away from what had quickly become my favorite place. You see, Bass Lake, with its calm, crystal-blue-morning water and its choppy, loud, and fun-filled afternoons, is a truly magnificent place.

On our last day there, I got up early and walked the few steps from our rented log cabin to the dock on the lake for a final goodbye. At this hour, the lake was still. The water, a deep navy blue, had a glassy sheen to it that I hated to disturb. As I walked to the end of the dock, the wood planks creaked and gave slightly, causing small ripples in the water below.

Two small boats were tied to the dock—an old, messy rowboat and a speed boat ready to take its passengers for waterskiing adventures after dawn turned to day. On either side, not far from my dock, were other similar docks, quietly waiting for the day to begin. Homes old and new, large and small, lined the shore and rose up into the hills above it. In the distance, I heard a dog bark and thought it must be eager for its morning swim. Across the vast lake there were no homes, just pine trees bunched together thickly, leaving a dark impression of their outline in the water.

I took a deep breath, inhaling the strong scent of pine and the slightly fishy smell of the water. I also smelled the faint odor of fuel from the boat. Though the sun was quickly rising, the air was still crisp, and my toes caught a chill when I took off my shoes. I wanted to get one last feel of the lake's cool, clean water, a final reminder of my visit. I could see rocks below the surface of the lake as I carefully stuck my toe into its chilly bath. The rocks became blurry and faded from my view with the movement of the water, and I got up to leave for the last time.

Writing Traits in the Scoring Guide
(Student pages 176–177)

Note that scoring for test writing is based on writing traits much like the writing traits in the rubrics students have been using throughout the book. Ask a student to read the traits in the scoring guide on Student page 176. Tell students to think of the scoring guide in much the same way as they used the rubrics in other chapters. Ask students how a writer taking this test might get a poor score in the organization category. **Possible response: His or her paper is not well organized and does not flow smoothly.** Note that by using the scoring guide, students can ensure their test papers are well written.

Read the Model:
Writing Prompt Response

Point out that students will be studying the strategies for descriptive test writing in this chapter. A good descriptive writing test contains the traits listed in the scoring guide. Have them look for these traits as they read the model writing prompt response, "Sitting on the Dock."

Differentiating Instruction

English-Language Learners Explain that *setup* is a compound word made by joining two smaller words: *set* and *up*. In a writing prompt, *setup* means "a description of the situation." Have students name other compound words, such as *playground* and *sidewalk*. Also discuss synonyms for the word *task*, such as *job* and *assignment*.

Using the Scoring Guide to Study the Model

Now let's use the scoring guide to check Daniel's writing test, "Sitting on the Dock." Let's see how well his essay meets each of the six writing traits.

Information/Organization
• The writing is organized so that the essay flows smoothly.

Daniel's essay flowed smoothly. He begins by saying what a great place the lake turned out to be, and then goes on to describe the scene in detail.

> On our last day there, I got up early and walked the few steps from our rented log cabin to the dock on the lake for a final goodbye. At this hour, the lake was still. The water, a deep navy blue, had a glassy sheen to it that I hated to disturb. As I walked to the end of the dock, the wood planks creaked and gave slightly, causing small ripples in the water below.

Voice/Audience
• The writing has a clear purpose and is appropriate for the audience.

Daniel uses terms and descriptions that give me, the reader, a good idea of what Bass Lake looked like that morning. He doesn't give details that a reader might not understand had she never visited Bass Lake.

> Two small boats were tied to the dock—an old, messy rowboat and a speed boat ready to take its passengers for waterskiing adventures after dawn turned to day. On either side, not far from my dock, were other similar docks, quietly waiting for the day to begin. Homes old and new, large and small, lined the shore and rose up into the hills above it.

Content/Ideas
• The writing includes specific details about the subject.

Daniel does a good job providing specific details. For instance, he talks about how still the lake was. He even describes what it smelled like outside.

> At this hour, the lake was still. The water, a deep navy blue, had a glassy sheen to it that I hated to disturb.

> I took a deep breath, inhaling the strong scent of pine and the slightly fishy smell of the water. I also smelled the faint odor of fuel from the boat.

Word Choice/Clarity
• The writing is colorful and interesting.

Daniel makes his writing more interesting by using colorful, descriptive words. I know, for instance, that boats can't wait for the day to begin, but it helps to give the reader a clearer picture when Daniel uses descriptions like this.

> On either side, not far from my dock, were other similar docks, quietly waiting for the day to begin. Homes old and new, large and small, lined the shore and rose up into the hills above it. In the distance, I heard a dog bark and thought it must be eager for its morning swim. Across the vast lake there were no homes, just pine trees bunched together thickly, leaving a dark impression of their outline in the water.

Using the Scoring Guide to Study the Model

(Student pages 178–180)

Explain that the scoring guide is used to determine how well a test was written, much in the same way rubrics were used to assess the writing samples from other chapters. Point out that the scoring guide may not always include criteria for each of the six key areas students have been studying: Information/Organization, Voice/Audience, Content/Ideas, Word Choice/Clarity, Sentence Fluency, and Grammar/Mechanics. Still, students should think about each of these areas as they write for tests.

Tell students that in this writing prompt, all six key areas of assessment are addressed in the scoring guide. Have students read each of the bulleted points on Student pages 178–180 aloud. Then read Denise's comments under each bulleted item. For each point, ask students whether they agree with Denise's assessment or not. Ask them to look for other examples in the model. As a class, decide how you would rate the test overall based on how well the writer followed the traits listed in the scoring guide.

Differentiating Instruction

Enrichment Ask students to think about how writing can be made more colorful and interesting. Have them look through books, magazines, or articles on-line to find descriptive essays or articles in which the writing seems colorful and interesting. Ask them to bring in a paragraph from the article or story they find and read it aloud to the class. Have them share their writing examples with the class and note the words or descriptions in the text that make them decide that the writing is colorful and interesting.

Using the Scoring Guide to Study the Model

Sentence Fluency
- The writing stays on topic.

I think Daniel stayed on topic. For instance, I don't see any sentences that don't seem to belong in the story. Although the first paragraph doesn't describe the lake, it provides a good introduction to what Daniel will be describing, and why!

I really didn't want to spend my summer vacation with my family at Bass Lake—I wanted to stay home with my friends. But by the end of our vacation, my parents practically had to drag me away from what had quickly become my favorite place. You see, Bass Lake, with its calm, crystal-blue-morning water and its choppy, loud, and fun-filled afternoons, is a truly magnificent place.

Grammar/Mechanics
- The writing contains correct grammar, punctuation, capitalization, and spelling.

I didn't notice any mistakes in Daniel's writing. When you take a test, it's important to check for mistakes in your work, including errors in grammar, punctuation, capitalization, and spelling. Be sure to go through and edit your work before you turn it in!

Planning My Time

Before giving us a writing test prompt, my teacher tells us how much time we'll have to complete the test. Since I'm already familiar with the writing process, I can think about how much total time I have and then divide it up into the different parts of the writing process. If the test takes an hour, here's how I can organize my time. Planning your time will help you, too!

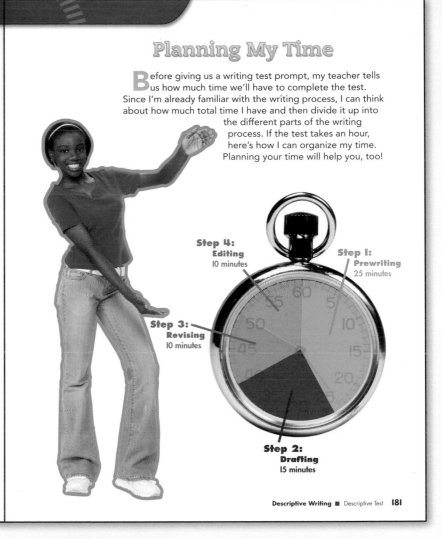

Step 4: Editing 10 minutes

Step 1: Prewriting 25 minutes

Step 3: Revising 10 minutes

Step 2: Drafting 15 minutes

Planning My Time
(Student page 181)

Explain to students that when they are writing for a test, they must organize their time as well as their notes and ideas. This chart offers a guide for various testing periods.

Total Test Minutes:	60	90	120
Prewriting	25	37	50
Drafting	15	23	30
Revising	10	15	20
Editing	10	15	20

Point out that drafting constitutes less than half of the allotted time for the entire test. Many students do poorly on writing tests because they begin writing before they have a plan and continue writing until they run out of time, without leaving any time for revising and editing.

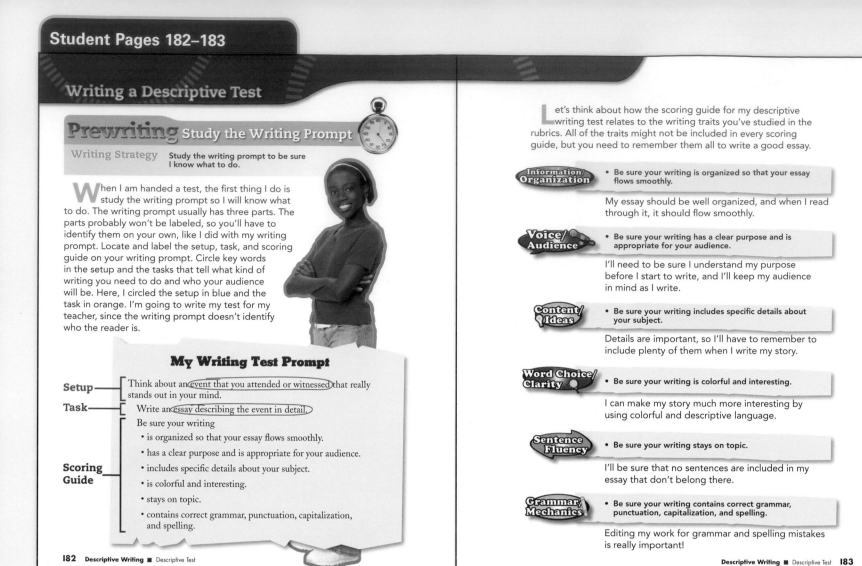

Study the Writing Prompt
(Student pages 182–183)

Ask students what they think *prewriting* means. **Possible response: what you do before you start writing or in preparation for writing** Note that studying the writing prompt is prewriting because it is a step that should be taken in preparation for writing for a test. Ask a student to read Denise's words on Student page 182. Stress the importance of studying the writing prompt before beginning to write for a test. Had Denise written an excellent essay on why she decided to attend an event, she would not have received a good grade because the writing prompt is asking her to describe the event in detail, not her reasons for going to the event.

Point out the three parts of the writing prompt. Ask which part of the prompt tells the students what to do. **the task**

Ask a student to read the scoring guide portion of the writing prompt. Note that Denise has gone over each of the traits in the scoring guide and stated them in her own words. This is to ensure that she fully understands what the prompt requires.

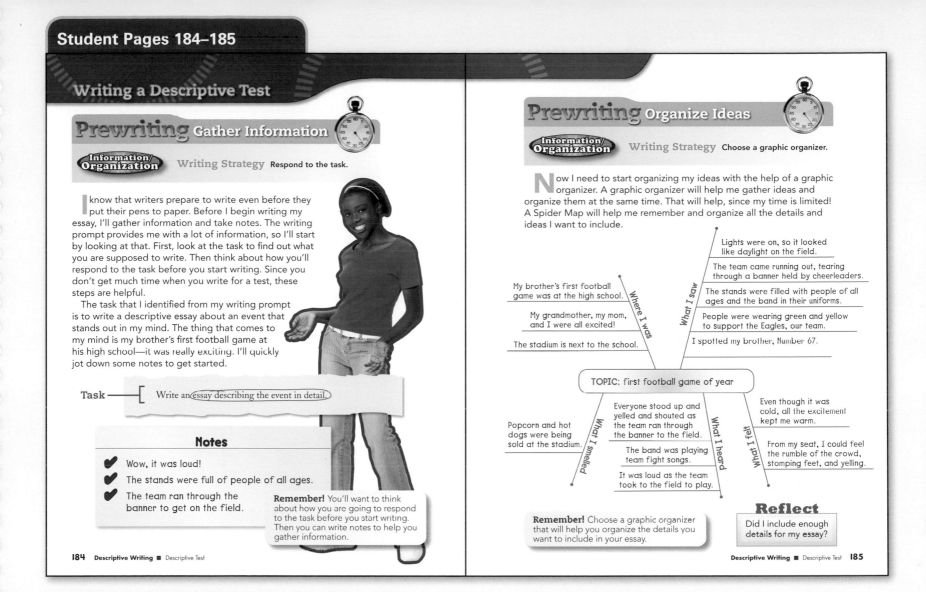

Gather Information and Organize Ideas

(Student pages 184–185)

Ask a student to read Denise's words on Student page 184. Note that she has highlighted the words *essay describing* on the task part of the scoring guide so she knows exactly what she is supposed to write about. This helps her to focus on a subject.

Ask students why they think it is helpful to jot down notes even before they start organizing the notes in a graphic organizer. **Possible responses: It helps to get the ideas that are coming to their minds down on paper. You'll want to have thoughts and ideas so that you can decide on and fill in a graphic organizer.**

Ask students why graphic organizers are important in writing, even when writing for a test. **Possible response: They help you organize your ideas before you start your draft.** Ask students why they think Denise decided to use a Spider Map to organize the information for her essay.

Possible response: It's a good way to get all the details about different aspects of the game organized. Point out that students will need to decide what type of graphic organizer to use for a test; they will not be told which kind to use. They will want to use a graphic organizer that they are familiar with and that will help them organize their ideas for the particular type of writing they will be doing.

Differentiating Instruction

Enrichment Discuss with students other types of graphic organizers that might be helpful for organizing the information Denise has listed in her Spider Map. Ask students to try organizing the information in another graphic organizer. List the graphic organizers students suggest on the board. Then, next to each type of graphic organizer, have students suggest the benefits of using that particular type of organizer.

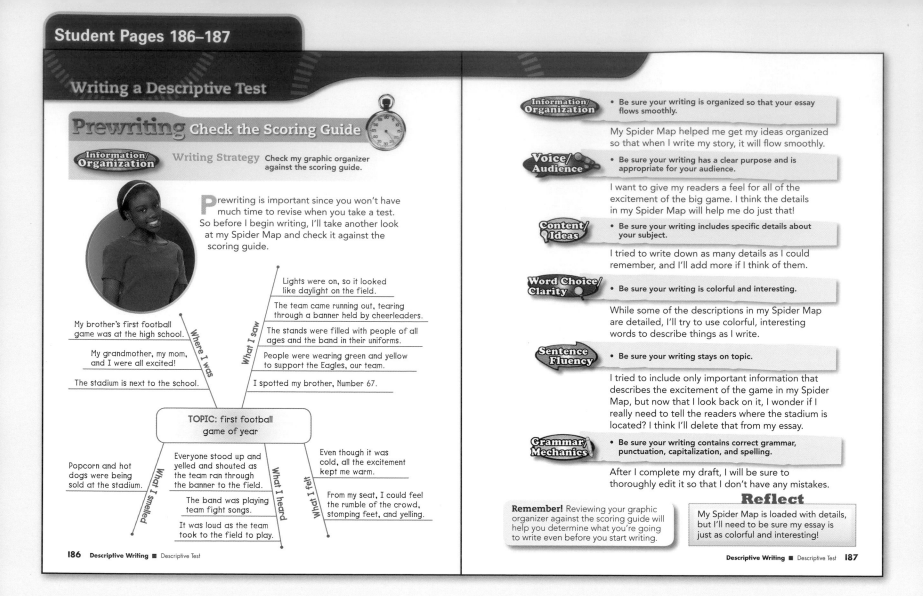

Check the Scoring Guide

(Student pages 186–187)

Make sure that students understand that the scoring guide is taken from the writing prompt. You can refer back to Student page 182 to point out the source.

Ask a student to read Denise's words on Student page 186. Note that checking the graphic organizer against the scoring guide helps ensure that they are following the instructions set forth in the scoring guide even before they begin to write. This will make writing the draft easier.

Ask students to read Denise's words on Student page 187 for each of the writing traits in the scoring guide. Have students try to find specific examples of each trait in Denise's Spider Map. Note that the graphic organizer can be adjusted to meet the requirements of the scoring guide. Remind students that some of the traits from the scoring guide, such as Grammar/Mechanics, will need to be checked in the editing and revising stage and not during prewriting.

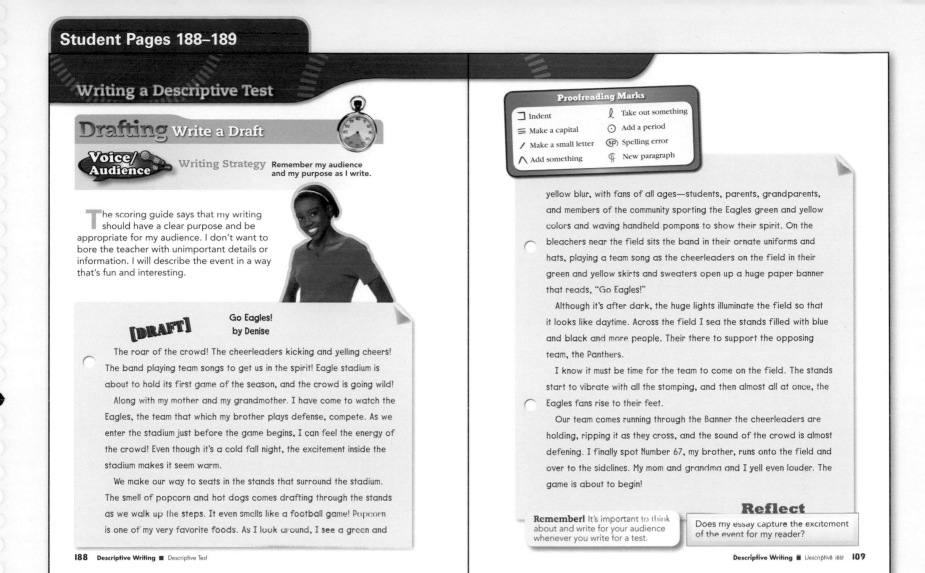

Drafting

(Student pages 188–189)

Point out that when writing for a test, students may not be able to recopy their tests. Encourage them to leave room between the lines when writing a draft in a testing situation. This will give them room to make corrections or to add and delete text as they revise and proofread. Note that although neatness is not a criterion in the scoring guide, they should nonetheless try to be neat so that test evaluators do not misread what they have written.

Discuss Denise's draft. Note that she paid attention to her audience and her purpose as she wrote. She focused on writing about the event in a way that was fun and interesting, so as not to bore her readers. Ask students to identify parts of the draft that they like and parts that could be improved. Ask if her essay seems to have a clear

purpose. Remind students that Denise is not too concerned with errors in spelling, grammar, and punctuation at this stage because she has given herself enough time to edit her essay later.

Differentiating Instruction

Support Some students may find the thought of taking a timed test intimidating. Assure them they have already learned many of the steps and strategies for effective test writing in the other chapters in the book. Stress, too, that if they plan their time accordingly, they will have ample time to go back over their essays and make any grammar, punctuation, and spelling edits and to make necessary revisions.

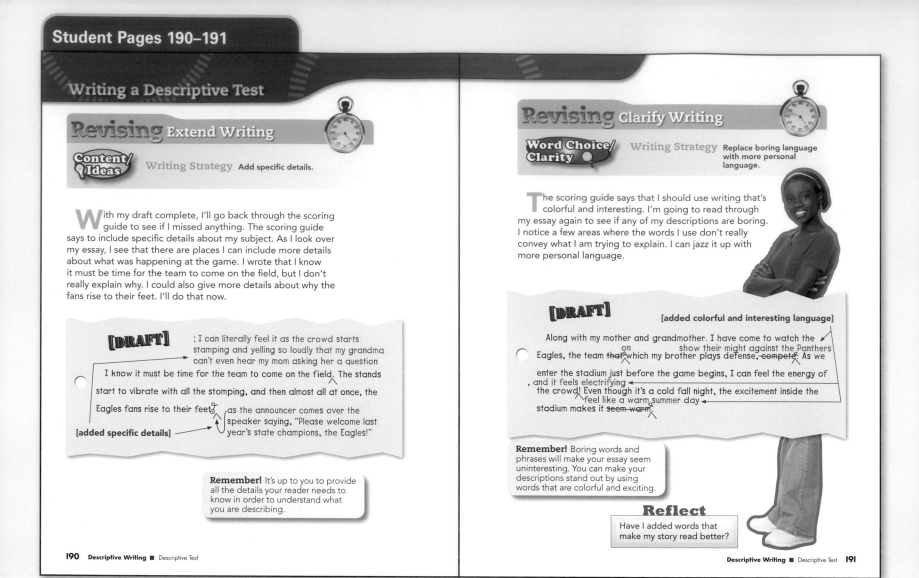

Revising

(Student pages 190–191)

Have a student to read Denise's words on Student page 190. Point out that when they are writing, it is sometimes easy to forget that the reader does not have as much knowledge about something as the writer does. They may need to provide details and explanations that help give the reader a better idea of what they are talking about. Read through the changes on Student page 190 that Denise made in her essay in order to add specific details. Ask students if they believe Denise's revisions help.

Now have a student read Denise's words on Student page 191. Note that Denise goes back over the scoring guide and sees that she needs to use writing that's colorful and interesting. Ask students what they think that means. Note that she wants to replace boring language with more personal language. Have students suggest examples of boring descriptions. Ask students if Denise has added words that make the story read better.

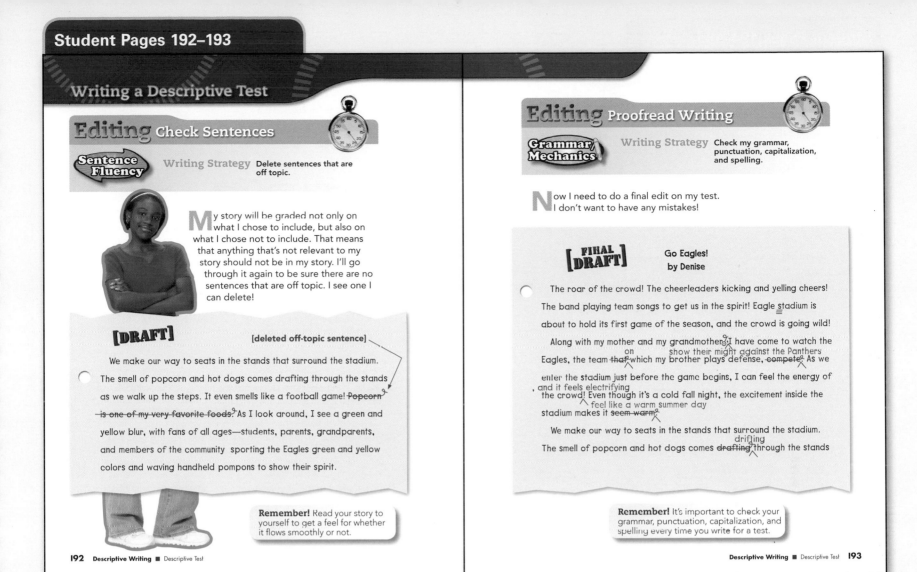

Editing

(Student pages 192–194)

Have a student read Denise's words on Student page 192. Ask students why they think that irrelevant, or off-topic, sentences should be removed. **Possible response: They take away from the story and seem out of place.** Ask students why they think Denise removed the line about popcorn. **Possible response: Her essay is about experiencing the game, and talking about her favorite food does not belong in the description.**

Point out that the final step in the editing process is to check the grammar, punctuation, capitalization, and spelling. Have a student read Denise's words on Student page 193. Urge students to allow enough time to edit and proofread their writing. Tell them to look for errors as they proofread their drafts and to make corrections on the test paper.

You may wish to review the grammar lessons students have learned in this chapter:

- correct use of appositives
- apostrophe use
- correct verb tense

Have students look for errors in these areas as well when they edit their test drafts.

Differentiating Instruction

Support Students should familiarize themselves with proofreading marks and how to make edits in their drafts using the proper proofreading marks. Have them refer to the proofreading marks box shown on Student page 189. Then ask them to write a paragraph that includes errors in each of the areas the proofreading marks box addresses. Instruct them to leave room between the lines so that they can make corrections. Have them use the proofreading marks to make clear and legible corrections to the paragraph.

FINAL [DRAFT]

as we walk up the steps. It even smells like a football game! ~~Popcorn is one of my very favorite foods?~~ As I look around, I see a green and yellow blur, with fans of all ages—students, parents, grandparents, and members of the community sporting the Eagles green and yellow colors and waving handheld pompons to show their spirit. On the bleachers near the field sits the band in their ornate uniforms and hats, playing a team song as the cheerleaders on the field in their green and yellow skirts and sweaters open up a huge paper banner that reads, "Go Eagles!"

Although it's after dark, the huge lights illuminate the field so that it looks like daytime. Across the field I ~~see~~ see the stands filled with blue and black and more people. ~~Their~~ They're there to support the opposing team, the Panthers. ; I can literally feel it as the crowd starts stamping and yelling so loudly that my grandma can't even hear my mom asking her a question I know it must be time for the team to come on the field. The stands start to vibrate with all the stomping, and then almost all at once, the Eagles fans rise to their feet as the announcer comes over the speaker saying, "Please welcome last year's state champions, the Eagles!" Our team comes running through the banner the cheerleaders are holding, ripping it as they cross, and the sound of the crowd is almost deafening ~~defening~~. I finally spot Number 67, my brother, as he runs onto the field and over to the sidelines. My mom and grandma and I yell even louder. The game is about to begin!

Reflect

This is my last chance! I'll take one more look at the scoring guide to be sure I didn't miss anything.

That's it! We've finished the test. Pretty easy, don't you think? Here are some helpful tips to remember when you write for a test.

TEST TIPS

1. **Study the writing prompt before you start to write.** Most writing prompts have three parts: the setup, the task, and the scoring guide. The parts probably won't be labeled. You'll have to figure them out for yourself!

2. **Make sure you understand the task before you start to write.**
   • Read all three parts of the writing prompt carefully.
   • Circle key words in the task part of the writing prompt that tell what kind of writing you need to do. The task might also identify your audience.
   • Make sure you know how you'll be graded.
   • Say the assignment in your own words to yourself.

3. **Keep an eye on the clock.** Decide how much time you will spend on each part of the writing process and try to stick to your schedule. Don't spend so much time on prewriting that you don't have enough time left to write.

4. **Reread your writing. Compare it to the scoring guide at least twice.** Remember the rubrics you have used all year? A scoring guide on a writing test is like a rubric. It can help you keep what's important in mind.

5. **Plan, plan, plan!** You don't get much time to revise during a test, so planning is more important than ever.

6. **Write neatly.** Remember, if the people who score your test can't read your writing, it doesn't matter how good your essay is!

Differentiating Instruction

Enrichment Ask students to create a sample test writing prompt for a descriptive writing test. Be sure that they include the setup, the task, and the scoring guide portions of the writing prompt. Have them swap their sample test writing prompts with a partner and ask the partner to identify the setup, task, and scoring guide parts of the writing prompt by circling or underlining each part and identifying it in the margin.

Test Tips

(Student page 195)

Read the test tips on Student page 195 aloud. Note that these tips can help students do well on tests, and students should remember the tips when they write for a test. You may wish to suggest that students write each of the tips on a single note card to help remember them.

Point out that students have already been learning good writing habits that will help them to do well on a writing test. They should already have the tools available to complete a writing test. Tests shouldn't be stressful for students if they remember that the scoring guide is similar to the rubrics they have been using to assess their writing and that they need to plan their time properly and keep an eye on the clock.

Books for Professional Development

Anderson, Carl. *How's It Going? A Practical Guide to Conferring with Student Writers.* Portsmouth: Heinemann, 2000.

Anderson provides samples that demonstrate various techniques and strategies that will help both teacher and students refine their participation in a conference.

Lane, Barry. *After THE END: Teaching and Learning Creative Revision.* Portsmouth: Heinemann, 1993.

The author stresses the importance of helping students take charge of their own writing. It is an idea book for upper elementary through high school. It guides the teacher in using specific revising techniques as part of the writing process.

McCarthy, Tara. *Teaching Genre: Explore 9 Types of Literature to Develop Lifelong Readers and Writers.* New York: Scholastic, 1996.

This book explores nine types of literature and is designed to develop lifelong readers and writers. A great deal of information is included in the book and it is accompanied by many quality reproducible worksheets. It is filled with creative and engaging writing assignments.

Portalupi, JoAnn, and Ralph Fletcher. *Nonfiction Craft Lessons: Teaching Information Writing K–8.* Portland: Stenhouse, 2001.

Divided into chapters for grades K–2, 3–4, and 5–8, this book includes more than 25 one-page descriptions of strategies for all aspects of the writing process. It focuses on informative writing, with lessons specific to persuasion, comparison, how-to writing, and biography.

School-Home Connection

Dear Family,

In this chapter of *Strategies for Writers,* your child is learning about how to write a descriptive essay. A descriptive essay gives a clear, detailed picture of a person, place, thing, or event. We'll be encouraging your child to be very observant in order to do this kind of writing. He or she will need to pay attention to details and describe them in a way that brings them to life for the reader.

Here are some easy ways you can help your child become more observant and learn about providing descriptive detail:

- Ask him or her to tell you about an event that happened that day, such as something at school or during an after-school activity. As he or she relates this event, have him or her point out sensory details. Ask what sounds he or she heard; was there a smell, feel, or taste he or she experienced? As your child describes what he or she saw, be sure he or she gives you details that give you a clear picture in your mind of what happened.

- As your child eats dinner, have him or her describe in detail what the meal tastes like. Have him or her give a detailed description of the meal, including the taste, smell, and sight of it.

- As you and your child observe ordinary objects, have him or her use metaphors to describe the object. Metaphors compare two different, usually non-related things. For example, your dog's swishing tail might be compared to a feather duster. Because metaphors help add to the description in a descriptive essay, this exercise will help your student write good descriptive essays.

Good descriptions are not just part of writing class; they are used every day. Encourage your child to help develop the skills that will not only improve his or her writing but will last a lifetime.

School-Home Connection

Dear Family,

In this chapter, your child will be learning and practicing descriptive writing. Descriptive writing paints pictures with words. It is meant to help the reader "see" what the writer is writing about. Descriptive writing can describe a person, place, event, or thing. Your child will be learning and practicing three examples of descriptive writing—a descriptive essay, an observation report, and a descriptive article.

A descriptive essay gives a clear, detailed picture of a person, place, thing, or event. In this type of writing, the writer must clearly communicate to the reader what he or she has observed.

In an observation report, the writer describes in detail an object, person, event, or process. Students will take notes on something they have observed, such as an experiment, and describe the step-by-step process for the reader.

A descriptive article, like a descriptive essay, gives a clear, detailed picture of a person, place, thing, or event. The descriptive article, though, is meant to inform readers of a newspaper, magazine, brochure, or other publication.

Throughout this chapter, we'll be asking your child to pay close attention to something specific in order to write a detailed report about it. He or she will be honing in on his or her observation skills and helping the reader get a visual picture of that something.

School-Home Connection

Dear Family,

Our class is learning and practicing many different kinds of writing. Writing is an opportunity for people to express their thoughts and feelings, as well as a chance to communicate information to others.

Encourage your child to think of himself or herself as a writer. Every piece of written material your child produces brings him or her one step closer to being a good communicator and a person who thinks creatively. Your support and encouragement mean a great deal.

Celebrate your child's writing. Here are some easy and fun ways you can encourage your child to write:

- Create a quiet place for your child to write. Set aside a small space where your child can daydream, take notes, doodle, and so on. It doesn't have to be anything fancy—just a spot where your child can go that's just for writing.

- Participate in your child's writing efforts. Offer to be interviewed for a writing assignment. Your memories or experiences may prove to be very valuable to your young writer.

- Post your child's writing in a special place at home. A refrigerator door is a great place to publish your child's work. Another great idea is a simple bulletin board.

- Finally, encourage your child to read. It doesn't matter what topic interests your child. Whatever it is, there are books about it. Try your public library for a great selection of books on any topic. People who love to read often become people who love to write.

Try these simple but effective ways to help your child become a better writer. You'll be surprised at how well they work!

School-Home Connection

Dear Family,

In this chapter, your child will be learning how to take a descriptive writing test. Sometimes the mere mention of the word *test* can stress out even the most well-prepared student. Throughout this chapter, we'll show how taking a test is similar to the other types of descriptive writing we have been studying throughout the chapter.

One of the biggest differences between writing for a test and writing for a class assignment is the amount of time students are given to complete a test. For that reason, we stress to students the importance of organizing their time.

You might be surprised to learn that actually writing the draft for the test should not take up a significant amount of the test-taker's time. Instead, we encourage students to spend more time on what is known as the prewriting stage. Prewriting involves studying the writing prompt (the instructions on what to write), gathering information, organizing the information into a graphic organizer, and checking the information in the graphic organizer against the scoring guide. In an hour-long test, the steps of prewriting, drafting, revising, and editing can be divided as follows:

Prewriting: 25 minutes
Drafting: 15 minutes
Revising: 10 minutes
Editing: 10 minutes

The revising and editing steps are an important part of test taking, and we encourage students to leave enough time for each of these steps. It is during these stages that students are able to fine-tune their drafts and ensure that they are error free.

We hope that by learning and practicing the steps in taking a descriptive writing test, your child will realize that taking a test doesn't have to be stressful.

EXPOSITORY writing strategies

IN THIS UNIT

1 Summary

- Read an article and take notes on the main points.
- Make a Spider Map from my notes.
- State the topic in the first sentence so the audience immediately knows my subject.
- Use only the most important details.
- Replace wordy phrases with succinct language.
- Combine short, choppy sentences to make the writing flow.
- Make sure the subject and verb agree in each sentence.

2 Cause-and-Effect Report

- Use the Internet to find credible sources of information on my topic.
- Make a Cause-and-Effect Chain to organize my notes.
- Begin with an interesting fact to grab the audience's attention.
- Add supporting facts.
- Use transition words to make cause-and-effect relationships clear.
- Rewrite long, confusing sentences.
- Check that subject and object pronouns are used correctly, especially *who* and *whom*.

3 Research Report

- Use an encyclopedia and at least two other sources to research my topic.
- Make an Outline to organize my notes.
- Provide details to interest my audience.
- Add a conclusion that summarizes the main points.
- Change passive voice to active voice.
- Use a variety of lively, energetic sentences.
- Make sure proper nouns and proper adjectives are capitalized correctly.

4 Writing for a Test

- Study the writing prompt to be sure I know what to do.
- Respond to the task.
- Choose a graphic organizer.
- Check my graphic organizer against the scoring guide.
- Clearly identify the topic for my audience at the beginning.
- Include details or facts that help explain each main idea.
- Use transition words to clarify connecting ideas.
- Include a variety of sentence patterns.
- Check the grammar, punctuation, capitalization, and spelling.

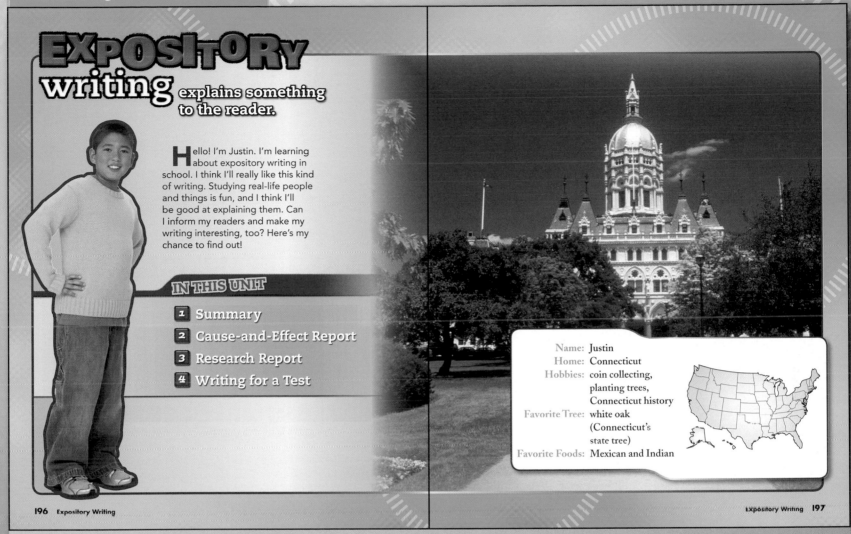

EXPOSITORY
writing explains something to the reader.

Hello! I'm Justin. I'm learning about expository writing in school. I think I'll really like this kind of writing. Studying real-life people and things is fun, and I think I'll be good at explaining them. Can I inform my readers and make my writing interesting, too? Here's my chance to find out!

IN THIS UNIT

1. Summary
2. Cause-and-Effect Report
3. Research Report
4. Writing for a Test

Name: Justin
Home: Connecticut
Hobbies: coin collecting, planting trees, Connecticut history
Favorite Tree: white oak (Connecticut's state tree)
Favorite Foods: Mexican and Indian

196 Expository Writing

Expository Writing 197

IN THIS UNIT

Summary This genre gives students the opportunity to explain, in their own words, the main ideas from a longer piece of writing.

Cause-and-Effect Report Students will learn to describe how a cause or causes produce certain effects.

Research Report This genre shows students how to gather information from multiple sources, organize it, and explain the main points to readers.

Expository Test Students will learn and practice how to read an expository test prompt and how to plan their time. They will also learn and practice writing strategies for successful expository test writing.

Meet Justin

Here, we introduce students to their student guide for this chapter, Justin, a boy from Connecticut. Review Justin's profile with students, and point out that Justin's hobbies, interests, and background will influence the topics he chooses to write about and the approach he will take when completing his writing assignments. Explain that this will help make his writing more real, as he will be better able to relate to his subjects. Point out that expository writing explains something to the reader. Remind students to write about something they know, or something in which they have an interest.

by Julie Coiro, Ph.D.
University of Connecticut

Locating Resources: Reading Within Search Engine Results

One of the most challenging aspects of on-line reading is understanding how to strategically evaluate a long list of search results to determine which link, if any, to pursue. You may wish to share these strategies with students:

- **Read the description, not just the link.** Some students only skim the blue underlined titles that appear in a search list entry. However, the description that follows often contains helpful clues, with keywords from the search in bold print. Students can avoid a link that's not useful by using the available descriptions to more accurately predict if the information actually meets their research needs. Several search engines use ellipses (. . .) at the end of descriptions; students should understand what ellipses mean and try to anticipate what the rest of the description might say.

- **Know how to read the parts of a Web site address.** Information can be gleaned from the dots, slashes, abbreviations, and words in the Web addresses that appear in search results. Show students how Web addresses can

be broken down, with each part providing identification of the path leading to the Web site host, as follows:

http://	school. discovery. com/	schooladventures/	geogame. html
type of protocol	domain name, or host	path or directory to the file	name and type of file

Once students understand these "clues," they can use them to determine which Web sites will be useful.

- **Use the clues to try a different search.** If nothing useful is found in the first ten or twenty sites in the search result list, it's time to try a new search with different keywords. Encourage students to think about words that appeared in the descriptions or within the Web sites they visited. Sometimes reading more about the topic on one Web site will help generate synonyms for different keywords that might yield better results in a new search.

Critical Evaluation: Evaluating Accuracy

Students should know that it is possible for credible individuals to make an inaccurate statement or a mistake. For this reason, you may wish to discuss strategies to help students evaluate the accuracy of on-line information. *Accuracy* refers to the extent to which information contains factual details that can be verified by another reliable source. Here are three tips you may wish to model for your students:

- **Read the Web site.** Read carefully. Searching for information requires skimming and scanning. Reading for accuracy requires close reading. Ask yourself the following questions: *Does the information make sense? When was it last updated? Is it free from spelling or grammatical errors? Does the author list the bibliographic sources for the information?*

- **Read other Web sites.** Can the information be verified at another Web site? Use a search engine and the keyword strategies covered in Unit 2 to search for other sites that contain similar facts.

- **Read a primary source Web site.** You may wish to spend a class period talking about the differences between

primary sources and secondary sources. Then, you can recommend that students include at least one primary source in their research report. **The Library of Congress American Memory Database Learning Page** at **http://memory.loc.gov/learn/lessons/psources/pshome. html** provides excellent lessons on primary sources for older students. A search for "Primary Sources" on the **ReadWriteThink** Web site at **www.readwritethink. org** also results in several comprehensive lessons using the American Memory Database. These include **Slave Narratives: Constructing U.S. History Through Analyzing Primary Sources** at **http://edsitement. neh.gov/view_lesson_plan.asp?id=364** and the **Boston Tea Party: Costume Optional?** at **http://edsitement.neh.gov/view_lesson_plan. asp?id=397**.

Finally, **QUICK (The QUality Information ChecKlist)** from the United Kingdom at **http://www.quick.org.uk/ menu.htm** is an additional resource for evaluating accuracy.

Communicating Globally: Publishing With Classroom Blogs and Podcasts

Blogs and podcasts are two exciting new ways for students to share their work with others around the world. *Blog* is short for *weblog,* which is an on-line journal that displays entries in reverse chronological order. You can publish a blog on the Internet without knowing hypertext code or having to upload anything on a special server. A podcast is an audio or video file that is broadcast on the Internet. You may wish to explore the links in this section to get an idea of how teachers and students have begun using these on-line publishing tools.

Examples of Classroom Blogs

- Mark Ahlness is a veteran teacher who has experience with integrating technology, including blogs, into his classroom. One example of his work is **Mighty Writers 2006–07** at **http://roomtwelve.com**.

- Anne Davis of Georgia State University created **The Write Weblog** at **http://itc.blogs.com/ thewriteweblog** with staff and students from J.H. House Elementary School in Conyers, Georgia. Anne's work at the school inspired Hillary Meeler to begin her own classroom blog project called **Blog Write** at **http:// jhh.blogs.com/blogwrite**.

Examples of Classroom Podcasts

- Podcast Central at **http://mabryonline.org/podcasts** features video-enhanced podcasts and a series of blogs by middle school students and their teachers, including **Sixceed** at **http://mabryonline.org/sixceed**.

- Students at Sandaig Primary School in Glasgow, Scotland, have joined together to publish both **Radio Sandaig Podcasts** at **http://www.sandaigprimary. co.uk/radio_sandaig/index.php** and **Sandaig Otters Weblog** at **http://www.sandaigprimary.co.uk/pivot/ index.php**.

If the above examples inspired you, you may wish to use the following introductory tutorial: "Introduction to Blogs and Blogging," written by Michael Stach of **TechLearning** at **http://www.techlearning.com/story/showArticle. php?articleID=18400984**.

Supporting and Extending Writing: Internet Project

Students can share what they are learning with others around the world through Internet Project. Internet Project may take place as you work with another class on a common learning activity. It may also take place when classes contribute data to a common site and then analyze and compare results. One way to get involved with Internet Project is to join one of the following projects that have already demonstrated success.

- **Monarch Watch** at **http://www.monarchwatch.org** invites students to raise, tag, and release butterflies; record observations about them; and sit back and watch while the data is used to track their annual migration.

- **Square of Life: Studies in Local and Global Environments** at **http://www.k12science.org/ curriculum/squareproj** invites students to investigate their local environment, share their findings with other participating classes, look for similarities and differences in the reported data, and prepare a final presentation to share with other students from around the world.

- **Journey North: A Global Study of Wildlife Migration and Seasonal Change** at **http://www.learner. org/jnorth** provides opportunities to explore animal migration or to track the growth patterns of tulips.

For access to a large database of other existing Internet projects across the curriculum, try **Global SchoolNet's Internet Projects Registry** at **http://www. globalschoolnet.org/GSH/pr/index.cfm**. This site enables you to search by grade level, content area, and collaboration type through projects conducted by teachers worldwide. This site's **Collaborative Learning Center** at **http://www.globalschoolnet.org/center** also provides an excellent overview of how to select partner classes.

For more information, you may wish to read Donald J. Leu, Jr.'s article titled "Internet Project: Preparing Students for New Literacies in a Global Village" at **http://www. readingonline.org/electronic/RT/3-01_Column/index. html**.

Summary Overview

In this chapter, students will learn how to write a summary. They will learn what's in a summary—length, organization, a clear beginning, and interest—and some reasons for writing a summary. Students will then use a summary rubric to assess a model writing sample.

Students will then follow the student guide as he goes through the writing stages—prewriting, drafting, revising, editing, and publishing. Students will follow as the student guide learns new writing strategies in each step. Then they will be directed to practice the strategies in their own writing. Students will read an article and take notes on the main points. They will organize their notes in a Spider Map and then use the Spider Map to write their drafts. As they revise their drafts, students will ensure their writing contains only the most important details and that their language is concise. In the editing stage, students will learn how to make their sentences flow smoothly. Next, they will edit their drafts for spelling, punctuation, capitalization, and grammar and ensure that all subjects and verbs agree. After editing their drafts, they will write a final draft for publishing.

You may wish to send to families the School-Home Connection Letter for this chapter, located at the end of this unit in the Teacher Edition.

Summary Writing Traits

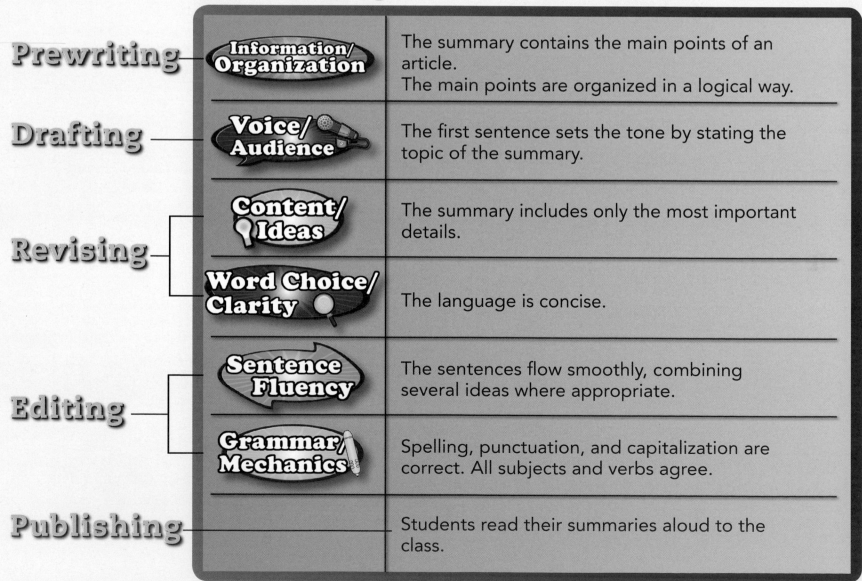

Prewriting	Information/Organization	The summary contains the main points of an article. The main points are organized in a logical way.
Drafting	Voice/Audience	The first sentence sets the tone by stating the topic of the summary.
Revising	Content/Ideas	The summary includes only the most important details.
	Word Choice/Clarity	The language is concise.
Editing	Sentence Fluency	The sentences flow smoothly, combining several ideas where appropriate.
	Grammar/Mechanics	Spelling, punctuation, and capitalization are correct. All subjects and verbs agree.
Publishing		Students read their summaries aloud to the class.

Summary Time Management

WEEK 1

Day 1	Day 2	Day 3	Day 4	Day 5
Learning Objectives				
Students will: • learn the components of a summary.	Students will: • learn how to gather information for a summary.	Students will: • practice gathering information for their own summaries.	Students will: • learn how to make a Spider Map to organize their notes.	Students will: • practice organizing their notes into a Spider Map.
Activities				
• Discuss the elements and traits of a summary (Students pages 198–200). • Use the rubric to study the model (Student pages 201–207).	• Read and discuss **Prewriting: Gather Information** (Student pages 208–210).	• Select an article to summarize, and take notes on the main points. • Work with a partner to gather information.	• Read and discuss **Prewriting: Organize Ideas** (Student page 211).	• Look at the notes for summaries. • Determine the main points to include in summaries. • Make a Spider Map to organize the notes.

WEEK 2

Day 1	Day 2	Day 3	Day 4	Day 5
Learning Objectives				
Students will: • learn how to state the topic of the summary in the first sentence.	Students will: • practice writing their drafts.	Students will: • learn how to delete any unnecessary details from their summaries.	Students will: • learn to include only the most important details.	Students will: • learn how to keep their language concise.
Activities				
• Read and discuss **Drafting: Write a Draft** (Student pages 212–213).	• Use Spider Map to write a draft. • State the topic in the first sentence.	• Read and discuss **Revising: Extend Writing** (Student page 214).	• Add only the most important details, and delete any unnecessary details.	• Read and discuss **Revising: Clarify Writing** (Student page 215).

WEEK 3

Day 1	Day 2	Day 3	Day 4	Day 5
Learning Objectives				
Students will: • practice replacing wordy phrases with succinct language.	Students will: • learn how to make their writing flow by using sentences that flow smoothly.	Students will: • learn to make the subject and verb agree in their sentences.	Students will: • practice editing their drafts for spelling, punctuation, and capitalization.	Students will: • learn different ways to publish their summaries.
Activities				
• Reread drafts, looking for wordy phrases. • Replace wordy phrases with succinct language.	• Read and discuss **Editing: Check Sentences** (Student page 216). • Make sure drafts contain sentences that flow smoothly.	• Read and discuss **Editing: Proofread Writing** (Student page 217). • Check subject-verb agreement.	• Fix any spelling, punctuation, or capitalization errors in their drafts. • Fix any subject-verb agreement problems in drafts.	• Read and discuss **Publishing: Share Writing** (Student pages 220–222).

* To complete the chapter in fewer days, teach the learning objectives and activities for two days in one day.
This planning chart, correlated to your state's writing standards, is available on-line at http://www.zaner-bloser.com/sfw.

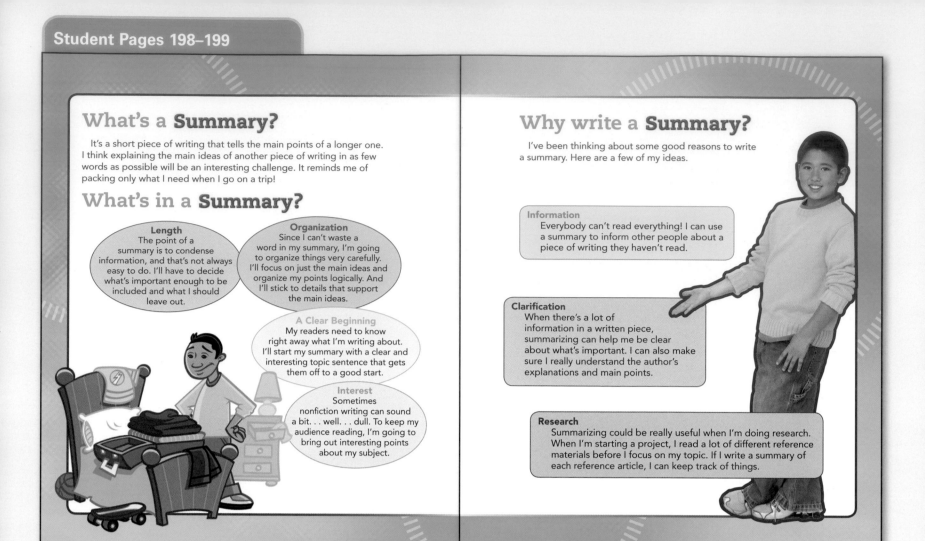

Define the Genre

(Student page 198)

Summary

Review the definition of summary with students. Ask students if they have ever seen a good movie they wanted to tell a friend about. Tell them that if they've ever described the details of a movie to another person, chances are they recounted only the main points and left out any unnecessary details—otherwise the description would last as long as the movie. Point out that when students summarize a longer work, they are using the summary genre.

Elements of the Genre

Summary

Read and discuss the elements of a summary with the students. Explain that these elements can also be found in news stories they might read on the front page of a newspaper. Have the students think about a current event and discuss how each of these elements might be present in a story about that current event.

Authentic Writing

(Student page 199)

Summary

Read and discuss with students the reasons for writing a summary on Student page 199. Point out that all writing has a purpose and the purpose for writing can affect the tone of the writing. In writing a summary, especially, the reasons have to do with condensing information and clarifying the meaning of a longer piece of writing. Point out that when the students write their own summaries, they should include the most important information about the article or story which they are summarizing. As students write their summaries, they should keep in mind why they are writing the summary and understand how that affects the tone and focus of their writing.

Summary
Writing Traits

There are six traits of good writing. But what makes a good summary? I'll use the list below when I write my summary.

Information/Organization	The summary contains the main points of an article. The main points are organized in a logical way.
Voice/Audience	The first sentence sets the tone by stating the topic of the summary.
Content/Ideas	The summary includes only the most important details.
Word Choice/Clarity	The language is concise.
Sentence Fluency	The sentences flow smoothly, combining several ideas where appropriate.
Grammar/Mechanics	Spelling, punctuation, and capitalization are correct. All subjects and verbs agree.

Let's see how Keesha used these traits to help her write the summary on the next page.

Summary Model

"A Touch of Genius"

by Patricia Millman
Summary by Keesha Kane

Organization · *Clear beginning* · *Short length*

Michael Naranjo is a Native American sculptor in Santa Fe, New Mexico. He chose his career when he was a boy helping his mother make pottery in the pueblo. At age 23, however, Naranjo was wounded in the Vietnam War. He was blinded and left without the complete use of one hand.

Interesting point

Naranjo was unsure if he would still be able to sculpt. While recovering in the hospital, he molded several clay sculptures of animals. One was so good that it was photographed for the newspaper. That convinced him to pursue his dream. · *Smooth writing holds interest*

Although he cannot see, he can remember images from his past. His mind carries the images to his fingertips. · *Interesting point*

Naranjo has won awards for his work and leads sculpture workshops. His sculptures are displayed in museums and public buildings around the world. Private collectors also seek his art.

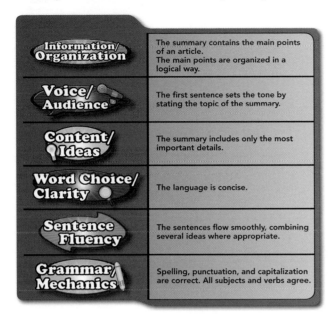

Michael A. Naranjo

Writing Traits
(*Student pages 200–201*)

Summary

Read aloud the traits of a good summary on Student page 200. Point out the six categories, and be sure students are clear on their meaning in the context of writing. Possible points to discuss:

- Information/Organization: In a summary, the organization of the main points must be clear and logical.

- Voice/Audience: Because a summary is brief, the writer should set the tone by stating the topic in the first sentence.

- Content/Ideas: Since the goal of the summary is to be brief and concise, only the most important details should be included.

- Word Choice/Clarity: A good writer uses only clear and concise language and eliminates wordy phrases.

- Sentence Fluency: To make their sentences flow smoothly, students should combine several ideas into one sentence where appropriate.

- Grammar/Mechanics: Writers who ensure that all subjects and verbs agree make their writing easier and more enjoyable to read.

Ask students to listen for these traits as you read aloud the summary of "A Touch of Genius," starting on Student page 201.

A Touch of Genius
by Patricia Millman

Michael Naranjo is a Native American, a Vietnam War veteran, and "a sculptor who happens to be blind." Behind this statement lies a remarkable story.

Michael grew up in the Tewa Indian pueblo of Santa Clara, New Mexico. As a boy, he roamed the scenic foothills west of the pueblo community and explored the Rio Grande, a river to the south and east. His world was enriched by the beautiful sights and sounds of the desert country.

This artist sees with his hands.

Michael's love of sculpting was born at the pueblo, too. "My mother was a potter, and I would help her fix clay," he recalls. "She gathered her clay in a place in the hills that only she knew about. Every potter has their own source of clay, and when they find that clay, they're very secretive about it.

"My mother would bring in the clay and screen it to get out anything that didn't belong, and then she would soak it in tubs. After that, she'd put the clay into a square of canvas cloth, and she'd sprinkle a different white kind of clay on top. Then she would fold this square of canvas and press on it this way and that way, and when she unfolded the canvas I could see this little log of clay inside.

"Then I would take off my shoes and perform a little dance with the clay. I would sidestep on this log of clay. I could feel the moist clay on the side of my foot and between my toes. And when I reached the other end, I'd step off the square of canvas, and she'd fold it and push it this way and that way and refold it, and I would have this little log of clay again. And once again I would perform my little dance."

Michael's dance served a very important purpose. He was blending the white clay and the brown clay to make it stronger. With this strong clay, his mother could make pots that would last a long time.

"That's probably how I started sculpting. . . playing with clay," Michael says. "Not long after that, I wanted to make figures of animals. And as they became more detailed, they became sculptures. So even way back then, I knew that what I wanted to do was be an artist someday."

One More by Michael A. Naranjo

Seeing with His Hands

Michael's goal would not be reached easily. While serving with the Army in Vietnam, Michael was badly wounded in battle. He lost his sight and partial use of one hand. For the first time, Michael wondered if he could ever be a sculptor.

One day, while recovering in the hospital, Michael asked if he could have a small piece of clay. From it he made an inchworm.

The next sculpture Michael made, an Indian on a horse, was so good it was photographed by the newspapers. Lucky thing! Because when

Michael enjoys teaching sculpting workshops. "One step at a time and you can do it," he reminds his students.

Michael decided to make his next sculpture, he found that the hospital didn't have any more clay. So he reshaped the Indian on a horse into a bear with a fish in its mouth.

Today, Michael has lots of material to use to make his memories come to life. "I was able to see until I was twenty-three years old, so I have a very good idea of what most things look like," he said. "So I sit, and I think about it, and I get a picture in my mind. If you close your eyes and think of. . . well, if you have a cat or a dog, you can picture this pet. The same process happens with me.

"Once you have the material in your hand that you can mold and shape, then you can carry it over from your mind to your fingertips; and your mind tells your fingers, 'Make that bigger or smaller. . .' until this whole process slowly starts happening.

"Nowadays, when I make animals, I sit there and think about the days when I'd take a moment sitting on a cliff side and look down and see a deer down there or watch some turkeys walk through the forest. Or the time I followed a mountain stream and a deer stopped in this pool of water and looked at me with his huge brown eyes. It lasted just a few moments, but it's one of those moments that I draw on for inspiration."

Michael inspires others by leading sculpture workshops for children and adults, veterans and seniors, both sighted and visually impaired.

In 1999, Michael was named the Outstanding Disabled Veteran of the Year and received the LIFE Presidential Unsung Hero Award. His sculptures can be seen in museums and public buildings across the United States, in the Vatican, and in the White House.

A Special Fan

Many people like to collect Michael's work, but Michael fondly remembers one special young "collector."

"It was maybe twenty years ago at the Indian Market in Santa Fe. One day there was this little boy who came, and he was looking at my work and I was telling him about it. Next year, he came back and said, 'I was here last year. Do you remember me?' And I said, 'Yes.' He said, 'I want to buy that little buffalo.' And I said, 'OK.' I told him how much it was.

"As he paid for it, he said, 'I worked all last summer and this summer, and saved my money.' I had no words to describe the emotion I felt. I still can't describe what a moment like that feels like."

Does Michael have one piece of sculpture that is his very favorite? Could it be the buffalo from the Santa Fe Indian Market? Or the bear with a fish in its mouth?

"You know, it's the same as with children," Michael said. "If you have more than one, you love them all equally. That's how I feel about my sculptures."

Differentiating Instruction

English-Language Learners To help students understand subject/verb agreement, develop flash cards. On one side of a card, write a singular or a plural subject, the infinitive form of a regular verb, and the word *past* or *present*. On the reverse side, include the subject and the correct verb form. Have students practice with the cards before they write their summaries.

Support To help students identify the main points of a piece of writing, prepare a summary of a newspaper article. For each sentence in the summary, have students identify the section of the article from which it was taken and highlight it. Then ask them to underline the most important point in the highlighted section. Explain that they are underlining the main point.

Summary Rubric

The traits of a good summary from page 200 have been used to make the rubric below. By using 1, 2, 3, or 4 check marks to judge each trait, you can decide how well any summary was written.

	Excelling ✓✓✓✓	Achieving ✓✓✓	Developing ✓✓	Beginning ✓
Information/ Organization	The summary contains the main points of an article and is organized logically.	The summary contains most of the main points and is mostly organized.	The summary contains some of the main points and is loosely organized.	The summary needs to be more focused and better organized.
Voice/ Audience	The first sentence sets the tone by clearly stating the topic.	The first sentence contains the topic.	The topic is stated, but not in the first sentence.	The first sentence needs to state the topic to set the tone.
Content/ Ideas	The summary includes only the most important details.	The summary includes some of the necessary details.	The summary includes several necessary details.	The summary contains too many unnecessary details.
Word Choice/ Clarity	The language is consistently concise.	Most of the language is concise.	Some of the language is concise.	The language needs to be concise.
Sentence Fluency	All sentences flow smoothly.	Most sentences flow smoothly.	Some sentences flow smoothly.	Few sentences flow smoothly.
Grammar/ Mechanics	Spelling, grammar, and subject-verb agreement are correct.	There are a few errors in spelling, grammar, and subject-verb agreement.	There are several errors in spelling, grammar, and subject-verb agreement.	There are many errors in spelling, grammar, and subject-verb agreement.

204 Expository Writing ■ Summary

Using the Rubric to Study the Model

Let's use the rubric to check Keesha's summary, "A Touch of Genius." I want to see how she used each trait in her writing. How many check marks would you give her for each trait?

 Information/ Organization
- The summary contains the main points of an article.
- The main points are organized in a logical way.

Keesha does a good job of summarizing the main points of the article. She also organizes her summary in a logical way. She follows the organization of the article, which makes a lot of sense.

[from the writing model]

Naranjo was unsure if he would still be able to sculpt. While recovering in the hospital, he molded several clay sculptures of animals. One was so good that it was photographed for the newspaper. That convinced him to pursue his dream.

 Voice/ Audience
- The first sentence sets the tone by stating the topic of the summary.

The topic of the article—and of the summary—is Michael Naranjo, a Native American sculptor. Did you notice how the writer tells the audience the topic in her very first sentence?

[from the writing model]

Michael Naranjo is a Native American sculptor in Santa Fe, New Mexico. He chose his career when he was a boy helping his mother make pottery in the pueblo. At age 23, however, Naranjo was wounded in the Vietnam War. He was blinded and left without the complete use of one hand.

Expository Writing ■ Summary 205

Using the Rubric
(Student page 204)

Explain that a rubric helps the reader evaluate a piece of writing. The rubric on Student page 204 can be used to evaluate a summary. It is based on the same traits for a summary that students read on Student page 200.

Review the row for Content/Ideas. Point out that in a summary, only the most important details should be included. Remind students of the need to be concise when writing their summaries. Unlike genres that encourage elaboration, including too many details in a summary will warrant a lower score.

Study the Model
(Student pages 205–207)

Explain that Student pages 205–207 show how the summary writing model meets all six traits of the rubric. Read the section on Information/Organization with the students. Have students identify the main points of the article that Keesha used in her summary on Student page 201.

Read each of the other sections with the students. Ask students how many check marks they would give Keesha for each of the traits in the rubric.

Remind students that it is important for them to use the rubric when they are writing their summaries. Explain that they should think about each of the writing traits in the rubric as they go through each of the writing steps.

Summary

Content/Ideas
- The summary includes only the most important details.

The writer includes just enough details to support the main points. For example, the paragraph below tells how successful the sculptor is, without a lot of unnecessary detail. See how she does it? It's nice and brief.

[from the writing model]

> Naranjo has won awards for his work and leads sculpture workshops. His sculptures are displayed in museums and public buildings around the world. Private collectors also seek his art.

The article includes details about how the sculptor mixed his mother's clay. It also tells about a little boy who saved money to buy a sculpture. The writer knew those details did not support any of the main points, so she left them out of the final draft.

Word Choice/Clarity
- The language is concise.

Keesha knows that a summary needs to be as short as possible, so she made sure her writing was not wordy. For the second sentence below, she might have written, "He sits and thinks about the image in his mind. After he gets a picture of it, the image goes to his fingertips." Instead, she carefully chose her words and used as few of them as possible.

[from the writing model]

> Although he cannot see, he can remember images from his past. His mind carries the images to his fingertips.

Sentence Fluency
- The sentences flow smoothly, combining several ideas where appropriate.

Keesha avoided short, choppy sentences. In some places, she combined ideas and wrote longer sentences. For example, Keesha could have written her last paragraph this way: "Naranjo has won awards for his work. He leads sculpture workshops. His sculptures are displayed in museums. They are also displayed in public buildings around the world. Private collectors also seek his art." You can read below how she really wrote the paragraph. See how she made her sentences flow smoothly?

[from the writing model]

> Naranjo has won awards for his work and leads sculpture workshops. His sculptures are displayed in museums and public buildings around the world. Private collectors also seek his art.

Grammar/Mechanics
- Spelling, punctuation, and capitalization are correct. All subjects and verbs agree.

I checked Keesha's summary for mistakes, but I couldn't find any. She did a great job on spelling, punctuation, and capitalization. And the subjects and their verbs definitely agree. For example, look at the sentence below. **His mind** is a singular subject, so it needs the singular verb **carries**. She wrote it just right.

[from the writing model]

> His mind carries the images to his fingertips.

My Turn! I'm going to write a summary using good writing strategies. I'll also use what I learned from the rubric and good writing strategies. Follow along and see how I do it.

Differentiating Instruction

Support To help students understand how to combine ideas into one longer sentence, write the following on the board:

She was going to be away from home for two weeks.
She needed someone to come over and water her plants.
She also needed someone to take care of her cat.

Ask students to create longer sentences using two or three of the sentences above. **Possible reponse: Because she was going to be away from home for two weeks, she needed someone to come over to water her plants and take care of her cat.**

Point out that combining short, choppy sentences can often help make the writing flow more smoothly. Have students review their drafts to see if they can combine short sentences.

Writing a Summary

Prewriting Gather Information

Information/Organization

The summary contains the main points of an article.

Writing Strategy

Read an article and take notes on the main points.

My teacher asked us to write a summary of an article. I chose the article below because it combines my interests in trees, the history of my state, and coins. As I read the article, I found the main points in it. On page 210, you will see the notes I took as I read.

The Tree That Saved History
by Jane Sutcliffe

An unusual funeral took place in Hartford, Connecticut, on August 21, 1856. The city's bells tolled in mourning, and a band played funeral hymns. It was an outpouring of grief fit for a hero—except that this hero was a tree, a white oak to be exact.

For nearly 169 years this special tree had been known simply as the Charter Oak in honor of the part it played in the history of colonial America.

The Charter Oak was an old and respected tree even before colonial times. Native Americans of the area held meetings under its branches. And when the tree's new leaves were as big as a mouse's ear, they knew that it was time to plant corn.

In time, the English came to the valley surrounding the big oak. They settled there and founded the colony of Connecticut. Every colony had to obtain a contract, called a charter, from the king of England. The charter helped to protect the colony's rights. The charter given to Connecticut by King Charles II in 1662 was the pride of the colony. It allowed the colonists to govern themselves by their own constitution. More than a century before the Declaration of Independence, the charter treated Connecticut almost as if it were an independent country.

Then, in 1685, King Charles died. The new English ruler, King James II, not only disapproved of Connecticut's charter but he also disliked having so many colonies. He thought it would be better to combine the colonies of the northeast into one big colony.

King James ordered Sir Edmund Andros, the governor of the Dominion of New England, to seize any documents recognizing the colonies' old rights. Most colonies felt they had no choice and turned over their charters. Only Connecticut delayed. Again and again, Andros demanded that Connecticut give up its charter to him. Again and again, the colonists politely but firmly refused. Finally, Andros had enough. On All Hallow's Eve, 1687, Andros and more than sixty British soldiers marched into Hartford.

Connecticut Governor Robert Treat was waiting for Andros at the door of the meetinghouse, where leaders of the colony were assembled. Politely he escorted Andros inside. Andros wasted no time. He demanded that Connecticut obey the king and surrender its charter.

By now a crowd of townspeople had gathered outside. As they strained to hear every word, Governor Treat spoke passionately about the struggles of the people to build their colony, and about their love of freedom. Giving up the charter, he said, would be like giving up his life. Andros was unmoved. At dark, candles were lit so that the meeting could continue, but Andros had heard enough. He demanded to see the charter. The colonists could delay no longer. They brought out the charter and placed it on the table before him.

Suddenly all the candles in the room went out. In the darkness, a young patriot, Captain Joseph Wadsworth, snatched the charter and jumped out an open window. Carefully wrapping the document in his cloak, he placed it in the hollow of the great white oak. Had the brave captain simply seized the opportunity provided by the sudden darkness, or had it all been a clever plan? No one would ever know. By the

Captain Joseph Wadsworth carefully placed Connecticut's charter in the hollow of the great white oak.

time the candles were lit again, Andros was looking at nothing but innocent faces.

If Andros was furious at being outsmarted, he did not show it. With or without the charter, he said that the government of the colony was over. Fortunately, King James was soon overthrown. Andros was imprisoned and then sent back to England. The new rulers, King William III and Queen Mary II, agreed that since Connecticut had never surrendered its charter, the colony could take up its old freedoms again.

The Charter Oak became a beloved symbol of freedom throughout the land. After it was blown down in a storm on August 21, 1856, people requested keepsakes of its wood. There was plenty to go around—so much, in fact, that author Mark Twain said there was enough "to build a plank road from here (Hartford) to Great Salt Lake City."

Craftsmen fashioned pianos, chairs, and even a cradle of Charter Oak wood. One of the fanciest pieces was an elaborately carved chair that is still used in the Senate Chamber in the State Capitol Building in Hartford. It occupies a place of honor in memory of the Charter Oak, one of the most unusual heroes in our country's struggle for liberty.

The Charter Oak appears on the Connecticut quarter, issued in 1999 by the U.S. Mint. Connecticut became a state in 1788.

Prewriting
(Student pages 208–209)

Read aloud the paragraph on Student page 208. Point out that Justin chose an article that combined his interest in trees, Connecticut history, and coins. Tell students that if possible, they should choose a subject they are interested in when they decide on a longer article to summarize. Suggest that students first read through the article they are going to summarize and take notes on the main points, as Justin plans to.

As students read the article "The Tree That Saved History" on Student pages 208–209, ask them to identify the main points from the article.

More Practice!

For more practice with these writing strategies, you may wish to have students use the Strategy Practice Book. See the appendix for reduced Strategy Practice Book pages.

Differentiating Instruction

English-Language Learners **Preteach** the words *colony, charter, liberty,* and *constitution* with students. Help students understand these terms as they relate to American history. Remind students that they will sometimes encounter unfamiliar terms. Although many times context clues can help them better understand, or guess, the meaning of a word, point out that they will sometimes need to look for definitions elsewhere. Ask students to look for context clues in the article "The Tree That Saved History" in order to find clues about the meanings of the terms listed above. Point out these clues within the text that help define the terms:

They settled there and founded the <u>colony</u> of Connecticut.
Every colony had to obtain a contract, called a <u>charter</u>… the charter helped to protect the colony's rights.
It allowed the colonists to govern themselves by their own <u>constitution</u>.
…the <u>charter</u> treated Connecticut almost as if it were an independent country.
…one of the most unusual heroes in our country's struggle for <u>liberty</u>.

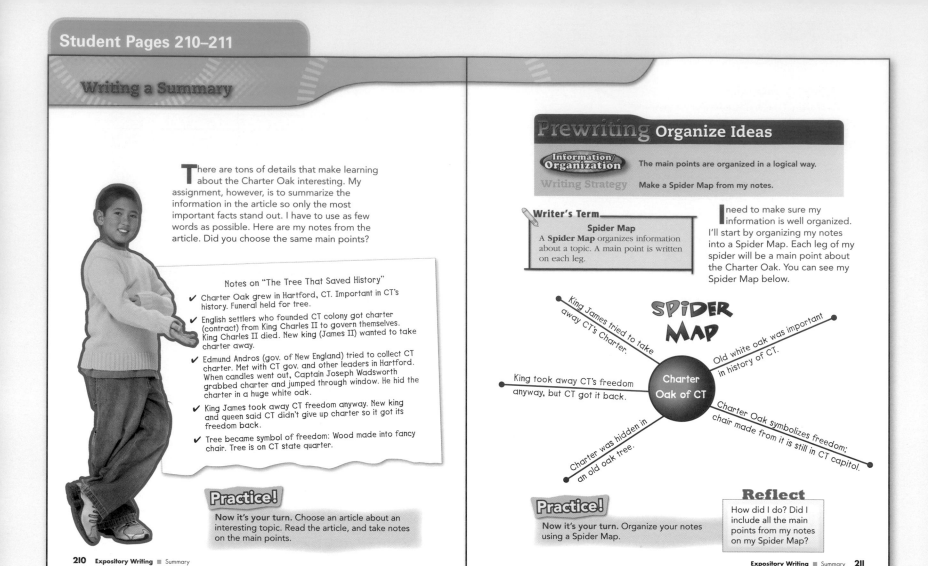

Prewriting
(Student pages 210–211)

After students read the article "The Tree That Saved History" on Student pages 208–209, review the article together. Have a student volunteer orally summarize the article. Next, review the notes that Justin jotted down about the article. Ask students if they think he covered all the main points. Ask if they think any of the notes he has written down seem unnecessary.

Then look at the Spider Map that Justin created. To help your students better understand how to complete a Spider Map, read aloud a short article from a newspaper or magazine. Have the class identify the main points of the article and write them on the board. Work with them to develop a Spider Map on the board to organize these ideas. Write the topic, or main idea, in the center, and have student volunteers suggest points to write on each of the legs.

WORK with a PARTNER Have students select an article to summarize. Have them work with another student to review the article and identify its main points. Then have the partners work together to fill in a Spider Map to organize the main points of their article.

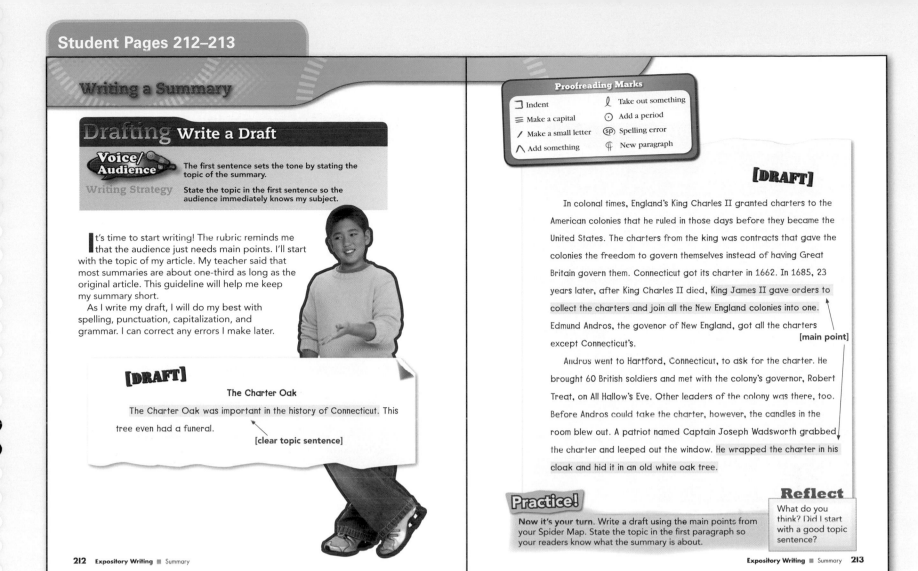

Writing a Summary

Drafting — Write a Draft

Voice/Audience The first sentence sets the tone by stating the topic of the summary.

Writing Strategy State the topic in the first sentence so the audience immediately knows my subject.

It's time to start writing! The rubric reminds me that the audience just needs main points. I'll start with the topic of my article. My teacher said that most summaries are about one-third as long as the original article. This guideline will help me keep my summary short.

As I write my draft, I will do my best with spelling, punctuation, capitalization, and grammar. I can correct any errors I make later.

[DRAFT]

The Charter Oak

The Charter Oak was important in the history of Connecticut. This tree even had a funeral.

[clear topic sentence]

Proofreading Marks

⊐ Indent
≡ Make a capital
/ Make a small letter
∧ Add something
ℓ Take out something
⊙ Add a period
SP Spelling error
¶ New paragraph

[DRAFT]

In colonal times, England's King Charles II granted charters to the American colonies that he ruled in those days before they became the United States. The charters from the king was contracts that gave the colonies the freedom to govern themselves instead of having Great Britain govern them. Connecticut got its charter in 1662. In 1685, 23 years later, after King Charles II died, King James II gave orders to collect the charters and join all the New England colonies into one. Edmund Andros, the govenor of New England, got all the charters except Connecticut's. [main point]

Andros went to Hartford, Connecticut, to ask for the charter. He brought 60 British soldiers and met with the colony's governor, Robert Treat, on All Hallow's Eve. Other leaders of the colony was there, too. Before Andros could take the charter, however, the candles in the room blew out. A patriot named Captain Joseph Wadsworth grabbed the charter and leeped out the window. He wrapped the charter in his cloak and hid it in an old white oak tree.

Practice!

Now it's your turn. Write a draft using the main points from your Spider Map. State the topic in the first paragraph so your readers know what the summary is about.

Reflect

What do you think? Did I start with a good topic sentence?

Drafting
(Student pages 212–213)

Remind students that writing a draft allows writers to get their ideas on paper without worrying too much about mistakes that can be corrected later.

Note that Justin is paying attention to the traits listed on Student page 200 as he prepares to write his draft. Remind students to pay attention to the writing traits and rubric as they do their own writing.

Look at Justin's draft on Student page 213. Point out that Justin stated his topic in the first sentence for his audience. Read the second sentence aloud. Ask students what the purpose of this next sentence might be. Suggest that it helps to make the story more interesting to draw readers in. Note that a good lead paragraph that is interesting and that contains the main topic entices the audience to read further.

Writing Across the Curriculum

Social Studies Justin writes about the importance of the Charter Oak in Connecticut history. The tree became a symbol of the state's struggle for independence and was even considered a state hero. For that reason, it is not surprising that many products and businesses in the state choose to use the name Charter Oak in association with their product. Have students use the Internet to research Connecticut businesses using the name or symbol of Charter Oak. Have them select a business associated with the Charter Oak and write a short summary of why they think this business chose to use the name or symbol.

Writing a Summary

Revising Extend Writing

Content/Ideas The summary includes only the most important details.

Writing Strategy Use only the most important details.

Writer's Term

Details
The **details** are the words used to describe a person, persuade an audience, explain a process, or in some way support a main idea.

When I checked the rubric again, I noticed that it says to include only important details. That's when I realized that I had added too many unnecessary details to my summary. Do you see all the details I crossed out below? When you write a summary, the idea is to skip unnecessary details, not to add them!

[DRAFT]

[deleted unnecessary details]

Andros went to Hartford, Connecticut, to ask for the charter. He ~~brought 60 British soldiers and~~ met with the colony's governor, ~~Robert Treat, on All Hallow's Eve.~~ Other leaders of the colony was there, too. Before Andros could take the charter, however, the candles in the room blew out. A patriot named ~~Captain~~ Joseph Wadsworth grabbed the charter and leeped out the window. He ~~wrapped the charter in his~~ the charter ← [added an important detail] ~~cloak and~~ hid ~~it~~ in an old white oak tree.

Practice!

Now it's your turn. Check your summary for unnecessary details and eliminate them.

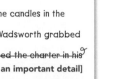

Revising Clarify Writing

Word Choice/Clarity The language is concise.

Writing Strategy Replace wordy phrases with succinct language.

Writer's Term
Succinct Language
Succinct language is brief and to the point; there are no wasted words.

If you want a piece of writing to be concise, you have to get rid of any extra words. I read my paper aloud to myself to listen for wordy phrases and sentences. I heard a lot of extra words! I got rid of them in this paragraph and in others, too. I also substituted some more exact words for language that wasn't succinct.

[DRAFT]

[wordy]

In colonal times, England's King Charles II granted charters to the American colonies ~~that he ruled in those days before they became the United States.~~ The charters from the king was contracts that gave the colonies the freedom to govern themselves ~~instead of having Great Britain govern them.~~ Connecticut gained its charter in 1662. In 1685, ~~23 years later,~~ after King Charles II died, King James II gave orders to seize ← [succinct] ~~colleet~~ the charters and join all the New England colonies into one.

Practice!

Now it's your turn. Take out any wordy phrases in your summary and use succinct language instead.

Reflect
Did I replace all the wordy phrases? Is my language concise?

Revising

(Student pages 214–215)

Read aloud the description of *details* from the Writer's Term box on Student page 214. Then have a student volunteer read Justin's words from the same page. Explain that a summary should include only the main points and a few important details. Remind students that in a summary, the goal is not to add any more details than are necessary to explain the main idea.

Have students look for places in their summaries where they can eliminate unnecessary details.

Next, ask a student to read Justin's words on Student page 215. Explain that one way to make writing clearer is to eliminate wordiness, or using too many words to say something. This is especially important in summaries, which should be as short as possible. Go over the material that Justin crossed out. Point out that these details are not necessary in the summary.

Now have students check their drafts for wordiness, and have them replace wordy phrases with more succinct language.

Differentiating Instruction

Enrichment Challenge students to summarize a chapter in a nonfiction book or article that includes facts and opinions. Have students identify the individual or organization that stated the opinion.

Support To help students better understand how to identify and summarize the main idea of an article, tell them about the Hollywood pitch rule. Explain that when writers pitch movie ideas, they need to be able to summarize the whole point, or main idea, of the movie, in one sentence. Ask students to think about their favorite movies. See if they can summarize the main idea of their favorite movies in just one sentence. **Possible response: Charlie and the Chocolate Factory: A young boy wins a tour through the most magnificent chocolate factory in the world, led by the worlds most unusual candy maker.**

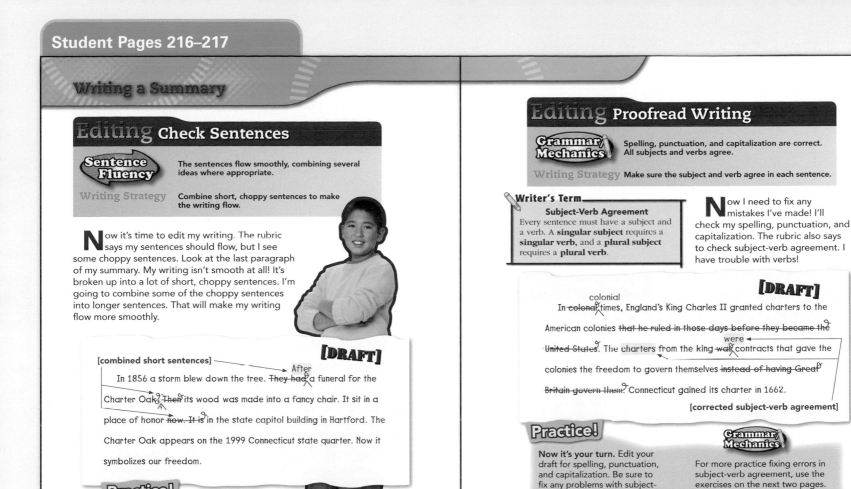

Editing

(Student pages 216–217)

Discuss the difference between revising and editing. Make sure students understand that in the revising step, they reread their draft to look for ways to make it more complete, clearer, or, in the case of summaries, shorter. In the editing step, they look for errors in sentence structure, spelling, grammar, and punctuation.

Ask a student volunteer to read Justin's words on Student page 216. Point out that as Justin rereads his draft, he is able to spot areas where the writing does not flow smoothly. This is not a content problem or a problem with the information he has chosen to include, but rather a sentence structure problem, one that he can fix in the editing process. Note how Justin combined the shorter sentences into longer sentences that flowed better.

Next, have a student volunteer read the Writer's Term box on Student page 217. Write the following sentence on the board: *The cats from the shelter was declawed.* Ask if this sentence is grammatically correct. **no** Ask a student volunteer to fix the sentence so that it is correct. **The cats from the shelter were declawed.** Remind students of the importance of subject-verb agreement in their writing.

If some of your students are having trouble understanding subject-verb agreement, you may wish to teach the Mini-Lesson on page 166 of this Teacher Edition. Then have students complete the exercises on Student pages 218–219. Review the answers and possible rewrites with them.

Have students begin checking their summaries for subject-verb agreement. Remind students to check their drafts for correct spelling, punctuation, and capitalization.

WORK with a **PARTNER** Have students swap their drafts with another student. Each student should read the other's summary to check for mistakes in sentence construction, spelling, punctuation, and capitalization.

 Practice!

Subject-Verb Agreement

 KNOW the RULE

Every sentence must have a subject and a verb. A **singular subject** requires a **singular verb**, and a **plural subject** requires a **plural verb**.

In many sentences, a prepositional phrase comes between the subject and the verb. A prepositional phrase is a group of words that begins with a preposition and ends with an object. Do not mistake the object of the preposition for the subject of the sentence. The verb in every sentence must agree with its subject, not the object of the preposition (op).

Incorrect: The charters from the king was contracts.

Correct: The charters from the king were contracts.

Incorrect: One of the patriots were named Joseph Wadsworth.

Correct: One of the patriots was named Joseph Wadsworth.

Practice the Rule

Number your paper 1–5, and write the correct verb form for each sentence.

1. Connecticut (is/are/am) one of six New England states.
2. Maine (was/were) the last New England colony to become a state.
3. The U.S. Mint (is/are) issuing a quarter for each state.
4. The first quarter for the New England states (was/were) for Connecticut.
5. Many people in this country (collect/collects) state quarters.

Apply the Rule

Read the following summary. Correct any problems with subject-verb agreement, and rewrite the summary on another sheet of paper.

Not Your Ordinary Tree

The white oak is a common tree, but it is uncommon in its beauty and usefulness. The tree grow all over the eastern United States. A variety of climates and soils suit the white oak, and it can reach an impressive size. Some white oaks grows 100 feet in height and four feet in diameter.

The white oak is important to American wildlife. The acorns of the white oak serves as food for many birds and mammals. Rabbits, squirrels, chipmunks, raccoons, and blue jays all enjoys these acorns. Like many other trees, the white oak provide cover for small animals. Sometimes a hollow white oak become a den for a raccoon or an opossum.

People values the white oak for its natural beauty and for its practical usefulness. White oaks make good ornamental trees, and they provides a lot of shade. The strong wood of white oaks are used to make hardwood floors, boats, furniture, barrels, and cabinets. Long ago, Native Americans made flour from its acorns. The USS Constitution was called "Old Ironsides," but most of this ship were made from white oak.

 Mini-Lesson

(Student pages 218–219)

Subject-Verb Agreement

Explain to the students that every sentence must contain a subject and a verb and that singular verbs must be used with singular subjects, just as plural verbs must be used with plural subjects.

Write the following on the board: *The new puppies was very hungry.*

Ask students if the subject-verb agreement is correct. **no** Ask students what the subject is. **the puppies** Ask them if it's singular or plural. **plural.** Have them change the sentence so that the subject and verb agree. **The new puppies were very hungry.**

Answers for Practice the Rule

1. is   2. was   3. is   4. was   5. collect

Answers for Apply the Rule

The white oak is a common tree, but it is uncommon in its beauty and usefulness. The tree grows all over the eastern United States. A variety of climates and soils suit the white oak, and it can reach an impressive size. Some white oaks grow 100 feet in height and four feet in diameter.

The white oak is important to American wildlife. The acorns of the white oak serve as food for many birds and mammals. Rabbits, squirrels, chipmunks, raccoons, and blue jays all enjoy these acorns. Like many other trees, the white oak provides cover for small animals. Sometimes a hollow white oak becomes a den for a raccoon or an opossum.

People value the white oak for its natural beauty and for its practical usefulness. White oaks make good ornamental trees, and they provide a lot of shade. The strong wood of white oaks is used to make hardwood floors, boats, furniture, barrels, and cabinets. Long ago, Native Americans made flour from its acorns. The USS Constitution was called "old Ironsides," but most of this ship was made from white oak.

 For more practice with grammar/mechanics skills, see Zaner-Bloser's *G.U.M.* materials.

Writing a Summary

Publishing Share Writing

Read my summary to the class.

There are a lot of different ways I could publish my summary. I could include it in my scrapbook about Connecticut or read it to my grandparents who are interested in history. But since we're doing a social studies unit on our state history, I think I'll share the summary with my class. My classmates and I are going to read our summaries aloud so we can all learn from the articles we've read. Before we do, I want to check my summary one last time. I'll use this checklist to help me.

My Checklist

✔ My summary is well focused and organized.

✔ I start out with a clear topic sentence.

✔ My writing is tight, with concise language and good sentence flow.

✔ I stick to details that support the main ideas.

✔ My spelling, punctuation, and capitalization are all correct. I made sure my subjects and verbs agree throughout the summary.

Practice!

Now It's your turn. Make a checklist to help you check your summary. How did you do?

220   Expository Writing ■ Summary

"The Tree That Saved History" by Jane Sutcliffe

Summary by Justin

The Charter Oak was important in the history of Connecticut. This tree even had a funeral.

In colonial times, England's King Charles II granted charters to the American colonies. The charters were contracts that gave the colonies the freedom to govern themselves. Connecticut gained its charter in 1662. In 1685, after King Charles II died, King James II gave orders to seize the charters and join all the New England colonies into one. Edmund Andros, the governor of New England, collected all the charters except Connecticut's.

Andros went to Hartford, Connecticut, to ask for the charter. He met with the colony's governor and other leaders. Before Andros could take the charter, however, the candles in the room blew out. A patriot named Joseph Wadsworth grabbed the charter and leaped out the window. He hid the charter in the hollow of an old white oak tree.

King James II didn't get the charter, but he took away Connecticut's freedom anyway. Soon another English king and queen came into power. They ruled that the colony could have its freedom back because it never surrendered its charter.

In 1856 a storm blew down the tree. After a funeral for the Charter Oak, its wood was carved into many things. A beautiful chair made from the Charter Oak now sits in the state capitol. The Charter Oak also appears on the 1999 Connecticut state quarter. The famous tree still symbolizes our freedom.

Reflect

What do you think? Did I use all the traits of a good summary in my writing? Check it against the rubric. Don't forget to use the rubric to check your own summary.

Expository Writing ■ Summary   221

Publishing

(Student pages 220–221)

Ask a student to read Justin's words on Student page 220. Ask students if they can guess where Justin's checklist came from. **Possible response: from the writing traits** Remind students that a checklist will help them make sure that they have not missed any important points from the writing traits. Just as Justin has done, they should review their final drafts one last time before they publish them.

Have students make a checklist to check their own summaries.

Tips for the Writing Classroom

Purposeful Journal Writing

by Ken Stewart, *Master Teacher*

For journal writing to be a worthwhile activity, your students must be totally engaged in the subject matter. You can provide a variety of inspirational activities that stimulate the imagination. These activities might include

1. engaging the students in meaningful service learning, such as working with the elderly, protecting the environment, or sharing with the mentally challenged.

2. inviting people from the community to speak on such topics as their jobs, overcoming obstacles, and so on.

3. planning special events that involve family members, such as setting up after-school sessions for sharing writing or sponsoring a grandparents' day.

You can also help every student develop his/her writing voice. Encourage students to write from the heart. Allow them to make spelling and other errors in their initial journal entries. Later, give them an opportunity to make corrections.

Ways to Publish a
Summary

I decided to read my summary to my class, but maybe you have a different audience in mind for your writing. Thinking about who will be reading your summary can help you figure out how to publish it. Here are some of my ideas!

✓ Read your summary to your family.

✓ Use your summary to start a research project about the topic. Read and summarize other articles until you narrow the topic. Then use the summaries to help you decide which references you'll use for the final project.

✓ Make your summary part of a scrapbook on a relevant subject.

✓ Work with your classmates to create a hallway display of all your summaries.

✓ Share your summary with a friend from another class.

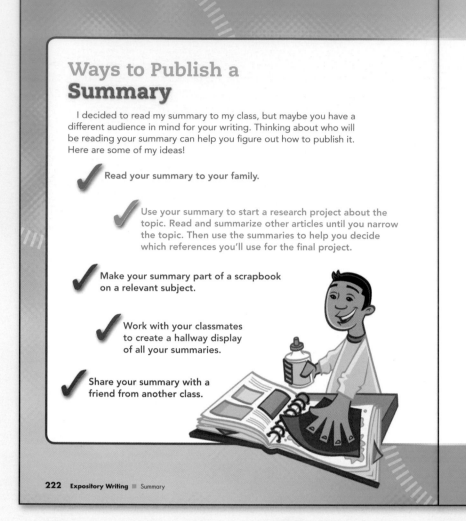

Writing Across the Content Areas
Summary

Summarizing is a skill you can use in almost any subject. Writing a summary can help you organize ideas and learn information. Here are a few suggestions for how you could use this kind of writing in some of your subjects. Can you think of other ideas?

Math
- Find an article about how to make a budget. Read and summarize the article, and then try to follow what it says.
- For a few weeks, follow the newspaper coverage of one athlete. Then summarize his/her performance in a short article, including all the important statistics.

Social Studies
- Read an important historical document and write a short, clear summary of its main points.
- Sum up a magazine article about current news, and publish the summary in your school newspaper.

Art or Music
- Watch a play or a movie and write a review that includes a recap of the plot.
- Study a famous painter and summarize the main events in his/her life.

Ways to Publish
(Student page 222)

Read and discuss with students the different publishing options on Student page 222. Ask student volunteers to tell the class about their summaries and other options they might consider for publishing them. Tell students that the summaries they have created and shared with the class have helped to provide classmates with a breadth of knowledge about many different subjects in a short amount of time and space.

Writing Across the Content Areas
(Student page 223)

Point out that the ability to write a clear and concise summary will help students not just in writing but in many other subjects as well. Have student volunteers read aloud the information on Student page 223. Have students consider using one of the content areas listed to write another summary. Ask them to suggest how a summary might be helpful in other subjects.

Books for Professional Development

Freeman, Marcia S. *Listen to This: Developing an Ear for Expository*. Gainesville: Maupin, 1997.

This author suggests adding an auditory component to writing. She encourages teachers to read aloud sample essays in a variety of informative, narrative, and persuasive genres. Students are guided to analyze these essays and then use them as models for their own writing.

Urquhart, Vicki, and Monette McIver. *Teaching Writing in the Content Areas*. Alexandra: ASCD, 2005.

This book shows how to quickly integrate writing assignments into content areas by using strategic practical tools. Included in the book are 35 classroom strategies that will help teachers guide students through the steps of preparing written assignments, getting their thoughts down, and refining their work. It will help students learn good writing habits and how to use them during writing conferences.

King, Laurie, and Dennis Stovall. *Classroom Publishing: A Practical Guide to Enhancing Student Literacy*. Hillsboro: Blue Heron, 1992.

The authors offer many suggestions in a wide range of genres and forms of publications. Six chapters describe classroom publishing projects for grades 6–8. Other ideas in this resource are adaptable to different levels.

Bromley, Karen, Linda Irwin-De Vitis, & Marcia Modlo. *Graphic Organizers: Visual Strategies for Active Learning*. New York: Scholastic, 1995.

The authors provide tips on using graphic organizers in teaching across the curriculum. They also describe organizing techniques that students can use to plan their writing in the content areas, including various genres of descriptive writing.

Cause-and-Effect Report Overview

In this chapter, students will learn how to write a cause-and-effect report. First, they will learn different elements of a cause-and-effect report—connections, interest, and research—and some reasons for writing a cause-and-effect report. They will review the cause-and-effect model writing sample against a rubric to understand what makes a good cause-and-effect report.

As the student guide goes through the process of writing a cause-and-effect report, including prewriting, drafting, revising, editing, and publishing, students will have a chance to follow along and practice these strategies in their own writing. They will use the Internet to find credible sources for a topic about which to write. Then they will organize their ideas in a Cause-

and-Effect Chain, which they will use to write their drafts. Revising their reports will involve adding supporting facts and transition words to make cause-and-effect relationships clear. Next, students will edit their drafts, rewriting long, confusing sentences and ensuring that subject and object pronouns are used correctly. They will also check for correct spelling, punctuation, and capitalization. After completing their cause-and-effect reports, they will explore ways to publish their drafts.

You may wish to send to families the School-Home Connection Letter for this chapter, located at the end of this unit in the Teacher Edition.

Cause-and-Effect Report Writing Traits

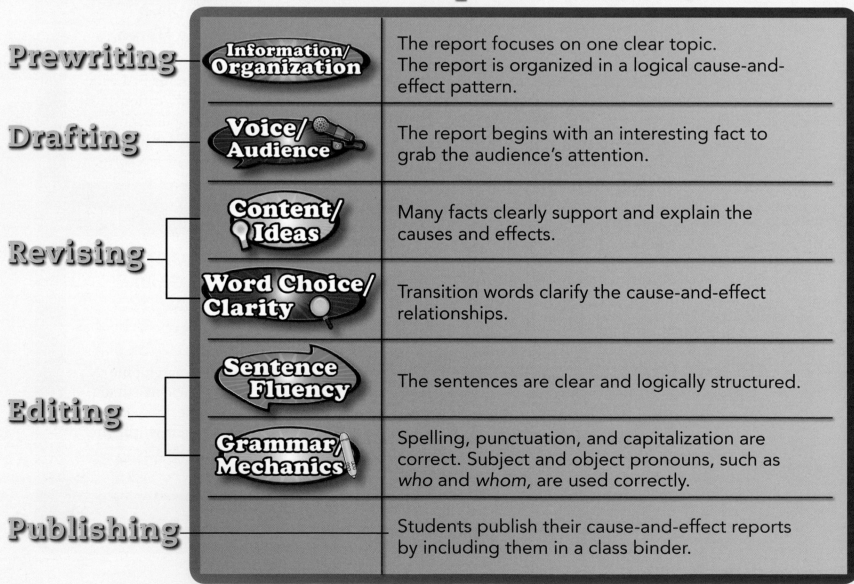

Prewriting	Information/Organization	The report focuses on one clear topic. The report is organized in a logical cause-and-effect pattern.
Drafting	Voice/Audience	The report begins with an interesting fact to grab the audience's attention.
Revising	Content/Ideas	Many facts clearly support and explain the causes and effects.
	Word Choice/Clarity	Transition words clarify the cause-and-effect relationships.
Editing	Sentence Fluency	The sentences are clear and logically structured.
	Grammar/Mechanics	Spelling, punctuation, and capitalization are correct. Subject and object pronouns, such as *who* and *whom*, are used correctly.
Publishing		Students publish their cause-and-effect reports by including them in a class binder.

Cause-and-Effect Report Time Management

WEEK 1

	Day 1	Day 2	Day 3	Day 4	Day 5
Learning Objectives	Students will: • learn the components of a cause-and-effect report.	Students will: • learn how to find credible sources of information for a cause-and-effect report.	Students will: • practice researching and gathering information for their reports.	Students will: • learn how to make a Cause-and-Effect Chain to organize their notes.	Students will: • practice organizing their notes to make a Cause-and-Effect Chain.
Activities	• Discuss the elements and traits of a cause-and-effect report (Student pages 224–226). • Use the rubric to study the model (Student pages 227–231).	• Read and discuss **Prewriting: Gather Information** (Student pages 232–233).	• Research the Internet and choose a cause-and-effect report to share. • Gather information and take notes.	• Read and discuss **Prewriting: Organize Ideas** (Student pages 234–235).	• Look at the notes on a cause-and-effect report. • Use notes to fill in a Cause-and-Effect Chain.

WEEK 2

	Day 1	Day 2	Day 3	Day 4	Day 5
Learning Objectives	Students will: • learn how to begin their reports with an interesting fact.	Students will: • practice writing their drafts.	Students will: • learn how to add supporting facts.	Students will: • practice adding facts to support and explain the causes and effects.	Students will: • learn how to use transition words to make cause-and-effect relationships clear.
Activities	• Read and discuss **Drafting: Write a Draft** (Student pages 236–237)	• Use Cause-and-Effect Chain to write a draft. • Begin reports with an interesting fact to grab the audience's attention.	• Read and discuss **Revising: Extend Writing** (Student page 238).	• Add facts and reasons that support the cause-and-effect relationships.	• Read and discuss **Revising: Clarify Writing** (Student page 239).

WEEK 3

	Day 1	Day 2	Day 3	Day 4	Day 5
Learning Objectives	Students will: • practice adding transition words to their drafts.	Students will: • learn how to rewrite long, confusing sentences to make their writing clearer.	Students will: • learn how to correctly use subject and object pronouns.	Students will: • practice editing their drafts for spelling, punctuation, and capitalization.	Students will: • learn different ways to publish their cause-and-effect reports.
Activities	• Reread drafts to see where transition words will make writing clearer. • Add transition words where appropriate.	• Read and discuss **Editing: Check Sentences** (Student page 240). • Reread drafts for long, confusing sentences and rewrite them.	• Read and discuss **Editing: Proofread Writing** (Student page 241). • Make sure any subject and object pronouns are used correctly.	• Fix any spelling, punctuation, or capitalization errors. • Fix any subject and object pronoun mistakes.	• Read and discuss **Publishing: Share Writing** (Student pages 244–245).

* To complete the chapter in fewer days, teach the learning objectives and activities for two days in one day.

This planning chart, correlated to your state's writing standards, is available on-line at http://www.zaner-bloser.com/sfw.

What's a Cause-and-Effect Report?

A cause-and-effect report tells how a cause or causes produce certain effects. It might also describe certain effects and trace them back to their causes. This kind of writing really makes you think!

What's in a Cause-and-Effect Report?

Connections
Cause-and-effect writing is about showing connections. I really have to understand the cause-and-effect relationships and make them clear to my readers. So it's important to organize my report well and to include plenty of supporting details.

Interest
To capture my audience's attention from the start, I'll begin my report with a fascinating fact. Once I have them interested, I'll keep them reading with good reasoning and smooth writing.

Research
A cause-and-effect report isn't based on opinions. I'll have to do some research to find facts that support the cause-and-effect relationships. I'll use a variety of references to get the whole story on my topic. And I won't use just any source—I need reliable references I can trust!

Why write a Cause-and-Effect Report?

I can think of a lot of reasons for writing a cause-and-effect report, and I've listed some of them below. What's my reason? I'm still thinking about that!

Reasoning Skills
To write a cause-and-effect report, I have to really think things through. Looking at causes and figuring out their effects or looking at effects and examining their causes makes me use my reasoning skills. I have to think logically and make sure all my points are valid. This is the kind of thinking I need in all my subjects—and in life!

Information
A cause-and-effect report is a good way to inform other people about our world—and about why things happen the way they do. I can help others learn about nature, current events, historical happenings, and many other things with this kind of writing.

Practice
I've had to write cause-and-effect reports in Social Studies, Science, and English. I'm sure I'll be assigned more of this kind of writing in the future. So I can use the practice!

Define the Genre
(Student page 224)

Cause-and-Effect Report

Ask students to recall something that they saw happen that morning. Then have them think about why it happened. Tell them that if they wrote about the event, telling what caused it and what effect it might have, they would be writing a cause-and-effect report. Explain that cause-and-effect reports are one type of expository writing in which writers present information to their readers.

Elements of the Genre

Cause-and-Effect Report

Read and discuss each of the elements of a cause-and-effect report with the students. Ask students how a cause-and-effect report differs from a personal essay. **Possible response: Personal essays include personal opinions or observations, while cause-and-effect reports present facts.** Point out that cause-and-effect reports do not include the writer's opinion. Cause-and-effect reports present information in an objective way.

Authentic Writing
(Student page 225)

Cause-and-Effect Report

Ask the students what they think some of the reasons are for writing a cause-and-effect report. Point out that all writing has a purpose, and review some of the purposes for writing a cause-and-effect report found on Student page 225. Note that the reasons for writing a cause-and-effect report benefit both the writer and the reader. For the readers, the benefit is information about a process that can help them learn more about something. For the writers, the benefit is learning reasoning skills and getting practice in a type of writing that they will likely have to do again in the future. Ask students what they think the tone of a cause-and-effect report written for the reasons listed on Student page 225 would likely be. **Possible responses: informational, logical** Tell them that when they are writing their own cause-and-effect reports, they should try to present the information clearly and logically.

Cause-and-Effect Report
Writing Traits

Good writing includes these six traits. I want to write a good cause-and-effect report, so I'll use the traits listed below to help me.

Information/Organization	The report focuses on one clear topic. The report is organized in a logical cause-and-effect pattern.
Voice/Audience	The report begins with an interesting fact to grab the audience's attention.
Content/Ideas	Many facts clearly support and explain the causes and effects.
Word Choice/Clarity	Transition words clarify the cause-and-effect relationships.
Sentence Fluency	The sentences are clear and logically structured.
Grammar/Mechanics	Spelling, punctuation, and capitalization are correct. Subject and object pronouns such as **who** and **whom** are used correctly.

Let's see how Julia Tazzi used these traits to help her write the cause-and-effect report on the next page.

Cause-and-Effect Report Model

Understanding the Barrier Islands
by Julia Tazzi

Interesting beginning ↘

The barrier islands are called the "children of the sea." Born after the last ice age, they stretch along the Atlantic coast in long, narrow chains. Some of these chains extend for 100 miles or more. The islands have been around for nearly 18 centuries, but they may not exist forever. ← *Research*

What caused the islands to form? At the end of the ice age, the air ← *Cause* warmed and the glaciers melted. The melting ice caused rivers and streams to rise. As they flooded over the beaches, they carried sand and sediment to shallow areas just off the Atlantic coast. Ridges formed there. Then waves deposited more sand on the ridges. The ridges slowly became islands. Ocean currents pushed the sand up and down the islands. That caused them to lengthen into narrow strips. *Effects*

The barrier islands have broad beaches and dunes on the ocean side. They have mud flats and salt marshes on the mainland side. This low, sandy structure is vulnerable to erosion. However, plants in the dunes, flats, and marshes help stabilize the islands. The plants and the dunes themselves slow the wind. As the wind slows down, it is not strong enough to pick up sand and carry it away. Plant roots also hold the sand in place.

Natural erosion isn't the only danger to these islands. People who enjoy the beach love to vacation on the barrier islands. To build houses, hotels, and roads for them, developers flatten the dunes. As they fill in mud flats and marshes, they bury the plants growing there. As they change the islands, developers increase the erosion that occurs.

Since communities want to save their islands, they try to stop the erosion with "beach nourishment." This involves dumping many truckloads of sand on eroding beaches. However, this only helps for a while. The erosion starts up again because there are no dunes to break the wind or plants to hold the sand in place. The new sand is soon washed away. As a result, the islands continue to be in danger. *Research*

Erosion has caused many changes in the islands. For example, the Cape Hatteras Lighthouse had to be moved. The beach had eroded, so in 1999, the lighthouse was moved about one-half mile inland.

We need to learn ways to deal with the relentless force of erosion so we can preserve these sandy national treasures.

Writing Traits
(Student pages 226–227)

Cause-and-Effect Report

Ask students to explain their school's procedures for a fire drill. Tell them to explain the information as though they were educating a new student on the process. Write their responses on the board. **Possible responses: Students stop what they are doing, follow their teacher, gather outside together, and wait until they are allowed to enter their classrooms again.** Explain that if they were writing this information in a cause-and-effect report, they would need to organize it logically so the new student would not be confused. Ask them to suggest an interesting fact about the process that might grab this new student's attention and get him or her to want to read the report. **Possible response: If you don't know what to do in a fire drill, you might be in trouble when the real thing happens.**

Review with students the writing traits of a cause-and-effect report, relating them to the students' ideas about a fire drill cause-and-effect report. Remind them that they will need to include facts, logically structured sentences, and transition words to help make the cause-and-effect relationships clear. Point out that the traits listed on Student page 226 are what make a good cause-and-effect report.

Have students identify these traits as you read aloud "Understanding the Barrier Islands" on Student page 227.

Differentiating Instruction

English-Language Learners One clue that students can look for in a cause-and-effect report to indicate a cause or an effect is the use of the word "cause" within the report. After you have read "Understanding the Barrier Islands" aloud, have students go through and try to locate the word "cause" or "caused" within the report. Write down the sentences containing these words:

The melting ice caused rivers and streams to rise.
That caused them to lengthen into narrow strips.
Erosion has caused many changes in the islands.

For each of the sentences, have students identify the cause-effect relationship being discussed. Then have them review the remainder of the report to find other cause-and-effect relationships.

Cause-and-Effect Report
Rubric

The traits of a good cause-and-effect report from page 226 have been used to make the rubric below. By using 1, 2, 3, or 4 check marks to judge each trait, you can decide how well any cause-and-effect report was written.

	Excelling ✓✓✓✓	Achieving ✓✓✓	Developing ✓✓	Beginning ✓
Information/ Organization	The report focuses on one clear topic and is organized logically by cause and effect.	The report focuses on one topic and is mostly organized by cause and effect.	The report focuses on more than one topic, and some events are organized by cause and effect.	The report needs clarity and better organization.
Voice/ Audience	The report begins with an interesting fact.	The report begins with a somewhat interesting fact.	The report begins with a fact, but it is not interesting.	The report needs to begin with an interesting fact.
Content/ Ideas	Many facts clearly support and explain the causes and effects.	Some facts support and explain the causes and effects.	A few facts are included, but they do not explain the causes or effects.	Facts need to be included in the report.
Word Choice/ Clarity	Transition words clarify the cause-and-effect relationships throughout.	Some transition words are used throughout.	Few transition words are used.	Transition words need to be used.
Sentence Fluency	All sentences are clear and logically structured.	Most sentences are clear and logically structured.	Some sentences are clear and logically structured.	Few sentences are clear and logically structured.
Grammar/ Mechanics	Spelling, grammar, and subject and object pronouns are correct.	There are few errors in spelling, grammar, and subject and object pronouns.	There are some errors in spelling, grammar, and subject and object pronouns.	There are many errors in spelling, grammar, and subject and object pronouns.

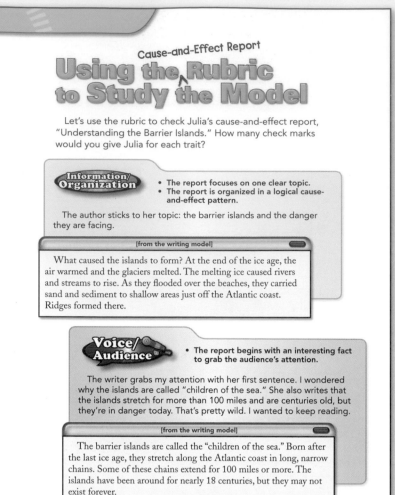

Cause-and-Effect Report
Using the Rubric to Study the Model

Let's use the rubric to check Julia's cause-and-effect report, "Understanding the Barrier Islands." How many check marks would you give Julia for each trait?

Information/ Organization
- The report focuses on one clear topic.
- The report is organized in a logical cause-and-effect pattern.

The author sticks to her topic: the barrier islands and the danger they are facing.

[from the writing model]

What caused the islands to form? At the end of the ice age, the air warmed and the glaciers melted. The melting ice caused rivers and streams to rise. As they flooded over the beaches, they carried sand and sediment to shallow areas just off the Atlantic coast. Ridges formed there.

Voice/ Audience
- The report begins with an interesting fact to grab the audience's attention.

The writer grabs my attention with her first sentence. I wondered why the islands are called "children of the sea." She also writes that the islands stretch for more than 100 miles and are centuries old, but they're in danger today. That's pretty wild. I wanted to keep reading.

[from the writing model]

The barrier islands are called the "children of the sea." Born after the last ice age, they stretch along the Atlantic coast in long, narrow chains. Some of these chains extend for 100 miles or more. The islands have been around for nearly 18 centuries, but they may not exist forever.

Using the Rubric
(Student page 228)

Have students review the writing traits listed on Student page 226. Then ask them how these traits relate to the rubric on Student page 228. **Possible response: The writing traits match the excelling marks on the rubric.** Remind students of the importance of following the writing traits and rubric when they are doing their own writing.

Point out that as students compare the student model on Student page 227 to the rubric, they will be able to assess how well the cause-and-effect report was written. This will help them improve their own writing.

Study the Model
(Student pages 229–231)

Ask students whether they think the student model was well written. Now explain that you will compare the model to the rubric for an actual assessment of the student model. Read Student pages 229–231 with your students to compare the writing model with the rubric. As you review each of the traits, ask students as a group to determine how many check marks they would give the writer. Encourage students to explain their responses.

Cause-and-Effect Report

Content/Ideas • Many facts clearly support and explain the causes and effects.

The writer includes all sorts of facts and reasons to explain the causes and effects in her report. One fact that stood out for me was the need to move the Cape Hatteras Lighthouse. Erosion must have really washed away the beach around that lighthouse! I bet it was hard to move, too!

[from the writing model]

Erosion has caused many changes in the islands. For example, the Cape Hatteras Lighthouse had to be moved. The beach had eroded, so in 1999, the lighthouse was moved about one-half mile inland.

Word Choice/Clarity • Transition words clarify the cause-and-effect relationships.

Transition words or phrases tie ideas together. They signal to the reader that the writing is moving from one idea to the next. Julia did a good job of using the transition words *since, because,* and *as a result* in the paragraph below. See how smoothly she moves from one idea to another?

[from the writing model]

Since communities want to save their islands, they try to stop the erosion with "beach nourishment." This involves dumping many truckloads of sand on eroding beaches. However, this only helps for a while. The erosion starts up again because there are no dunes to break the wind or plants to hold the sand in place. The new sand is soon washed away. As a result, the islands continue to be in danger.

Sentence Fluency • The sentences are clear and logically structured.

The author wrote easy-to-understand sentences, not long, confusing ones. If she had connected the sentences below with *ands,* I would have quit reading before I got to the end. The shorter, clearer sentences are much easier to read, and they keep me interested.

[from the writing model]

The barrier islands have broad beaches and dunes on the ocean side. They have mud flats and salt marshes on the mainland side. This low, sandy structure is vulnerable to erosion.

Grammar/Mechanics • Spelling, punctuation, and capitalization are correct. Subject and object pronouns such as *who* and *whom* are used correctly.

The spelling, punctuation, and capitalization are all correct in this report. And this author can handle pronouns! In this part, for example, she uses *who,* not *whom,* as the subject of the verb **enjoy.** Then she uses **them,** not **they,** as the object of the preposition **for.** That's tricky!

[from the writing model]

Natural erosion isn't the only danger to these islands. People who enjoy the beach love to vacation on the barrier islands. To build houses, hotels, and roads for them, developers flatten the dunes.

My Turn! I'm going to write a cause-and-effect report! I'll use the rubric and good writing strategies to help me. Follow along and learn with me.

Differentiating Instruction

Enrichment Explain to students that rubrics are not just for analyzing writing. Rubrics can be found in other venues, even non-educational venues such as restaurants and supermarkets. Ask students to imagine that they are restaurant critics and are dining at a restaurant they plan to review. Have them identify the qualities that might be in a restaurant critic's rubric. **Possible responses: atmosphere, décor, service, menu choices, taste** Once they have identified qualities for the critic's rubric, have them develop a rubric listing the traits that would enable a restaurant to get a four-star rating versus a one-star rating.

Writing a Cause-and-Effect Report

Prewriting Gather Information

Information/Organization

The report focuses on one clear topic.

Writing Strategy

Use the Internet to find credible sources of information on my topic.

Writer's Term

Credible Source

A **credible source** is one that can be trusted to have accurate, unbiased, up-to-date information. School librarians can help you find credible sources if you need some guidance.

When our teacher asked us to write a cause-and-effect report, I thought about what I wanted to do. Then I zeroed in on the topic of irrigation in Nevada. I got interested in that subject last year when I visited my cousins in Nevada. It was fun to stay on their farm and learn about a completely different way of life!

I wanted to do some of my research on the Internet. My teacher told us that some Web sites might not be good. Some sites are too complicated for me to understand. Other sites are out of date. Our librarian says we can trust a Web site run by a government agency, most news organizations, an encyclopedia, or an educational organization (like a university or a museum).

I found two credible sources for my topic on the Internet.

Then I carefully took notes from my sources. I put the notes for each source on a separate sheet of paper. You can see some of my notes below. I found other sources, too, so I will have more pages of notes for my report.

I might not use all the facts in these notes. I will choose the ones that best explain the causes and effects in my report.

Notes From the US Geological Service—Water Science for Schools: Irrigation Water Use

http://ga.water.usgs.gov/edu/wuir.html

1. About 60 percent of the world's fresh water is used for irrigation.
2. About 40 percent of the fresh water used in the United States is used to irrigate crops.
3. Farms could not feed the world without irrigation from rivers, lakes, reservoirs, and wells.
4. Of the water used for flood irrigation, one half is lost through evaporation or in transit (leaking pipes).

Notes From Colorado River Water Users Association: Nevada

http://crwua.org/nv/crwua_nv.htm

1. Nevada gets less rainfall than any other state, an average of 9 inches a year.
2. Building Hoover Dam on the Colorado River helped Nevada with water supply and hydroelectric power.
3. Agriculture uses 78 percent of the water in Nevada.
4. Water conservation is common and necessary in Nevada.

Practice!

Now it's your turn. Choose a topic that interests you and gather information about it from credible sources, including the Internet. Take notes on what you read.

Prewriting

(Student pages 232–233)

Read aloud the definition of *credible source* in the Writer's Term box on Student page 232. Tell students that they will be using the Internet to research information for their cause-and-effect reports. Remind them that not all sources on the Internet are credible. Some Web sites are written by people who may not have all the correct facts about a topic, or the information on the Web site might be out of date. Ask students to suggest Internet sites that likely have credible information. **Possible responses: major newspaper sites, government sites, educational sites, on-line encyclopedias** Tell students that as they research their topics, they should be sure to use trusted sites to gather information.

WORK with a PARTNER

Students can work together to research the topics they have chosen to use for their cause-and-effect reports. Suggest that they work with a partner and split the resources so that they do not cover the same information. For example, while one of the partners searches through the library for information, the other partner can be looking on the Internet.

Differentiating Instruction

Support Some students may have trouble selecting a topic that presents a cause-and-effect relationship. Remind them that they can use a topic in which they have an interest and find a cause-and-effect relationship that has to do with that topic. For instance, if they are interested in music, they might want to focus on the effects that being able to download music one song at a time has had on the recording industry. Ask student volunteers to name topics that interest them. Work together as a class to list suggestions about that topic that would be appropriate for a cause-and-effect report.

Enrichment Help students practice their research skills by providing a cause-and-effect topic for them to research and take notes on. For example, suggest that they research the effect that bark beetles are having on the nation's pine trees. Point out that they can use search engine sites to start their searches, but that the sites they use for research must be credible. Have them organize their notes on the subject in a Cause-and-Effect Chain.

Writing a Cause-and-Effect Report

Prewriting Organize Ideas

Information/Organization The report is organized in a logical cause-and-effect pattern.

Writing Strategy Make a Cause-and-Effect Chain to organize my notes.

As I looked over my notes, I noticed how some things cause other things. For example, Nevada gets little rain, so the farmers have to use irrigation.

The rubric reminds me to organize my report into a cause-and-effect pattern. This will help me show what causes what. I know that sometimes one cause has several effects, like when a storm blows down trees, causes rivers to overflow, and brings lightning.

Other times, several causes lead to the same effect. One example I can think of is when you pay attention in class, read the assigned chapters, and do your homework. What's the effect? You get good grades! (You also learn more, of course!)

A Cause-and-Effect Chain shows how events connect. The effect of one event can become the cause of the next event. The events link together in a chain.

You can see part of my chain on the next page.

Writer's Term
Cause-and-Effect Chain A Cause-and-Effect Chain shows actions and their results. One effect can have several causes, and one cause can have several effects.

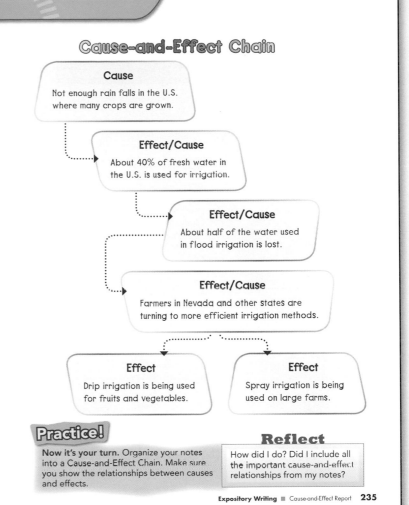

Cause-and-Effect Chain

Cause — Not enough rain falls in the U.S. where many crops are grown.

Effect/Cause — About 40% of fresh water in the U.S. is used for irrigation.

Effect/Cause — About half of the water used in flood irrigation is lost.

Effect/Cause — Farmers in Nevada and other states are turning to more efficient irrigation methods.

Effect — Drip irrigation is being used for fruits and vegetables.

Effect — Spray irrigation is being used on large farms.

Practice!
Now it's your turn. Organize your notes into a Cause-and-Effect Chain. Make sure you show the relationships between causes and effects.

Reflect
How did I do? Did I include all the important cause-and-effect relationships from my notes?

Prewriting

(Student pages 234–235)

Point out that the graphic organizer used in this chapter, the Cause-and-Effect Chain, helps students to see the sequential order of events, one leading to another. Looking forward, the chain shows the effects. Looking backward traces the causes.

Tell students that the structure of cause-and-effect reports is often chronological. One or more things happen, causing other things to happen. Some reports follow this pattern, explaining how one cause leads to an effect, which causes another effect, which causes another effect, and so on. Another common approach is to explain an effect and then describe the causes of it. Sometimes the writer then explains another related effect and shows the causes of it. The report may end by describing how the various effects may or may not cause other effects.

More Practice!

For more practice with these writing strategies, you may wish to have students use the Strategy Practice Book. See the appendix for reduced Strategy Practice Book pages.

Differentiating Instruction

Enrichment Challenge students to work backward with the student model on Student page 227, creating a Cause-and-Effect Chain based on the information presented in the report. Have them reread the student model and then fill in a Cause-and-Effect Chain using the information from the report. Once they have completed their Cause-and-Effect Chains, ask them to identify whether the information is presented chronologically or if the writer explained effects and the causes of them and then went on to explain other related effects.

Support Have students color-code their Cause-and-Effect Chains. Each cause should be written in a certain color. Its effect should be underlined in that same color. Have them continue this code as they write the drafts for their reports. Point out that some effects will also be causes and that some effects may be underlined with more than one color.

Writing a Cause-and-Effect Report

Drafting Write a Draft

Voice/Audience

The report begins with an interesting fact to grab the audience's attention.

Writing Strategy Begin with an interesting fact to grab the audience's attention.

Now it's time to start writing. I'll use my Cause-and-Effect Chain to show how each cause leads to an effect. I'll add facts and details along the way.

I'll also think of a way to begin that grabs the attention of my audience—my classmates, in this case. They may not have to irrigate crops, but natural resources like water are important to everyone. I'll start with a question that gets them thinking about how we use our water. Then I'll include interesting facts that will keep them reading.

I'll do my best with spelling, punctuation, and grammar now and check for mistakes when I edit my draft.

You can read the beginning of my draft on the next page.

236 **Expository Writing** ■ Cause-and-Effect Report

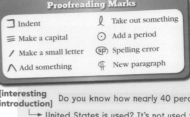

Proofreading Marks

⌐ Indent   ℓ Take out something
≡ Make a capital   ⊙ Add a period
／ Make a small letter   SP Spelling error
∧ Add something   ¶ New paragraph

[DRAFT]

[interesting introduction] Do you know how nearly 40 percent of the fresh water in the United States is used? It's not used for drinking or baths or swimming pools. It's used for irrigation! Many areas in the United States don't get enough rainfall to grow crops, so the land must be irrigated.

[cause] Most irrigation is in the western states. Water is scarce there. Nevada gets less rainfall than any other state. Farmers in nevada must depend on irrigation to grow their crops. ↑ [effect]

The oldest and cheapest type of irrigation is flood irrigation. In this method, water is allowed to flow along rows of plants. However, about half of the water used in this type of irrigation evaporates or runs off the feelds. To keep water from running off there feelds, farmers whom live in hilly areas make there feelds as level as possible. They also release water at intervals. This reduces runoff, too. In addition, some farmers capture the runoff in ponds. There it is stored for they to use again. ↓ [cause]

To conserve water, farmers across the West have experimented with irrigation. Many of they now use more efficient methods. ← [effect]

Practice!

Now it's your turn. Write a draft that shows the cause-and-effect relationships in your graphic organizer. Grab your reader's attention with an interesting fact right at the beginning.

Reflect

What do you think? Did I include enough interesting facts to hold the reader's interest?

Expository Writing ■ Cause-and-Effect Report 237

Drafting

(Student pages 236–237)

Review the purpose of a draft. Stress that writers will have several opportunities to change or correct their drafts as they follow the steps in the writing process. Then ask a student to read aloud Justin's draft on Student page 237.

Ask students why Justin is not worried about making mistakes in this draft. **Possible response: He's more concerned with showing how each cause leads to an effect; he knows he can come back later and edit the draft; he is more focused at this stage on writing a report that will hold the reader's attention.**

Point out how Justin used his graphic organizer to write his draft. If you wish, refer to his Cause-and-Effect Chain on Student page 235 and have students note how he used the graphic organizer to write his draft. Ask if they think Justin has followed the points from his Cause-and-Effect Chain.

Writing Across the Curriculum

Geography Researching and writing a cause-and-effect report will enable students to explore other subjects they may be studying. In Justin's case, he is uncovering information that he might also learn about when studying geography. Challenge students to learn about other forms of irrigation used by farmers in the western United States. What are challenges each form of irrigation poses to farmers? How have methods of irrigation improved recently? Suggest that they start their research by looking at the US Geological Survey's Water Science for Schools Web site. Refer to http://ga.water.usgs.gov/edu.

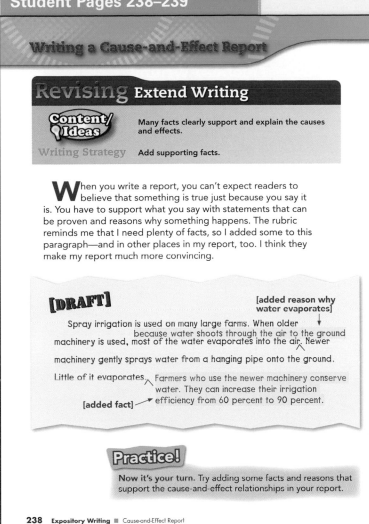

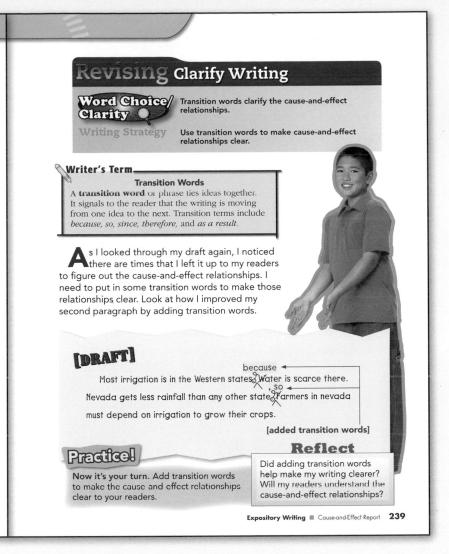

Revising

(Student pages 238–239)

Ask students to read Justin's words on Student page 238. Ask them why facts and reasons are important in a cause-and-effect report. **Possible response: They help readers better understand causes and effects, and they make the report more interesting.**

Remind students of the need to use facts and reasons in their reports. Point out that cause-and-effect reports should be based on facts and reasons, and their notes and research should provide them with the facts to include in their reports.

Next, have students read Justin's words on Student page 239. Read aloud the definition of *transition words* in the Writer's Term box. Write the following sentences: *The phone rang. I picked it up.* Now ask students to rewrite the sentences using a transition word to show what effect the phone ringing had on the narrator. **Possible response: The phone rang, so I picked it up.** Explain that in a cause-and-effect report, the cause-and-effect relationships should be clear and identifiable. Transition words can help make this relationship clear.

Have students read through their drafts to identify places they can make the cause-and-effect relationships clearer by adding transition words.

Differentiating Instruction

Support To help students understand how to use transition words to clarify cause-and-effect relationships, have them complete the following exercise. On the board, write: *My brother was studying. He asked me to turn my music down. I turned it down. I couldn't hear it. I turned it back up. He complained again. I put on my headphones. We were both happy.*

Now have them review the transition words listed in the Writer's Term box on Student page 239. Ask them to rewrite the story using transition words to show cause-and-effect relationships. **Possible response: My brother was studying, so he asked me to turn my music down. Because I turned it down, I couldn't hear it. Therefore, I turned it back up. Since he complained again, I put on my headphones. As a result, we were both happy.**

Writing a Cause-and-Effect Report

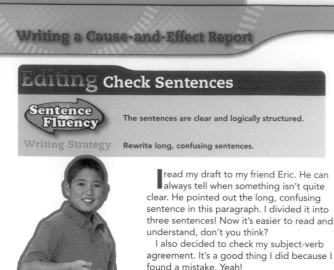

Editing Check Sentences

Sentence Fluency

The sentences are clear and logically structured.

Writing Strategy Rewrite long, confusing sentences.

I read my draft to my friend Eric. He can always tell when something isn't quite clear. He pointed out the long, confusing sentence in this paragraph. I divided it into three sentences! Now it's easier to read and understand, don't you think?

I also decided to check my subject-verb agreement. It's a good thing I did because I found a mistake. Yeah!

[DRAFT] [corrected error in subject-verb agreement]

Many farmers, including those in Nevada, now ~~uses~~ use drip irrigation for fruits and vegetables. The water runs through plastic pipes laid along crop rows or buried in the soil and holes in the pipes allow the water to drip directly into the soil and the water soaks into the ground instead of running off or evaporating.

[rewrote long sentence]

Practice!

Now it's your turn. Do you have any long, confusing sentences in your report? If you do, rewrite them and make them clearer and easier to understand.

Editing Proofread Writing

Grammar Mechanics Spelling, punctuation, and capitalization are correct. Subject and object pronouns such as who and whom are used correctly.

Writing Strategy Check that subject and object pronouns are used correctly, especially who and whom.

✏️ **Writer's Term**

Subject and Object Pronouns
A **subject pronoun** takes the place of the subject in a sentence. An **object pronoun** replaces the object of a verb or a preposition.

Okay, it's time to do the nitty-gritty stuff—spelling, capitalization, punctuation, and grammar. I also have to check that I used subject and object pronouns correctly. I have problems with **who** and **whom**.

[DRAFT] [changed to a subject pronoun]

or runs off the feelds. To keep water from running off ~~there~~ their fields, farmers ~~whom~~ who live in hilly areas make their ~~feelds~~ fields as level as possible. They also release water at intervals. This reduces runoff, too. In addition, some farmers capture the runoff in ponds. There it is stored for ~~they~~ them to use again.

[changed to an object pronoun]

Practice!

Now it's your turn. Edit your draft for spelling, punctuation, and capitalization errors. Be sure to correct any problems with subject and object pronouns.

Grammar Mechanics

For more practice fixing subject and object pronouns, use the exercises on the next two pages.

Reflect

What do you think? Is my report clear and interesting? Are my sentences easier to read as shorter sentences or as one long one? Do my subjects and verbs agree?

Editing

(Student pages 240–241)

Ask a student to read Justin's words on Student page 240 to the class. Explain that one way to make writing clearer is to avoid rambling sentences. These could discourage readers from reading further.

Next, have a student read Justin's words on Student page 241 to the class. Then read aloud the description of subject and object pronouns in the Writer's Term box on that page. Point out that since this is the stage of writing where writers look for and correct mistakes, Justin is looking not only for grammatical and spelling errors, but also to make sure that his subject and object pronouns are correct.

Justin has problems with *who* and *whom,* so he will pay close attention to these words in his writing. If any of your students are having trouble with subject and object pronouns, you may wish to teach the Mini-Lesson on page 181 of this Teacher Edition. Then have students complete the exercises on Student pages 242–243. Review the answers and possible rewrites with them.

WORK with a **PARTNER** Point out that Justin chose to read a draft of his report to his friend Eric. He thought Eric could tell when something wasn't quite clear. Explain that sometimes it is easier for someone else to identify weaknesses in your writing. Have students read their reports to a partner to see if the other person can find places in the report that need to be edited.

Practice!

Subject and Object Pronouns

KNOW the RULE

A **subject pronoun** takes the place of the subject in a sentence.
    Example: **Leanne** lives near Hoover Dam.
             She lives near Hoover Dam.

An **object pronoun** replaces the object of a verb or a preposition.
    Example: The dam helps **farmers** irrigate.
             The dam helps **them** irrigate.

Use **who** as a subject pronoun. Use **whom** as an object pronoun.
    Examples: Herbert Hoover, **who** was president then, made a speech. He talked to farmers for **whom** the dam would make a huge difference. (*Who* is the subject of the verb *was. Whom* is the object of the preposition *for.*)

Practice the Rule

Number your paper 1–5. Choose the correct pronoun for each sentence and write it on your paper. Add **S** if you chose a subject pronoun or **O** if you chose an object pronoun.

1. People (who/whom) live in the desert value water.
2. (I/me) grew up in the Mojave Desert in Nevada.
3. Hoover Dam was built near (us/we) in the early 1930s.
4. For (who/whom) was Hoover Dam built?
5. It was built for all of (we/us) in the Southwest.

Apply the Rule

Read the following cause-and-effect report about Herbert Hoover. Correct any problems with subject or object pronouns, and rewrite the paragraphs on another sheet of paper. Watch out for *who* and *whom*!

The Great Humanitarian

Before Herbert Hoover ever became president of the United States, he earned the nickname "The Great Humanitarian." In 1914, Hoover helped thousands of Americans whom were stranded in Europe because of World War I. After their were safe at home in the U.S., Hoover moved on to the job of getting food to the people of Belgium and France, many of who were starving as a result of the war.

After the war, Hoover continued his humanitarian work by helping Europeans who didn't have enough food because of the post-war devastation. President Wilson put him in charge of an organization that fed millions of people.

Hoover, whom was asked to be Secretary of Commerce by both presidents Harding and Coolidge, helped many Americans in the 1920s. During that time, he supervised relief for people whom had lost their homes because of flooding along the Mississippi River. It was Hoover who urged the building of a huge dam to control the Colorado River. Later, the dam was named for Hoover, whom was president when construction started.

Grammar/Mechanics Mini-Lesson

(Student pages 242–243)

Subject and Object Pronouns

Explain to the students that subject pronouns take the place of the subject in a sentence, while object pronouns replace the object of a verb or preposition.

Write on the board: *He rode his new bike to school.*
Ask students whether the *he* in the sentence is a subject or object pronoun. **subject pronoun**
Write on the board: *The bike rack at school helps them keep their bikes safe.*
Ask students whether *them* in this sentence is a subject or object pronoun. **object pronoun**
Write on the board: *Joe, ____ was an avid cyclist, loved riding his bike. It was cyclists like Joe for ____ the bike rack was installed.*
Ask students to supply the correct missing pronouns.
who; whom

 For more practice with grammar/mechanics skills, see Zaner-Bloser's *G.U.M.* materials.

Answers for Practice the Rule
1. who   2. I   3. us   4. whom   5. us

Answers for Apply the Rule

Before Herbert Hoover ever became president of the United States, he earned the nickname "The Great Humanitarian." In 1914, Hoover helped thousands of Americans who were stranded in Europe because of World War I. After they were safe at home in the U.S., Hoover moved on to the job of getting food to the people of Belgium and France, many of whom were starving as a result of the war.

After the war, Hoover continued his humanitarian work by helping Europeans who didn't have enough food because of the post-war devastation. President Wilson put him in charge of an organization that fed millions of people.

Hoover, who was asked to be Secretary of Commerce by both presidents Harding and Coolidge, helped many Americans in the 1920s. During that time, he supervised relief for people who had lost their homes because of flooding along the Mississippi River. It was Hoover who urged the building of a huge dam to control the Colorado River. Later, the dam was named for Hoover, who was president when the construction started.

Writing a Cause-and-Effect Report

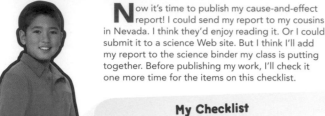

Publishing Share Writing

Add my cause-and-effect report to the class binder.

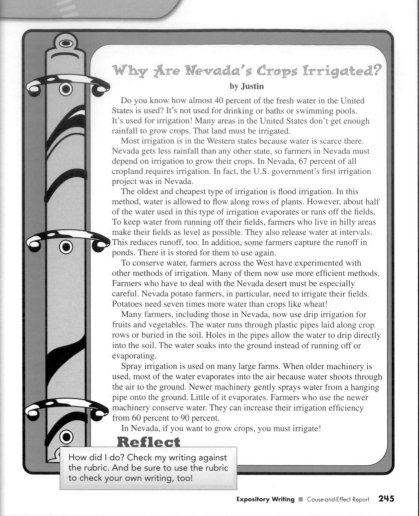

Now it's time to publish my cause-and-effect report! I could send my report to my cousins in Nevada. I think they'd enjoy reading it. Or I could submit it to a science Web site. But I think I'll add my report to the science binder my class is putting together. Before publishing my work, I'll check it one more time for the items on this checklist.

My Checklist

✔ The report is focused and organized in a clear cause-and-effect pattern.

✔ The beginning captures the interest of the audience.

✔ The cause-and-effect relationships are made clear with supporting details and transition words.

✔ I've eliminated long, confusing sentences and replaced them with clear, logically structured sentences.

✔ Spelling, capitalization, and punctuation are all correct. I've used subject and object pronouns such as **who** and **whom** correctly.

Practice!

Now it's your turn. Make a checklist to check your own cause-and-effect report. Then make a final draft to publish.

244 **Expository Writing** ■ Cause-and-Effect Report

Why Are Nevada's Crops Irrigated?
by Justin

Do you know how almost 40 percent of the fresh water in the United States is used? It's not used for drinking or baths or swimming pools. It's used for irrigation! Many areas in the United States don't get enough rainfall to grow crops. That land must be irrigated.

Most irrigation is in the Western states because water is scarce there. Nevada gets less rainfall than any other state, so farmers in Nevada must depend on irrigation to grow their crops. In Nevada, 67 percent of all cropland requires irrigation. In fact, the U.S. government's first irrigation project was in Nevada.

The oldest and cheapest type of irrigation is flood irrigation. In this method, water is allowed to flow along rows of plants. However, about half of the water used in this type of irrigation evaporates or runs off the fields. To keep water from running off their fields, farmers who live in hilly areas make their fields as level as possible. They also release water at intervals. This reduces runoff, too. In addition, some farmers capture the runoff in ponds. There it is stored for them to use again.

To conserve water, farmers across the West have experimented with other methods of irrigation. Many of them now use more efficient methods. Farmers who have to deal with the Nevada desert must be especially careful. Nevada potato farmers, in particular, need to irrigate their fields. Potatoes need seven times more water than crops like wheat!

Many farmers, including those in Nevada, now use drip irrigation for fruits and vegetables. The water runs through plastic pipes laid along crop rows or buried in the soil. Holes in the pipes allow the water to drip directly into the soil. The water soaks into the ground instead of running off or evaporating.

Spray irrigation is used on many large farms. When older machinery is used, most of the water evaporates into the air because water shoots through the air to the ground. Newer machinery gently sprays water from a hanging pipe onto the ground. Little of it evaporates. Farmers who use the newer machinery conserve water. They can increase their irrigation efficiency from 60 percent to 90 percent.

In Nevada, if you want to grow crops, you must irrigate!

Reflect

How did I do? Check my writing against the rubric. And be sure to use the rubric to check your own writing, too!

Expository Writing ■ Cause-and-Effect Report 245

Publishing
(Student pages 244–245)

Note that Justin is once again reviewing the writing traits for a cause-and-effect report. He wants to be sure, before he publishes his report, that his report is well written. Remind students to review their drafts against their own checklists to be sure that they have not missed anything that could affect their score.

Challenge students to identify other ways that Justin could publish his report. Who else might benefit from learning about irrigation in Nevada?

TiPS for the Writing Classroom

Listening Skills
by Ken Stewart, *Master Teacher*

When you introduce the significance of communicating effectively to your class, emphasize to your students the importance of developing good listening skills. Your students must understand that attentive listening is just as important as clearly voicing their ideas. In the classroom, most educators constantly have their students respond to direct questioning or give their opinions about a particular topic. Since listening is fifty percent of effective oral communication, then it is imperative that you establish good listening skills.

With your guidance, have your class discuss the rules of good listening. Use the following questions to guide the discussion.

1. How important is listening?

2. What are some classroom rules about listening?

List responses on the board/overhead projector, and transfer them to a poster board to be displayed and referred to throughout the year.

Note: Rules should include remaining silent while another person speaks, looking at the speaker, nodding or smiling to show understanding, asking for clarification when necessary, and restating what you heard or think you heard.

Ways to Publish a
Cause-and-Effect Report

To pick the best format for publishing your cause-and-effect report, think about who your audience will be. If you need more ideas for publishing your report, try one of the suggestions below.

✓ Send your report to friends or relatives who live far away. Follow up with a letter to get their reactions.

✓ Make your own science binder. Your cause-and-effect report can come first in the binder, but include other science reports you write this year.

✓ Display your report in the library near the shelf that holds books on science topics.

✓ Include your cause-and-effect report as part of a multimedia presentation to your class or another class.

✓ Gather a group of your classmates. Take turns reading your cause-and-effect reports to one another.

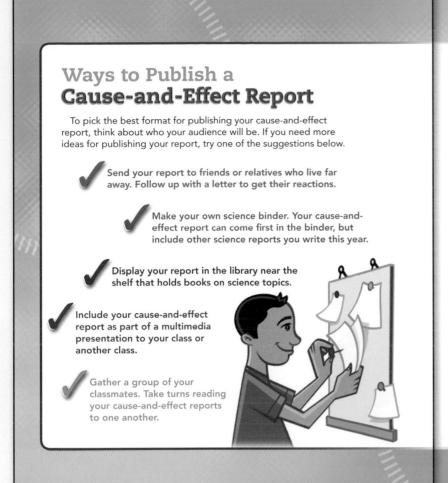

Writing Across the Content Areas
Cause-and-Effect Report

Understanding cause-and effect relationships is important in every subject. Here are some of my ideas for cause-and-effect writing. Can you think of some more ideas?

Math
- Make a budget for yourself, and write about the effects of the budget on your life.
- Write a cause-and-effect report on how different ways of managing time affect your life or our society.

Social Studies
- Choose an important historical event. Write about what caused the event to occur or explain the effects the event had on history.
- Write a cause-and-effect report about a time you were successful in school, at home, or in your friendships. Why were you successful? What impact did your success have?

English
- Read a short story and focus on the protagonist's problem. Write a cause-and-effect report about why the character has this problem and how his/her problem affects others.
- Choose a favorite author and research his/her life. What caused this person to become a writer and to write about his/her chosen topics? What effects has reading this author's works had on you?

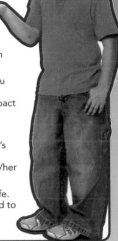

Ways to Publish
(Student page 246)

Student page 246 contains a list of suggestions for publishing the students' cause-and-effect reports. Go through the list with students. Ask them to think about other places to publish their cause-and-effect reports. You may wish to gather all of the students' cause-and-effect reports and create a binder for them so that the students can see each other's work. Suggest that students research Web sites that might want to publish cause-and-effect reports, such as sites that educate others about how things work. Encourage your students to find other places to publish their cause-and-effect reports.

Writing Across the Content Areas
(Student page 247)

Remind students that cause-and-effect reports can be useful in other subjects as well. Review the ideas and subjects on Student page 247 with the class. Ask students to think about cause-and-effect relationships as they explore other subjects in school or even at home. As they think about why things happen, they will be able to come up with many ideas for exploring how and why to write a cause-and-effect report.

Research Report Overview

Students will learn about writing research reports in this chapter. First, they will look at different elements of a research report, including multiple and varied sources, organization, lively writing, and fully cited sources. To help them understand how all writing has a purpose, they will look at some of the reasons for writing a research report—information, mastery, and going deeper. The writing model in this chapter will give students the opportunity to better understand the traits that make up a good research report.

Justin, the student guide for this chapter, will go through each of the stages involved in writing a research report, including prewriting, drafting, revising, editing, and publishing. Students will follow along and practice these steps in writing

their own research reports. They will use an encyclopedia and at least two other sources to research their topics and then organize their notes in an Outline. They will write and then revise their drafts, focusing on using interesting details and adding a conclusion that summarizes the main points and changing passive voice to active voice. As they edit, they will check to be sure their sentences are lively and that proper nouns and proper adjectives are capitalized. Finally, they will correct any spelling and grammatical errors and publish their final reports.

You may wish to send to families the School-Home Connection Letter for this chapter, located at the end of this unit in the Teacher Edition.

Research Report Writing Traits

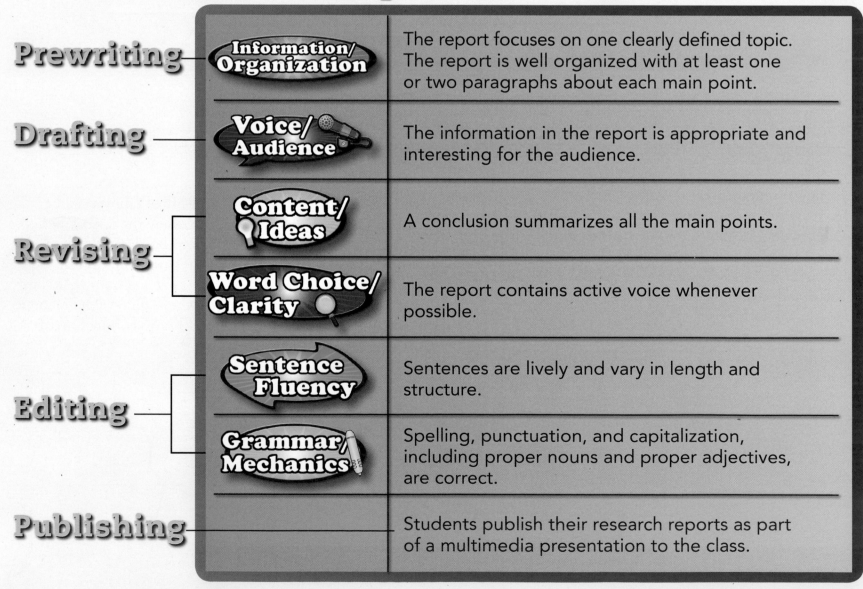

Prewriting	Information/Organization	The report focuses on one clearly defined topic. The report is well organized with at least one or two paragraphs about each main point.
Drafting	Voice/Audience	The information in the report is appropriate and interesting for the audience.
Revising	Content/Ideas	A conclusion summarizes all the main points.
	Word Choice/Clarity	The report contains active voice whenever possible.
Editing	Sentence Fluency	Sentences are lively and vary in length and structure.
	Grammar/Mechanics	Spelling, punctuation, and capitalization, including proper nouns and proper adjectives, are correct.
Publishing		Students publish their research reports as part of a multimedia presentation to the class.

Research Report Time Management

WEEK 1

Day 1	Day 2	Day 3	Day 4	Day 5
Learning Objectives				
Students will: • learn the components of a research report.	Students will: • learn how to gather information for a research report.	Students will: • practice researching and gathering information for their research reports.	Students will: • learn how to make an Outline to organize their notes.	Students will: • practice organizing their notes to make an Outline.
Activities				
• Discuss the elements and traits of a research report (Student pages 248–250). • Use the rubric to study the model (Student pages 251–257).	• Read and discuss **Prewriting: Gather Information** (Student pages 258–259).	• Brainstorm ideas and choose a research report. • Gather information and take notes.	• Read and discuss **Prewriting: Organize Ideas** (Student pages 260–261).	• Look at the notes on a research report. • Use notes to fill in an Outline.

WEEK 2

Day 1	Day 2	Day 3	Day 4	Day 5
Learning Objectives				
Students will: • learn how to provide details to interest their audience.	Students will: • practice writing their drafts.	Students will: • learn how to add a conclusion that summarizes the main points.	Students will: • practice writing a conclusion that summarizes the main points in their reports.	Students will: • learn how to change passive voice to active voice.
Activities				
• Read and discuss **Drafting: Write a Draft** (Student page 262).	• Use Outlines to write a draft. • Make sure to provide details to interest the audience.	• Read and discuss **Revising: Extend Writing** (Student page 264).	• Summarize the main points in conclusions.	• Read and discuss **Revising: Clarify Writing** (Student page 265).

WEEK 3

Day 1	Day 2	Day 3	Day 4	Day 5
Learning Objectives				
Students will: • practice replacing passive voice with active voice.	Students will: • learn about using sentences that are lively and energetic.	Students will: • learn how to correctly capitalize proper nouns and proper adjectives.	Students will: • practice editing their drafts for spelling, punctuation, and capitalization.	Students will: • learn different ways to publish their research reports.
Activities				
• Reread drafts to check for use of passive voice. • Replace passive voice with active voice whenever possible.	• Read and discuss **Editing: Check Sentences** (Student page 266). • Check to be sure there's a variety of lively, energetic sentences.	• Read and discuss **Editing: Proofread Writing** (Student page 267). • Make sure any proper nouns and proper adjectives are correctly capitalized.	• Fix any spelling, punctuation, or capitalization errors.	• Read and discuss **Publishing: Share Writing** (Student page 270).

* To complete the chapter in fewer days, teach the learning objectives and activities for two days in one day.

This planning chart, correlated to your state's writing standards, is available on-line at http://www.zaner-bloser.com/sfw.

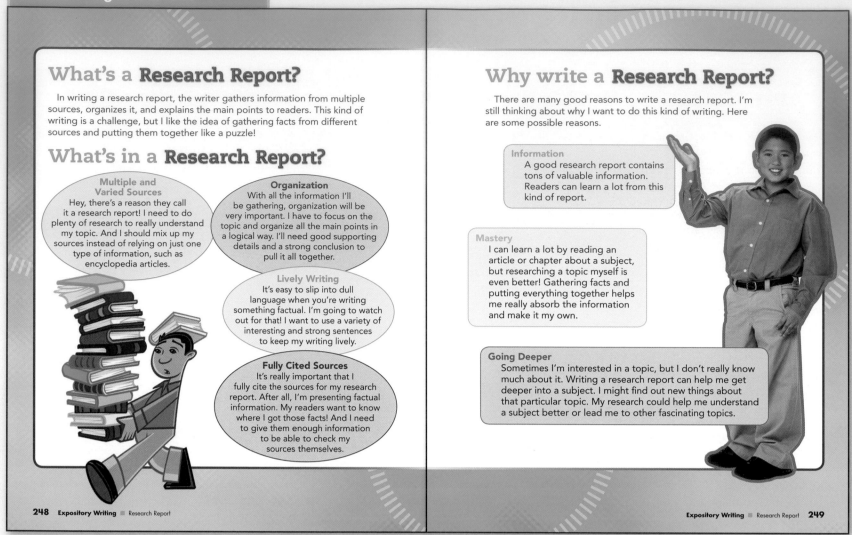

Define the Genre
(Student page 248)

Research Report

Ask students to explain how scientists, businesspeople, salespeople, government committees, and other professionals find answers to their questions. **Possible responses: They do research, talk to experts, go to the library, read a book, look on the Internet.** Ask students to suggest ways those people might share what they learn from their research. **Possible responses: post an article on the Internet, have a meeting, write a report.** Explain that a written account of factual information gathered on a topic is called a *research report*, which is a form of expository writing.

Tell students that this chapter will help them learn how to write an effective research report.

Elements of the Genre

Research Report

Read and discuss elements of a research report with the students. Point out the importance of using multiple and varied sources when writing a research report and crediting these sources by citing or fully identifying them. That means students will have to spend time researching before they can write their reports.

Authentic Writing
(Student page 249)

Research Report

Have student volunteers read each of the reasons for writing a research report listed on Student page 249. Ask them which of the reasons listed benefit the reader and which benefit the writer. **Information benefits the reader; mastery and going deeper benefit the writer.** Tell students that when they research and write their research reports, they should think about why they are writing. They want to educate their readers, so they should be sure to load the reports with interesting and reliable information. They are also writing research reports to learn more about a subject themselves and to dig deeper into a topic that they may not know about. This means that they will likely be spending more time doing research on the topic than they would do when writing for a different genre, such as a short story or an eyewitness account.

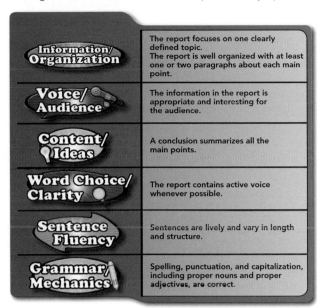

Research Report
Writing Traits

A good research report needs to have the six traits of good writing. I'll use the traits listed below to help me write my report.

Information/Organization	The report focuses on one clearly defined topic. The report is well organized with at least one or two paragraphs about each main point.
Voice/Audience	The information in the report is appropriate and interesting for the audience.
Content/Ideas	A conclusion summarizes all the main points.
Word Choice/Clarity	The report contains active voice whenever possible.
Sentence Fluency	Sentences are lively and vary in length and structure.
Grammar/Mechanics	Spelling, punctuation, and capitalization, including proper nouns and proper adjectives, are correct.

Let's see how Peter Nuan used these traits to help him write the research report that begins on the next page.

250   **Expository Writing** ■ Research Report

Research Report Model

Digging Into Backyard Archaeology

by Peter Nuan

Lively writing

With a toothbrush, Jan Haas carefully removed dirt from a little lump in her hand. The object under the dirt glinted in the sunlight. Was it a piece of gold jewelry? She continued to brush off the soil hiding the object. The shape became clear. It was round and fairly flat. Then she saw a design. Soon it was clear that the object was a tarnished brass button.

It had been buried six inches deep in Jan's backyard in Baltimore, Maryland. She dug it up near an old washhouse. The washhouse had been built in the mid-1700s. Later, Jan learned the button was from the Colonial period.

As a backyard archaeologist, Jan was pleased with her find. Backyard archaeologists are amateurs. Like the professionals, they search for and study objects made by people long ago.   *Organization—main point*

Across America, people like Jan Haas are digging up their backyards. They hope to find treasures. These treasures will probably not be gold or diamonds. More likely, they will be old buttons or chipped glass. They are still valuable, though. They tell about an area's history and culture. A dig in the backyards of Alexandria, Virginia, uncovered items from more than a century ago. They included marbles, medicine bottles, and pottery shards. Before the Civil War, free African American people lived in the area. "By studying these artifacts, we were able to trace the development of this neighborhood and the lifestyles of its inhabitants," said the city's archaeologist, Pamela J. Cressey, Ph.D.

Archaeologists urge people who dig as a hobby to follow a few guidelines. If amateurs just start digging, they may destroy valuable old objects.

First, property owners should research their site. Town records may provide facts about former owners. Many libraries and museums may have collections of news clippings and photos. Information about early Native American groups living in the region is usually available at history museums.

Organization—main point

Organization—supporting details

Expository Writing ■ Research Report   **251**

Writing Traits
(Student pages 250–251)

Research Report

Review with students the writing traits listed on Student page 250. Explain to students that they will be studying strategies for writing research reports. They will also be using these strategies to write their own research reports. Point out that a good research report contains the traits listed on Student page 250.

Tell students to try to identify these traits in the report "Digging Into Backyard Archaeology" on Student page 251 as they read it.

Research Report

Backyard archaeologists should then contact authorities and explain what they have learned about the site. The state archaeologist is a good person to contact. Other possible contacts are historical societies and college archaeology departments. An expert will often arrange a survey of the site.

Some backyard sites contain valuable objects. Unless such a site is in danger of being destroyed, archaeologists usually ask property owners not to dig there. They believe the past should be left untouched so it will be preserved for the future. If the site is in danger, the archaeologists may conduct a dig. They often ask the property owner to help.

Whatever diggers find at the site belongs to the property owners. Some backyard archaeologists donate the items to a historical society or museum. There, trained professionals can catalog and care for the items. Objects removed from the ground may dry out, rot, or get moldy. Professionals know how to preserve these objects. They can keep them safe for study and display. *(Lively writing)*

Some backyard archaeologists get started by volunteering at a dig site. Several government agencies offer a chance to work in the field. For example, Passport in Time (PIT) is a volunteer program of the U.S. Forest Service. Its aim is to preserve landmarks and historical sites in national forests. PIT volunteers work with archaeologists on sites around the country. Linda Ruys volunteered at a PIT site in Idaho. She learned a lot about the people of the past—and made friends in the present! "The words 'kindred spirits' and 'family' were repeated often in a group that had just met," she said. She found joy in working with these people. "We understood our connectedness as human beings—a life lesson worth learning." *(Organization—main point)*

School programs are another place to learn the basics of archaeology. Sixth-grade students at Blake Middle School in Medfield, Massachusetts, learn through a hands-on experience. Each fall they work in teams on an old trash heap owned by a local family. They have found old nails, jars, and pieces of an old toy bank. *(Organization—supporting details)*

The students learn to use the correct tools and methods. They are shown how to mark the site into square plots. They learn how to properly dig with a trowel. They also practice sifting buckets of soil through screens. Any objects in the soil remain on the screen while the dirt falls through. Finally, they learn to record what they find and where they find it.

Another place to learn about archaeology is a Web site called "Dr. Dig." This Web site is about archaeology in general, but the advice on the site can help backyard archaeologists, too. For example, Dr. Dig suggests using tools that fit the location and the job in order to avoid damaging artifacts. Dr. Dig once used a tongue depressor to excavate some flint! "As a general rule," says Dr. Dig, "small tools are used to uncover small artifacts, large-scale tools for large artifacts." He also cautions amateurs to contact their local utility companies before starting to dig. This will protect any buried wires on their property.

Archaeology requires patience and attention to detail. It requires caring about the past and the future. Many backyard archaeologists love their hobby for these reasons. Some professional archaeologists worry about what might be lost if the amateurs are not careful. However, amateurs can learn how to dig the right way by consulting experts and working as volunteers in the field. As Dr. Dig might say to backyard archaeologists, every tarnished button counts, so be careful! *(Organization—strong conclusion)*

Works Consulted

"Archaeology." *Encyclopedia Britannica.* 2007 ed.
Ask Dr. Dig. DIG Magazine. 6 Dec. 2006 <http://www.digonsite.com/drdig>
Atkin, Ross. "Kids dig history." *Christian Science Monitor.* 23 Nov. 1999: 22.
Haas, Jan. Personal interview. 12 Sept. 2001.
Kersting, Jane. "The PIT Experience: Life Lessons and So Much More." *Passport in Time.* 6 Dec. 2006 <http://www.passportintime.com>
Proeller, Marie. "Backyard Archaeology." *Country Living.* Aug. 1998: 40.

(Multiple and varied sources, fully cited)

Differentiating Instruction

English-Language Learners Ask a student to read aloud the title of the student model. Explain that the students can conclude by the title of the essay that it will contain some archaeology terms that they may not be familiar with. Before they read the essay, it would be helpful to review new terms or terms that have a different meaning in this context. Some terms to preteach include *site, dig, archaeology, tools, trowel, artifact.* Explain to students that sometimes words can have different meanings in different contexts. For instance, they may be familiar with the word "dig" as it refers to breaking ground, but in archaeology, "dig" means an archaeological excavation or its site. When students are going to read a report about a new topic, its often helpful if they learn terms about this topic before reading the report.

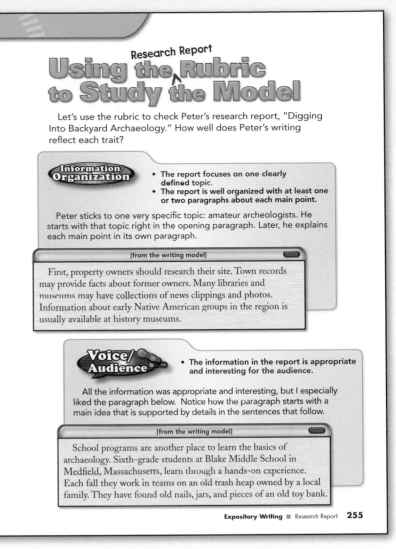

Using the Rubric
(Student page 254)

Review with students the qualities of a good research report shown in the rubric on Student page 254. Remind students that the rubric is a useful tool in determining if a research report is well written or not. Point out that they will be using this rubric to determine whether the student model is well written and if the student writer included all of the traits that comprise a good research report.

Have them use the rubric to review the student model.

Study the Model
(Student pages 255–257)

Read the bulleted points on Student pages 255–257. Discuss whether students agree with Justin's assessment of the research report on each point. For example, do they feel that there are areas in the report where the writer could have changed the sentence length or structure to make the sentences livelier? Have them present specific examples from the writing model.

Tell students that the rubric focuses on the capitalization and punctuation of proper nouns and proper adjectives. Have them identify examples of proper nouns and proper adjectives within the writing model.

Remind students that as they write, edit, and revise their stories, they will continually refer to the rubric to be sure that they do not forget to include any of the traits listed.

Research Report

Content/Ideas
• A conclusion summarizes all the main points.

The writer made a lot of good points in his research report. Then he brought them all together in a concluding paragraph that summed everything up!

[from the writing model]

Archaeology requires patience and attention to detail. It requires caring about the past and the future. Many backyard archaeologists love their hobby for these reasons. Some professional archaeologists worry about what might be lost if the amateurs are not careful. However, amateurs can learn how to dig the right way by consulting experts and working as volunteers in the field. As Dr. Dig might say to backyard archaeologists, every tarnished button counts, so be careful!

Word Choice/Clarity
• The report contains active voice whenever possible.

The writer could have used mostly passive voice. For example, he could have written "The items are donated by some backyard archaeologists to a historical society or museum. There, the items can be cataloged and cared for by trained professionals." Instead, he uses active voice. See how he does it? The sentences are much clearer in active voice.

[from the writing model]

Some backyard archaeologists donate the items to a historical society or museum. There, trained professionals can catalog and care for the items.

Sentence Fluency
• Sentences are lively and vary in length and structure.

Peter does a good job of making his sentences lively. Look at how he does it in the following paragraphs. He uses short sentences and long sentences. Some sentences start with dependent clauses; some do not. Peter mixes up the structure of his sentences, too, using different patterns throughout the report.

[from the writing model]

It had been buried six inches deep in Jan's backyard in Baltimore, Maryland. She dug it up near an old washhouse. The washhouse had been built in the mid-1700s. Later, Jan learned the button was from the Colonial period.

As a backyard archaeologist, Jan was pleased with her find. Backyard archaeologists are amateurs. Like the professionals, they search for and study objects made by people long ago.

Grammar/Mechanics
• Spelling, punctuation, and capitalization, including proper nouns and proper adjectives, are correct.

I couldn't find any mistakes in spelling, punctuation, or capitalization in Peter's report. He even wrote all the proper nouns and proper adjectives correctly!

[from the writing model]

A dig in the backyards of Alexandria, Virginia, uncovered items from more than a century ago. They included marbles, medicine bottles, and pottery shards. Before the Civil War, free African American people lived in the area. "By studying these artifacts, we were able to trace the development of this neighborhood and the lifestyles of its inhabitants," said the city's archaeologist, Pamela J. Cressey, Ph.D.

My Turn!

Now it's my turn! I'm going to write a research report on my own topic. With the help of the rubric and good writing strategies, I think I'll write a good one. Follow along and see how I do it!

Differentiating Instruction

Support To help students understand active versus passive voice, ask them to read through a newspaper, book, or magazine and locate sentences written in the passive voice. Note that passive voice uses constructions such as *are, is, has been, and will be…by.* Ask them to determine who or what is doing the action, if they can. Then help them rewrite the sentences in active voice.

Writing a Research Report

Prewriting: Gather Information

Information/Organization

The report focuses on one clearly defined topic.

Writing Strategy

Use an encyclopedia and at least two other sources to research my topic.

As soon as I heard we were going to write research reports, I thought of India because I love Indian food! I figured there was a lot about India that would be interesting to my classmates. They will be my audience.

When I looked up the word *India* in an encyclopedia, I found a long list of topics! They included India's people, geography, climate, natural resources, religions, history, government—the list went on and on. I needed to narrow my topic!

I noticed there was a section about Indian food. Maybe I could focus on just that area. But then I realized that even Indian food was too broad a topic for my report. There are so many kinds!

I learned from the encyclopedia that people in different parts of India eat different dishes. I decided to narrow my topic to regional foods of India. I think my classmates will find that interesting. They love anything that has to do with food!

In addition to the encyclopedia, I checked two other sources. As I read, I took notes on note cards. Each card had one piece of information and its source. Here are two of my note cards.

Writer's Term

Note Card

A **note card,** usually an index card, should include the topic, information about the topic (either summarized or directly quoted), and the source of the information. Use one note card for each piece of information.

> **Regional Food in India—South India**
>
> source: Voros, Sharon. "Fare of the Country: The Vegetarian Snacks of South India."
> http://query.nytimes.com
>
> foods made from rice:
> "Idlis, which resemble spongy dumplings, are always served in pairs. Dosas are crepelike pancakes served neatly rolled."

> **Regional Food in India—Introduction**
>
> source: Kanitkar, V.P. Indian Food and Drink/ New York: Bookwright Press, 1987.
>
> Religion and climate are two things that determine food habits in each region.

Practice!

Now it's your turn. Choose a topic and look it up in the encyclopedia. Narrow the topic. Then check two more sources and start making note cards.

Prewriting

(Student pages 258–259)

Review Student page 258 with the students. Remind students that when they first met Justin, they learned about his interests and hobbies and discussed how these would influence the topics he chose to write about. In this case, he is turning his love for Indian food into a topic for a research report. As Justin has, students should focus on a topic that interests them. Note that students may also have to target something specific within their chosen topic, as Justin has.

Look at Justin's notes on Student page 259 with your students. Point out that Justin used note cards to jot down specific information for his report, and he wrote down the source of the information so that he could cite it in his report.

WORK with a PARTNER Encourage students to work with partners to come up with ideas for their research reports. Once a student has come up with a general topic, have the student work with another to brainstorm specific research report ideas based on this topic.

Differentiating Instruction

Support You may want to point out to students that not all of the information they present in their research reports needs to be credited. Note that writers' opinions and widely known facts don't need to be cited. Have your students read the following sentences. Then ask them which sentences would likely need to include a source if they were used in a research report.

1. *Indian food is delicious.* **does not need source**
2. *India is a country in South Asia.* **does not need source**
3. *India has an estimated population of 1.1 billion, making it the second most populous country in the world, behind China.* **needs source**

More Practice!

For more practice with these writing strategies, you may wish to have students use the Strategy Practice Book. See the appendix for annotated Strategy Practice Book pages.

Writing a Research Report

Prewriting Organize Ideas

Information/Organization
The report is well organized with at least one or two paragraphs about each main point.

Writing Strategy
Make an Outline to organize my notes.

The best way to organize my report is to organize my notes, right? I considered several different graphic organizers and decided to use an Outline to organize the body of my report. That way, I can put details under the main points. Then I'll write one or two paragraphs about each main point and its details. I'll write the introduction and conclusion of my report later.

To get started, I made a separate pile of note cards for each main point. Then I wrote the Outline you see on the next page.

Writer's Term

Outline
An **Outline** organizes notes by main points and supporting details. Each main point has a Roman numeral. The supporting details under each main point have capital letters. Any information listed under a supporting detail gets a number.

Outline

Regional Food in India

I. Regional foods are determined by many things.
   A. One main influence is religion.
      1. Most people are vegetarian Hindus.
      2. Immigrants from other religions who eat meat influence the Hindu diet.
   B. India's many different climates also affect food production.
II. The North has a strong Muslim influence.
   A. Muslims live in the North.
      1. They eat lamb, chicken, beef and fish.
      2. Many do not eat pork.
   B. Dates, nuts, and milk are used in sweets (desserts).
   C. Hindu bread and vegetarian dishes are also common.
III. Food in the South has a more traditional Hindu style.
   A. Rice is cooked in many ways.
   B. Two popular dishes are dosas and idlis.
   C. Vegetables served with rice include soupy dishes made from peas or beans.
IV. Coastal Indian food has many influences.
   A. Fish dishes are common and varied.
   B. They include carp with chilies, prawns with mustard seed, and fish curry.
   C. Some foods are made with coconut.

Practice!

Now it's your turn. Look through your note cards. Then organize your notes into an Outline.

Reflect
How did I do? Are my main points and supporting details well organized?

Prewriting
(Student pages 260–261)

Explain that a graphic organizer, such as an Outline, is one way to organize information in preparation for writing.

Review the definition of Outline in the Writer's Term box on Student page 260. Note that an Outline helps students group and organize related information. It can help them determine where to put the supporting details they gather. In addition, they can judge how many supporting details to include for each major point in their report. Direct your students' attention to Justin's outline. Discuss how it is organized by main points and supporting details.

Differentiating Instruction

Support To help students understand how to create an Outline, demonstrate the structure of an outline on the board. Start with the main topic as the title. Then, for Roman Numerals I, II, and III, write down "Main Point." For the letters that follow, write "Supporting detail for Main Point." Finally, under each letter, write the numbers 1 and 2. Next to each number, write "Additional information on supporting detail." Have students use this model as they develop outlines for their reports.

Writing a Research Report

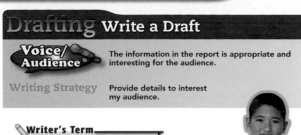

Drafting — Write a Draft

Voice/Audience The information in the report is appropriate and interesting for the audience.

Writing Strategy Provide details to interest my audience.

Writer's Term_____

Body
The **body** is the main part of your report. The body comes between the introduction and the conclusion and develops your main points.

Now I'll write one or two paragraphs for each point in my Outline. This will be the body of my report. I'll make sure there's plenty of good information to interest my audience. Later, I'll add an introduction and a strong conclusion. I'll also watch out for subject-verb agreement. Look at the start of my draft on the next page.

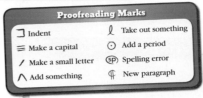

Proofreading Marks

⌐ Indent ℓ Take out something
≡ Make a capital ⊙ Add a period
/ Make a small letter SP Spelling error
∧ Add something ⁋ New paragraph

[DRAFT]

The foods people eat in each region of India are determined by many things. Religion is a big thing. **[interesting detail]** In India, 80 percent of the population is hindu, and strict hindus are vegetarians and do not eat meat. Immigrants whom practice other religions have come to India. Many of these people do eat meat. They have influenced the traditional hindu diet in some places. **[interesting detail]** Another big thing is climate. The type of food production of a region is affected by the climate there. For example, rice is grown mostly in the tropical south and the rainy northeast, and wheat is an important crop in the dry northern plains. **[interesting detail]** The North has a strong muslim influence. Muslims eat lamb, chicken, **[correct subject verb agreement]** beef, and fish but not pork. One favorite dish is lamb kebab. Lamb kebab is pieces of mildly spiced meat roasted on skewers. Another favorite is tandoori chicken, spiced chicken cooked in a clay oven. Dates, nuts, and milk are in many deserts called milk sweets. The milk comes from water buffalos. They are the main source of milk in India. Kheer is a milk sweet similar to rice pudding.

Practice!

Now it's your turn. Write a draft using your Outline as a guide. Be sure to write plenty of interesting details for your audience.

Reflect
What do you think? Will my details hold the reader's interest?

Drafting
(Student pages 262–263)

Review what it means to write a draft. Point out that a draft is a temporary form of writing that will be corrected later. Have a student read aloud Justin's words on Student page 262.

Next, read the definition of *body* from the Writer's Term box. Have students identify the main points in the body of Justin's report on Student page 263. Explain that some main points require two or more paragraphs because they include several supporting details.

Ask students to look for the supporting details from Justin's Outline within the draft on Student page 263.

Ask students whether they see any errors, such as spelling or capitalization mistakes, in Justin's draft. Note that Justin is not worried about these mistakes at this point because he knows he will have the chance to go back and edit the report later. Instead, he is more concerned about getting the details from his Outline into his report.

Writing Across the Curriculum

Geography Researching and writing a research report will enable students to explore other subjects they may be studying. In Justin's case, he is uncovering information that he might also learn about when studying geography. Challenge students to learn about a culture in another country, particularly the types of food they eat. Have students research why certain foods, such as rice, fish, or even insects, are prevalent in some countries and not in others. What kinds of climates and geographic locations lend themselves to those foods? How has the culture in a particular country evolved around that food? Suggest students start at http://www.nationalgeographic.com.

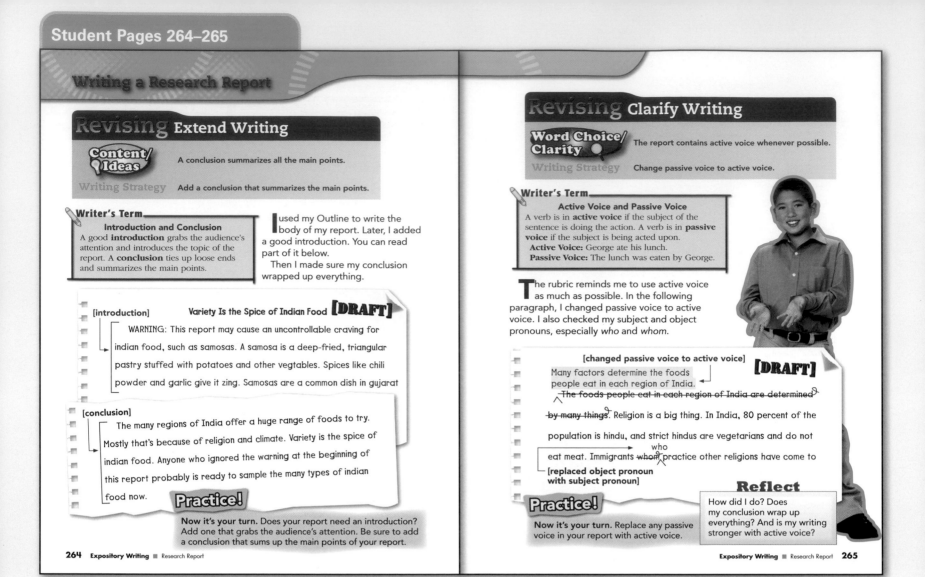

Writing a Research Report

Revising Extend Writing

Content/Ideas

A conclusion summarizes all the main points.

Writing Strategy

Add a conclusion that summarizes the main points.

Writer's Term

Introduction and Conclusion
A good **introduction** grabs the audience's attention and introduces the topic of the report. A **conclusion** ties up loose ends and summarizes the main points.

I used my Outline to write the body of my report. Later, I added a good introduction. You can read part of it below.
Then I made sure my conclusion wrapped up everything.

[introduction]   Variety Is the Spice of Indian Food **[DRAFT]**

WARNING: This report may cause an uncontrollable craving for indian food, such as samosas. A samosa is a deep-fried, triangular pastry stuffed with potatoes and other vegtables. Spices like chili powder and garlic give it zing. Samosas are a common dish in gujarat

[conclusion]

The many regions of India offer a huge range of foods to try. Mostly that's because of religion and climate. Variety is the spice of indian food. Anyone who ignored the warning at the beginning of this report probably is ready to sample the many types of indian food now.

Practice!

Now it's your turn. Does your report need an introduction? Add one that grabs the audience's attention. Be sure to add a conclusion that sums up the main points of your report.

264 Expository Writing ■ Research Report

Revising Clarify Writing

Word Choice/Clarity

The report contains active voice whenever possible.

Writing Strategy

Change passive voice to active voice.

Writer's Term

Active Voice and Passive Voice
A verb is in **active voice** if the subject of the sentence is doing the action. A verb is in **passive voice** if the subject is being acted upon.
Active Voice: George ate his lunch.
Passive Voice: The lunch was eaten by George.

The rubric reminds me to use active voice as much as possible. In the following paragraph, I changed passive voice to active voice. I also checked my subject and object pronouns, especially *who* and *whom*.

[changed passive voice to active voice]   **[DRAFT]**

Many factors determine the foods people eat in each region of India. ~~The foods people eat in each region of India are determined by many things.~~ Religion is a big thing. In India, 80 percent of the population is hindu, and strict hindus are vegetarians and do not eat meat. Immigrants ~~whom~~ who practice other religions have come to

[replaced object pronoun with subject pronoun]

Practice!

Now it's your turn. Replace any passive voice in your report with active voice.

Reflect

How did I do? Does my conclusion wrap up everything? And is my writing stronger with active voice?

Expository Writing ■ Research Report **265**

Revising

(Student pages 264–265)

Point out that Justin did not write an introduction or a conclusion in his draft. Instead, as he notes on Student page 264, he will use the information from the body of his report to create his introduction and to write a conclusion that summarizes the main points. Read Justin's conclusion aloud. Ask students if they feel his conclusion wraps things up by summarizing the main points.

Next, review with your students the information on Student page 265. Read the definitions of active voice and passive voice in the Writer's Term box. Read the first line from Justin's draft on this page before it was corrected. Point out that the phrase "are determined by" is a clue that the sentence was written in passive voice, as "the foods people eat in each region of India" are being acted upon by "many things." Next, read how Justin changed his sentence to active voice. Explain that now the subject of the sentence is doing the action. Note that the sentence is clearer in active voice.

Instruct students to go through their own stories to find places where they can change passive voice into active voice.

Differentiating Instruction

Enrichment Challenge students to try using unusual introductions in their reports, just as Justin has done. Have them read the introductions of ten articles in various magazines to get ideas. Suggest that they try a narrative or a descriptive introduction.

Writing a Research Report

Editing — Check Sentences

Sentence Fluency

Sentences are lively and vary in length and structure.

Writing Strategy Use a variety of lively, energetic sentences.

According to the rubric, I should use lively sentences that vary in length and structure. When I reread this section of my report, I realized I wasn't doing that at all. Many of my sentences are the same length, and they follow the same pattern. Look at how I rewrote this part of my report to spice up the sentences!

[DRAFT]

[changed sentences for variety]

Coastal indian food has many influences. ~~People on the coast of~~
Naturally, people there
~~indic~~ live near rivers as well as the bay of Bengal
eat a lot of fish. The residents of west Bengal ~~eat fish from the~~
enjoy
~~rivers, too.~~ They ~~like~~ Another favorite Bengali recipe is
carp cooked with chilies. ~~They also like~~ prawns,
which are large shrimp, spiced with mustard seeds.

[changed sentences for variety]

Practice!

Now it's your turn. Do a lot of your sentences sound alike? Are too many of them a similar length? Vary your sentences, and make your writing more lively!

Editing — Proofread Writing

Grammar/Mechanics

Spelling, punctuation, and capitalization, including proper nouns and proper adjectives, are correct.

Writing Strategy Make sure proper nouns and proper adjectives are capitalized correctly.

Writer's Term

Proper Nouns and Proper Adjectives
Proper nouns name a specific person, place, thing, or idea. **Proper adjectives** are formed from proper nouns.

Now I'll check my spelling, grammar, and punctuation. I'll make sure I capitalized and punctuated proper nouns and proper adjectives correctly.

[capitalized proper noun]   [capitalized proper adjective]   **[DRAFT]**

Food in the south has a more traditional hindu style. Rice is used all the time, and it's cooked in many different ways. VoPo (Hemant) Kanitkar, author of Indian Food and Drink, says "Rice grains simply boiled may appear to us to be a poor meal, but different processes like grinding, pounding, steaming, and frying transform rice and other cereals into tasty dishes."

[capitalized proper initials]

Practice!

Now it's your turn. Edit your draft for spelling, punctuation, and capitalization. Be sure to check proper nouns and proper adjectives.

Grammar/Mechanics

For more practice with proper nouns and proper adjectives, use the exercises on the next two pages.

Reflect

I replaced dull sentences with lively, energetic sentences and edited my draft for errors. How did I do?

Editing

(Student pages 266–267)

Ask a student to read Justin's words on Student page 266. Then read Justin's draft on Student page 266 before his edits. Point out that in his draft, Justin uses sentences that begin with a subject and end with a preposition. He also uses the word "like" in two sentences. Note that reading a report that contained all the same types of sentences and repeated the same words throughout would be very dull for the reader. Just as Justin has done, writers can enliven their writing by changing the length and structure of sentences.

Read Justin's revised paragraph on Student page 266. Ask if students feel that the paragraph reads better now that the sentences have been revised.

Have a student read the definitions of proper nouns and proper adjectives from the Writer's Term box on Student page 267. Ask students to give examples of each. Note how Justin had to capitalize a proper noun and a proper adjective in his report. If students are having trouble with proper nouns and proper adjectives, you may wish to have them complete the Grammar/Mechanics Practice! on Student pages 268–269.

At this point, students should also read through their research reports to be sure that there are no grammatical or spelling mistakes. Have them check for correct spelling and punctuation. Remind students that they should always proofread their reports.

WORK with a PARTNER Students may find it helpful to have another person read through their reports to check for grammar, spelling, punctuation, and capitalization mistakes. Suggest that students swap their papers with another student and edit each other's reports.

Proper Nouns and Proper Adjectives

KNOW the RULE

1. Capitalize **proper nouns**.
   Example: My family immigrated to the **United States** from **India**.
2. Capitalize **proper adjectives**.
   Example: Have you ever tasted **Indian** food?
3. Capitalize **titles of respect** when they are used before a person's name.
   Example: Mr. Raj Chopra gave a presentation to our class.
4. Capitalize **proper abbreviations** (words in addresses such as *street* and *avenue*, days, months, and parts of business names in informal notes). End the abbreviations with a period.
   Example: Sakthi's address is 247 Fourteenth **St.**
5. Capitalize an **initial** when it replaces the name of a person or place. Follow the initial with a period.
   Example: Our new neighbor's name is **P. R.** Phalke.

Practice the Rule

Number a separate sheet of paper 1–5. Read each sentence below. Find the error or errors in proper nouns or proper adjectives and write that part of the sentence correctly on your paper. Add the number of the rule you followed.

1. The indian film industry is over 100 years old.
2. The French Lumière brothers showed six short silent films at a bombay hotel in 1886.
3. Shortly afterwards, Hiralal Sen and H S. Bhatavdekar started making films.
4. india's first talkie, *Alam Ara*, was released in march 1931.
5. Imperial Film Co was the producer of that film.

Apply the Rule

Read the following research report. Rewrite it on your paper, correcting any errors in the use of proper nouns or proper adjectives.

New Neighbors

The number of asian Indians in the United states is growing at a rapid pace. According to the Us census Bureau, the indian american population doubled between 1990 and 2000. And the growth shows no sign of slowing down today!

This population increase is part of a general trend for asian Americans, who are the fastest growing group in the country. The numbers of vietnamese Americans, Chinese americans, filipino americans, and korean Americans have all increased significantly. But the Indian american population has shown the most growth—and continues to outpace other asian american groups. Some experts predict there will be 4.5 million asian Indians in the U S by 2010.

Why do so many Asian indians come here? Mr P khandhar, who works for the asian American federation in new york, says, "One obvious factor for the growth in the Indian American community is the importing of the hi-tech workers." mr. a Bhatt of the Indo-American Commerce trade Council agrees. "I think the numbers reflect the need of the united States for highly skilled workers more than anything else."

(Student pages 268–269)

Proper Nouns and Proper Adjectives

Read through the Know the Rule section on Student page 268. Explain that students should capitalize proper nouns and proper adjectives in their writing.

Write the following on the board: *The tourists visited Mayan ruins.*
Ask students to identify the proper adjective in this sentence. **Mayan**

Write the following on the board: *There are ruins to explore outside of Cancun.*
Ask students to identify the proper noun in the sentence. **Cancun**

Point out that in each of these cases, the proper noun or proper adjective is capitalized.

 For more practice with grammar/mechanics skills, see Zaner-Bloser's *G.U.M.* materials.

Answers for Practice the Rule

1. Indian, rule 2
2. Bombay, rule 2
3. H.S., rule 5
4. Indias, rule 1
5. Co., rule 4

Answers for Apply the Rule

The number of Asian Indians in the United States is growing at a rapid pace. According to the U.S. Census Bureau, the Indian American population doubled between 1990 and 2000. And the growth shows no sign of slowing down today!

This population increase is part of a general trend for Asian Americans, who are the fastest growing group in the country. The numbers of Vietnamese Americans, Chinese Americans, Filipino Americans, and Korean Americans have all increased significantly. But the Indian American population has shown the most growth—and continues to outpace other Asian American groups. Some experts predict there will be 4.5 million Asian Indians in the U.S. by 2010.

Why do so many Asian Indians come here? Mr. P. Khandhar, who works for the Asian American Federation in New York, says, "One obvious factor for the growth in the Indian American community is the importing of hi-tech workers." Mr. A. Bhatt of the Indo-American Commerce Trade Council agrees. "I think the numbers reflect the need of the United States for highly skilled workers more than anything else."

Writing a Research Report

Publishing · Share Writing

Include my written report as part of a multimedia presentation to the class.

Publishing with multimedia doesn't mean you have to use a computer, although I plan to. It just means that you present information in more than one way. For example, you could use pictures and sound.

When I give my presentation, I'm going to offer samples of Indian food and play some Indian music in the background. I'm also going to hand out maps showing the regions of India. Before I do all that, I want to check over my report one more time. I'll use this checklist to help me make sure my report is ready for publication.

My Checklist

✓ The report is focused and well organized.

✓ I've included plenty of details to make the report interesting.

✓ A strong conclusion summarizes all the main ideas.

✓ I used active voice and varied my sentences to make my writing energetic.

✓ Spelling, capitalization, and punctuation are all correct. I've used proper nouns and proper adjectives correctly.

Practice!

Now it's your turn. Check your research report against your own checklist. Then make a final draft to publish.

Variety Is the Spice of Indian Food

By Justin

WARNING: This report may cause an uncontrollable craving for Indian food, such as samosas. A samosa is a deep-fried, triangular pastry stuffed with potatoes and other vegetables. Spices like chili powder and garlic give it zing. Samosas are a common dish in Gujarat, one of India's many regions. People eat different types of foods in different regions of India.

Many factors determine the foods people eat in each region of India. Religion is a major factor. In India, 80 percent of the population is Hindu. Strict Hindus are vegetarians and do not eat meat. Over the centuries, immigrants who practice other religions have come to India. Many of these people do eat meat. They have influenced the traditional Hindu diet in some places.

Another major factor is climate. The climate of a region affects the food production there. For example, people grow rice mostly in the tropical South and the rainy Northeast. Wheat is an important crop in the dry northern plains.

Publishing

(Student pages 270–271)

Review Student page 270 with students. Note that before Justin submits his multimedia presentation to the class, he once again reviews his draft. This time, he uses a checklist based on the rubric to ensure that he has not missed anything.

Ask students what they think about Justin's idea for publishing his report. How will some of his ideas make his report more interesting to the class? **Possible responses: The music and food will engage the students. Maps of the region will help students understand the information he presents in his report about the different regions' cuisines.**

Writing a Research Report

The North has a strong Muslim influence. Muslims eat lamb, chicken, beef, and fish, but not pork. One favorite dish is lamb kebab. Lamb kebab is pieces of mildly spiced meat roasted on skewers. Another favorite is tandoori chicken, spiced chicken cooked in a clay oven. Dates, nuts, and milk are in many desserts called milk sweets. The milk comes from water buffalo. They are the main source of milk in India. Kheer is a milk sweet similar to rice pudding.

Bread and vegetarian dishes from the Hindu tradition are also common in the North. Most breads don't have any yeast, so they don't rise. Parathas are flat cakes of wheat dough baked on a hot stone and then pan-fried. Purees are flat circles of wheat dough deep-fried in oil until they puff up like balloons. A dish of spiced rice and vegetables called pullao is also popular. In the North, the pullao vegetables are usually cauliflower and peas.

Food in the South has a more traditional Hindu style. Rice is prepared in many ways. V. P. (Hemant) Kanitkar, author of *Indian Food and Drink,* says, "Rice grains simply boiled may appear to us to be a poor meal, but different processes like grinding, pounding, steaming, and frying transform rice and other cereals into tasty dishes."

Two popular South Indian foods are made from rice. Dosas are thin rice-flour pancakes. Idlis are steamed rice dumplings. Vegetables served with rice include dal, which is a soupy dish made from split peas or beans.

Coastal Indian food has many influences. Naturally, people there eat a lot of fish. The residents of West Bengal live near rivers as well as the Bay of Bengal. They enjoy carp cooked with chilies. Another favorite Bengali recipe is prawns. These large shrimp are spiced with mustard seeds.

Goa has a strong Portuguese influence. Its fish curries are well known. A curry is a general term for a dish cooked with crushed spices and turmeric. Turmeric is an herb that adds a yellow color. Coconuts are plentiful in Kerala. Coconut milk is used in fish, rice, and vegetable curries.

Because of the influence of religion and climate, the many regions of India offer a huge range of foods. Variety is the spice of Indian food. Anyone who ignored the warning at the beginning of this report will now probably be ready to sample the many types of Indian food.

Works Consulted
"India." *The World Book Encyclopedia.* 2007 ed.
Kanitkar, V.P. (Hemant). *Indian Food and Drink.* New York: The Bookwright Press, 1987.
Voros, Sharon. "Fare of the Country; The Vegetarian Snacks of South India." *New York Times on the Web* 15 July 1990. 6 Dec. 2006 <http://query.nytimes.com/gst/fullpage.html?sec=travel&res=9C0CE4DC163EF936A2 5754C0A966958260>

Reflect
What do you think? Did I use all the traits of a good research report in my writing? Check it against the rubric. Don't forget to use the rubric to check your own research report.

TiPS for the Writing Classroom

Week-Long Due Dates and Student Input

by Ken Stewart, *Master Teacher*

By allowing your students the flexibility of turning in major writing assignments over a range of due dates, you may feel that you are creating more work for yourself by re-grading papers turned in early. However, you are really not grading the entire piece over. Ask the students to return the graded draft(s) with their corrected final copy. Then you need only check the sections you had marked for improvement on the draft.

Ways to Publish a
Research Report

Maybe your research report would make a good multimedia presentation for your class, too. Can you think of some different ways to publish your report? Here are my ideas.

✔ Research and find a Web site that fits your topic. Submit your report for publication.

✔ Create a display in the library, the office, or a display case in your school. Include your report and other materials that go along with the topic, such as maps, artifacts, photos, or models.

✔ If you don't already have a writing portfolio, use this report to start one.

✔ Read your report to your family to spice up a boring trip in the car.

✔ Let friends who are not in your class read the report and give you their reactions.

Writing Across the Content Areas
Research Report

You can write a report in any subject. What topics would you like to research? Do any of the ideas below appeal to you?

Science
- Choose an interesting chapter from your science book. Narrow the subject of the chapter until you have a clearly defined topic for writing a research report.
- Write a research report about fascinating natural phenomena, such as tornados, tidal waves, hurricanes, or volcanic eruptions.

Language Arts
- Use references to research the life of your favorite author. Take notes, make an outline, and write a research report about the person.
- After you have read a work of historical fiction, write a report about a real event, person, or time period from the book.

Social Studies
- What do you think is our country's biggest problem? Research the problem and write a report about it.
- Write a research report about a famous American. Combine it with reports by your classmates to make a book.

Ways to Publish
(Student page 274)

Read through the suggestions on Student page 274 for publishing a research report. As a class, you may wish to use one or more of these suggestions to publish the students' reports. For instance, you may want to create a poster board display or a showcase for each student's research report to share other material that relates to the topic. Display the reports in the classroom or in the school library. Challenge students to identify ways to publish their research reports, and suggest that they publish their reports in one of the ways suggested on this page or another way they feel would be appropriate.

Writing Across the Content Areas
(Student page 275)

Remind students that writing is not just for English or language arts class. Encourage students to think about how to write a research report on another subject they are studying, using the ideas on Student page 275 as inspiration. Students may wish to speak with other teachers for more ideas on writing in their content areas.

Expository Test Writing

In this chapter, students will learn about expository test writing. First, they will review the parts of a writing prompt—the setup, task, and scoring guide—and see how the writing prompt relates to the writing traits they have been studying throughout the unit. Students will then use the scoring guide to assess a model writing sample.

Students will join Justin, the student guide, as he completes the steps involved in writing for a writing test, including planning one's time, prewriting, drafting, revising, and editing.

You may wish to relate each of the steps in the test writing process to steps they have used in other chapters in this unit. Point out that many of the steps and strategies that they have learned in earlier chapters can be applied to writing tests as well.

You may wish to send to families the School-Home Connection Letter for this chapter, located at the end of this unit in the Teacher Edition.

Writing Traits in the Scoring Guide

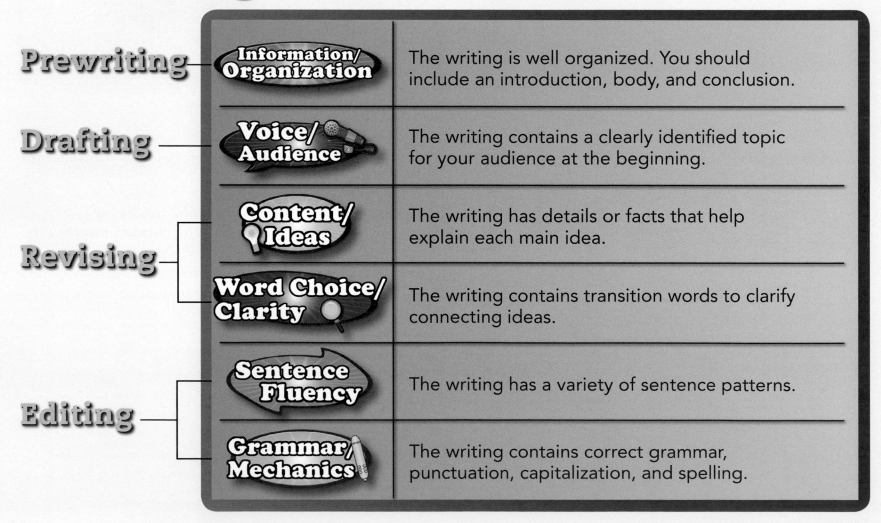

	Information/Organization	The writing is well organized. You should include an introduction, body, and conclusion.
Prewriting		
Drafting	Voice/Audience	The writing contains a clearly identified topic for your audience at the beginning.
Revising	Content/Ideas	The writing has details or facts that help explain each main idea.
	Word Choice/Clarity	The writing contains transition words to clarify connecting ideas.
Editing	Sentence Fluency	The writing has a variety of sentence patterns.
	Grammar/Mechanics	The writing contains correct grammar, punctuation, capitalization, and spelling.

Expository Test Writing Time Management

WEEK 1

	Day 1	Day 2	Day 3	Day 4	Day 5
Learning Objectives	Students will: • learn the components of a writing prompt.	Students will: • recognize the relationship of the scoring guide to the rubric and the six traits of writing. • read a model writing test response.	Students will: • apply the scoring guide to a model test response.	Students will: • apply the scoring guide to a model test response.	Students will: • learn how to budget their time during a writing test.
Activities	• Discuss the components of a writing prompt (Student pages 276–277).	• Read and discuss the scoring guide chart (Student page 278). • Read the model (Student page 279).	• Read and discuss **Using the Scoring Guide to Study the Model** (Student pages 280–281).	• Read and discuss **Using the Scoring Guide to Study the Model** (Student page 282).	• Read and discuss **Planning My Time** (Student page 283).

WEEK 2

	Day 1	Day 2	Day 3	Day 4	Day 5
Learning Objectives	Students will: • learn to read and understand a writing test prompt for test writing. • apply the six traits of writing to the writing prompt.	Students will: • learn how to respond to the task in the writing prompt.	Students will: • learn how to choose a graphic organizer for the writing prompt.	Students will: • learn how to check the graphic organizer against the scoring guide.	Students will: • use the graphic organizer to begin a writing test response report.
Activities	• Read and discuss **Prewriting: Study the Writing Prompt** (Student pages 284–285).	• Read and discuss **Prewriting: Gather Information** (Student page 286).	• Read and discuss **Prewriting: Organize Ideas** (Student page 287).	• Read and discuss **Prewriting: Check the Scoring Guide** (Student pages 288–289).	• Read and discuss **Drafting: Write a Draft** (Student pages 290–291).

WEEK 3

	Day 1	Day 2	Day 3	Day 4	Day 5
Learning Objectives	Students will: • add details or facts that help explain the main idea in their writing test response reports.	Students will: • use transition words to clarify connecting ideas in their writing test response reports.	Students will: • include a variety of sentence patterns in their writing test response reports.	Students will: • edit their writing test response for grammar and mechanics.	Students will: • review tips for writing for a test.
Activities	• Read and discuss **Revising: Extend Writing** (Student page 292).	• Read and discuss **Revising: Clarify Writing** (Student page 293).	• Read and discuss **Editing: Check Sentences** (Student page 294).	• Read and discuss **Editing: Proofread Writing** (Student pages 295–296).	• Read and discuss **Test Tips** (Student page 297).

* To complete the chapter in fewer days, teach the learning objectives and activities for two days in one day.

This planning chart, correlated to your state's writing standards, is available on-line at http://www.zaner-bloser.com/sfw.

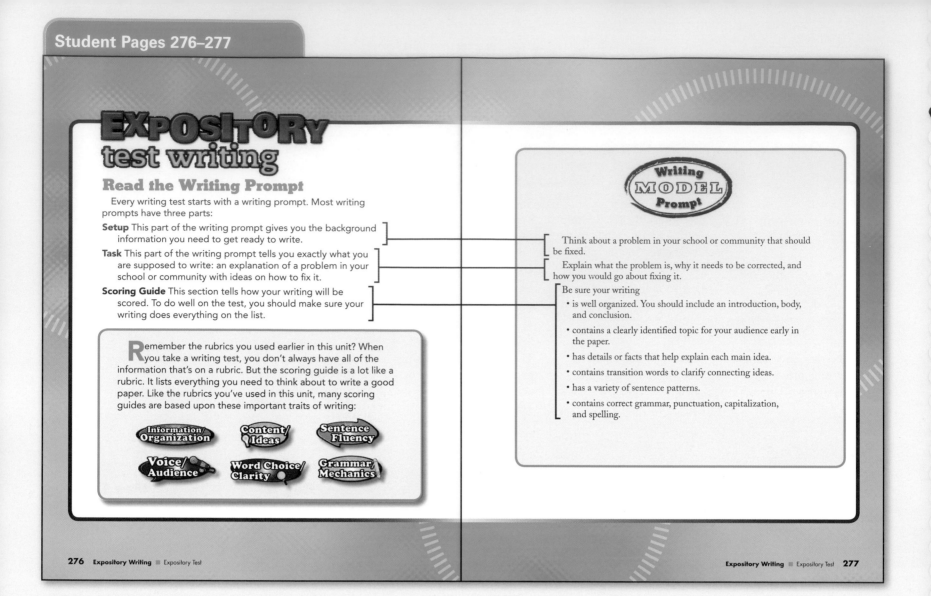

Introduce the Writing Prompt
(Student pages 276–277)

Expository Writing

Explain to students that when they are writing for a test, they will be given a writing prompt that will explain all they need to know in order to complete their tests. Read aloud the information on the writing prompt on Student page 276. Note that the setup, task, and scoring guide are probably not going to be labeled for them, but they will be able to identify these parts on their own by analyzing the writing prompt.

The first thing they will likely look for when they read their writing prompts is what exactly they are supposed to do. Note that this will be a specific instruction on what they are to do or write. Refer students to the model writing prompt on Student page 277. Tell students to ask themselves, "What am I supposed to write?" Ask a student to answer the question using the model writing prompt. **Explain a problem that should be fixed, why it needs to be corrected, and how you would go about fixing it.**

Tell students that they probably will need more information in order to write their tests. They might need some background information. This is the setup part of the writing prompt. In the case of the model writing prompt, the writer needs to think about a problem in the school or community.

Finally, test writing prompts usually tell students the elements of a good, well-written paper. This is the scoring guide section of the writing prompt, which tells students what they need to include in order to do well on the test. Ask a student to read the scoring guide section from the model writing prompt.

Differentiating Instruction

Enrichment To help students better understand the writing prompt, ask them to refer back to an earlier chapter in the expository writing unit and write one of the writing assignments from the chapter as a test writing prompt. Point out that they should use the information from the rubric as their scoring guide.

Writing Traits
in the Scoring Guide

Look back at the scoring guide in the writing prompt on page 277. Not every test prompt will include each of the writing traits, but this one does. You can use the following chart to help you better understand the connection between the scoring guide and the writing traits in the rubrics you've been using.

 **Information/Organization**
- Be sure your writing is well organized. You should include an introduction, body, and conclusion.

 **Voice/Audience**
- Be sure your writing contains a clearly identified topic for your audience at the beginning.

Content/Ideas
- Be sure your writing has details or facts that help explain each main idea.

Word Choice/Clarity
- Be sure your writing contains transition words to clarify connecting ideas.

Sentence Fluency
- Be sure your writing has a variety of sentence patterns.

Grammar/Mechanics
- Be sure your writing contains correct grammar, punctuation, capitalization, and spelling.

Look at Bonnie Campbell's essay on the next page. Did she follow the scoring guide?

278 **Expository Writing** ■ Expository Test

A Place for Us
by Bonnie Campbell

A big problem in our community is that many middle-school students have nowhere to go after school. I would like to explain my solution to this problem.

There are many kids in our town who would like to spend time together after school. I'm not talking about kids who play sports. I'm concerned about a whole group of other kids like me who have nothing to do after school. Our parents don't like us to get together at our homes when no adults are there, so where can we go?

There is no place for us to hang out without getting in trouble. If we go to the diner for a snack, we can't stay there very long. The servers complain that we don't spend enough money to take up the tables. If we go to the library, people complain that we are too noisy. If we get together outside the shops downtown, sometimes adults tell us to move. They say we're blocking the sidewalk.

Now that I've explained the problem, I'd like to explain my solution to it. There is an empty store on Main Street. If we could make this a drop-in center, it would keep students off the street. We could play table tennis and air hockey. There could also be quiet areas for kids to do their homework. In addition, it would be great if we had a little kitchen or some machines with snacks. I also know kids would like it if we could listen to music there and maybe watch some videos.

This way, kids would not have to go home to empty houses or apartments after school. They would not be on the street. Kids with no place else to go would not be bored and would stay out of trouble. There could be one or two adults at the center to make sure everyone behaves. We kids could even help out. We could keep the place clean and do other jobs like making snacks. We could help pay for the center by having fundraisers, such as car washes or bake sales.

With a special place for kids to go after school, everybody wins! Kids stay busy and have fun, and parents don't have to worry about them.

Expository Writing ■ Expository Test 279

Writing Traits in the Scoring Guide
(Student pages 278–279)

Tell students that a well-written test paper is much the same as a well-written essay or report. It will be organized, take into consideration the audience, include well-thought-out ideas and content, be clear to read, flow smoothly, and contain correct grammar and mechanics. Even if attention to all of these traits is not specifically mentioned in the scoring guide, students will still want to think about the lessons they have learned about expository writing throughout the unit.

Ask a student volunteer to read the traits in the scoring guide on Student page 278. Note that the scoring guide in this instance clearly identifies attention to each of the six writing traits they have been studying. The information in the scoring guide will guide students as they go through the test writing process. Remind students to think about each of the traits listed in the scoring guide as they write their test papers.

Read the Model:
Writing Prompt Response

Note that students will be studying the strategies for expository test writing in this chapter. A good expository writing test contains the traits listed in the scoring guide. Ask them to look for these traits as they read the model writing prompt response, "A Place for Us."

Differentiating Instruction

English-Language Learners During a test, students may have trouble understanding directions. Read the following line aloud: *Be sure your writing contains transition words to clarify connecting ideas.* Ask students what this means. **Possible response: Be sure that connecting ideas make sense.** Then explain that if transition words can make connecting ideas make sense, they must serve to bridge sentences and ideas together. Tell students that the teacher may be able to clarify directions for them if they ask. And they should also be prepared to find other ways to determine meanings while taking a test, such as looking at the context of words in the sentence.

Using the Scoring Guide to Study the Model

Let's use the scoring guide to check Bonnie's writing test, "A Place for Us." How well does her explanation meet each of the six writing traits?

 Information/Organization
• The writing is well organized. The writer includes an introduction, body, and conclusion.

A big problem in our community is that many middle-school students have nowhere to go after school. I would like to explain my solution to this problem.

In the body, Bonnie explains the problem, offers a solution, and then includes an explanation of the solution.
Finally, she uses her conclusion to wrap up all of her ideas.

With a special place for kids to go after school, everybody wins! Kids stay busy and have fun, and parents don't have to worry about them.

 **Voice/Audience**
• The writing contains a clearly identified topic for the audience at the beginning.

In the lead paragraph, Bonnie explains the problem. She also says that she has an idea for fixing it. This will be the topic of her explanation.

A big problem in our community is that many middle-school students have nowhere to go after school. I would like to explain my solution to this problem.

 Content/Ideas
• The writing has details or facts that help explain each main idea.

Bonnie expands her ideas by including details about how kids could help out at the center. These details helped me understand what she meant.

We kids could even help out. We could keep the place clean and do other jobs like making snacks. We could help pay for the center by having fundraisers, such as car washes or bake sales.

 **Word Choice/Clarity**
• The writing contains transition words to clarify connecting ideas.

Transition words help readers follow a writer's ideas. Can you find the transition words Bonnie used in this part of her explanation?

There could also be quiet areas for kids to do their homework. In addition, it would be great if we had a little kitchen or some machines with snacks. I also know kids would like it if we could listen to music there and maybe watch some videos.

Using the Scoring Guide to Study the Model

(Student pages 280–282)

Note that like a rubric, the scoring guide is used to determine how well a test was written. Students should understand that although scoring guides in writing prompts do not include the criteria for different levels of accomplishment, they do provide guidance in some or all of the key areas of assessment: Information/Organization, Voice/Audience, Content/Ideas, Word Choice/Clarity, Sentence Fluency, and Grammar/Mechanics.

Stress the importance of using a scoring guide when students are writing for a test.

Have students read each of the scoring guide traits on Student pages 280–282. Then for each of the traits, look at and discuss the ways that "A Place for Us" meets the traits listed in the scoring guide. Ask students whether they agree with Justin's assessment of the story for each of the traits in the scoring guide and, if possible, find other examples for each writing trait.

Differentiating Instruction

Support To help students better understand how to recognize and use a clearly identified topic at the beginning of a report, ask them to look at the editorial section of a newspaper. Have them select an editorial to bring to class and identify the topic at the start of the editorial. Ask students to read the topics aloud in class and note where in the editorial the topic is stated.

Using the Scoring Guide to Study the Model

Sentence Fluency
- The writing has a variety of sentence patterns.

Bonnie uses a variety of sentence patterns. She begins by stating that there's no place to go, and then she follows up with several "if" clauses that further explain her original statement. The clauses connect one sentence to the next, which makes the writing flow.

There is no place for us to hang out without getting in trouble. If we go to the diner for a snack, we can't stay there very long. The servers complain that we don't spend enough money to take up the tables. If we go to the library, people complain that we are too noisy. If we get together outside the shops downtown, sometimes adults tell us to move. They say we're blocking the sidewalk.

Grammar/Mechanics
- The writing contains correct grammar, punctuation, capitalization, and spelling.

As far as I can tell, Bonnie didn't make any mistakes in capitalization, punctuation, spelling, or grammar. But don't forget to check for mistakes in your own work. For example, if you know you often misspell words, you should pay close attention to spelling. Editing for grammar and mechanics at every step of the writing process will help you to avoid errors on your final test!

282 Expository Writing ■ Expository Test

Planning My Time

Before giving us a writing test prompt, my teacher tells us how much time we'll have to complete the test. Since I'm already familiar with the writing process, I can think about how much total time I need and then divide it up into the different parts of the writing process. If the test takes an hour, here's how I can organize my time. Planning your time will help you, too!

Step 4: Editing 10 minutes

Step 1: Prewriting 25 minutes

Step 3: Revising 10 minutes

Step 2: Drafting 15 minutes

Expository Writing ■ Expository Test 283

Planning My Time
(Student page 283)

Students should understand the importance of organizing their time when they are planning for a test. Because they will have a limited amount of time when they write for a test, they will need to budget their time accordingly so that they can complete the test. Note that the sample time organizer on Student page 283 is a good example of how one should plan time for an hour-long test.

Ask students where they have seen each of the sections called out on the stopwatch. **Possible response: They are the steps students took when writing for other sections.** Stress that even though they are taking a test, they still need to follow the appropriate steps in the writing process, including prewriting, drafting, revising, and editing. Students should leave appropriate time for each step as they plan their time for a test.

It may be helpful to put a chart on the board to show how much time has been allotted to each step in the test writing process. Then, next to the time in minutes, indicate the amount of time as a percentage of the total time.

This may be a helpful tool for students who have more or less than an hour to write for a test.

	Time	Percentage
Prewriting	25 minutes	42 percent
Drafting	15 minutes	25 percent
Revising	10 minutes	17 percent
Editing	10 minutes	17 percent

Writing an Expository Test

Prewriting — Study the Writing Prompt

Writing Strategy — Study the writing prompt to be sure I know what to do.

Once I have my writing prompt, I study it and make sure I know exactly what I'm supposed to do. Usually a writing prompt has three parts, but the parts aren't always labeled. You should find and label the setup, task, and scoring guide on your writing prompt, just like I did on mine below. Then you can circle key words in the setup and the task that tell what kind of writing you need to do and who your audience will be. I circled my topic in blue. I also circled what kind of writing I'll be doing (an explanation) in red. The writing prompt doesn't say who the reader is, so I'll write for my teacher.

My Writing Test Prompt

Setup — Suppose you have (an opportunity to travel on a space shuttle.)

Task — Write (an essay explaining why) you would or would not want to go on a space shuttle.

Scoring Guide — Be sure your writing

• is well organized. You should include an introduction, body, and conclusion.

• contains a clearly identified topic for your audience at the beginning.

• has details or facts that help explain each main idea.

• contains transition words to clarify connecting ideas.

• has a variety of sentence patterns.

• contains correct grammar, punctuation, capitalization, and spelling.

284 **Expository Writing** ■ Expository Test

Think about how the scoring guide relates to the writing traits you've studied in the rubrics. All of the traits might not be included in every scoring guide, but you need to remember them all to write a good essay!

Information/Organization
• Be sure your writing is well organized. You should include an introduction, body, and conclusion.

I want my reader to understand my explanation from beginning to end, so organization is important!

Voice/Audience
• Be sure your writing contains a clearly identified topic for your audience at the beginning.

The topic should be included in the lead paragraph because my reader will want to know what the piece is about right away.

Content/Ideas
• Be sure your writing has details or facts that help explain each main idea.

I have to remember to fully develop my ideas with plenty of interesting details and facts.

Word Choice/Clarity
• Be sure your writing contains transition words to clarify connecting ideas.

My reader will have an easier time following my explanation if I use transition words to identify how ideas connect.

Sentence Fluency
• Be sure your writing has a variety of sentence patterns.

I can add liveliness to my writing by using different kinds of sentences. This will keep my reader interested and help make my writing flow!

Grammar/Mechanics
• Be sure your writing contains correct grammar, punctuation, capitalization, and spelling.

I should always remember to check my grammar and mechanics any time I write!

Expository Writing ■ Expository Test 285

Study the Writing Prompt
(Student pages 284–285)

Ask a student to read Justin's words on Student page 284. Point out that the first step to take when writing for a test is to read and study the writing prompt.

Ask students why they think Justin has circled key words in the writing prompt. **Possible response: to clarify what he needs to do** Note that as he brainstorms what he is going to write and jots down notes, he will be thinking more about the setup and the task than he will be about the scoring guide. Later, before he starts to write, and as he drafts, revises, and edits, he will concentrate on the traits listed in the scoring guide.

Ask a student to read the scoring guide portion of the writing prompt. Have students think about how each of the traits relate to the six key areas of assessment. Ask students to read Justin's words on Student page 285 to note how he is thinking about each of the writing traits in the scoring guide even before he begins to write his draft.

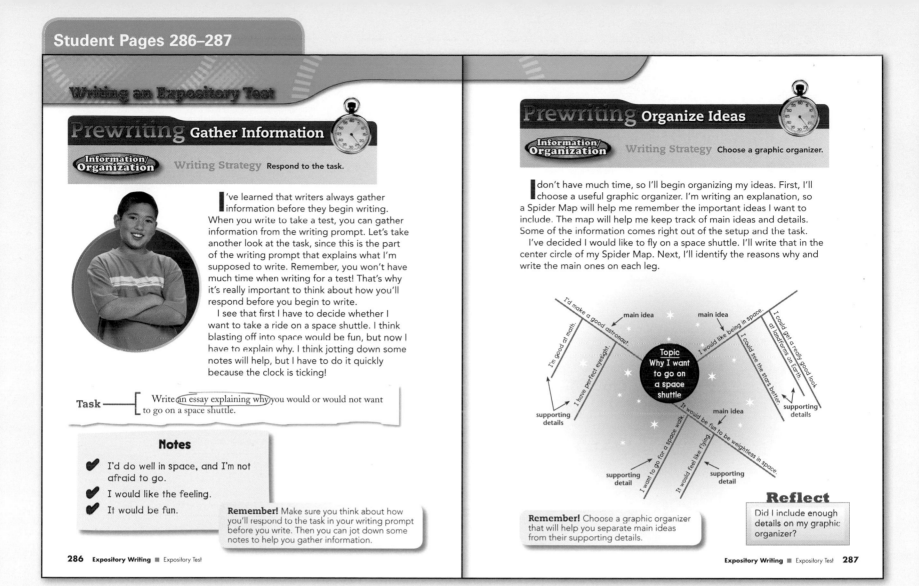

Gather Information and Organize Ideas

(Student pages 286–287)

Ask a student to read Justin's words on Student page 286. Note that Justin has to decide quickly what he is going to be writing about. Once he figures out how he is going to respond to the task, he begins to write down notes that can help him as he begins to gather information for his test.

Ask students why graphic organizers are important in writing, even when writing for a test. **Possible response: They help you organize your ideas before you start your draft.** Note that using a graphic organizer can actually help the students save time because it will ensure their essays are well-thought-out and organized before they begin their drafts.

Ask a student to read the information from Justin's Spider Map. In looking at the graphic organizer, what part of the Spider Map would Justin include in his introduction? **the information from the center, or body, of the spider** What might each of the paragraphs in the body of the essay include? **information from each of the legs**

Students should understand that during a writing test, they will not be told what kind of graphic organizer to use. They should think about the graphic organizers they are familiar with and come up with a useful graphic organizer for the type of writing they will be doing. It does not matter which graphic organizer they use, so long as it helps them organize their ideas.

Differentiating Instruction

Support To help students understand how ideas are organized in a graphic organizer, ask them to complete a Spider Map with the information in the model writing prompt response, "A Place for Us." You may wish to draw a Spider Map on the board and write *topic* in the center of it to help get students started. Note that they should find the topic of the essay in the first paragraph.

Writing an Expository Test

Prewriting Check the Scoring Guide

 Information/Organization

Writing Strategy Check my graphic organizer against the scoring guide.

In a test, you don't always get much time to revise. That makes prewriting more important than ever! So before I write, I'll check my Spider Map against the scoring guide in the writing prompt.

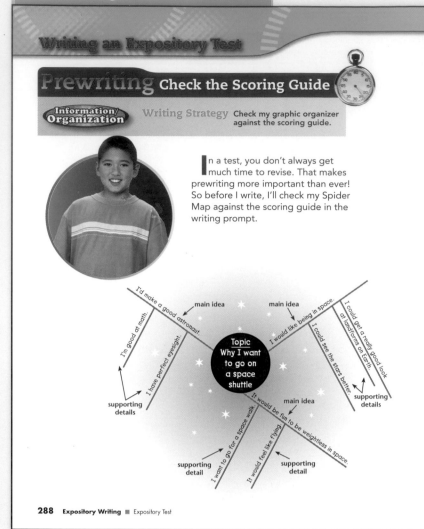

I'd make a good astronaut.

I'm good at math.

I have perfect eyesight.

main idea

main idea

I would like being in space.

I could get a really good look at landforms on Earth.

I could see the stars better

Topic Why I want to go on a space shuttle

supporting details

supporting details

main idea

It would be fun to be weightless in space.

I want to go for a space walk.

It would feel like flying.

supporting detail

supporting detail

 Information/Organization
- Be sure your writing is well organized. You should include an introduction, body, and conclusion.

I'll use the topic from my Spider Map to write an introduction and the main ideas from the legs to write the body. I'll wrap things up in my conclusion.

 Voice/Audience
- Be sure your writing contains a clearly identified topic for your audience at the beginning.

My topic is clearly labeled on my Spider Map.

 Content/Ideas
- Be sure your writing has details or facts that help explain each main idea.

I'll use the supporting details attached to each spider leg to fully develop the body of my explanation.

 Word Choice/Clarity
- Be sure your writing contains transition words to clarify connecting ideas.

My Spider Map doesn't show connecting sentences yet, but as I write, I'll remember to use transition words like *most important* and *finally*.

 Sentence Fluency
- Be sure your writing has a variety of sentence patterns.

I'll need to remember to do this when I start writing!

Grammar/Mechanics
- Be sure your writing contains correct grammar, punctuation, capitalization, and spelling.

I'll check for proper grammar and mechanics when I edit my draft.

Remember! Before you start to write, reread the scoring guide in the writing prompt to be sure you know what to do.

Reflect
My Spider Map doesn't include every point in the scoring guide, but I think it covers most of them. Is there anything else that I'm missing?

Check the Scoring Guide
(Student pages 288–289)

Ask a student to read Justin's words on Student page 288. Have students explain why they think Justin would take additional time to check his Spider Map before he starts writing a draft. **Possible responses: He wants to be sure he hasn't missed anything; it's easier to catch and change things now than after his paper is already written.**

Ask students to read Justin's words on Student page 289 for each of the writing traits in the scoring guide. Point out that Word Choice/Clarity, Sentence Fluency, and Grammar/Mechanics are areas he will need to think about as he is writing, revising, and editing his test. These areas would be hard to cover in a graphic organizer.

Writing an Expository Test

Drafting Write a Draft

Voice/Audience

Writing Strategy Clearly identify the topic for my audience at the beginning.

I already know my explanation needs an introduction, body, and conclusion. I can use the information from my Spider Map to write all three sections. But as I look back at the scoring guide, I can see that it's also important to identify my topic early in the paper. I think I'll use my opening sentence to do this. This way my reader will know what I'm writing about from the start!

[DRAFT]

The Sky's the Limit!

by Justin

[identified topic at the beginning]

If I ever had an opportunity to go on the Space Shuttle, I would jump at the chance. Actually, maybe I should say I would fly at the chance! There are several reasons why I think this would be the experience of a lifetime.

First of all, I think I would make a good astronaut. I like all of the rides at amusement parks, even the ones where you turn upside down. I'm also good in math, and I have perfect eyesight, so those are two more things in my favor.

I would be fascinated by the whole experience of being in space. I love looking at the stars from here on Earth. I can only imagine how

Proofreading Marks

⌐ Indent
≡ Make a capital
/ Make a small letter
∧ Add something
ℓ Take out something
⊙ Add a period
SP Spelling error
¶ New paragraph

much better stargazing would be up in the sky. The other astronauts and me could look down at Earth when we got tired of stargazing. I've read that you can see Rivers, Mountains, and other landforms from space.

I think that moving around without gravity wood be just like flying. My greatest dream is to go for a space walk. Walking in space would be just about the best thing I can imagine. Some people might be afraid of floating into space forever I don't think that would be a problem. The people who designed the space shuttle and all of it's equipment is very careful about everything they do.

I know that not many people would enjoy eating and drinking food from tubes especially while being cooped up with other people in such a small space. Those things wouldn't bother me, though. Instead, being in space would make me really appreciate what I have here on earth.

Remember! Any time you write an explanation, you should include an introduction, body, and conclusion. The topic should be identified in the introduction so that the reader will know right away what the writing is about.

Reflect

What do you think? Did I include my topic early enough? Is it clear?

Drafting

(Student pages 290–291)

Ask students which trait from the scoring guide will be on Justin's mind as he starts to write his draft. **Clearly identify the topic for my audience at the beginning.**

Because Justin has identified his topic in his Spider Map, he knows what he needs to include in his opening paragraph. Ask a student to read the first sentence from Justin's draft. Ask the students whether they feel Justin has clearly identified the topic for his audience at the beginning.

Remind students that although they will want to be neat when writing their drafts, they should not be overly concerned about grammar and mechanics as they get their ideas on paper; if they have organized their time well, they will have a chance to come back and revise and edit their drafts.

Differentiating Instruction

English-Language Learners Create a set of proofreading marks flashcards for the class. On one side, write the proofreading symbol. On the other, explain what the symbol means. Then write a sample showing how the mark is used. Go through the cards with students until they have memorized the different marks and how they are used.

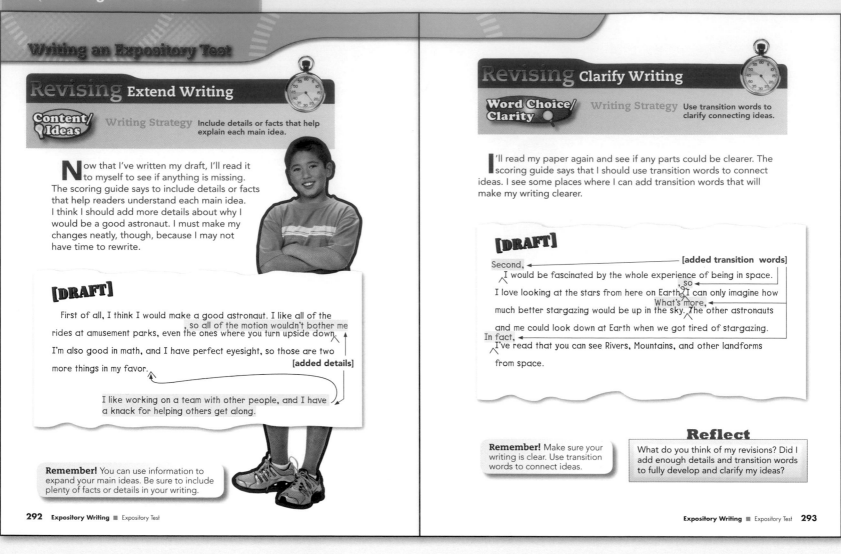

Writing an Expository Test

Revising Extend Writing

Content/Ideas · **Writing Strategy** Include details or facts that help explain each main idea.

Now that I've written my draft, I'll read it to myself to see if anything is missing. The scoring guide says to include details or facts that help readers understand each main idea. I think I should add more details about why I would be a good astronaut. I must make my changes neatly, though, because I may not have time to rewrite.

[DRAFT]

First of all, I think I would make a good astronaut. I like all of the rides at amusement parks, even the ones where you turn upside down, so all of the motion wouldn't bother me.

I'm also good in math, and I have perfect eyesight, so those are two more things in my favor.

[added details]

I like working on a team with other people, and I have a knack for helping others get along.

Remember! You can use information to expand your main ideas. Be sure to include plenty of facts or details in your writing.

Revising Clarify Writing

Word Choice/Clarity · **Writing Strategy** Use transition words to clarify connecting ideas.

I'll read my paper again and see if any parts could be clearer. The scoring guide says that I should use transition words to connect ideas. I see some places where I can add transition words that will make my writing clearer.

[DRAFT]

[added transition words]

Second, I would be fascinated by the whole experience of being in space. so
I love looking at the stars from here on Earth. I can only imagine how What's more, much better stargazing would be up in the sky. The other astronauts and me could look down at Earth when we got tired of stargazing.
In fact, I've read that you can see Rivers, Mountains, and other landforms from space.

Remember! Make sure your writing is clear. Use transition words to connect ideas.

Reflect

What do you think of my revisions? Did I add enough details and transition words to fully develop and clarify my ideas?

Revising

(Student pages 292–293)

Have a student read Justin's words on Student page 292. Ask students to identify the main idea in the paragraph from Justin's essay shown on Student page 292. **I think I would make a good astronaut.** Ask students why they think he added a line about the motion not bothering him to the sentence about amusement park rides. **Possible response: Otherwise, readers may not understand why he brought up amusement park rides.** Note that the other idea he added to this paragraph further explains the main idea of the paragraph by providing another example.

Now have a student read Justin's words on Student page 293. Point out that in this case, Justin needs to add transition words to clarify connecting ideas. He uses words such as *second, so, what's more,* and *in fact* to help connect the ideas in this paragraph. Ask students why he added the transition word *second* to the start of this paragraph. **Possible response: It connects this paragraph to the previous paragraph.**

Point out that at this point in the writing process, Justin is done revising his paper. All of his revisions have been added. Next, he will concentrate on editing the paper. Note the difference between editing and revising: In the revising step, students reread their drafts to look for ways to make them more polished or clearer; in editing, they look for and correct errors.

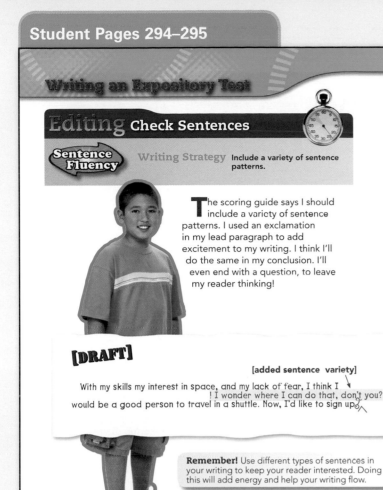

Writing an Expository Test

Editing Check Sentences

Sentence Fluency   **Writing Strategy** Include a variety of sentence patterns.

The scoring guide says I should include a variety of sentence patterns. I used an exclamation in my lead paragraph to add excitement to my writing. I think I'll do the same in my conclusion. I'll even end with a question, to leave my reader thinking!

[DRAFT]

[added sentence variety]

With my skills my interest in space, and my lack of fear, I think I ! I wonder where I can do that, don't you? would be a good person to travel in a shuttle. Now, I'd like to sign up.

Remember! Use different types of sentences in your writing to keep your reader interested. Doing this will add energy and help your writing flow.

294 Expository Writing ■ Expository Test

Editing Proofread Writing

Grammar/Mechanics   **Writing Strategy** Check the grammar, punctuation, capitalization, and spelling.

Now there's just one last step! The scoring guide says to use correct grammar and mechanics. I always leave plenty of time to check for errors in these important areas.

[FINAL DRAFT]

The Sky's the Limit!

by Justin

If I ever had an opportunity to go on the Space Shuttle, I would jump at the chance. Actually, maybe I should say I would fly at the chance! There are several reasons why I think this would be the experience of a lifetime.

First of all, I think I would make a good astronaut. I like all of the , so all of the motion wouldn't bother me rides at amusement parks, even the ones where you turn upside down. I'm also good in math, and I have perfect eyesight, so those are two more things in my favor. Second, I would be fascinated by the whole experience of being in space. I love looking at the stars from here on Earth, so I can only imagine how I like working on a team with other people, and I have a knack for helping others get along.

Remember! Check your grammar, punctuation, capitalization, and spelling every time you write for a test.

Expository Writing ■ Expository Test 295

Editing

(Student pages 294–295)

Ask a student to read Justin's words on Student page 294. Note that Justin has decided to end his essay with a question. Read aloud the question Justin inserted in the conclusion of his essay. Point out that using a question in your writing is a good way to engage the reader in the essay.

Next, ask a student to read Justin's words from Student page 295. Students should understand the importance of allowing enough time to edit and proofread their writing. Tell them to look for errors as they proofread their drafts and make corrections on the test paper. Stress that even when making corrections, they should try to keep their papers neat and legible. The person or persons scoring their papers needs to be able to read them!

Differentiating Instruction

Support If students are having trouble spotting and correcting errors in their writing, suggest that they save enough time to be able to go through their essays backwards. Point out that sometimes it's hard to spot mistakes after reading the same paper over and over. There is a natural tendency to skim through the paper when you already know what it says. By reading the paper backwards, it will be easier to spot incorrectly spelled words. Note, though, that this type of reading won't allow students to catch sentence fluency errors or some grammatical errors; they should still read through their essays thoroughly from front to back.

[FINAL DRAFT]

What's more,
much better stargazing would be up in the sky. The other astronauts
and me could look down at Earth when we got tired of stargazing.
In fact,
I've read that you can see rivers, mountains, and other landforms
from space.

I think that moving around without gravity would be just like flying.
, however,
My greatest dream is to go for a space walk. Walking in space would
be just about the best thing I can imagine. Some people might be
, but
afraid of floating into space forever I don't think that would be a
problem. The people who designed the space shuttle and all of it's
are
equipment is very careful about everything they do.

I know that not many people would enjoy eating and drinking food
from tubes, especially while being cooped up with other people in such
a small space. Those things wouldn't bother me, though. Instead, being
in space would make me really appreciate what I have here on earth.

With my skills, my interest in space, and my lack of fear, I think I
! I wonder where I can do that, don't you?
would be a good person to travel in a shuttle. Now, I'd like to sign up

Reflect

Is my writing missing anything? Check it against the scoring guide. Remember to use your writing prompt's scoring guide to check your writing any time you take a test!

We're finished! That wasn't so bad! Remember these important tips when you write for a test.

TEST TIPS

1. **Study the writing prompt before you start to write.** Most writing prompts have three parts: the setup, the task, and the scoring guide. The parts probably won't be labeled. You'll have to figure them out for yourself!

2. **Make sure you understand the task before you start to write.**
   - Read all three parts of the writing prompt carefully.
   - Circle key words in the task part of the writing prompt that tell what kind of writing you need to do. The task might also identify your audience.
   - Make sure you know how you'll be graded.
   - Say the assignment in your own words to yourself.

3. **Keep an eye on the clock.** Decide how much time you will spend on each part of the writing process and try to stick to your schedule. Don't spend so much time on prewriting that you don't have enough time left to write.

4. **Reread your writing. Compare it to the scoring guide at least twice.** Remember the rubrics you have used all year? A scoring guide on a writing test is like a rubric. It can help you keep what's important in mind.

5. **Plan, plan, plan!** You don't get much time to revise during a test, so planning is more important than ever.

6. **Write neatly.** Remember, if the people who score your test can't read your writing, it doesn't matter how good your essay is!

Differentiating Instruction

Enrichment Have students write an expository test using the writing prompt on Student page 284. Allow them one hour to complete the test, and have them structure their time according to the chart on Student page 283. Stress that students refer to the writing prompt throughout the test writing process to be sure they know what they are doing and have included everything from the scoring guide. Remind them of the importance of prewriting, revising, and editing their tests before submitting them. Once they have completed their writing tests, have them check their papers against the writing traits in the scoring guide. Ask if they followed the traits and whether they feel their papers would receive good grades.

Test Tips

Read the test tips on Student page 297 aloud. Tell students that they should keep in mind these six tips every time they complete a writing test.

This would be a good time to remind students that test writing is not so different from writing for a class assignment. Ask students what they think the biggest difference is. **Possible response: They need to keep an eye on the clock.** Note that although there may not be unlimited time to complete a test, planning and prewriting are still important parts of the writing process. Emphasize that there is no need to be fearful of writing tests. After all their practice throughout the other writing chapters, they have what it takes to be test-writing champs like Justin.

Books for Professional Development

McCarthy, Tara. *Expository Writing (Grades 4–8)*. New York: Scholastic, 1999.

This complete resource includes great activities, models, and reproducibles for helping students with their expository writing skills. They'll learn how to write accurate messages and announcements, well-organized expository paragraphs, and successful reports. Includes independent learning ideas, reinforcement activities, and self-assessment pages.

Peha, Steve and Margot Carmichael Lester. *Be a Better Writer: Power Tools for Young Writers!: Essential Tips, Exercises and Techniques for Aspiring Writers*. Bend: The Leverage Factory, 2006.

Packed with practical tips and techniques to help young writers build a solid foundation for writing, this fun, easy-to-use guide is a comprehensive introduction to the world of the written word. Students will learn how to generate interesting ideas, how to use descriptive detail, and how to beat writer's block. Plus, they will learn how to perform the five most important types of revision and develop other key skills.

Murray, Donald M. *Shoptalk: Learning to Write with Writers*. Portsmouth: Boynton/Cook, 1990.

This collection of quotations on all aspects of the writing process is taken from a wide variety of writers. It includes comments from writers both famous and obscure. One example is this quote from James Thurber: "Don't get it right, get it written."

Anderson, Carl. *How's It Going? A Practical Guide to Conferring With Student Writers*. Portsmouth: Heinemann, 2000.

Anderson provides samples that demonstrate various techniques and strategies to help both teacher and students refine their participation in a conference.

School-Home Connection

Dear Family,

In this unit of *Strategies for Writers,* your child will be learning and practicing expository writing. Expository writing is writing that explains or informs. It can be a research report, a cause-and-effect report, or a summary. Expository writing does not involve creating fictional stories or persuasive letters.

In this chapter, your student will be learning how to write a summary. He or she will select a longer article to summarize. When he or she summarizes a longer piece or writing, it's important to focus on only the main points of the longer article. Unlike with other types of writing that encourage elaboration, we'll be encouraging brevity when writing summaries. That means that each of the steps your child will take after the prewriting and draft writing steps will involve careful revising and editing.

As your child works on this project, we encourage you to read both the longer article and your child's summary of the article. If you have any questions about the material in this chapter, please let me know.

Thanks for your help in the writing process!

School-Home Connection

Dear Family,

Throughout the year, your child will have the opportunity to write a variety of essays and reports. Before your child even begins to write his or her draft, he or she will focus on pre-writing, the steps necessary to take before drafting. During the prewriting stage, students will be asked to come up with ideas, create notes on their ideas, and then organize their notes.

As your child organizes his or her notes, he or she will be working with a very important writing device—a graphic organizer. Graphic organizers are the charts, webs, tables, and other visual tools we use to help us make sense of information for our writing process. In this unit on expository writing, your child will be using the following graphic organizers:

- Spider Map—organizes information about one topic. The topic is written in the center of the "spider." Details related to the topic are written on the "legs" of the spider.

- Cause-and-Effect Chain—shows the reasons (causes) for specific events or results (effects).

- Outline—shows the main points and the supporting details of the paragraphs in an essay.

There are many more kinds of graphic organizers, and we will continue to use them throughout the year. Your child may show a preference for one kind over another. It doesn't matter which kind he or she uses, as long as the organizer helps your child make sense of information and improves his or her writing.

Thank you for helping your child in the writing process.

School-Home Connection

Dear Family,

In this chapter of *Strategies for Writers,* your child will get to practice his or her research skills in order to write a research report. These days, much of a student's research can be done using the Internet. Please keep in mind that when we have your student use the Internet to do research, we direct him or her to credible and reliable sources of information. Some of these sources include:

- Educational Web sites, such as college Web sites, museum sites, or sites ending in **.edu**.

- Government Web sites, such as those ending in **.gov**.

- Well-known online encyclopedias, such as *Britannica* and *Encarta*.

- Most news organization sites, such as online newspapers or journals.

Of course, we also encourage students to use the library to find research material. When writing a research report, in particular, students will need to use an encyclopedia and at least two other credible sources to research their topics.

Research takes time, and it is an important step in the prewriting process. In addition, knowing how to research is an important skill that your child will continually use in life. I hope this gives him or her the opportunity to practice and improve those skills.

If you have questions about the writing process, please contact me. Together, we can help your child become an effective writer.

School-Home Connection

Dear Family,

In this chapter of *Strategies for Writers,* your student will learn how to take an expository writing test. Many kinds of tests now require essay-style answers to questions. Standardized tests, such as proficiency and achievement tests, increasingly require students to write essays. That's why we're taking the time during the school year to help your writer learn and practice some specific skills that will help him or her write for a test.

Students must remember six basic things when they write for a test. They are outlined in the Test Tips section of this chapter.

1. Analyze the writing prompt before you start to write.

2. Make sure you understand the task before you start to write.

3. Keep an eye on the clock.

4. Reread your writing. Check it against the scoring guide at least twice.

5. Plan, plan, plan!

6. Write neatly.

You can help your child prepare for writing tests by following these six simple steps. Writing for a test doesn't have to be stressful. With the right tools and good writing habits, your child can feel good about writing for a test.

PERSUASIVE
writing strategies

IN THIS UNIT

1 Book Review: Response to Literature

- Pick a book I liked and find a similar book. Jot notes about the first book. Keep a response journal as I read the new book.
- Make a Venn diagram from my notes and response journal.
- Use a sincere tone to state my opinion in the first paragraph.
- Add facts or quotations to support my comparisons.
- Add transition words to make my comparisons clearer.
- Use a mix of sentence patterns.
- Check that all dependent clauses are part of complex sentences.

2 Persuasive Essay

- Choose an issue and find information to support my opinion.
- Use a Network Tree to organize my ideas.
- Begin by expressing my opinion in a convincing tone.
- Add facts and reasons to support my opinion.
- Replace loaded words with neutral words.
- Use question-and-answer sentence patterns.
- Make sure each pronoun has a clear antecedent.

3 Business Letter

- Pick something I would like a business to change. List reasons for the change.
- Use an Order-of-Importance Organizer to organize my reasons.
- Be sure to use correct business letter form and write with a businesslike tone.
- Add details to support my opinion.
- Restate my purpose for writing in the last paragraph.
- Make sure each sentence reflects the purpose of my letter.
- Make sure homophones are used correctly.

4 Writing for a Test

- Study the writing prompt to be sure I know what to do.
- Respond to the task.
- Choose a graphic organizer.
- Check my graphic organizer against the scoring guide.
- Tell my reader my position in the opening sentence.
- Strengthen any explanations that seem weak.
- Delete information that doesn't support my opinion.
- Make sure each sentence supports my position.
- Check the grammar, punctuation, capitalization, and spelling.

PERSUASIVE
writing convinces the reader to do something.

Hi, there! I'm Leila. I'm learning about persuasive writing in school. I really like to share my opinions with other people and get them to understand my point of view. I want to convince people through good reasoning, and this kind of writing should help me learn to do that better.

IN THIS UNIT

1. **Book Review: Response to Literature**
2. **Persuasive Essay**
3. **Business Letter**
4. **Writing for a Test**

Name:	Leila
Home:	Tennessee
Hobbies:	watching old movies, playing blues guitar, reading
Favorite Blues Song:	"Crossroad Blues" by Robert Johnson
Favorite Book:	*The Diary of Anne Frank*

298 Persuasive Writing

Persuasive Writing 299

IN THIS UNIT

Book Review Students will learn how to compare and contrast two books that they have read.

Persuasive Essay In this genre, students will learn to express their opinions on a topic and convince readers to agree with them.

Business Letter This genre shows students how to write a professional letter that expresses their opinion and persuades their reader to consider that opinion.

Persuasive Test Here, students will learn and practice how to read a persuasive test prompt. They will also learn and practice how to plan their time for a test and how to use writing strategies for successful persuasive test writing.

Meet Leila

Tell students that their student guide for this chapter is Leila, a girl from Tennessee. Have a student read aloud Leila's hobbies, favorite song, and favorite book. Remind students that we learn about the student guides' hobbies and interests because oftentimes they relate to the type of writing and the subject matter these student models will use. This will help make Leila's writing seem authentic. Point out that persuasive writing convinces the reader to do something.

by Julie Coiro, Ph.D.
University of Connecticut

Locating Resources: Reading Within Web Sites

Once students have located a relevant Web site, the challenge is to decide what to attend to first. Like previewing a book, scanning a Web site's homepage can give readers a sense of the structure and intended connections among different content linked within the site. Unlike reading a book, readers cannot rapidly page through large sections to get a sense of the text; they must think strategically about how to preview multiple levels of a Web site for their reading purposes.

The following strategy lesson invites students to stop, think, and anticipate where important information about a Web site's content might be found. Initially, you may wish to model for students these seven steps for previewing a Web site, thinking out loud to show the decision-making that accompanies each step.

1. Read both the title of the page and the title of the Web site in the margin at the top of the window.

2. To get a big picture of the information within the site, scan menu choices by holding your mouse over the navigational or topical menus that often appear along the sides of the frame or across the top of the window, but don't click yet.

3. Explore interactive features of dynamic images (animated images or images that change as a viewer holds the mouse over them), pop-up menus, and scroll bars that may reveal additional levels of information.

4. Identify the creator of the Web site and when the site was last updated. You can often find this information by clicking on a button on the homepage labeled "About This Site." Consider what this information indicates about the site.

5. Decide whether or not the site seems worthwhile. If the site looks worthwhile, decide which areas to explore first.

After several effective demonstrations, you may wish to have students practice these previewing strategies in their own on-line reading.

Critical Evaluation: Evaluating Commercial Bias

Many Web sites contain information that appears to be influenced by commercial interests for or against a certain product. Often, advertising is artfully woven into factual information or interactive games. This is known as *commercial bias*. It is critical that students, even young students, recognize the techniques businesses use to persuade and influence others who use the Internet for information.

Commercially biased Web sites share information, but they also sell products.

When determining commercial bias, encourage your students to consider questions such as the following:

- *Whose opinion does the information represent?*

- *What techniques does the business use to attract children to its Web site?*

- *What techniques does the business use to attract children to its products?*

- *Are there attempts to offer new ideas or teach something new?*

- *Why did the authors use these techniques?*

- *How does the advertising influence your opinions of the products sold on the site?*

- *Who benefits most from the different types of information provided at this site?*

For additional practice in considering persuasive marketing techniques, you may wish to have students explore **Kids. Gov: The Official Kids' Portal for the U.S. Government** at **http://www.kids.gov**. Here, resources for each topic are divided into categories, including Government, Organizations, Education, and Commercial Sites to help children distinguish among the different points of view. Encourage students to consider the questions above as they explore several Web sites in each category. Take time to compare and contrast the ways information is presented about the topic on Web sites created for education as compared to commercial sites, for example.

Communicating Globally: Persuasive Writing Opportunities

The Internet provides a number of opportunities for students to practice their persuasive writing techniques for a larger audience. One idea is to have students share their opinions about a book they have read in ways that persuade others to read (or perhaps not to read) the same book. Web sites that allow children to add their book reviews to a collection maintained by someone outside your school include the following:

- **The Book Zone** at **http://www.rif.org/ readingplanet/bookzone** is sponsored by Reading is Fundamental, Inc., the nation's oldest and largest nonprofit children's literacy organization. Children are invited to publish their book reviews by simply clicking on the "Review This Book" icon featured as part of the on-line book search tool. Other students can then search for their favorite book and compare the range of reviews available before they select what book they'd like to read next. Students can visit another part of the Web site to learn more about many popular authors and illustrators before or after writing their review.

- **Bookhooks** at **http://www.bookhooks.com/index. cfm**, created by Adrian Hoad-Reddick, is a free on-line book-reporting tool kit for young readers. A simple pop-up form allows one to compose his or her book review, add an illustration, rate the emotional impact of the book, and have it published alongside a growing list of other reviews sorted by genre and author. The site is rounded out by an on-line style guide and invitations to add a book-related quotation or word search puzzle to the collection.

- **World of Reading** at **http://www.worldreading.org**, sponsored by the Ann Arbor District Library in Ann Arbor, Michigan, accepts book reviews from students all around the world. Teachers are asked to e-mail the site's creators so that they can help set up the form for the appropriate school. Then, an on-line form walks students through the process of publishing their book reviews.

Supporting and Extending Writing: Online Instructional Resources

Teaching students about issues related to persuasion and commercial bias are complex and challenging. The Internet provides a number of comprehensive Web sites dedicated to helping teachers and parents understand these issues in order to better support children as they develop critical reading skills. One useful resource is called **Web Awareness** at **http://www.media-awareness.ca/english/special_ initiatives/web_awareness/index.cfm**. It was developed by the Canadian group Media Awareness Network to help parents, teachers, and librarians teach children how to locate good information, as well as how to question and evaluate on-line sources. The section for teachers focuses on teaching students about Internet safety, authenticating on-line information, and dealing with on-line marketing and privacy issues. The site also features links to background articles and to three interactive games that teach students how to make smart and ethical decisions about the Internet. This site is great for parents, too.

A second on-line resource you may find helpful is titled **Information and Its Counterfeits: Propaganda, Misinformation, and Disinformation** at **http://www. library.jhu.edu/researchhelp/general/evaluating/ counterfeit.html**. Library media expert Elizabeth Kirk at Johns Hopkins University wrote this helpful summary to review important strategies useful for distinguishing real information from three look-alikes.

Many Web sites also offer on-line lesson plans to extend the writing curriculum. A favorite among teachers is **ReadWriteThink** at **http://www.readwritethink.org**, established in partnership with several organizations including the International Reading Association. Each lesson is designed by a classroom teacher and grounded in research. Each also integrates helpful handouts, scoring rubrics, and Internet resources.

Book Review Overview

In this chapter, students will learn how to write a book review. First, they will learn elements of a book review—thesis statement, organization, supporting evidence, and clear writing. Then they will learn different reasons for writing a book review. Next, students will use a book review rubric to assess a model writing sample.

Students will follow Leila, the student guide, as she goes through the writing stages, including prewriting, drafting, revising, editing, and publishing. For each step, students will learn new writing strategies and have the opportunity to apply them in their own writing. Students will jot notes about a book they have read and keep a response journal on another similar book. They will organize their notes and compare the

books in a Venn diagram and then use the Venn diagram to write their drafts. In the revision stage, they will add facts or quotations to support their comparisons and transition words to make their comparisons clearer. They will then edit their drafts to be sure they have used a mix of sentence patterns and that all their dependent clauses are part of complex sentences. They will also edit their drafts for spelling, punctuation, and grammar. After editing their drafts, they will prepare their final drafts to publish.

You may wish to send to families the School-Home Connection Letter for this chapter, located at the end of this unit in the Teacher Edition.

Book Review Writing Traits

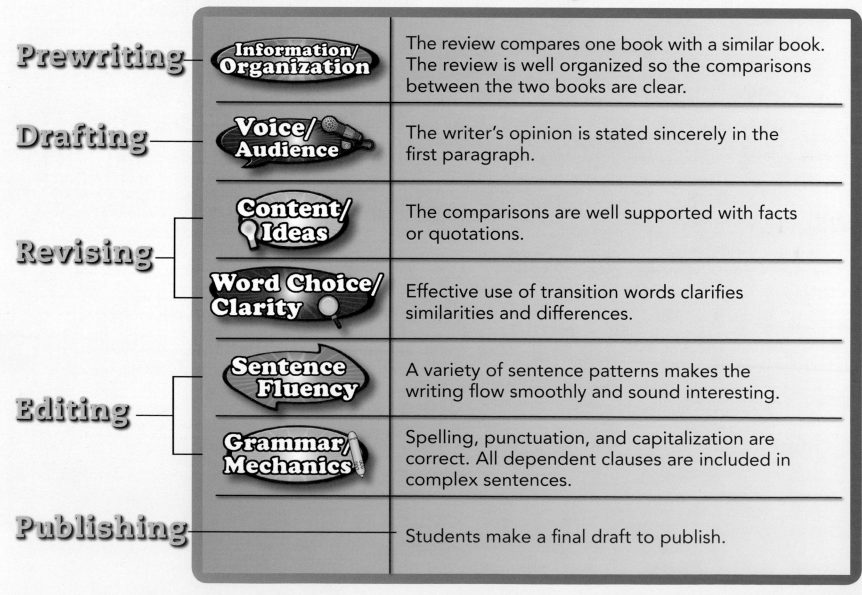

Prewriting — Information/Organization: The review compares one book with a similar book. The review is well organized so the comparisons between the two books are clear.

Drafting — Voice/Audience: The writer's opinion is stated sincerely in the first paragraph.

Revising — Content/Ideas: The comparisons are well supported with facts or quotations.

Word Choice/Clarity: Effective use of transition words clarifies similarities and differences.

Editing — Sentence Fluency: A variety of sentence patterns makes the writing flow smoothly and sound interesting.

Grammar/Mechanics: Spelling, punctuation, and capitalization are correct. All dependent clauses are included in complex sentences.

Publishing — Students make a final draft to publish.

Book Review Time Management

WEEK 1

Day 1	Day 2	Day 3	Day 4	Day 5
Learning Objectives				
Students will: • study the components of a book review.	Students will: • learn how to gather information for a book review.	Students will: • practice gathering information for their own book reviews.	Students will: • learn how to make a Venn Diagram to organize their notes.	Students will: • practice organizing their own notes into a Venn diagram.
Activities				
• Discuss the elements and traits of a book review (Student pages 300–302). • Use the rubric to assess the model (Student pages 303–307).	• Read and discuss **Prewriting: Gather Information** (Student pages 308–309).	• Select two books to compare. Jot notes on a book and keep a response journal on a similar book. • Work with a partner to gather information for the book reviews.	• Read and discuss **Prewriting: Organize Ideas** (Student pages 310–311).	• Look at notes made for the book review. • Make a Venn Diagram to organize notes and compare the two books.

WEEK 2

Day 1	Day 2	Day 3	Day 4	Day 5
Learning Objectives				
Students will: • learn how to use a sincere tone to state their opinions in the first paragraph.	Students will: • practice writing their own drafts.	Students will: • learn how to ensure comparisons are well supported with facts or quotations.	Students will: • learn to add facts or quotations to support their comparisons.	Students will: • learn how to effectively use transition words to clarify similarities and differences.
Activities				
• Read and discuss **Drafting: Write a Draft** (Student pages 312–313).	• Use Venn diagrams to write a draft. • State own opinion in the first paragraph.	• Read and discuss **Revising: Extend Writing** (Student page 314).	• Add facts or quotations to support comparisons.	• Read and discuss **Revising: Clarify Writing** (Student page 315).

WEEK 3

Day 1	Day 2	Day 3	Day 4	Day 5
Learning Objectives				
Students will: • practice adding transition words to make their comparisons clearer.	Students will: • learn how to make their writing flow and sound interesting by using a variety of sentence patterns.	Students will: • learn how to ensure dependent clauses are part of complex sentences.	Students will: • practice editing their drafts for spelling, punctuation, and capitalization.	Students will: • learn different ways to publish their book reviews.
Activities				
• Reread drafts, looking for areas to further clarify similarities and differences. • Add transition words to make comparisons clearer.	• Read and discuss **Editing: Check Sentences** (Student page 316). • Use a mix of sentence patterns.	• Read and discuss **Editing: Proofread Writing** (Student page 317). • Make sure that any dependent clauses are contained within complex sentences.	• Fix any spelling, punctuation, or capitalization errors. • Fix any dependent clause errors.	• Read and discuss **Publishing: Share Writing** (Student pages 320–323).

* To complete the chapter in fewer days, teach the learning objectives and activities for two days in one day.

This planning chart, correlated to your state's writing standards, is available on-line at http://www.zaner-bloser.com/sfw.

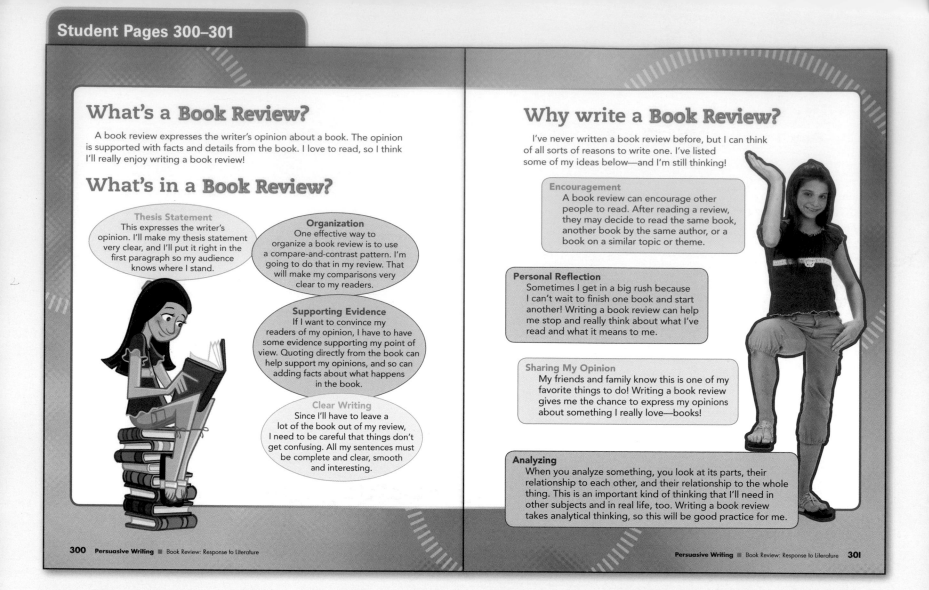

Define the Genre

(Student page 300)

Book Review

Ask students whether they have ever discussed a book with others. Encourage them to share why they discuss books with others. **Possible responses: to convince others to read or not read the book; to share their excitement or disappointment about the book** Ask what features of the book they discuss. **Possible responses: plot, characters, setting, theme, mood/tone**

Explain that if they wrote down the ideas they discussed in an organized way, they would have a book review. A book review is an example of persuasive writing because the writer expresses an opinion about a book and tries to convince others that the opinion is correct.

Elements of the Genre

Book Review

Read and discuss the elements of a book review with the students. Explain that many of these elements can also

be found in other forms of writing, such as a summary or a research report. Discuss how each of the elements is important in a well-written book review.

Authentic Writing

(Student page 301)

Book Review

Ask students about times when they have discussed two or more books with others—books they have read or books the other person has read. Ask what they compare about the books. **Possible responses: similarities and differences in plot, characters, setting, theme, mood/tone**

Explain that sharing their opinion with others is one of the reasons for writing a book review. Have students read aloud the reasons for writing a book review on Student page 301. Point out that these authentic purposes help shape their writing and set the tone for it. Encourage students to think about their reasons for writing a book review and how those reasons will affect the tone of their writing.

Book Review: Response to Literature
Writing Traits

One way to write a book review is to compare and contrast two books. It takes the traits below to make a good compare-and-contrast book review. I'm going to include each one when I write!

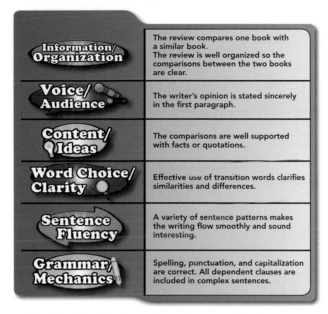

Information/Organization	The review compares one book with a similar book. The review is well organized so the comparisons between the two books are clear.
Voice/Audience	The writer's opinion is stated sincerely in the first paragraph.
Content/Ideas	The comparisons are well supported with facts or quotations.
Word Choice/Clarity	Effective use of transition words clarifies similarities and differences.
Sentence Fluency	A variety of sentence patterns makes the writing flow smoothly and sound interesting.
Grammar/Mechanics	Spelling, punctuation, and capitalization are correct. All dependent clauses are included in complex sentences.

Juan Perro's book review on the next page examines the similarities and differences between two books. Let's read the review, keeping the six writing traits in mind.

Book Review Model

Two Books by One Excellent Author
by Juan Perro

Virginia Hamilton has written a wide range of stories. *The House of Dies Drear*, for example, is a spellbinding mystery. In contrast, *Cousins* is an emotional story of love and betrayal. Although different, both books are ideal for middle graders. **Thesis statement** → **Organization—comparing characters**

These readers can easily identify with the young main characters in these two books. While these characters are both independent, they love their families. In *The House of Dies Drear*, Thomas Small attempts to unravel the dark secrets of his new house by himself. Thomas wants to prove that he is brave and smart, like his father. He also wants to protect his family from dangers in the house. In *Cousins*, on the other hand, young Cammy loves being her mother's "baby." Like Thomas, though, she also enjoys freedom. She wants to visit her grandmother whenever she pleases. Unlike Thomas, Cammy rarely sees her father. Instead, she looks up to her big brother. Sometimes she feels "like she would burst with love" for him. **Clear writing**

Supporting evidence **Organization—comparing settings**

The settings of both books combine the familiar and the unfamiliar. Thomas's new home is a mysterious old house. The huge mansion had been a stop on the Underground Railroad. It has a homey kitchen, but it also has secret passages. The house looms over the story, creating a dark mood. In contrast, the pleasant little town in *Cousins* creates a sunny mood. As in *The House of Dies Drear*, however, that setting can turn threatening. In *Cousins*, a river swallows one of Cammy's cousins. **Organization—comparing themes**

Each book addresses the theme of dealing with changes. Many middle-grade readers can identify with this theme, as they are also dealing with changes. Thomas has to overcome his fears about moving to a new place. Similarly, Cammy copes with her grief over the death of her cousin.

Virginia Hamilton tells stories that middle graders can understand and enjoy. Read *The House of Dies Drear*, *Cousins*, or any of Hamilton's other novels. You will see how the characters, settings, and themes make her stories so appealing. **Clear writing**

Writing Traits
(Student pages 302–303)

Book Review

Bring in a copy of a published book review to share with your students. Read aloud some of the review in which the writer draws upon passages or quotations from the book. Ask students why they think the writer uses examples from the book in his or her review. **Possible response: Examples from the book help support the writer's opinion.** Point out that a well-written book review includes quotations or examples from the book which support the writer's opinion.

Tell students that they will be studying strategies for writing book reviews. They will be using these strategies to write their own book reviews. Point out that a good book review will contain the traits listed on Student page 302. Have student volunteers read the traits and their descriptions.

Have students listen for these traits as you read aloud "Two Books by One Excellent Author" on Student page 303.

Differentiating Instruction

English-Language Learners As students learn the traits of a good book review and practice writing their own book reviews, they will need to call upon some of the elements present in a book. In particular, they will want to note the plot, characters, settings, and themes in a book. Help your students get a better understanding of these elements by examining each in detail.

Plot: What is the story about?

Characters: Who are the main characters? What are their backgrounds, personalities, and situations? Are they strong or weak characters?

Settings: Where do the books take place? Are they historical, set in a previous time, or set in the present? Do they take place in a home, a town, in outer space, etc.?

Themes: What are the issues that the book deals with? Are there themes that run throughout the book?

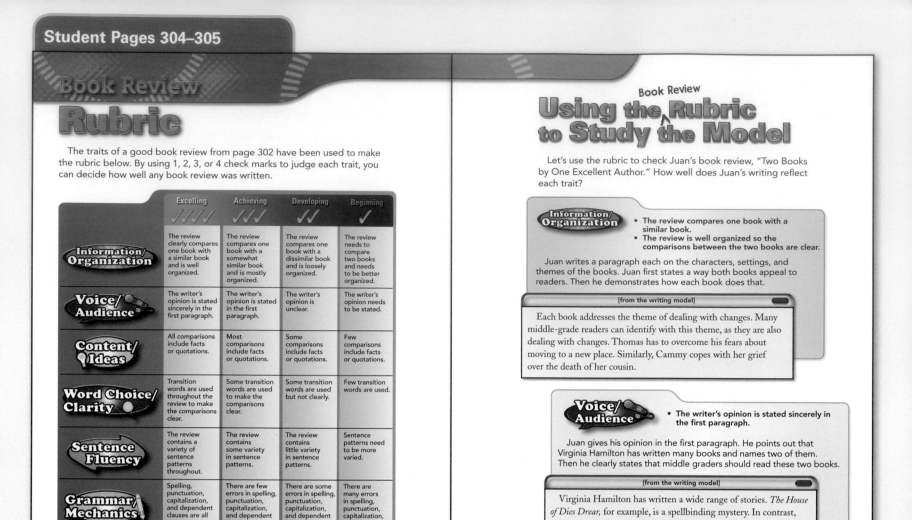

Book Review
Rubric

The traits of a good book review from page 302 have been used to make the rubric below. By using 1, 2, 3, or 4 check marks to judge each trait, you can decide how well any book review was written.

	Excelling ✓✓✓✓	Achieving ✓✓✓	Developing ✓✓	Beginning ✓
Information/ Organization	The review clearly compares one book with a similar book and is well organized.	The review compares one book with a somewhat similar book and is mostly organized.	The review compares one book with a dissimilar book and is loosely organized.	The review needs to compare two books and needs to be better organized.
Voice/ Audience	The writer's opinion is stated sincerely in the first paragraph.	The writer's opinion is stated in the first paragraph.	The writer's opinion is unclear.	The writer's opinion needs to be stated.
Content/ Ideas	All comparisons include facts or quotations.	Most comparisons include facts or quotations.	Some comparisons include facts or quotations.	Few comparisons include facts or quotations.
Word Choice/ Clarity	Transition words are used throughout the review to make the comparisons clear.	Some transition words are used to make the comparisons clear.	Some transition words are used but not clearly.	Few transition words are used.
Sentence Fluency	The review contains a variety of sentence patterns throughout.	The review contains some variety in sentence patterns.	The review contains little variety in sentence patterns.	Sentence patterns need to be more varied.
Grammar/ Mechanics	Spelling, punctuation, capitalization, and dependent clauses are all correct.	There are few errors in spelling, punctuation, capitalization, and dependent clauses.	There are some errors in spelling, punctuation, capitalization, and dependent clauses.	There are many errors in spelling, punctuation, capitalization, and dependent clauses.

304   **Persuasive Writing** ■ Book Review: Response to Literature

---

Book Review
Using the Rubric to Study the Model

Let's use the rubric to check Juan's book review, "Two Books by One Excellent Author." How well does Juan's writing reflect each trait?

Information/ Organization
- The review compares one book with a similar book.
- The review is well organized so the comparisons between the two books are clear.

Juan writes a paragraph each on the characters, settings, and themes of the books. Juan first states a way both books appeal to readers. Then he demonstrates how each book does that.

> **[from the writing model]**
>
> Each book addresses the theme of dealing with changes. Many middle-grade readers can identify with this theme, as they are also dealing with changes. Thomas has to overcome his fears about moving to a new place. Similarly, Cammy copes with her grief over the death of her cousin.

Voice/ Audience
- The writer's opinion is stated sincerely in the first paragraph.

Juan gives his opinion in the first paragraph. He points out that Virginia Hamilton has written many books and names two of them. Then he clearly states that middle graders should read these two books.

> **[from the writing model]**
>
> Virginia Hamilton has written a wide range of stories. *The House of Dies Drear*, for example, is a spellbinding mystery. In contrast, *Cousins* is an emotional story of love and betrayal. Although different, both books are ideal for middle graders.

Persuasive Writing ■ Book Review: Response to Literature   305

Using the Rubric
(Student page 304)

By now, students should understand that a rubric is a tool that helps the reader evaluate a piece of writing. The rubric shown on Student page 304 can be used to evaluate a book review. Note that it is based on the traits for a book review that students read on Student page 302.

Point out that not only is the quality of their writing important in a book review, but also the books which they choose to compare. Read the four descriptors for Information/Organization. Note that students will want to find two similar books to review when they write their own book reports.

Study the Model
(Student pages 305–307)

Point out that Student pages 305–307 show how the book review writing model meets all six traits of the rubric. Read each section with students. Have students try to find other examples of each trait in the writing model.

Ask students to refer to the rubric to determine how many check marks they would assign the writing model for each trait. As a class, decide how you would rate the writing model overall.

Remind students of the importance of using the rubric as they write their book reviews. Referring to the rubric will ensure that they are meeting all six writing traits.

Book Review

Content/Ideas
- The comparisons are well supported with facts or quotations.

Juan uses facts from the books to support his comparisons. In this paragraph about the characters, he also uses a quotation. That makes the comparison even more interesting.

[from the writing model]

In *The House of Dies Drear*, Thomas Small attempts to unravel the dark secrets of his new house by himself. Thomas wants to prove that he is brave and smart, like his father. He also wants to protect his family from dangers in the house. In *Cousins*, on the other hand, young Cammy loves being her mother's "baby." Like Thomas, though, she also enjoys freedom. She wants to visit her grandmother whenever she pleases. Unlike Thomas, Cammy rarely sees her father. Instead, she looks up to her big brother. Sometimes she feels "like she would burst with love" for him.

Word Choice/Clarity
- Effective use of transition words clarifies similarities and differences.

Juan uses quite a few transition words to make sure the reader knows he's comparing and contrasting two things. In these two sentences, he's comparing how the setting creates the mood in each book. See how he uses the transition words *In contrast* to make the comparisons clear?

[from the writing model]

The house looms over the story, creating a dark mood. In contrast, the pleasant little town in *Cousins* creates a sunny mood.

Sentence Fluency
- A variety of sentence patterns makes the writing flow smoothly and sound interesting.

Juan uses a good variety of sentences throughout his review to keep things flowing smoothly, but I especially like this paragraph. The sentences are well written and clear, and none of them follow the same pattern. There's even a command in there!

[from the writing model]

Virginia Hamilton tells stories that middle graders can understand and enjoy. Read *The House of Dies Drear*, *Cousins*, or any of Hamilton's other novels. You will see how the characters, settings, and themes make her stories so appealing.

Grammar/Mechanics
- Spelling, punctuation, and capitalization are correct. All dependent clauses are included in complex sentences.

I didn't find any dependent clauses used as sentences. That would be an error! This sentence, for example, begins with a dependent clause, but the clause is part of a complex sentence. That makes it correct!

[from the writing model]

While these characters are both independent, they love their families.

Now it's my turn to write! How can I apply good writing strategies in my own book review? Just watch! I'm going to use what I learned from the rubric and some good writing strategies.

Differentiating Instruction

Enrichment Have students locate several compare-and-contrast book reviews in magazines or on the Internet. Ask them to highlight comments about each book in a separate color. Then ask them to underline each major point of comparison or contrast. Ask them to judge the review for Voice/Audience and Content/Ideas based on the traits in the rubric found on Student page 304. This activity should help them understand the ways these book reviews can be organized.

Writing a Book Review

Prewriting — Gather Information

Information/Organization

Writing Strategy

The review compares one book with a similar book.

Pick a book I liked and find a similar book. Jot notes about the first book. Keep a response journal as I read the new book.

Recently, I read *Number the Stars* by Lois Lowry. I chose it because it was about my Jewish heritage. I wanted to find a book kind of like that to use for my next writing assignment: a book review that compares two books.

The review on page 303 compares two books by the same author. I decided to compare two fiction books on the same topic by different authors. *Good Night, Maman* is a fiction book like *Number the Stars*, but it's by a different author, Norma Fox Mazer. I wrote these notes from memory about *Number the Stars* before I read *Good Night, Maman*.

My Notes on Number the Stars

✔ World War II: Nazi soldiers all over Copenhagen, Denmark

✔ 1943: Nazis begin arresting Jews. Jewish Rosens leave their daughter Ellen with her friend Annemarie Johansen and her family. Johansens pretend Ellen is their daughter.

✔ Annemarie and her mom take Ellen to Uncle Henrik's house at the coast. Ellen's parents come there. They have a fake funeral so Jews can gather at the house disguised as mourners. Nazis investigate; girls are terrified, but brave.

✔ Annemarie's parents, Uncle Henrik, and others help Jews hide on fishing boats to escape to Sweden.

✔ Annemarie meets Nazis in woods; she is frightened, but brave. Rosens get to Sweden safely.

Instead of taking notes as I read my second book, I'm keeping a response journal. That way, I can write down my thoughts as I read the book. This book is also about a Jewish girl and her family hiding from the Nazis during World War II. I included my own reactions and lots of quotations (with the page numbers where I found them). See what I've written so far?

Writer's Term

Response Journal

A **response journal** is a notebook or other place where someone jots down his or her impressions about an experience, such as reading a book.

My Response Journal for Good Night, Maman
(page 1)

I couldn't stay quiet for a year like Karin Levi did in that attic closet. I guess she just had to.

Maman is strict but sweet. You can see why Karin loves her so much. Marc acts so mature. He's trying to be the man since his dad was shot.

It must have been terrible to run from your home, begging for food, with no place to live. Karin said, "It had been weeks since I'd slept on a real bed, in a real room." (p. 31) She said, "We were free and unfree. We were in our own beloved land, but it was not ours." (p. 36)

It was so sad when Karin kissed Maman goodbye. Karin was worried Maman wouldn't find them after she got better. "How was she going to do that? Find us where?" Karin said. (p. 58)

I thought everyone who helped the Jews was nice to them, but Madame Zetain wasn't. The farmer and Maria Theresa were. Maria Theresa even told them about a ship that could take them to America.

Practice!

Now it's your turn. Choose a book you've already read and liked, and make notes on it. Then keep a response journal as you read a second book that you plan to compare with it.

Prewriting

(Student pages 308–309)

Read Leila's words on Student page 308 aloud. Discuss her reasons for choosing those two books. Point out that students might decide to compare a fiction and a nonfiction book on the same topic, two books by the same author, two books with the same illustrator, two books with similar main characters, two books set in the same period, and so on.

Ask students to compare and contrast Leila's notes and response journal. **Possible responses: Her notes are brief but full of information. Her response journal is more conversational and includes her opinions and quotations.**

More Practice!

For more practice with these writing strategies, you may wish to have students use the Strategy Practice Book. See the appendix for reduced Strategy Practice Book pages.

Differentiating Instruction

English-Language Learners Create word-bank cards with compare-and-contrast signal words. On one side, write words that show comparison; on the other side, contrast. Create a separate card with sentences that use the words. Help students use the words in their writing.

Support To help students better understand response journals, ask them to keep a response journal that notes their impressions about something they will experience in the next few days. Point out that it can be something like watching a favorite television show, reading a book or newspaper article, witnessing a sporting event, etc. Note that they should complete their response journals as they are experiencing the event, as opposed to after the event. Ask student volunteers to share their response journals with the class.

WORK with a PARTNER

Have students work with a partner to help identify the books they will be comparing. Students should share information about books they have read and enjoyed. Their partners can then suggest other books which offer some similarities or would make for a good compare-and-contrast book review.

Writing a Book Review

Prewriting Organize Ideas

Information/Organization

Writing Strategy

The review is well organized so the comparisons between the two books are clear.

Make a Venn Diagram from my notes and response journal.

The rubric stresses the importance of organizing my book review. I'll review my notes and my response journal and organize the important points into a Venn Diagram. This diagram will help me keep track of the ways that the books are similar and different.

Writer's Term

Venn Diagram
A **Venn Diagram** is two overlapping circles that show how two things are similar and different. Ways the things are similar are described in the overlapping section. Ways they are different are described in the outside part of each circle.

One of the first things I notice is that *Number the Stars* is set in Denmark, but *Good Night, Maman* is set in France and other countries. That's one way the two books are different. I'll put that information in each outside circle.

However, both books take place during World War II. That's one way they are the same. I'll write that in the overlapping part of the circles. I already have a good start on my Venn Diagram!

Here is my completed Venn Diagram. Besides the settings, I compared the characters, the main events, and the themes. I decided that the theme is the same in both books: Hope and bravery help the children survive.

VENN DIAGRAM
Comparing My Books

Number the Stars
- set in Denmark
- Annemarie and Ellen are warm and fed.
- Rosens are together and safe.
- Rosens escape to Sweden.

Both Books
- 10-year-old girls
- set in WWII
- Nazis are searching for Jews.
- People help Jews escape.
- Hope and bravery help the children survive.

Good Night, Maman
- set in France, Italy, USA
- Karin and Marc are homeless and hungry.
- Levi family splits up; mother dies later.
- Karin and Marc escape to USA.

Now it's your turn. Organize your ideas by using a Venn Diagram.

Reflect
How did I do? Does my Venn Diagram make the major similarities and differences clear?

Prewriting
(Student pages 310–311)

Explain that writing can be organized in many different ways. A graphic organizer, such as a Venn Diagram, can help organize information in preparation for writing.

Review the definition of *Venn Diagram*. Help students recognize the kind of information that should be placed in each section of the circles. Then direct attention to Leila's diagram. Point out that students may not always have equivalent information to list in each portion of the circles, such as "set in Denmark," "set in France, Italy, USA," and "Set in WWII."

Writing a Book Review

Drafting Write a Draft

Voice/Audience The writer's opinion is stated sincerely in the first paragraph.

Writing Strategy Use a sincere tone to state my opinion in the first paragraph.

The rubric reminds me that my opinion, or thesis statement, should sound sincere and clear to my audience. My classmates are my audience, so I'll state my opinion about the books in a way they will understand. Also, I'll put my thesis statement in the first paragraph, as the rubric suggests.

After looking at my notes and response journal, I think I like *Good Night, Maman* better than *Number the Stars*. That will be my thesis statement!

Next, I'll summarize the plot of *Number the Stars* and the plot of *Good Night, Maman*. Then I'll point out ways they are the same and different. I'll show why I think *Good Night, Maman* is better in some ways, so my comparisons support my thesis statement. The first part of my draft is on the next page.

Writer's Term

Thesis Statement
A **thesis statement** is the opinion the writer is attempting to prove. The writer tries to convince readers to accept or believe his or her opinion or thesis statement.

312 **Persuasive Writing** ■ Book Review: Response to Literature

Proofreading Marks

⊐ Indent	ℓ Take out something
≡ Make a capital	⊙ Add a period
/ Make a small letter	SP Spelling error
∧ Add something	¶ New paragraph

[DRAFT]

Bravery and Hope

Number the Stars, by Lois Lowry, and Good Night, Maman, by Norma Fox Mazer, tell about brave young girls during World War II. I prefer Good Night, Maman. It shows better than Number the Stars that children needed both hope and bravery to get through terrible experiences during the war. ← [thesis statement]

In Number the Stars, Annemarie Johansen and Ellen Rosen are friends. They are 10 years old and live in Copenhagen, Denmark. It is 1943, and the Nazis have started arresting Jews in Copenhagen. The Rosens are Jewish.

Ellen stays with Annemarie and pretends to be her sister. Although scared, Annemarie and Ellen face the Nazis when they come to the Johansens' apartment.

Practice!

Now it's your turn. Write a draft using your Venn Diagram. Be sure to state your thesis statement sincerely in the first paragraph.

Reflect

What do you think? Does my thesis sentence seem sincere? Does it make my opinion clear?

Persuasive Writing ■ Book Review: Response to Literature 313

Drafting

(Student pages 312–313)

Begin by reviewing the purpose of a draft. Make sure students understand that a draft is a temporary form of a piece of writing. A draft should be changed and corrected several times before it is finished. Then have a student read Leila's words for the class.

Have students read the definition of thesis statement. Ask whether they think Leila has written a clear thesis statement. Point out that she is beginning her review by summarizing the main points in one of the books, *Number the Stars*. Then she will summarize the main points in *Good Night, Maman,* comparing and contrasting them with the points she covered in *Number the Stars*.

Have students use the information from their Venn Diagrams to write their drafts. Remind them to state their thesis statement sincerely in the first paragraph.

Writing Across the Curriculum

Social Studies Leila is comparing two books about children during World War II. Challenge your students to research how World War II affected children throughout the world. You may wish to separate the class into small groups and assign each group a particular country to research. For example, one group may wish to research how children in the USA dealt with the war and how it affected their lives. Have them find stories, photos, and quotations from children during this time period. Have each group create a poster board displaying what they have learned.

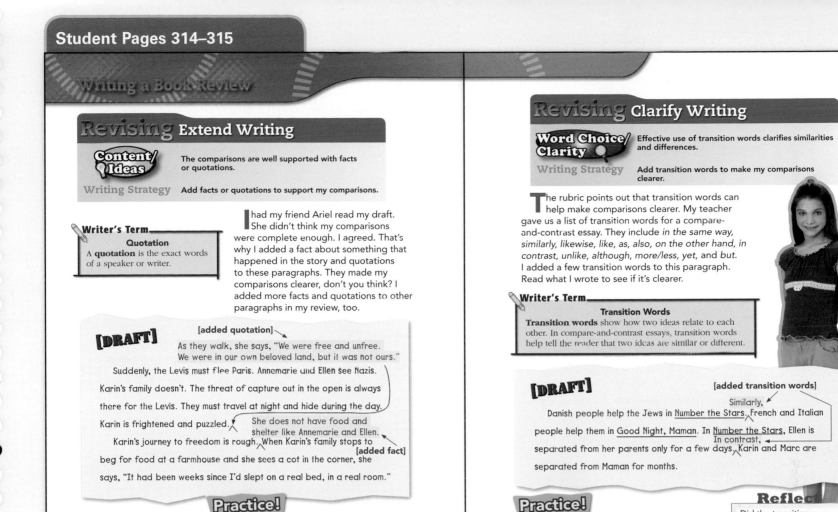

Writing a Book Review

Revising Extend Writing

Content/Ideas The comparisons are well supported with facts or quotations.

Writing Strategy Add facts or quotations to support my comparisons.

Writer's Term___
Quotation
A **quotation** is the exact words of a speaker or writer.

I had my friend Ariel read my draft. She didn't think my comparisons were complete enough. I agreed. That's why I added a fact about something that happened in the story and quotations to these paragraphs. They made my comparisons clearer, don't you think? I added more facts and quotations to other paragraphs in my review, too.

[DRAFT]

[added quotation]
As they walk, she says, "We were free and unfree. We were in our own beloved land, but it was not ours."
Suddenly, the Levis must flee Paris. Annemarie and Ellen see Nazis. Karin's family doesn't. The threat of capture out in the open is always there for the Levis. They must travel at night and hide during the day. Karin is frightened and puzzled.
She does not have food and shelter like Annemarie and Ellen.
Karin's journey to freedom is rough. When Karin's family stops to [added fact] beg for food at a farmhouse and she sees a cot in the corner, she says, "It had been weeks since I'd slept on a real bed, in a real room."

Practice!
Now it's your turn. Try adding some facts or quotations to support your comparisons.

Revising Clarify Writing

Word Choice/Clarity Effective use of transition words clarifies similarities and differences.

Writing Strategy Add transition words to make my comparisons clearer.

The rubric points out that transition words can help make comparisons clearer. My teacher gave us a list of transition words for a compare-and-contrast essay. They include *in the same way, similarly, likewise, like, as, also, on the other hand, in contrast, unlike, although, more/less, yet,* and *but.* I added a few transition words to this paragraph. Read what I wrote to see if it's clearer.

Writer's Term___
Transition Words
Transition words show how two ideas relate to each other. In compare-and-contrast essays, transition words help tell the reader that two ideas are similar or different.

[DRAFT]

[added transition words]
Similarly,
Danish people help the Jews in Number the Stars. French and Italian people help them in Good Night, Maman. In Number the Stars, Ellen is
In contrast,
separated from her parents only for a few days. Karin and Marc are separated from Maman for months.

Practice!
Now it's your turn. Add transition words to clarify the similarities and differences in your review.

Reflect
Did the transition words I added make my comparisons clearer?

Revising

(Student pages 314–315)

Ask a student to read Leila's words on Student page 314 to the class. Point out that Leila has asked a friend to read her draft and offer advice. Suggest that students have another person read their draft and offer ideas for improvement.

Explain to students that one good way to convince readers that your opinion is correct is to elaborate on it by including facts and quotations. Ask students why they think facts or quotations are important to support comparisons. **Possible response: This kind of support is evidence that your opinions are based on facts or quotations from the source.**

Have students look for places in their book reviews where they can add facts or quotations to support their comparisons.

Next, have students read Leila's words on Student page 315 to the class. Remind students that unclear comparisons can be confusing. One way to make writing clearer is to use transition words. Have students read the definition of *transition words* in the Writer's Term box.

Ask them how transition words can help in a compare-and-contrast book review. **Possible response: Readers will know whether you are explaining how things are the same or how they are different.**

Have students check their drafts to see if there are places where they can add transition words to make comparisons clearer.

Differentiating Instruction

Enrichment To further understand transition words, ask students to locate a compare-and-contrast book review in a book, magazine, or on the Internet. Have them underline transition words that the writer used to compare two books. Then have them circle transition words that the writer used to contrast the two books.

Support To help students support their comparisons, provide a chart with three columns. They will write each comparison statement in the wide left column and place a check mark in one or both of the remaining two narrow columns, headed *fact* and *quotation*. At least one column should be checked for each comparison statement.

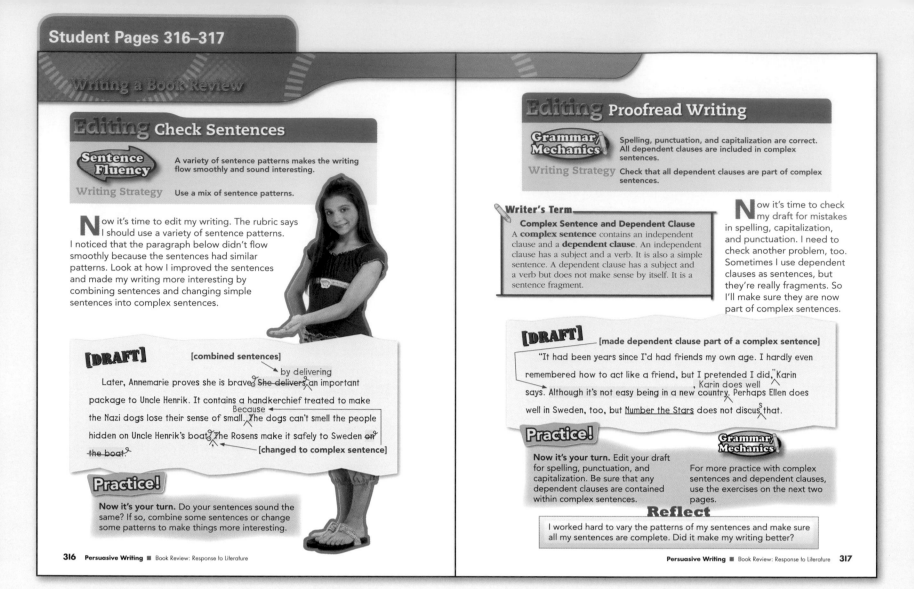

Editing

(Student pages 316–317)

Write the following sentences on the board: *We packed up the car. We filled the car with gas. We started driving to our grandparents' house. They live six hours away.* Ask students whether the sentence structure in these sentences is similar or different. **similar** Explain to students that their writing will flow better if they use a mix of sentence patterns.

Have students change the sentence patterns in the above sentences to make the writing more interesting. **Possible response: We packed up the car and filled it with gas. At long last, we started the six-hour drive to our grandparents' house.**

Have students read through their drafts and identify sentence patterns they could change to make their writing flow smoothly and sound more interesting.

Next, have students read Leila's words on Student page 317. Read aloud the description of *complex sentence* and *dependent clause* from the Writer's Term box on that page. Remind students that dependent clauses should not be used as complete sentences. As students read through their drafts to check for spelling, punctuation, and capitalization errors, ask them to check that dependent clauses are contained within complex sentences.

If some of your students are having trouble identifying complex sentences and dependent clauses, you may wish to teach the Mini-Lesson on page 233 of this Teacher Edition. Then have students complete the exercises on Student pages 318–319. Review the answers and possible rewrites with them.

WORK with a PARTNER Have students swap their drafts with another student. Each student should read through the other's draft to be sure that there are no errors. Students may also wish to point out any ways that the reviews can be clearer, more complete, or better organized.

Complex Sentences

KNOW the RULE

A **complex sentence** contains an independent clause and a dependent clause. An **independent clause** has a subject and a verb. It is also a simple sentence. A **dependent clause** has a subject and a verb but does not make sense by itself. It is one kind of **sentence fragment**. Dependent clauses begin with **subordinating conjunctions** such as *although, because, if, as, so, before,* or *when.*

A dependent clause should be combined with an independent clause to create a complex sentence.

Example:
Independent clause:
You will make wise decisions.
Dependent clause (sentence fragment):
If you think carefully.
Dependent clause + independent clause = complex sentence:
If you think carefully, you will make wise decisions.

Practice the Rule

Number your paper 1–5. Read each group of words and write **CX** if it is a complex sentence or **F** (fragment) if it is a dependent clause.

1. Although Lois Lowry has written many books, *Number the Stars* was her first to win the Newbery Award.
2. When Lowry learned about the World War II rescue of Jews in Denmark.
3. After the Nazis began to threaten the Danish Jews, the Danish Resistance smuggled nearly 7,000 Jews to safety.
4. If you were a Jew in Denmark during the early 1940s.
5. A resistance is a secret organization because it works against a government.

Apply the Rule

Read the following paragraphs from a book review. Write the paragraphs on your paper, correcting any errors in using dependent clauses.

Books of Hope

Although death is a controversial topic. Many young-adult authors have tackled it in their books. Because cancer is a common terminal illness. Some of these authors have chosen to write about the death of a family member by cancer. Two excellent books on this topic are After the Rain by Norma Fox Mazer and A Summer to Die by Lois Lowry. Although the authors face the pain and grief of death head-on. Both books offer hope and healing, too.

It's easy to relate to the main characters of these books. Because they both seem so real. In After the Rain, Rachel is down on herself. She dreams of being a writer, but she never gets more than the beginning of a story written. Since her older parents are sensitive. She should be more thoughtful of their feelings, but she hurts them anyway. She feels she's never had a real boyfriend. Because she has no personality.

Meg, the main character in A Summer to Die, doesn't think a lot of herself either. Since her older sister, Molly, got all the good qualities she doesn't have. Meg says, "I represent the leftovers." While Molly is pleasant and charming. Meg sees herself as impatient and angry. Rachel and Meg also have something really heartbreaking in common: someone in each girl's family is dying of cancer.

Grammar/Mechanics Mini-Lesson

(Student pages 318–319)
Complex Sentences

Explain to students that complex sentences contain independent clauses and dependent clauses. The independent clause contains a subject and a verb and can stand alone as a sentence. A dependent clause has a subject and a verb but does not make sense by itself. Instead, it is a sentence fragment.

Write the following on the board: *When you get home, you should finish your homework.*

Ask students to identify the independent clause in the sentence above. **You should finish your homework.** Ask students to identify the dependent clause. **when you get home**

Explain to the students that dependent clauses begin with subordinating conjunctions such as *although, because, if, as, so, before,* or *when.*

Write the following on the board: *You can watch TV after you have completed your homework.*

Ask students to identify the subordinating conjunction, dependent clause, and independent clause in the sentence above. **subordinating conjunction: after; dependent clause: after you have completed your homework; independent clause: You can watch TV.**

Answers for Practice the Rule

1. **CX**
2. **F**
3. **CX**
4. **F**
5. **CX**

Answers for Apply the Rule

Although death is a controversial topic, many young-adult authors have tackled it in their books. Because cancer is a common terminal illness, some of these authors have chosen to write about the death of a family member by cancer. Two excellent books on this topic are *After the Rain* by Norma Fox Mazer and *A Summer to Die* by Lois

(Answers continue on page 234.)

Writing a Book Review

Publishing Share Writing

Publish my review in the school newspaper.

I like to share my opinions about what I read. The school newspaper seems like the best place to do that. A lot of people can read my review there!

Before publishing my work, I want to check it over one last time. I'll use this checklist to help me.

My Checklist

✔ The review concentrates on important similarities and differences between the books.

✔ My thesis statement is sincere and appears in the first paragraph.

✔ The review is well organized with clear comparisons, effective use of transition words, and good supporting facts or quotations.

✔ My writing flows smoothly because my sentences are varied and interesting.

✔ Spelling, capitalization, and punctuation are all correct. There are no fragments because dependent clauses are all in complex sentences.

Practice!

Now it's your turn. Make a checklist to check your book review. Then make a final draft to publish.

BOOK REVIEW CORNER

Bravery and Hope
by Leila

Number the Stars by Lois Lowry and *Good Night, Maman* by Norma Fox Mazer tell about brave young girls during World War II. I prefer *Good Night, Maman.* It shows better than *Number the Stars* that children needed both hope and bravery to get through terrible experiences during the war.

In *Number the Stars,* Annemarie Johansen and Ellen Rosen are friends. They are 10 years old and live in Copenhagen, Denmark. It is 1943, and the Nazis have started arresting Jews in Copenhagen. The Rosens are Jewish.

Ellen stays with Annemarie and pretends to be her sister. Although scared, Annemarie and Ellen face the Nazis when they come to the Johansens' apartment.

The Johansens then take Ellen to Uncle Henrik's house by the sea. There Ellen is reunited with her parents. Annemarie realizes her family and friends are in danger, but she is unsure that she is brave enough to help them. Uncle Henrik says, "I think you are like your mama, and your papa, and like me. Frightened, but determined, and if the time came to be brave, I am quite sure you would be very, very brave."

Later, Annemarie proves she is brave by delivering an important package to Uncle Henrik. It contains a handkerchief treated to make the Nazi dogs lose their sense of smell. Because the dogs can't smell the people hidden on Uncle Henrik's boat, the Rosens make it safely to Sweden.

The main character in *Good Night, Maman* is also a 10-year-old girl. Karin Levi lives in Paris, France, with her mother (Maman) and her brother, Marc. The Nazis have also occupied this country and have been searching for Jewish people like the Levis. They have shot Karin's father already. Her family must hide in a

---

(Answers continued from page 233.)

Lowry. Although the authors face the pain and grief of death head-on, both books offer hope and healing, too.

It's easy to relate to the main characters of these books because they both seem so real. In *After the Rain,* Rachel is down on herself. She dreams of being a writer, but she never gets more than the beginning of a story written. Since her older parents are sensitive, she should be more thoughtful of their feelings, but she hurts them anyway. She feels she's never had a real boyfriend because she has no personality.

Meg, the main character in *A Summer to Die,* doesn't think a lot of herself, either. Since her older sister, Molly, got all the good qualities she doesn't have, Meg says, "I represent the leftovers." While Molly is pleasant and charming, Meg sees herself as impatient and angry. Rachel and Meg also have something really heartbreaking in common: someone in each girl's family is dying of cancer.

✔ For more practice with grammar/mechanics skills, see Zaner-Bloser's *G.U.M.* materials.

Publishing
(Student pages 320–321)

Ask a student to read Leila's words on Student page 320. Ask students if they like Leila's choice for sharing her book review. Ask them to think of other places Leila might consider publishing her review.

Read aloud Leila's checklist. Have students make a checklist to check their own book reviews. Once they have completed their drafts, students might submit their book review to the school newspaper to be published.

tiny attic closet for a year. This is worse than anything Annemarie or Ellen goes through, but Karin stays hopeful.

Suddenly, the Levis must flee Paris. Annemarie and Ellen see Nazis. Karin's family doesn't. On the other hand, the threat of capture out in the open is always there. They must travel at night and hide during the day. Karin is frightened and puzzled. As they walk, she says, "We were free and unfree. We were in our own beloved land, but it was not ours."

Karin's journey to freedom is rough. She does not have food and shelter like Annemarie and Ellen. When Karin's family stops to beg for food at a farmhouse and she sees a cot in the corner, she says, "It had been weeks since I'd slept on a real bed, in a real room."

Danish people help the Jews in *Number the Stars*. Similarly, French and Italian people help them in *Good Night, Maman*. In *Number the Stars*, Ellen is parted from her parents only for a few days. In

contrast, Karin and Marc are separated from Maman for months.

The separation becomes wider when Karin and Marc board a ship taking Jewish refugees to the United States. Annemarie and Ellen can depend on their parents for help, but Karin has only Marc. She begins writing letters to Maman. The letters show how brave and strong she is. In her first letter, she writes, "I never wanted to go so far away from you. I didn't want to get on this boat. But Marc said we wouldn't be safe anywhere in Europe until the war was over, and that you would absolutely want us to do this."

In the United States, Karin and Marc stay in a refugee camp and learn American ways. Karin still writes to Maman, but she also is determined to make new friends. "It had been years since I'd had friends my own age. I hardly even remembered how to act like a friend, but I pretended I did," Karin says. Although it's not easy being in a new country, Karin does well. Perhaps

Ellen does well in Sweden, too, but *Number the Stars* does not discuss that.

Finally, Karin learns the truth: her mother is dead. Marc has known about it for a few months. He helps Karin handle her grief.

When the war ends, Annemarie waits for Ellen to come back to Copenhagen. Karin plans to live in California with her aunt. Although Karin has no parents, she has bravery and hope. Karin says, "I thought about everything I had learned

about people—some bad, some good. And I had learned that you can't look back for too long. You just have to keep going."

Both of these books are about 10-year-old Jewish girls coping with life in countries occupied by the Nazis. While I enjoyed reading both of them, I liked *Good Night, Maman* a little better because I thought the ending was more realistic. Many Jewish families were separated forever by that war, and *Good Night, Maman* showed that clearly.

Reflect

What do you think? Did I use all the traits of a good book review in my writing? Check it against the rubric. Then use the rubric to check your own book review.

TiPS for the Writing Classroom

Creating Personal Journals
by Ken Stewart, *Master Teacher*

Journal writing can be fun! So why do so many students seem to abhor the idea of putting their thoughts down into a journal? How can the teacher make this an enjoyable activity?

One thing that seems to "turn off" students is the fact that many educators want them to journal on a daily basis. Although this is an admirable concept, it is probably an unrealistic practice for most students. To many of your students, it will become a monotonous, forced task over time. Why not have fewer purposeful journaling times and encourage free (anytime) personal journaling?

Make a distinction between "purposeful journaling" and "free personal journaling." Purposeful journaling occurs when the teacher gives a prompt or direction on what to write about. Free journaling takes place when the student writes about personal (not private) experiences. These entries, although personal, can be shared with the teacher or other classmates when desired.

No matter what type of journal writing is being explored, it is a time for students to work on developing their own voice.

For this reason, it is recommended that you not grade student journals as you would regular assignments. You could, however, consider including student journals as part of a class grade or extra credit.

To further personalize journals, ask students to create their own journals and design their own covers. (Zaner-Bloser has excellent blank journals for this activity.) Also, encourage your students to draw, cut or paste, put in pockets, and add photographs to the pages to express themselves in other ways. The goal is to make the journal an interactive record that truly displays your students' feelings.

Here are four easy steps to good journal writing:

1. Define purposeful and personal journaling.

2. Journal with a purpose only once or twice a week.

3. Encourage personal journaling as often as students want.

4. Establish (ideally with the class) how the journals will be evaluated.

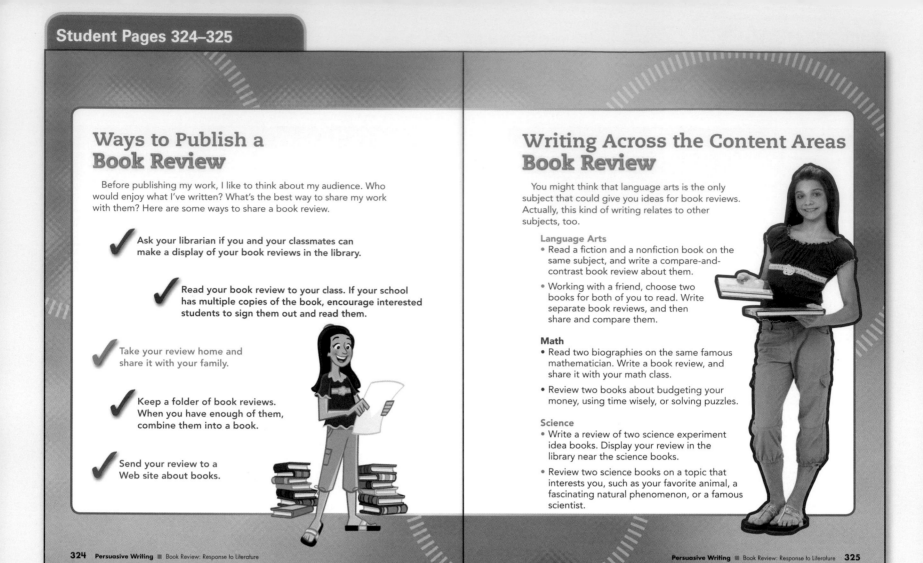

Ways to Publish
(Student page 324)

Read and discuss with students the different publishing options on Student page 324. Encourage your students to consider some of these options when publishing their own writing. You may also wish to have students share their book reviews with the class. Place copies of each book in the front of the class, with the reviews underneath them. Point out that students can use these book reviews to help find books they may wish to read. Have students research Web sites that publish student book reviews. Suggest that they submit their book reviews to these sites to be published.

Writing Across the Content Areas
(Student page 325)

Remind your students that writing is not just for English or language arts class. There are many other subjects that contain ideas, characters, and events that students may want to write about. Have students consider using one of the content areas on Student page 325 to write another book review. Students may wish to consult with other teachers for more ideas on writing in their content areas.

Books for Professional Development

Hyerle, David. *Visual Tools for Constructing Knowledge.* Alexandria: ASCD, 1996.

This book provides a deeper understanding of the use and application of graphic organizers, including some that may be new to many teachers. The author also offers many possible variations on the more familiar organizers.

Kiester, Jane Bell. *Blowing Away the State Writing Assessment Test: Four Steps to Better Scores for Teachers of All Levels.* 2nd ed. Gainesville: Maupin 2000.

The author offers reproducible pages for narrative, expository, and persuasive topics in elementary and middle school, as well as information on how students can use rubrics to evaluate their work.

Parsons, Les. *Revising & Editing: Using Models and Checklists to Promote Successful Writing Experiences.* Markam: Pembroke, 2001.

This source provides reproducible pages for eight series of revision models labeled "junior" or "intermediate." The author covers narratives, essays, projects or extended assignments, poetry, the entire drafting process, and peer conferencing.

Van Zile, Susan. *Awesome Hands-on Activities for Teaching Literary Elements.* New York: Scholastic, 2001.

In this resource, a teacher shares 30 hands-on activities for instructing students about literary elements. These activities build on students' different learning styles, giving all students a chance to learn information in the way they learn best. It also includes reproducible student direction sheets and rubric.

Persuasive Essay Overview

In this chapter, students will learn how to write a persuasive essay. They will learn different elements of a persuasive essay—clear opinion, good reasoning, neutral language, question-and-answer pattern—and some reasons for writing a persuasive essay. Students will then use a persuasive essay rubric to assess a model writing sample.

Next, students will follow the student guide as she goes through the various writing stages for a persuasive essay, including prewriting, drafting, revising, editing, and publishing. At each stage, students will be directed to practice the strategies in their own writing. They will begin by choosing an issue and finding information to support their opinions. Next, they will use a Network Tree to organize their ideas and write a draft using the information from their Network Trees. During the revising stage, they will add facts and reasons to support their opinions and replace loaded words with neutral words. After that, they will edit their drafts to include question-and-answer sentence patterns and be sure that each pronoun has a clear antecedent. They will also edit their drafts for correct spelling, punctuation, and capitalization and correct punctuation of quotations. Finally, they will explore ways to publish their persuasive essays.

You may wish to send to families the School-Home Connection Letter for this chapter, located at the end of this unit in the Teacher Edition.

Persuasive Essay Writing Traits

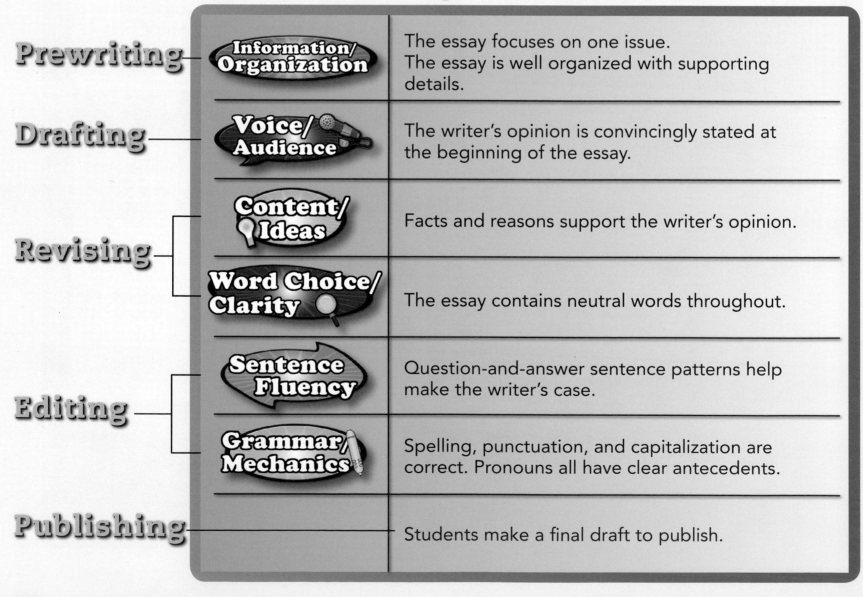

Prewriting	**Information/Organization**	The essay focuses on one issue. The essay is well organized with supporting details.
Drafting	**Voice/Audience**	The writer's opinion is convincingly stated at the beginning of the essay.
Revising	**Content/Ideas**	Facts and reasons support the writer's opinion.
	Word Choice/Clarity	The essay contains neutral words throughout.
Editing	**Sentence Fluency**	Question-and-answer sentence patterns help make the writer's case.
	Grammar/Mechanics	Spelling, punctuation, and capitalization are correct. Pronouns all have clear antecedents.
Publishing		Students make a final draft to publish.

Persuasive Essay Time Management

WEEK 1

	Day 1	Day 2	Day 3	Day 4	Day 5
Learning Objectives	Students will: • study the components of a persuasive essay.	Students will: • learn how to gather information for a persuasive essay.	Students will: • practice gathering information for their persuasive essays.	Students will: • learn how to make a Network Tree to organize their notes.	Students will: • practice organizing their notes to make a Network Tree.
Activities	• Discuss the elements and traits of a persuasive essay (Student pages 326–328). • Use the rubric to assess the model (Student pages 329–333).	• Read and discuss **Prewriting: Gather Information** (Student page 334).	• Choose an issue and find information to support opinions. • Gather information and take notes.	• Read and discuss **Prewriting: Organize Ideas** (Student page 335).	• Look at notes on a persuasive essay. • Use notes to fill in a Network Tree.

WEEK 2

	Day 1	Day 2	Day 3	Day 4	Day 5
Learning Objectives	Students will: • learn how to begin their essay by expressing their opinions in a convincing tone.	Students will: • practice writing their own drafts.	Students will: • learn to add facts and reasons to support their opinions.	Students will: • practice adding facts and reasons to support their opinions.	Students will: • learn to replace loaded words with neutral words.
Activities	• Read and discuss **Drafting: Write a Draft** (Student pages 336–337).	• Use Network Tree to write a draft. • Begin essays by expressing opinions in a convincing tone.	• Read and discuss **Revising: Extend Writing** (Student page 338).	• Add convincing facts and reasons to drafts.	• Read and discuss **Revising: Clarify Writing** (Student page 339).

WEEK 3

	Day 1	Day 2	Day 3	Day 4	Day 5
Learning Objectives	Students will: • practice replacing loaded words with neutral words.	Students will: • learn how using question-and-answer patterns help make the writer's case.	Students will: • learn how to make sure each pronoun has a clear antecedent.	Students will: • practice editing their drafts for spelling, punctuation, and capitalization.	Students will: • learn different ways to publish their persuasive essays.
Activities	• Reread drafts to see if there are any loaded words. • Replace any loaded words with neutral words.	• Read and discuss **Editing: Check Sentences** (Student page 340). • Add question-and-answer sentence patterns to drafts.	• Read and discuss **Editing: Proofread Writing** (Student page 341). • Make sure pronouns have clear antecedents.	• Fix any spelling, punctuation, or capitalization errors. • Fix pronoun and antecedent errors.	• Read and discuss **Publishing: Share Writing** (Student page 344).

* To complete the chapter in fewer days, teach the learning objectives and activities for two days in one day.

This planning chart, correlated to your state's writing standards, is available on-line at http://www.zaner-bloser.com/sfw.

What's a **Persuasive Essay?**

A persuasive essay expresses a writer's opinion on a topic. It tries to convince readers to agree with the writer and maybe even act in a certain way. For example, a persuasive essay might try to convince readers to conserve energy in specific ways.

I think I'll like writing a persuasive essay. I get to act like a lawyer and present a case for my opinion!

What's in a **Persuasive Essay?**

Clear Opinion
I need to decide exactly what I think of the issue I'm writing about. Then I have to make that opinion clear to my readers. That means stating the opinion convincingly so my audience knows just where I stand.

Good Reasoning
Readers aren't going to be convinced that my opinion is right just because I say so. I need to write a well-organized essay with plenty of supportive details and good, logical reasons for my opinions.

Neutral Language
When you're expressing an opinion on something you care about, it's easy to get emotional. But negative language or emotionally loaded words just turn readers off. I'll use neutral language in my essay so my audience will be willing to consider my opinion.

Question-and-Answer Pattern
Facts are important in this kind of writing, but I don't want my essay to be boring! I'm going to use a question-and-answer pattern to keep things interesting.

Why write a **Persuasive Essay?**

I enjoy convincing people of an opinion I think is right, but there are other reasons to write a persuasive essay. I've listed a few suggestions here to give you some ideas.

Changing Lives
Maybe that sounds a bit dramatic, but I really think a persuasive essay can do this! A good essay can change someone's point of view—and even encourage him or her to do something differently.

Reasoning Skills
You really have to think things through to write a persuasive essay. So this kind of writing gives me some good practice in reasoning skills, such as organizing my thoughts, backing up a point, and following a logical train of thought.

Informing
Even if a persuasive essay doesn't change a reader's opinion, it gives him or her more information on the topic. He or she might learn something completely new—or develop a deeper understanding of the issue.

Avoiding Arguments
Writing a persuasive essay helps make a disagreement about an issue less emotional and personal. This kind of writing turns things into a debate instead of a fight!

Define the Genre
(Student page 326)

Persuasive Essay

Ask students to suggest ways they could present their opinions about an issue to the school or community. **Possible responses: write an article about it for the school or local newspaper; talk about it on school or community cable TV; talk about it at a school assembly or town meeting** Ask what type of information they would offer to convince their audience that their opinion was correct. **Possible responses: other students' or towns-people's opinions; related news articles**

Explain that whether they are speaking or writing, they are trying to convince or persuade an audience that their opinion is correct. The written form of persuasion is called a persuasive essay. Tell them that most essays are short. Ask them why. **Possible response: Readers, especially those who disagree with the writer's opinion, are more likely to read an essay if it is short and to the point.**

Elements of the Genre
Persuasive Essay

Read and discuss the elements of a persuasive essay with the students. As you review the elements, ask students why they think each is important in a persuasive essay.

Authentic Writing
(Student page 327)

Persuasive Essay

Read and discuss with students the reasons for writing a persuasive essay on Student page 327. Remind students that all writing has a purpose and that the tone and focus of their writing will be shaped by their reasons for writing a persuasive essay. Point out that one reason for writing a persuasive essay—to practice reasoning skills—enables students to practice a skill that they will be using throughout their lives. A well-written persuasive essay can also affect others, by changing lives and by informing them of something of which they were unaware. Have students think about reasons they would write a persuasive essay. Remind them that these reasons will help set the tone of their essay.

Persuasive Essay Writing Traits

A persuasive essay has six traits, which are listed below. I plan to include all of them as I write.

Information/Organization	The essay focuses on one issue. The essay is well organized with supporting details.
Voice/Audience	The writer's opinion is convincingly stated at the beginning of the essay.
Content/Ideas	Facts and reasons support the writer's opinion.
Word Choice/Clarity	The essay contains neutral wording throughout.
Sentence Fluency	Question-and-answer sentence patterns help make the writer's case.
Grammar/Mechanics	Spelling, punctuation, and capitalization are correct. Pronouns all have clear antecedents.

Let's see how Arina Zubatova used these traits in her persuasive essay on the next page.

Persuasive Essay Model

The Right Angle on the Triangle
by Arina Zubatova

Question / *Answer*

When you think about the Bermuda Triangle, what comes to your mind? Do you picture mysterious forces, time warps, and the underwater city of Atlantis? That is how some people explain the disappearances of boats and planes in the Bermuda Triangle. However, the dangers there are natural, not supernatural. — *Clear opinion*

The corners of the Bermuda Triangle are Bermuda, Puerto Rico, and Fort Lauderdale, Florida. About 100 boats and planes have disappeared in this region. About 1,000 people have died there in the past century. However, that is only ten people a year, not a high number for such a large area. If this region were especially dangerous, insurance companies would charge higher rates for crafts that pass through it. They do not. *Logical reasoning*

Question Why did those 100 boats and planes disappear in the Triangle? The *Answer* causes were natural, not supernatural. In the tropics, sudden storms—even giant waterspouts—can destroy ships and aircraft. The Gulf Stream, a strong ocean current, can pull amateur sailors far off course. In addition, the region has trenches thousands of feet deep. In fact, the deepest trench in the Atlantic Ocean is in the Bermuda Triangle. Remains of boats and planes may be buried in these trenches. — *Neutral language*

Despite these facts, many accidents in the Bermuda Triangle have been described as mysterious. The 1945 disappearance of five Navy bombers off the coast of Florida was one of them. The planes disappeared during a training flight for rookies. The flight was led by an experienced pilot. However, radio transcripts show that his compass was not working. It caused him to lead the group out to sea instead of toward Florida. Then a storm blew in. The planes vanished, and no wreckage was ever found.

What happened to those Navy bombers? The planes probably ended up far out in the Atlantic. There they ran out of gas and fell into the sea. Sharks took the pilots. A trench swallowed the wreckage. In spite of this logical explanation, this and many other disappearances have been blamed on mysterious forces in the Triangle. — *Neutral language*

People like a good story. Still, we must not ignore the facts about the Bermuda Triangle. The dangers are real, not supernatural. — *Clear opinion*

Writing Traits

(Student pages 328–329)

Persuasive Essay

Ask students if they have ever read or heard an argument or essay that has changed their opinion about something. Ask them to recall why they changed their opinion. You may wish to share a personal anecdote if students cannot recall an incident.

Tell students that they will be studying strategies for writing persuasive essays. They will also be using these strategies to write their own persuasive essays. Point out that a good persuasive essay will have the traits listed on Student page 328. Have one or more volunteers read aloud the traits and their descriptions.

Have students listen and try to identify these traits as you read aloud "The Right Angle on the Triangle" on Student page 329.

Differentiating Instruction

English-Language Learners **Preteach** key words such as *supernatural* and *trench*. After reading "The Right Angle on the Triangle," help English-language learners understand the story by reviewing additional vocabulary with them. For example, you may wish to define the phrase *time warps* for students. Ask them to guess the meaning of the word *rookies* and to give examples of other instances where the word *rookies* might be used.

Remind students of the importance of using context clues to help decipher the meanings of words. For instance, in order to understand the meaning of the word *supernatural* in the first paragraph of this essay, students can refer back to the question, *"Do you picture mysterious forces, time warps, and the underwater city of Atlantis?"* This provides some explanation of *supernatural*, as does the comparison to the word *natural* in the sentence in which it appears. Students looking at these context clues might surmise that *supernatural* has to do with something not natural, or something mysterious. As ELLs continue to read these essays, they will come to realize that they do not need to know every word in a story in order to grasp the meaning.

Persuasive Essay
Rubric

The traits of a good persuasive essay from page 328 have been used to make the rubric below. By using 1, 2, 3, or 4 check marks to judge each trait, you can decide how well any persuasive essay was written.

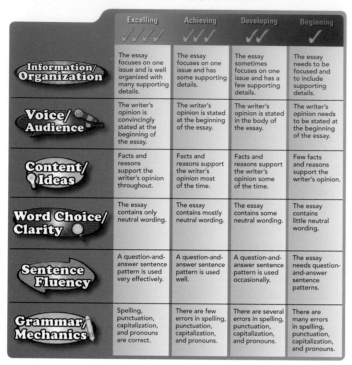

	Excelling ✓✓✓✓	Achieving ✓✓✓	Developing ✓✓	Beginning ✓
Information/Organization	The essay focuses on one issue and is well organized with many supporting details.	The essay focuses on one issue and has some supporting details.	The essay sometimes focuses on one issue and has a few supporting details.	The essay needs to be focused and to include supporting details.
Voice/Audience	The writer's opinion is convincingly stated at the beginning of the essay.	The writer's opinion is stated at the beginning of the essay.	The writer's opinion is stated in the body of the essay.	The writer's opinion needs to be stated at the beginning of the essay.
Content/Ideas	Facts and reasons support the writer's opinion throughout.	Facts and reasons support the writer's opinion most of the time.	Facts and reasons support the writer's opinion some of the time.	Few facts and reasons support the writer's opinion.
Word Choice/Clarity	The essay contains only neutral wording.	The essay contains mostly neutral wording.	The essay contains some neutral wording.	The essay contains little neutral wording.
Sentence Fluency	A question-and-answer sentence pattern is used very effectively.	A question-and-answer sentence pattern is used well.	A question-and-answer sentence pattern is used occasionally.	The essay needs question-and-answer sentence patterns.
Grammar/Mechanics	Spelling, punctuation, capitalization, and pronouns are correct.	There are few errors in spelling, punctuation, capitalization, and pronouns.	There are several errors in spelling, punctuation, capitalization, and pronouns.	There are many errors in spelling, punctuation, capitalization, and pronouns.

Persuasive Essay
Using the Rubric to Study the Model

Let's use the rubric to check Arina's persuasive essay, "The Right Angle on the Triangle." How many check marks would you give her for each trait?

Information/Organization
- The essay focuses on one issue.
- The essay is well organized with supporting details.

Arina focuses on only one specific issue: the strange disappearances in the Bermuda Triangle. Every single sentence in her essay relates to that topic! The essay is well organized, too, and it includes a number of supporting details that helped convince me of her opinion.

[from the writing model]

> The corners of the Bermuda Triangle are Bermuda, Puerto Rico, and Fort Lauderdale, Florida. About 100 boats and planes have disappeared in this region. About 1,000 people have died there in the past century. However, that is only ten people a year, not a high number for such a large area.

Voice/Audience
- The writer's opinion is convincingly stated at the beginning of the essay.

This writer lets us know her opinion in the very first paragraph. See how the last sentence in this paragraph really tells you what she thinks?

[from the writing model]

> When you think about the Bermuda Triangle, what comes to your mind? Do you picture mysterious forces, time warps, and the underwater city of Atlantis? That is how some people explain the disappearances of boats and planes in the Bermuda Triangle. However, the dangers there are natural, not supernatural.

Using the Rubric
(Student page 330)

Ask students to look at the rubric on Student page 330. Remind students that the rubric contains the same traits that are shown on Student page 328. Ask students what kind of marks a student would receive for following all of the writing traits on Student page 328 in his or her essay. **Excelling, or four checks**

Stress to students the importance of using a rubric when writing their own essays.

Review with students the traits under each level for the Grammar/Mechanics row. Point out that students will need to ensure their essays are free of grammar and mechanics errors when they write their final drafts. Note that they should look for grammar/mechanics errors every step of the way as they are writing their essays, especially during the editing stage.

Have students refer to the rubric as they assess the student model.

Study the Model
(Student pages 331–333)

Read Student pages 331–333 with your students to compare the writing model to the rubric. As you review each of the traits, ask students as a group to determine how many check marks they would give the writer. Have students explain their responses.

Tell students to look for other examples of each trait in the writing model.

As you read the Voice/Audience box on Student page 331, ask students to determine what the writer's opinion on the dangers of the Bermuda Triangle is. **that the dangers are natural, not supernatural** Note that the writer has very clearly stated her opinion early on in her essay.

Persuasive Essay

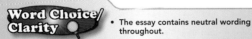
• Facts and reasons support the writer's opinion.

This writer carefully chose which facts to include. For example, she could have told us the name of the pilot leading the flight, but she didn't. She knew that would not help convince us that the dangers in the Bermuda Triangle are natural. Did you notice how she mentioned the storm, though? It's a good reason to think the planes' disappearance wasn't supernatural.

[from the writing model]

Despite these facts, many accidents in the Bermuda Triangle have been described as mysterious. The 1945 disappearance of five Navy bombers off the coast of Florida was one of them. The planes disappeared during a training flight for rookies. The flight was led by an experienced pilot. However, radio transcripts show that his compass was not working. It caused him to lead the group out to sea instead of toward Florida. Then a storm blew in. The planes vanished, and no wreckage was ever found.

Word Choice/ Clarity
• The essay contains neutral wording throughout.

Arina might have used loaded, negative words, like *idiot*, to show that she is amazed that some people believe there are mysterious forces in the Bermuda Triangle. However, she doesn't say, "Some idiots will believe anything." Instead, she simply says this:

[from the writing model]

People like a good story. Still, we must not ignore the facts about the Bermuda Triangle. The dangers are real, not supernatural.

Sentence Fluency
• Question-and-answer sentence patterns help make the writer's case.

Arina makes good use of a question-and-answer sentence pattern. It's as if she's asking the questions we would like to ask and then answering them! Read the following paragraph, and you'll see what I mean.

[from the writing model]

What happened to those Navy bombers? The planes probably ended up far out in the Atlantic. There they ran out of gas and fell into the sea. Sharks took the pilots. A trench swallowed the wreckage.

Grammar/ Mechanics
• Spelling, punctuation, and capitalization are correct. Pronouns all have clear antecedents.

I didn't find a single mistake in spelling, punctuation, or capitalization. The writer was also careful with pronouns. Can you tell what the pronoun *it* refers to in the first sentence below? It refers to *region*, right? *It* and *region* are both singular, so they agree. In the second sentence, it's clear that *They* refers to *companies*. These words are both plural, so they agree.

[from the writing model]

If this region were especially dangerous, insurance companies would charge higher rates for crafts that pass through it. They do not.

Now it's my turn to write a persuasive essay. I'll use what I learned from the rubric and good writing strategies. Follow along with me to see how I do it.

Differentiating Instruction

Support To help students understand the importance of keeping words neutral in a persuasive essay, write the following on the board: *The idea to increase the school day by half an hour is completely idiotic. I mean, who would come up with such an idea? Students already have enough on our plates without having to stay at school longer.* Ask students how they think the person who came up with the idea of increasing the school day would feel if he or she read this information. Do they think it would make this person want to change his or her mind? Why or why not? **Possible responses: It would probably put the person on the defensive and not make him or her want to even consider the other side.** Ask students how they think they could present a much more effective argument instead. **Possible responses: Leave out words such as *idiotic* and focus instead on facts and solid information about how this would not be a good idea.** Note that students should refrain from using loaded, negative words in their arguments, as such words will not help them to win their case.

Writing a Persuasive Essay

Prewriting Gather Information

Information/Organization The essay focuses on one issue.

Writing Strategy Choose an issue and find information to support my opinion.

I live in Tennessee, but California is the main location of one of my hobbies—old movies. My favorite aunt lives in California, too, and I visit her whenever I can.

Some people think that all Californians care only about how they look and what the latest fads are. That upsets me.

When our teacher asked us to write a persuasive essay, I decided to try to convince my classmates not to stereotype people based on where they live. I read some articles about California and took these notes.

Notes on Stereotyping and Californians

- CA's population grew 50 percent between 1970 and 1990.
- CA has more immigrants from other countries than any other state.
- Californians come in all shapes and sizes.
- One in four Californians is Hispanic.
- In 1990 census, nearly 5 million Californians had German ancestors; 3.5 million were from Irish families.
- 1990 census: more than half of the people living in CA were not born there.
- Migrants come from all over the nation, especially the South and Northeast.

Practice!

Now it's your turn. Choose an issue about which you have an opinion. Do some research and find facts to support your opinion.

334 **Persuasive Writing** ■ Persuasive Essay

Prewriting Organize Ideas

Information/Organization The essay is well organized with supporting details.

Writing Strategy Use a Network Tree to organize my ideas.

Writer's Term

Network Tree A **Network Tree** organizes information about a topic. The topic or opinion goes at the top, with main ideas or reasons on the next level. The bottom level contains facts to support the main ideas or reasons.

A Network Tree can help me get my ideas in order. I'll put my opinion at the top, the reasons for my opinion under that, and supportive facts underneath each reason. As I write, I can look at my Network Tree and see the reasons and facts I need to include in my essay.

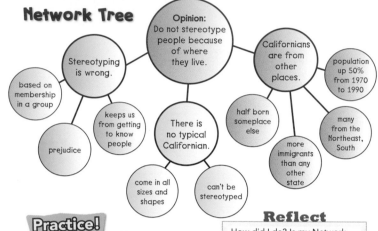

Network Tree

Practice!

Now it's your turn. Organize your ideas by using a Network Tree.

Reflect

How did I do? Is my Network Tree well organized? Will it help me write a convincing essay?

Persuasive Writing ■ Persuasive Essay 335

Prewriting

(Student pages 334–335)

Read Leila's words on Student page 334 aloud. Discuss her reasons for choosing this topic. Ask students to comment on her notes. **Possible responses: Her notes are brief but include many facts to support her opinion.**

Explain that writing can be organized in many different ways. A graphic organizer, such as a Network Tree, is one way to organize information in preparation for writing.

Ask a student to read the definition of *Network Tree* from the Writer's Term box on Student page 335. Then direct attention to Leila's Tree. Discuss how she organized her notes on the Network Tree.

Differentiating Instruction

Enrichment Challenge students to write a type of persuasive essay called the problem-solution essay, in which they present a problem and offer a workable solution. Encourage them to ask their audience to take an action that is part of the solution.

Enrichment Help students better understand how to use a Network Tree by having them create one from a newspaper editorial or a letter to the editor. Explain that many columns found on the editorial pages of a newspaper are persuasive in nature, presenting an opinion and then reasons, supported by facts. Have them present their Network Trees in class.

More Practice!

For more practice with these writing strategies, you may wish to have students use the Strategy Practice Book. See the appendix for reduced Strategy Practice Book pages.

WORK with a PARTNER

Have students select an issue that they wish to discuss in their persuasive essays. Then ask them to work with a partner to try to come up with facts and reasons to support their position. They should use the information to jot down notes for their essays, just as Leila has done.

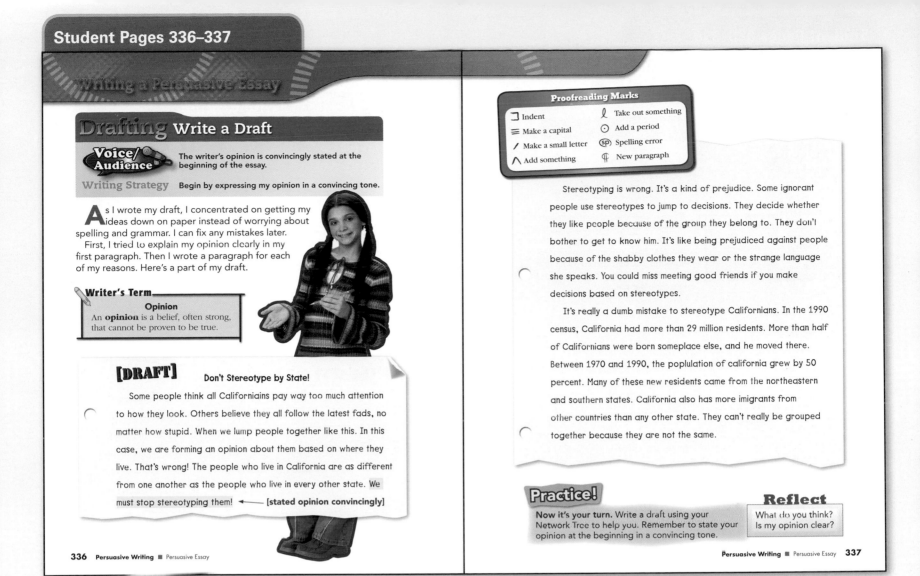

Drafting

(Student pages 336–337)

Have a student read Leila's words on Student page 336. Ask students why Leila is not worried about mistakes when she writes her draft. **Possible response: It's just a first draft, and she will be able to fix mistakes in the editing and revising stages.** Remind students that when they write their drafts, they should not be concerned about making mistakes, either; it's more important at this stage to get their ideas down on paper.

Ask students where in her Network Tree Leila would find the information to include at the beginning of her essay. **Possible response: from the top level of her Network Tree** Point out that after writing her first paragraph based on the information from the top level of her Tree, Leila went on to draft a separate paragraph for each of her supporting reasons. This is a good way to ensure that she has a well-organized essay.

Have students use the information from their Network Tree to write the draft of their persuasive essays. Remind them to state their opinions convincingly at the beginning of their essays.

When students begin to edit their drafts, encourage them to use the proofreading marks shown in the box on Student page 337.

> ## Writing Across the Curriculum
>
> **Geography** Leila states the population of California, as well as information on immigration, in her essay. Note that population and immigration statistics are part of the geography of California. Ask students to point out other information that is part of a region's geography. **Possible responses: landforms, climate, land area** Have students research other aspects of California's geography.

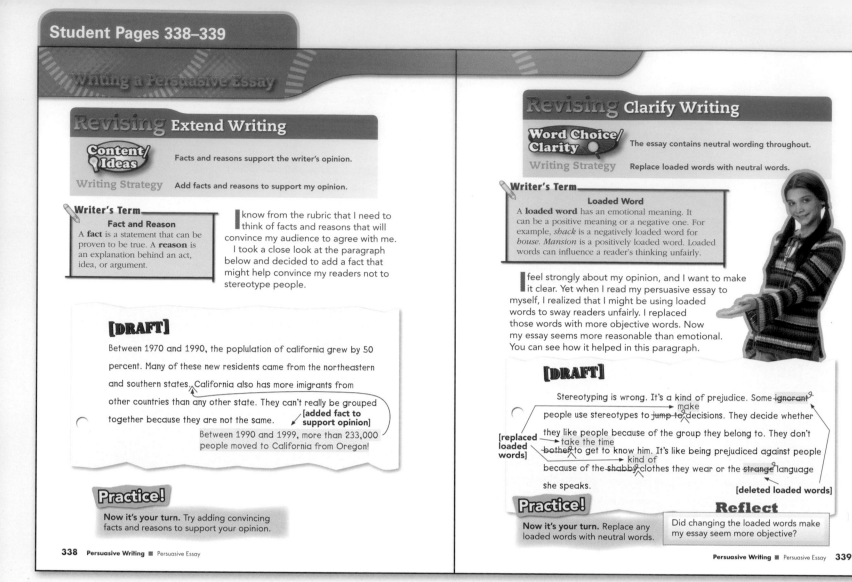

Revising

(Student pages 338–339)

Ask a student to read Leila's words on Student page 338. Explain that one good way to convince readers of your opinion is to present facts and reasons that support it. Ask students why facts and reasons are convincing. **Possible response: They are evidence that your opinions are based on facts or are shared by knowledgeable people. Without supporting facts and reasons, your opinions can seem like just your personal thoughts.**

Ask students to review their drafts to see if there are any areas where they can add convincing facts and reasons to support their opinion.

Next, have a student read Leila's words on Student page 339. Then read aloud the definition of *loaded word* from the Writer's Term box. Ask how avoiding loaded words makes their writing not only clearer but fairer. **Possible response: Loaded words use emotions, rather than logic, to sway readers' opinions. Using these words often backfires by distracting or angering readers. Readers are more likely to be convinced by facts, not emotions.**

Ask students to review their drafts to be sure there are no loaded words. Have them replace loaded words with neutral words.

Differentiating Instruction

English-Language Learners Students may need extra help in recognizing loaded words. Ask them to translate several loaded words into their native languages. (Note: Some loaded words are idiomatic, so translation may not be direct.) Then do the same with neutral words that could replace loaded words. English-language learners might ask students who are proficient in English to help them check their drafts for loaded words until they are able to recognize them on their own.

Support To help students include clear antecedents for each pronoun, ask them to write the antecedent in parentheses above each pronoun. Encourage students to use this strategy in all drafts but the final one.

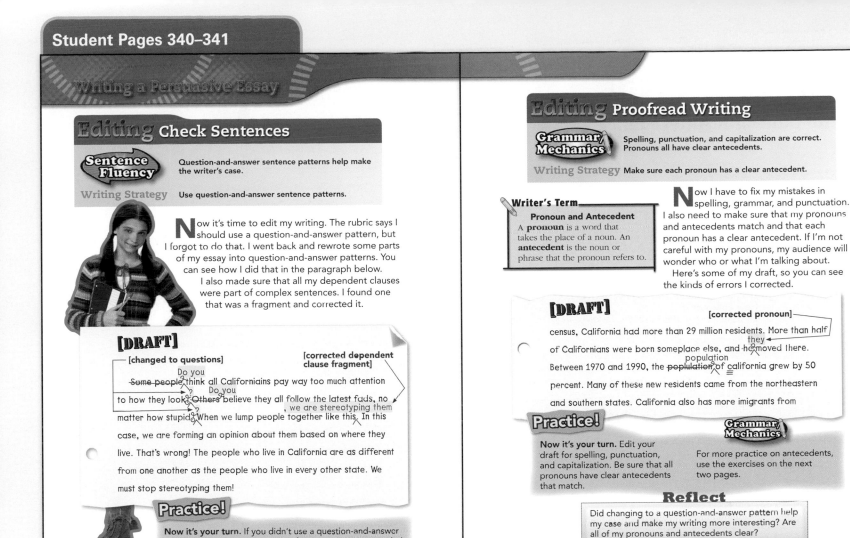

Editing

(Student pages 340–341)

Remind students that in the revising step, they reread their draft to look for ways to make it clearer and better organized. In the editing step, they correct errors or omissions from their writing.

Ask a volunteer to read Leila's words on Student page 340 aloud to the class. Note that Leila once again refers to the rubric to find out if she has missed anything in her essay. Because she has not included question-and-answer sentence patterns, she goes back and includes some now. Point out that question-and-answer sentence patterns help make the writer's case and keep it more interesting. Ask students to look at how Leila edited her draft to include question-and-answer sentence patterns. Encourage students to go through their drafts and be sure they have included sentences with a question-and-answer pattern.

Next, have a student read the definitions of *pronoun* and *antecedent* from the Writer's Term box on Student page 341. If any of your students are having trouble understanding pronouns and antecedents, you may wish to teach the Mini-Lesson on page 248 of this Teacher Edition. Then have students complete the exercises on Student pages 342–343 of their books. Review the answers and possible rewrites with them.

Have students read their persuasive essay drafts to be sure that they have used pronouns correctly. Direct them to check for correct spelling, punctuation, and capitalization.

WORK with a **PARTNER** Ask students to swap their drafts with a partner at this stage. Point out that a partner may be able to find mistakes that the writer has not spotted. Have each partner read the other's paper and note any errors.

Grammar Mechanics Practice!

Pronouns and Antecedents

KNOW the RULE

A pronoun must agree with its antecedent in two ways:
- The pronoun is singular if its antecedent is singular. The pronoun is plural if its antecedent is plural.
- The pronoun is female if its antecedent is female—or male if its antecedent is male.

Example:
Stereotyping might lead a girl to choose **her** friends based on the clothes **they** wear. (*Her* is singular and female, so it agrees with its singular antecedent, *girl*. *They* is plural and agrees with its plural antecedent, *friends*.)

When you use a pronoun, make sure its antecedent is clear.
Example of unclear antecedent:
Mark's friend is named Jamal. **He** lives down the street. (It is unclear whether *He* refers to *Mark* or *Jamal*.)
The sentence is clearer this way:
Mark's friend Jamal lives down the street. (Sometimes the best way to correct an unclear antecedent is not to use a pronoun at all!)

Practice the Rule

Identify the antecedent for the underlined pronoun in each sentence, and write it on your paper.

1. Stereotyping is a part of our culture. <u>It</u> is something we should try to change.
2. Stereotyping occurs when people are grouped together. Perhaps <u>they</u> are grouped because they all play football or chess.
3. We make poor judgments when we stereotype individuals. We do not respect <u>them</u>.
4. Stereotypes can be positive or negative, but <u>they</u> are almost always unfair.
5. Victims of stereotyping often do not know what to do about <u>it</u>.

Apply the Rule

Rewrite the following paragraphs from a persuasive essay. Correct any errors in unclear antecedents.

Some people believe teenagers are more likely to use stereotypes to choose their friends, but they are wrong. They don't rely on stereotypes more than any other group does. However, just like people of all ages, some teens do use them to make judgments about strangers and to decide whether to approach him in friendship.

Like everybody else, teenagers sometimes base their judgments about others on physical appearance. People tend to choose friends who look like himself. If a stranger wears fashions similar to yours, you are more likely to consider them a potential friend. Some teenagers won't even give her a chance if the unfamiliar people aren't in style! Even worse, racial bias is sometimes the cause for rejection of them though it has been proven wrong again and again.

Stereotypes hurt the victim of the prejudice and the person who is judging them. He could become a good friend, but they are closing the door to that friendship. They are losing a big opportunity!

Everyone has prejudices, but they can change. Many teens today are trying to set it aside and get to know them before judging him. Hopefully they will have a good influence on our society. Wouldn't it be nice if it became a thing of the past?

Grammar Mechanics Mini-Lesson

(Student pages 342–343)

Pronouns and Antecedents

Explain to the students that a pronoun must be singular if its antecedent is singular and plural if its antecedent is plural.

Write the following on the board: *When the students heard the bell ring, he/she/they hurried to class.*

Ask students to select the correct pronoun for this sentence. **they**

Explain to the students that the pronoun should be female if the antecedent is female and male if it is male.

Write the following on the board: *When Ben gets home from practice, he/it has a snack.*

Ask students to select the correct pronoun for this sentence. **he**

Explain to the students that the antecedent must be clear when you are using a pronoun.

Write the following on the board: *James and Will are both going to try out for the soccer team. He has played soccer for many years now, but he is just starting.* Note that the antecedent *he* is unclear in both instances in the second sentence.

Ask students to make the phrase clearer. **James and Will are both going to try out for the soccer team. James has played soccer for many years now, but Will is just starting.**

Answers for Practice the Rule

1. **stereotyping**
2. **people**
3. **individuals**
4. **stereotypes**
5. **stereotyping**

Answers for Apply the Rule

Some people believe teenagers are more likely to use stereotypes to choose their friends, but they are wrong. Teenagers don't rely on stereotypes more than any other group does. However, just like people of all ages, some teens do use stereotypes to make judgments about strangers and to decide whether to approach them in friendship.

(Answers continue on page 249.)

Writing a Persuasive Essay

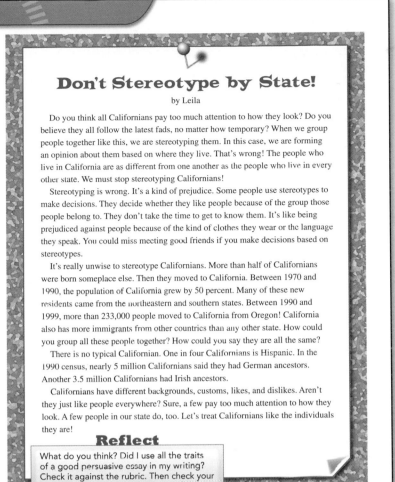

Publishing Share Writing

Post my essay on a class bulletin board.

Now it's time to publish my persuasive essay! I could share it with my writing partner or submit it for publication to a newspaper or a Web site, but I think I'll post my essay on the class bulletin board so all my classmates can read it. Before I do that, I want to read it over one last time to make sure it includes all of the items on this checklist.

My Checklist

✔ The essay is focused and organized.

✔ My opinion is clearly stated at the beginning.

✔ I supported my opinion with good reasons and appropriate facts.

✔ I used a question-and-answer pattern, neutral words, and good arguments to make my case.

● Spelling, capitalization, and punctuation are all correct. Pronouns are correct and have clear antecedents.

Practice!

Now it's your turn. Make a checklist and use it to check your persuasive essay. Then make a final draft to publish.

344 Persuasive Writing ■ Persuasive Essay

Don't Stereotype by State!

by Leila

Do you think all Californians pay too much attention to how they look? Do you believe they all follow the latest fads, no matter how temporary? When we group people together like this, we are stereotyping them. In this case, we are forming an opinion about them based on where they live. That's wrong! The people who live in California are as different from one another as the people who live in every other state. We must stop stereotyping Californians!

Stereotyping is wrong. It's a kind of prejudice. Some people use stereotypes to make decisions. They decide whether they like people because of the group those people belong to. They don't take the time to get to know them. It's like being prejudiced against people because of the kind of clothes they wear or the language they speak. You could miss meeting good friends if you make decisions based on stereotypes.

It's really unwise to stereotype Californians. More than half of Californians were born someplace else. Then they moved to California. Between 1970 and 1990, the population of California grew by 50 percent. Many of these new residents came from the northeastern and southern states. Between 1990 and 1999, more than 233,000 people moved to California from Oregon! California also has more immigrants from other countries than any other state. How could you group all these people together? How could you say they are all the same?

There is no typical Californian. One in four Californians is Hispanic. In the 1990 census, nearly 5 million Californians said they had German ancestors. Another 3.5 million Californians had Irish ancestors.

Californians have different backgrounds, customs, likes, and dislikes. Aren't they just like people everywhere? Sure, a few pay too much attention to how they look. A few people in our state do, too. Let's treat Californians like the individuals they are!

Reflect

What do you think? Did I use all the traits of a good persuasive essay in my writing? Check it against the rubric. Then check your own persuasive essay against the rubric.

Persuasive Writing ■ Persuasive Essay 345

(Answers continued from page 248.)

Like everybody else, teenagers sometimes base their judgments about others on physical appearance. People tend to choose friends who look like themselves. If a stranger wears fashions similar to yours, you are more likely to consider him or her a potential friend. Some teenagers won't even give them a chance if the unfamiliar people aren't in style! Even worse, racial bias is sometimes the cause for rejection of strangers, though racial bias has been proven wrong again and again.

Stereotypes hurt the victims of the prejudice and the person who is judging them. They could become good friends, but the person is closing the door to that friend-ship. He or she is losing a big opportunity!

Everyone has prejudices, but people can change. Many teens today are trying to set prejudices aside and get to know people before judging them. Hopefully they will have a good influence on our society. Wouldn't it be nice if prejudice became a thing of the past?

For more practice with grammar/mechanics skills, see Zaner-Bloser's *G.U.M.* materials.

Publishing
(Student pages 344–345)

Have a student read Leila's words on Student page 344. Challenge students to come up with other ways Leila may have chosen to publish her story.

Note that Leila takes a final look at her essay, reviewing it against a checklist she has made that is based on the writing traits for a persuasive essay. Suggest that students create a checklist based on the rubric to compare against their own essays.

Ways to Publish a Persuasive Essay

Because there are so many possible audiences for your persuasive essay, there are many ways you could publish it. Think about your audience, and choose the best way to share your essay. Here are a few of my ideas.

✓ Share your essay with your writing partner or another friend. Then discuss his or her reactions.

✓ Submit your account to the editorial page of your local newspaper.

✓ Read your essay on your school's radio or television station, at an assembly, or at a parents' meeting.

✓ Send a copy of your persuasive essay to a relative along with a letter asking his or her opinion about the issue.

✓ Combine your essay with those of your classmates and publish your own persuasive/opinion magazine.

Writing Across the Content Areas Persuasive Essay

The subjects you study in school can give you a lot of ideas for persuasive essays. I've listed some of my suggestions below. What ideas do you have?

Social Studies
- Choose an issue that affects our society and write a persuasive essay about your opinion on that issue. Find a classmate who disagrees and ask him or her to write an essay, too. Share your essays, and discuss your differences.
- Who was our most important president? Write a persuasive essay to support your opinion.

Art and/or Music
- Write a persuasive essay about the impact of your favorite kind of music.
- Should art or music classes be dropped from schools to make more time for other subjects? Write an essay to express your opinion on this issue.

Science
- Think of an environmental issue that concerns you. Write a persuasive essay to convince others about your opinion.
- Write a persuasive essay about the scientific discovery you feel has saved the most lives or done the most to make our lives easier.

Ways to Publish
(Student page 346)

Review the suggestions for publishing a persuasive essay shown on Student page 346. Ask volunteers to state what their essays are about, and ask the class as a group to come up with ideas for where that essay might be published. Challenge your students to explore options for publishing their persuasive reports, including the ideas listed on this page.

Writing Across the Content Areas
(Student page 347)

Explain to students that writing a persuasive essay can apply to other subjects as well. Read the ideas and subjects on Student page 347 with the class. Ask student volunteers to come up with a story suggestion based on one of the ideas on the page. Encourage them to talk to teachers of other subjects to get more ideas on writing a persuasive essay for that content area.

Books for Professional Development

Buss, Kathleen, and Lee Karnowski. *Reading and Writing Literary Genres.* **Newark: IRA, 2000.**

The authors discuss in detail six fiction genres: realistic, mystery, traditional folk tale, pourquoi stories and fable, modern folk tale, and fantasy. This source includes examples of each genre, an extensive bibliography, and many graphic organizers.

Nancy, Ted L. *Letters from a Nut.* **New York: Harper Collins, 1999.**

This book of humorous letters is an excellent resource for letter-writing assignments. The name of the author is a pseudonym, perhaps for Jerry Seinfeld, who wrote the introduction. The book is appropriate for middle school grades and above.

Peregoy, Suzanne, and Owen Boyle. *Reading, Writing, and Learning in ESL: A Resource Book for K–12 Teachers.* **4th ed. Boston: Pearson/Allyn & Bacon, 2005.**

This is an outstanding resource book for elementary and secondary teachers who work with ESL students.

Sizoo, Bob. *Teaching Powerful Writing: 25 Short Read-Aloud Stories With Lessons That Motivate Students to Use Literary Elements in Their Writing.* **New York: Scholastic, 2001.**

This book will help teachers work with students who have trouble using a novel's literary techniques in their own writing. It includes personal narratives which are meant to be read aloud, with each highlighting a different writing technique.

Business Letter Overview

This chapter explains how to write a business letter. Students will learn different elements of a business letter—organization, correct form, businesslike tone, supporting details—and some reasons for writing a business letter. By comparing the writing model to the rubric, students will learn how to assess the qualities of a business letter.

Students will follow along as the student guide goes through the writing stages for a business letter, including prewriting, drafting, revising, editing, and publishing. They will be directed to practice the strategies in their own writing as they write a business letter of their own. Following the lead of the student guide, they will put their ideas in an Order-of-Importance Organizer and use the Organizer to write a draft. Then they will revise their drafts by adding details to support their opinion and restating their purpose for writing in the last paragraph. They will edit their drafts to ensure that each sentence reflects the purpose of their letter and that homophones are used correctly. They will also correct any spelling, punctuation, and capitalization errors. Finally, they will explore ways to publish their business letters.

You may wish to send to families the School-Home Connection Letter for this chapter, located at the end of this unit in the Teacher Edition.

Business Letter Writing Traits

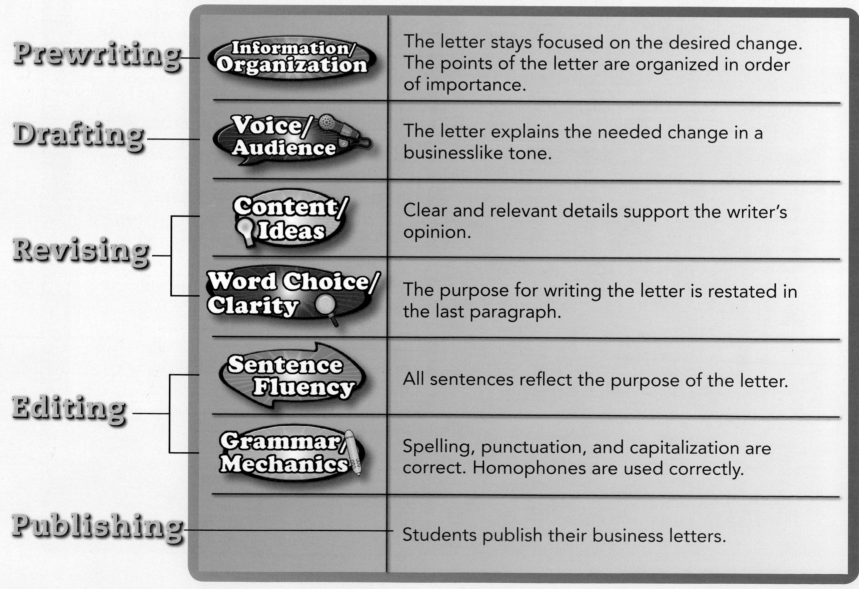

Prewriting	Information/ Organization	The letter stays focused on the desired change. The points of the letter are organized in order of importance.
Drafting	Voice/ Audience	The letter explains the needed change in a businesslike tone.
Revising	Content/ Ideas	Clear and relevant details support the writer's opinion.
	Word Choice/ Clarity	The purpose for writing the letter is restated in the last paragraph.
Editing	Sentence Fluency	All sentences reflect the purpose of the letter.
	Grammar/ Mechanics	Spelling, punctuation, and capitalization are correct. Homophones are used correctly.
Publishing		Students publish their business letters.

Business Letter Time Management

WEEK 1

Day 1	Day 2	Day 3	Day 4	Day 5
Learning Objectives				
Students will: • study the components of a business letter.	Students will: • learn how to gather information for a business letter.	Students will: • practice gathering information for their business letters.	Students will: • learn how to make an Order-of-Importance Organizer to organize their notes.	Students will: • practice organizing their notes to make an Order-of-Importance Organizer.
Activities				
• Discuss the elements and traits of a business letter (Student pages 348–350). • Use the rubric to assess the model (Student pages 351–355).	• Read and discuss **Prewriting: Gather Information** (Student page 356).	• Brainstorm ideas and choose something a business should change. • Gather information and take notes.	• Read and discuss **Prewriting: Organize Ideas** (Student page 357).	• Look at the notes made on a business letter. • Use notes to fill in an Order-of-Importance Organizer.

WEEK 2

Day 1	Day 2	Day 3	Day 4	Day 5
Learning Objectives				
Students will: • learn how to explain the needed change in a businesslike tone.	Students will: • practice writing their drafts.	Students will: • learn how to add clear and relevant details to support their opinion.	Students will: • practice adding supporting details to their drafts.	Students will: • learn how to restate their purpose for writing the letter in the last paragraph.
Activities				
• Read and discuss **Drafting: Write a Draft** (Student pages 358–359).	• Use Order-of-Importance Organizer to write a draft. • Use correct business letter form and write with a businesslike tone.	• Read and discuss **Revising: Extend Writing** (Student page 360).	• Add details to support their opinion.	• Read and discuss **Revising: Clarify Writing** (Student page 361).

WEEK 3

Day 1	Day 2	Day 3	Day 4	Day 5
Learning Objectives				
Students will: • practice restating their purpose in the last paragraph.	Students will: • make sure all sentences reflect the purpose of the letter.	Students will: • learn how to use homophones correctly.	Students will: • practice editing their drafts for spelling, punctuation, and capitalization.	Students will: • learn different ways to publish their business letters.
Activities				
• Make sure opinion is restated in the last paragraph. • Restate purpose for writing in the last paragraph, and re-emphasize it.	• Read and discuss **Editing: Check Sentences** (Student page 362). • Take out or rewrite sentences that don't reflect purpose for writing.	• Read and discuss **Editing: Proofread Writing** (Student page 363). • Make sure homophones are used correctly.	• Fix any spelling, punctuation, or capitalization errors. • Fix any incorrectly used homophones.	• Read and discuss **Publishing: Share Writing** (Student page 366).

* To complete the chapter in fewer days, teach the learning objectives and activities for two days in one day.

This planning chart, correlated to your state's writing standards, is available on-line at http://www.zaner-bloser.com/sfw.

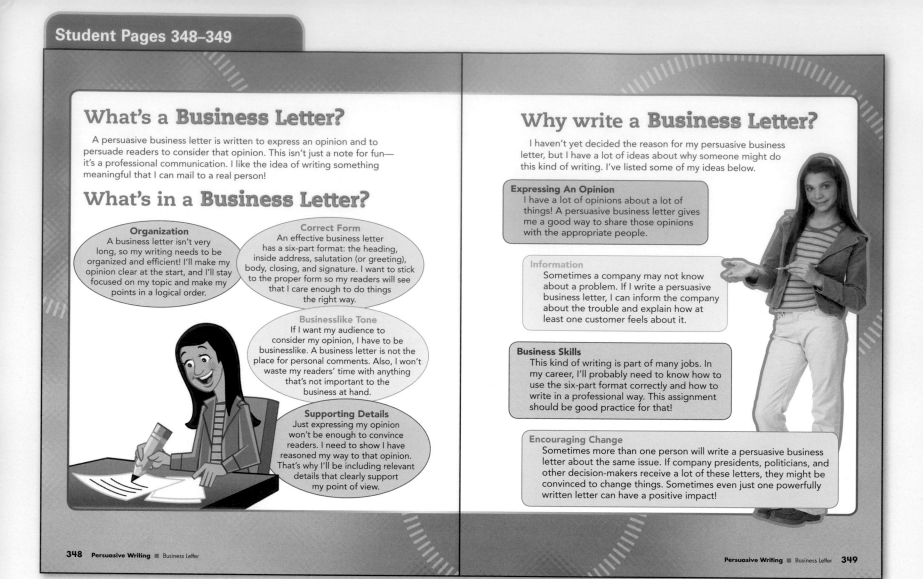

What's a **Business Letter**?

A persuasive business letter is written to express an opinion and to persuade readers to consider that opinion. This isn't just a note for fun—it's a professional communication. I like the idea of writing something meaningful that I can mail to a real person!

What's in a **Business Letter**?

Organization
A business letter isn't very long, so my writing needs to be organized and efficient! I'll make my opinion clear at the start, and I'll stay focused on my topic and make my points in a logical order.

Correct Form
An effective business letter has a six-part format: the heading, inside address, salutation (or greeting), body, closing, and signature. I want to stick to the proper form so my readers will see that I care enough to do things the right way.

Businesslike Tone
If I want my audience to consider my opinion, I have to be businesslike. A business letter is not the place for personal comments. Also, I won't waste my readers' time with anything that's not important to the business at hand.

Supporting Details
Just expressing my opinion won't be enough to convince readers. I need to show I have reasoned my way to that opinion. That's why I'll be including relevant details that clearly support my point of view.

348   **Persuasive Writing** ■ Business Letter

Why write a **Business Letter**?

I haven't yet decided the reason for my persuasive business letter, but I have a lot of ideas about why someone might do this kind of writing. I've listed some of my ideas below.

Expressing An Opinion
I have a lot of opinions about a lot of things! A persuasive business letter gives me a good way to share those opinions with the appropriate people.

Information
Sometimes a company may not know about a problem. If I write a persuasive business letter, I can inform the company about the trouble and explain how at least one customer feels about it.

Business Skills
This kind of writing is part of many jobs. In my career, I'll probably need to know how to use the six-part format correctly and how to write in a professional way. This assignment should be good practice for that!

Encouraging Change
Sometimes more than one person will write a persuasive business letter about the same issue. If company presidents, politicians, and other decision-makers receive a lot of these letters, they might be convinced to change things. Sometimes even just one powerfully written letter can have a positive impact!

Persuasive Writing ■ Business Letter   349

Define the Genre
(Student page 348)

Business Letter

Ask students what form of written communication people might use to express their opinion about a company to the business. Most students will probably suggest a letter. Explain that letters written to people whom they don't know very well tend to be business letters. A persuasive business letter is one in which the writer is expressing his or her opinion and requesting change.

Elements of the Genre

Business Letter

Read and discuss each of the elements of a business letter with the students. Ask students what they think is meant by the term *businesslike tone*. **Possible response: It's more formal and doesn't contain slang.** Explain that when you write a business letter, you want to be sure that it is structured correctly and not full of unnecessary personal comments.

Authentic Writing
(Student page 349)

Business Letter

Explain that every day, thousands and thousands of business letters written for a variety of purposes change hands. Ask students to imagine why some of these business letters are sent. **Possible responses: people looking for jobs, trying to sell something, expressing their opinions** Point out that all writing has a purpose and that there are many different reasons that people write business letters. Persuasive business letters are often written for the reasons shown on Student page 349. Read and review each of these reasons with students. Remind them to think about the reasons they are writing a business letter as they write. This will help set the tone for the writing.

Business Letter Writing Traits

What makes a good persuasive business letter? My teacher says it takes the traits listed below, so I'm going to use them as I write my letter.

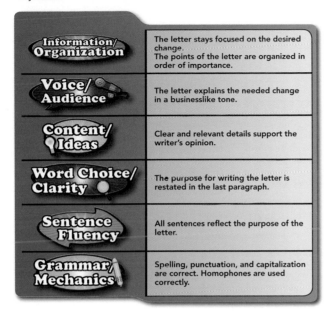

Information/Organization	The letter stays focused on the desired change. The points of the letter are organized in order of importance.
Voice/Audience	The letter explains the needed change in a businesslike tone.
Content/Ideas	Clear and relevant details support the writer's opinion.
Word Choice/Clarity	The purpose for writing the letter is restated in the last paragraph.
Sentence Fluency	All sentences reflect the purpose of the letter.
Grammar/Mechanics	Spelling, punctuation, and capitalization are correct. Homophones are used correctly.

Let's see how Jean Silverstone used these traits when she wrote the persuasive business letter on the next page.

Business Letter Model

Tiny Tikes Daycare Center
333 Willow Park Road
Lexington, KY 40509
May 4, 2006 — **Heading**

Customer Service Manager
Real Cereal, Inc.
2128 N. Jarvis St.
Trenton, NJ 08620 — **Inside address**

Dear Customer Service Manager: — **Salutation**
Businesslike tone

I own a daycare center that serves breakfast cereal to children in the morning. I am usually pleased with Real Cereal products. However, the "new and improved" Oaty Boats is not satisfactory. I refuse to continue to buy Oaty Boats until Real Cereal addresses its problems. — **Clear opinion**

The boats now have little taste, and they sink instead of floating. Furthermore, the food dye in the new boats turns the milk in the bowl greenish brown. — **Supporting details**

In addition, I do not like a recent commercial that shows Oaty Boats as destroyers in a battle. What does your ad tell children about the uses of a boat? It tells them only that a boat is used to fight.

There are sailboats, tugboats, and freighters in Oaty Boats, too. It would be more positive and educational to show children a range of boats and a range of uses. You're as responsible for molding their young minds as I am. I would like to see more thoughtful advertising from Real Cereal. Remember, it takes a community to raise a child. Please change the cereal back to its original flavor and natural color. Also, think more carefully about how you use boats in your advertising. Until Oaty Boats is returned to its original form, I will no longer purchase it for the children in my daycare center. — **Clear opinion**

Body

Closing → Sincerely,
Signature → *Jean Silverstone*
Jean Silverstone, Director

Writing Traits

(Student pages 350–351)

Business Letter

Ask students to imagine that the local ice cream parlor has just stopped selling their favorite flavor, chocolate brownie explosion. They decide to write a letter to the owner, requesting that she bring back the flavor. What details might they include in the letter? **Possible responses: how much they enjoy the flavor and how often they come to buy it; opinions of other people who also like the flavor; the desire for a varied selection of flavors; the fact that there are many chocolate lovers out there who look for chocolate ice cream when they shop** Ask them how they might end the letter. **Possible response: with a request that for all the reasons they have stated, the parlor bring back the chocolate brownie explosion ice cream**

Explain to students that these elements—details to support their opinion, restating their purpose in the last paragraph—are elements of good persuasive business letters. Review the writing traits of a business letter on Student page 350. Tell students that they will be studying strategies for writing business letters. They will also be using these strategies to write their own business letters. Point out that a good business letter contains the traits listed on Student page 350.

Have students look for these traits in the business letter on Student page 351 as you read it aloud.

Differentiating Instruction

English-Language Learners It is worth noting to students that business letters in English may vary slightly from business letters written in other languages, especially in how addresses and names are placed and punctuated and the terms used for greetings and salutations. You may wish to provide students with a model letter that shows the correct format of business letters in English. Note how addresses are placed, in particular the lack of commas after each line. Also go over the salutation, which should include the line *Dear/To [name of person]*. Provide options to use when the name of the person is unknown, such as *To whom it may concern* or *Dear Customer Service Manager*. Note the use of the word *Sincerely* as a closing for business letters.

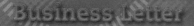

Business Letter
Rubric

The traits of a good persuasive business letter from page 350 have been used to make the rubric below. By using 1, 2, 3, or 4 check marks to judge each trait, you can decide how well any persuasive business letter was written.

	Excelling ✓✓✓✓	Achieving ✓✓✓	Developing ✓✓	Beginning ✓
Information/ Organization	The letter stays focused, and points are organized in order of importance.	The letter stays focused, and many points are organized.	The letter is somewhat focused and organized.	The letter needs to be more focused and better organized.
Voice/ Audience	The overall tone is always businesslike.	The overall tone is mostly businesslike.	The overall tone is somewhat businesslike.	The overall tone is seldom businesslike.
Content/ Ideas	Many clear and relevant details support the writer's opinion.	Some clear and relevant details support the writer's opinion.	A few relevant details support the writer's opinion, but they are not clear.	Clear and relevant details need to support the writer's opinion.
Word Choice/ Clarity	The purpose for writing the letter is clearly restated in the last paragraph.	The purpose for writing is restated in the last paragraph.	The purpose for writing is restated in another paragraph.	The last paragraph needs to restate the purpose for writing the letter.
Sentence Fluency	Every sentence reflects the purpose of the letter.	Most sentences reflect the purpose of the letter.	Some sentences reflect the purpose of the letter.	Few sentences reflect the purpose of the letter.
Grammar/ Mechanics	Spelling, punctuation, capitalization, and homophones are used correctly.	There are few errors in spelling, punctuation, capitalization, and homophones.	There are some errors in spelling, punctuation, capitalization, and homophones.	There are many errors in spelling, punctuation, capitalization, and homophones.

Business Letter
Using the Rubric to Study the Model

We can check Jean's persuasive business letter with the rubric. How many check marks do you think she should receive for each trait?

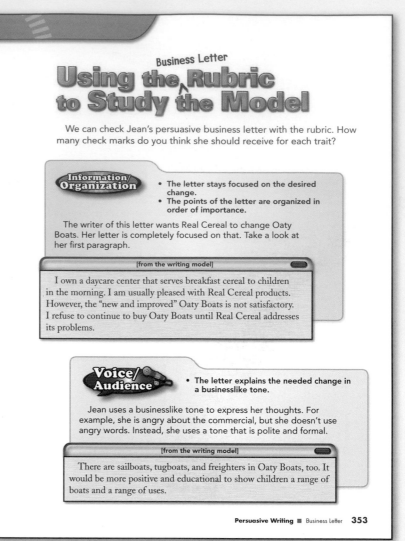

Information/ Organization
- The letter stays focused on the desired change.
- The points of the letter are organized in order of importance.

The writer of this letter wants Real Cereal to change Oaty Boats. Her letter is completely focused on that. Take a look at her first paragraph.

[from the writing model]

I own a daycare center that serves breakfast cereal to children in the morning. I am usually pleased with Real Cereal products. However, the "new and improved" Oaty Boats is not satisfactory. I refuse to continue to buy Oaty Boats until Real Cereal addresses its problems.

Voice/ Audience
- The letter explains the needed change in a businesslike tone.

Jean uses a businesslike tone to express her thoughts. For example, she is angry about the commercial, but she doesn't use angry words. Instead, she uses a tone that is polite and formal.

[from the writing model]

There are sailboats, tugboats, and freighters in Oaty Boats, too. It would be more positive and educational to show children a range of boats and a range of uses.

Using the Rubric
(Student page 352)

Read aloud the paragraph about the rubric on Student page 352. Note that students should keep the rubric in mind as they write their business letters, striving to write a letter that falls under the Excelling category. Have a student read all the traits under the Excelling column. Next, have a student read the traits under the Beginning column. Be sure students understand what makes a good business letter and what makes a poor business letter.

Tell students that they are going to be using the rubric to assess the model business letter shown on Student page 351.

Study the Model
(Student pages 353–355)

Read each section on Student pages 353–355 with students. Explain that each section is showing how the model letter meets each of the traits shown in the rubric. When appropriate, have students look for other examples in the model.

As you compare each of the writing traits in the rubric against the letter, ask students how they would rate the model. After completing all of the sections, ask students how they would rate the model overall. Did it meet the traits set forth in the rubric?

Remind students that as they write, edit, and revise their letters, they will continually refer to the rubric to be sure that they do not forget to include any of the traits listed.

Business Letter

Content/Ideas
- Clear and relevant details support the writer's opinion.

Jean does a good job of supporting her opinion of the new Oaty Boats. She uses enough details to prove her point, but she doesn't distract her reader with details that aren't important to the issue. In the paragraph below, she gives some relevant details about why the cereal is now unsatisfactory.

[from the writing model]

The boats now have little taste, and they sink instead of floating. Furthermore, the food dye in the new boats turns the milk in the bowl greenish brown.

Word Choice/Clarity
- The purpose for writing the letter is restated in the last paragraph.

My teacher told us that business people want to know right away why you're writing. That's why Jean begins by saying she won't buy the new Oaty Boats until the company fixes the problems with it. Her purpose for writing the letter is clear from the start.

Then she repeats her purpose for writing in her last paragraph. This reminds the reader of the change that she wants and emphasizes the seriousness of her concerns.

[from the writing model]

Please change the cereal back to its original flavor and natural color. Also, think more carefully about how you use boats in your advertising. Until Oaty Boats is returned to its original form, I will no longer purchase it for the children in my daycare center.

Sentence Fluency
- All sentences reflect the purpose of the letter.

The writer doesn't waste the time of the busy customer service manager at the cereal company. She makes sure that each and every sentence of her letter relates to the business at hand. For example, in the section of the letter shown below, the writer could have started talking about how difficult it is to be responsible for young children, but that would not have reflected the purpose of her letter. Take a look.

[from the writing model]

You're as responsible for molding their young minds as I am. I would like to see more thoughtful advertising from Real Cereal. Remember, it takes a community to raise a child.

Grammar/Mechanics
- Spelling, punctuation, and capitalization are correct. Homophones are used correctly.

I went back and checked the letter to see if there were any mistakes, but I couldn't find any. Spelling, punctuation, and capitalization are all correct. The writer also used homophones correctly. When she had to choose among words such as *to/too/two* and *your/you're,* she chose the right word every time.

[from the writing model]

There are sailboats, tugboats, and freighters in Oaty Boats, too.

My Turn!

I'm going to write a persuasive business letter about a change I'd like a business to make. Follow along and see how I use the rubric and good writing strategies to do it!

Differentiating Instruction

Support To help students better understand homophones, have them reread the model letter and find words that are homophones. Ask them to develop a list of the homophones in the letter, including the words that are pronounced the same but have different meanings from those used in the letter. **Possible responses: to/two/too, your/you're, buy/by, dye/die, do/due, would/wood, see/sea** Go over the list with the students. Have them give additional examples of when each word should be used and when it should not be used.

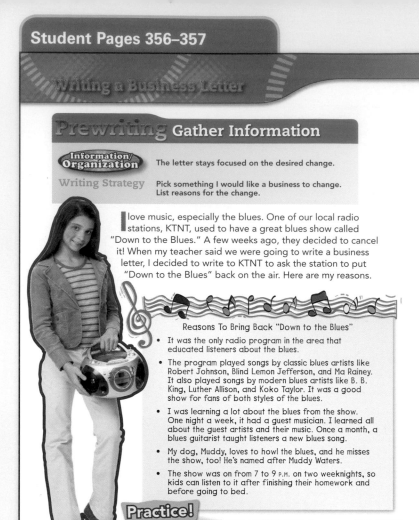

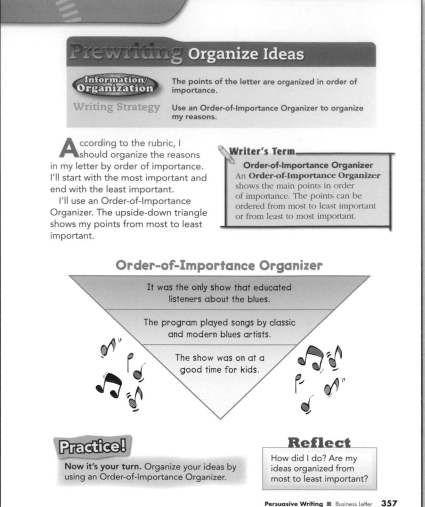

Prewriting

(Student pages 356–357)

Review Student page 356 with the students. Discuss the reasons why Leila likes the blues show. Point out that she was specific about what she likes about the show. Ask students what information Leila has jotted down in her notes that might not be important enough to include in her letter to KTNT. **Possible response: the fact that her dog likes the music and is named after Muddy Waters**

Tell students that writing can be organized in many ways and that one way is to list the main points in order of importance. An Order-of-Importance Organizer will help students do this. At this point, Leila might realize that some of her notes, such as her dog's interest in the show, might not be appropriate.

More Practice!

For more practice with these writing strategies, you may wish to have students use the Strategy Practice Book. See the appendix for reduced Strategy Practice Book pages.

Differentiating Instruction

Support To help students identify which points they are making are most important and which are least important, ask them to review each of the points in their list of notes. Have them think about which items are more likely to affect many people or to show how many people feel about the change. These should appear near the top of the Organizer. Explain that personal opinions or feelings should be near the bottom of the organizer because they are least likely to effect change. Statistics or facts that support their opinion should also be near the top of their Organizers because they carry more weight. Students may wish to work with a partner to complete their Order-of-Importance Organizers.

Enrichment Challenge students to try an inverted triangle as their Order-of-Importance Organizer. In this form, the writer moves from the least important item to the most important item, ending with the strongest point. The reasoning behind this approach is that the last item described is the one that readers remember best.

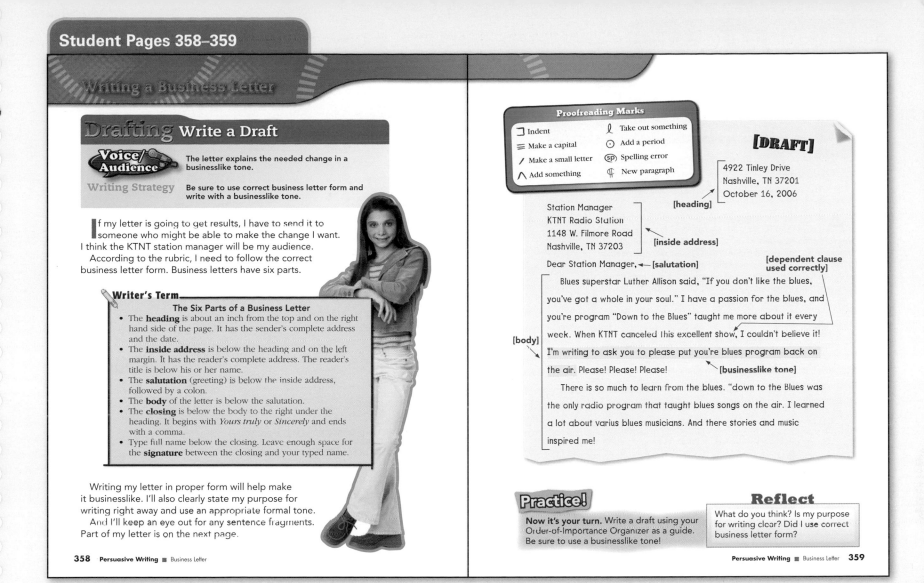

Drafting

(Student pages 358–359)

Be sure that students understand that a draft is a temporary form of writing. They need not worry about making mistakes at this time.

Have a student read Leila's words on Student page 358. Point out that Leila repeatedly refers to the rubric as she writes. Encourage students to get in the habit of using the rubrics to help them guide their writing.

As you read *The Six Parts of a Business Letter* from the Writer's Term box on Student page 358, refer to Leila's draft on Student page 359 to show how each of these looks in a business letter. Ask students what Leila's closing will likely look like if she follows the correct form. **Sincerely, or Yours truly, (new line) Leila Hirsch**

Have students write a draft using the information from their Order-of-Importance Organizers. Be sure they use correct business letter form to structure their letters.

Writing a Business Letter

Revising Extend Writing

Content/Ideas Clear and relevant details support the writer's opinion.

Writing Strategy Add details to support my opinion.

After I read over my draft, I looked at the rubric again. It says I should include relevant details to support my opinion. I found a part of my letter that didn't have enough details. Also, I took out a detail that wasn't relevant at all.

While I was working on details, I also noticed a few problems with pronouns and antecedents. I corrected those mistakes and checked the antecedents in the rest of my letter, too.

[DRAFT]

songs by classic blues artists and modern blues artists, too **[added detail]**

I really liked it that the show played different songs by different
The good mix
blues artists. They made "Down to the Blues" entertaining four any blues fan. **[replaced unclear antecedent]**

The timing of the program was perfect for me and other kids, to. The 7 P.M. time slot was late enough that I could finish my homework before the program started, but it didnt keep me up to late either.

I have to get up at six o'clock in the morning. **[took out irrelevant detail]**

Practice!

Now it's your turn. Try adding some relevant details to support your opinions. Take out any details that aren't relevant.

360 **Persuasive Writing** ■ Business Letter

Revising Clarify Writing

Word Choice/Clarity The purpose for writing the letter is restated in the last paragraph.

Writing Strategy Restate my purpose for writing in the last paragraph.

When I checked the rubric, I realized I hadn't restated my purpose for writing in my last paragraph. I know this is an effective way to wrap things up and to stress my opinion. Read below to see how I fixed the problem.

[DRAFT]

[restated purpose for writing]

I hope KTNT will return "Down to the Blues" to its evening programming. All kinds of blues fans enjoy the program and learn so much from listening, especially us kids!

Practice!

Now it's your turn. Restate your purpose for writing in your last paragraph, and emphasize your opinion.

Reflect

Is my last paragraph stronger now that I've restated my purpose?

Persuasive Writing ■ Business Letter **361**

Revising

(Student pages 360–361)

Have a student read Leila's words on Student page 360. Ask students why they feel Leila decided to take out the line about the show playing different songs by different artists. **Possible response: It is vague and irrelevant; most music stations do that.** Ask them why they feel the line she added in her letter is better. **Possible response: It gives more specific information about the show and why the show was so good.**

As students review their drafts, instruct them to look for areas in which they can add relevant details to make their argument stronger. Also have them remove any details that do not belong in their letters.

Next, have a student read aloud Leila's words on Student page 361. Ask students why they feel the conclusion is the best place to restate the purpose. **Possible response: The conclusion is the writer's last chance to stress important ideas, especially the purpose for writing.**

Have students read their closing paragraphs to make sure that they have restated their purpose for writing and re-emphasized their opinions.

Differentiating Instruction

Support To help students with business letter formatting, create a template that shows each part of the letter in a different color. Post the template in a prominent place or distribute color photocopies.

Enrichment Ask students to find a sample business letter from home. Tell them it could be a piece of "junk" mail, such as a subscription solicitation or a promotion for a new community. If they are unable to locate one at home, ask them to look for sample business letters on the Internet. Ask them to find a letter in which the last paragraph restates the writer's purpose for writing the letter. Have them share the letters with the class, noting how the writer stressed his or her purpose in the last paragraph.

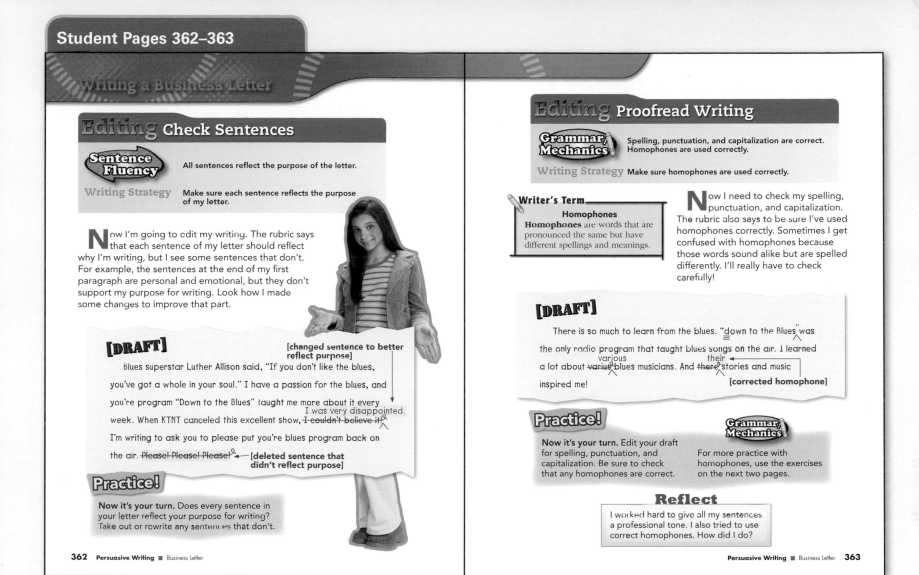

Editing

(Student pages 362–363)

Ask a student to read Leila's words on Student page 362. Then read the sentences that she changed in her letter. Ask students why they think she took out the line *"Please! Please! Please!"* **Possible response: It is not a good argument as to why the show should be brought back on the air.** Ask students why they feel that personal or emotional comments should not be included in persuasive business letters. **Possible responses: They might weaken the argument; they do not reflect the purpose of the letter.**

Have students read through their drafts and identify any sentences that do not reflect the purpose of their letter, in particular those that are personal or emotional. Have them change the sentences to reflect their purpose for writing.

Next, read aloud the definition of *homophone* from the Writer's Term box on Student page 363. Ask students to name some homophones. If any of your students are

having trouble understanding homophones, you may wish to teach the Mini-Lesson on page 262 of this Teacher Edition. Then have students complete the exercises on Student pages 364–365 of their books. Review the answers and possible rewrites with them.

At this point, students should also read through their business letters to be sure that there are no grammatical or spelling mistakes. Have them check for correct spelling, punctuation, and capitalization. Remind students that they should always proofread their letters.

WORK with a **PARTNER** Have students exchange their letters with a partner to check for grammar and mechanics errors.

Grammar/Mechanics Practice!

Homophones

KNOW the RULE

Homophones are words that are pronounced the same but have different spellings and meanings.

Here are some examples of homophones and their meanings. Make sure you are using the correct word.

its—possessive pronoun meaning "belonging to it"
it's—contraction of *it is* or *it has*

there—adverb meaning "in that place"
their—possessive pronoun meaning "belonging to them"
they're—contraction of *they are*

your—possessive pronoun meaning "belonging to you"
you're—contraction of *you are*

whose—possessive pronoun meaning "belonging to someone"
who's—contraction of *who is* or *who has*

Practice the Rule

Number your paper 1–6. On another sheet of paper, write the correct word to complete each sentence below.

1. Three chords and a simple pattern give the blues (its/it's) unique form.
2. (It's/Its) one of the oldest forms of American music.
3. (There/Their/They're) are several views about the origins of the blues.
4. The songs are called the blues because (there/their/they're) often sad.
5. At first, only people in the South sang or listened (two/to/too) the blues.
6. By the 1920s, people in the North were enjoying the blues, (two/to/too).

Apply the Rule

Read the following paragraphs from a persuasive business letter. Correct any mistakes in the use of homophones.

I loved the first issue of you're knew music magazine! Its an exciting blend of articles, photos, interviews, and sheet music from many types of music. Theirs just won little thing I didn't like. In your introduction too the magazine, you wrote that you won't bee including much information about the blues because its to sad. I hope to convince you that your wrong about the blues and persuade you to make the blues a big part of you're knew publication.

Of coarse, some blues songs are sad, but some are happy, two. Have you ever herd of Koko Taylor? She is a grate performer whose considered won of the best blues singers. Music fans no her as the "Queen of Chicago Blues." When you listen to her music, you don't feel sad at all. You want to get up and dance! They're is nothing more joyful than her foot-stomping blues.

Your knot going to bee sorry if you let you're readers no about Koko Taylor, and there knot going too bee sad. In fact, their going to be delighted that you're magazine introduced them two such a talented singer. Won't you consider making you're publication a good source of news on the blues?

Grammar/Mechanics Mini-Lesson

(Student pages 364–365)

Homophones

Remind students that homophones are words that are pronounced the same but have different spellings and meanings. Students should try to become familiar with homophones and their correct use.

Write the following on the board: *I sea that they have changed the menu at my favorite restaurant.*

Ask students to correct the misused homophone in the sentence. **change *sea* to *see***

Explain to students that contractions of some words form commonly misused homophones, such as *they're* and *there* or *it's* and *its*. Note that a contraction is a shortened form of two words with the missing letters often replaced by an apostrophe. *It's* means *it is*, and *they're* means *they are*.

Write the following on the board: *I hope their still going to feature clam chowder on Fridays.*

Ask students to correct the misused homophone in the sentence. **change *their* to *they're***

Answers for Practice the Rule

1. **its**
2. **It's**
3. **There**
4. **they're**
5. **to**
6. **too**

Answers for Apply the Rule

I loved the first issue of your new music magazine! It's an exciting blend of articles, photos, interviews, and sheet music from many types of music. There's just one little thing I didn't like. In your introduction to the magazine, you wrote that you won't be including much information about the blues because it's too sad. I hope to convince you that you're wrong about the blues and persuade you to make the blues a big part of your new publication.

(Answers continue on page 263.)

Writing a Business Letter

Publishing Share Writing

Mail my business letter to my reader.

Now that I've finished my persuasive business letter, I can't wait to mail it to the station manager! Before I do that, I want it to be perfect. I'm going to check my letter over one last time to be sure it includes all of the items on the checklist below. Then I'll make a good copy and mail it.

My Checklist

✔ The letter is focused and well organized.

✔ I've used the six-part business letter form correctly.

✔ My tone is professional throughout the letter.

✔ I stick to the business at hand in each and every sentence.

✔ My points are well supported with relevant details, and my purpose for writing is clear.

✔ Spelling, capitalization, and punctuation are all correct. I used homophones correctly.

Practice!

Now it's your turn. Make a checklist to check your persuasive business letter. Then make a final draft to publish.

4922 Tinley Drive
Nashville, TN 37201
October 16, 2006

Station Manager
KTNT Radio Station
1148 W. Filmore Road
Nashville, TN 37203

Dear Station Manager:

Blues superstar Luther Allison said, "If you don't like the blues, you've got a hole in your soul." I have a passion for the blues, and your program "Down to the Blues" taught me more about it every week. When KTNT canceled this excellent show, I was very disappointed. I'm writing to ask you to please put your blues program back on the air.

There is so much to learn about the blues. "Down to the Blues" was the only radio program that taught blues songs on the air. I learned a lot about various blues musicians. And their stories and music inspired me!

I really liked it that the show played songs by classic blues artists and modern blues artists, too. The good mix made "Down to the Blues" entertaining for any blues fan.

The timing of the program was perfect for me and other kids, too. The 7 P.M. time slot was late enough that I could finish my homework before the program started, but it didn't keep me up too late either.

I hope KTNT will return "Down to the Blues" to its evening programming. All kinds of blues fans enjoy the program and learn so much from listening, especially us kids!

Yours truly,

Leila Hirsch

Leila Hirsch

Reflect

What did you think? Did I use all the traits of a good persuasive business letter in my writing? Check it against the rubric. Then use the rubric to check your own persuasive business letter.

(Answers continued from page 262.)

Of course, some blues songs are sad, but some are happy, too. Have you ever heard of Koko Taylor? She is a great performer who's considered one of the best blues singers. Music fans know her as the "Queen of Chicago Blues." When you listen to her music, you don't feel sad at all. You want to get up and dance! There is nothing more joyful than her foot-stomping blues.

You're not going to be sorry if you let your readers know about Koko Taylor, and they're not going to be sad. In fact, they're going to be delighted that your magazine introduced them to such a talented singer. Won't you consider making your publication a good source of news on the blues?

✔ For more practice with grammar/mechanics skills, see Zaner-Bloser's *G.U.M.* materials.

Publishing

(Student pages 366–367)

Review Student page 366 with students. Point out that before Leila mails her letter to her reader, she takes another look at her checklist to be sure she hasn't missed anything. Encourage students to use their checklists to review their final drafts. Have students read Leila's final draft of her business letter to KTNT, using her checklist to assess the letter. Did she include all of the items on her checklist?

Encourage your students to publish their final drafts by mailing them to their readers.

Ways to Publish a Business Letter

Publishing a letter usually means mailing it, but there are other ways to publish this kind of writing. Here are some of my ideas about how to publish a persuasive business letter.

 If your topic would interest a lot of people, send a copy of your letter to the editor of your local newspaper.

 Instead of complaining to your parents, teachers, or other people in your life, write a persuasive business letter about what you'd like them to change. Leave the letter someplace where they can easily find it.

If your letter is about a needed change at your school, submit it for publication in your school newspaper.

 Ask classmates to write persuasive business letters about your topic. Collect the letters and mail them in one big envelope to someone who can help change things.

Writing Across the Content Areas Business Letter

Often a persuasive business letter is written about a "real-life" problem, but your school subjects can give you many ideas for this kind of writing.

Math
- Write a persuasive business letter about a change that would make your math textbook better for future students.
- If your school doesn't have a math team or club, write a letter to persuade a teacher or the principal to start one.

Social Studies
- Write your town's mayor a persuasive business letter about something that will make your community better.
- Think about a historical person who made a decision with far-reaching effects. Write a letter to that person and persuade him or her to do something different.

Art and/or Music
- Write a letter to a radio station or television network, and persuade them to change their programming.
- Choose a famous artist, composer, or musician from the past. Write the person a convincing letter about why he or she should become a teacher at your school.

Ways to Publish
(Student page 368)

Point out that while mailing a letter to its intended recipient is the most common way to publish a business letter, there are also other ways to publish this kind of writing. Ask a student or students to read the suggestions listed on Student page 368. Have students come up with specific examples for each of the suggestions. Ask students whether they feel that any of their letters might be suitable for publication in one of these ways. Have them share the topics of their letters and explain why these ways might be appropriate.

Writing Across the Content Areas
(Student page 369)

Point out that school subjects can also provide ideas for writing business letters. Many of the subjects they are learning can provide inspiration for writing a business letter. Encourage students to consider one of the content areas listed on Student page 369 to write and publish a business letter. You might also suggest that students look within their homes for ideas and inspiration for business letters they can write.

Books for Professional Development

Jorgensen, Karen L. *The Whole Story: Crafting Fiction in the Upper Elementary Grades*. Portsmouth: Heinemann, 2001.

This book focuses on moving away from writing that overly emphasizes action by developing and refining character development in children's stories. The author outlines procedures for introducing scene writing to facilitate character-driven fiction. She emphasizes observation as a critical element to writing with depth.

National Writing Project. *Writing for a Change: Boosting Literacy and Learning Through Social Action*. San Francisco: Jossey-Bass, 2006.

This publication shows teachers how to engage students in real-world problem-solving activities that can help them acquire voice, authority, and passion for both reading and writing practices. In collaboration with the Center for Social Action in England, the authors describe innovative strategies for encouraging students to collaborate on problems of their own choosing—to develop action, to discover solutions, and finally to reflect on their work.

Robb, Laura. *Brighten Up Boring Beginnings and Other Quick Writing Lessons (Grades 4 and up)*. New York: Scholastic, 2003.

Robb's book contains one-page mini-lessons—perfect for chart paper or overhead lessons—and companion reproducible activities that zero in on improving key writing skills. It also covers sentence combining, improving leads, strong verbs, getting rid of clutter, and more.

Robb, Laura. *Easy-to-Manage Reading & Writing Conferences (Grades 4–8)*. New York: Scholastic, 1999.

Written by a veteran teacher, this book delivers a plan for reading and writing conferences that won't eat up precious class time. It includes practical ideas for ways to make conferring with children more manageable and effective, such as spotlighting conferences, making-the-rounds, and debriefing talks.

Persuasive Test Writing

Students will learn about persuasive test writing in this chapter. First, they will review the parts of a writing prompt—setup, task, and scoring guide—and see how the writing prompt relates to the writing traits they have been studying throughout the chapter. Students will then use the scoring guide to assess a model writing sample.

Next, students will follow the student guide as she goes through the writing stages for a persuasive writing test, including planning one's time, prewriting, drafting, revising, and editing.

One of the goals of this chapter is to show students there is no reason to be concerned about writing tests. Each of the steps in the test writing process can be related to steps they have followed in other chapters in this unit. Emphasize that they already possess much of the knowledge they need to successfully complete a persuasive writing test.

You may wish to send to families the School-Home Connection Letter for this chapter, located at the end of this unit in the Teacher Edition.

Writing Traits in the Scoring Guide

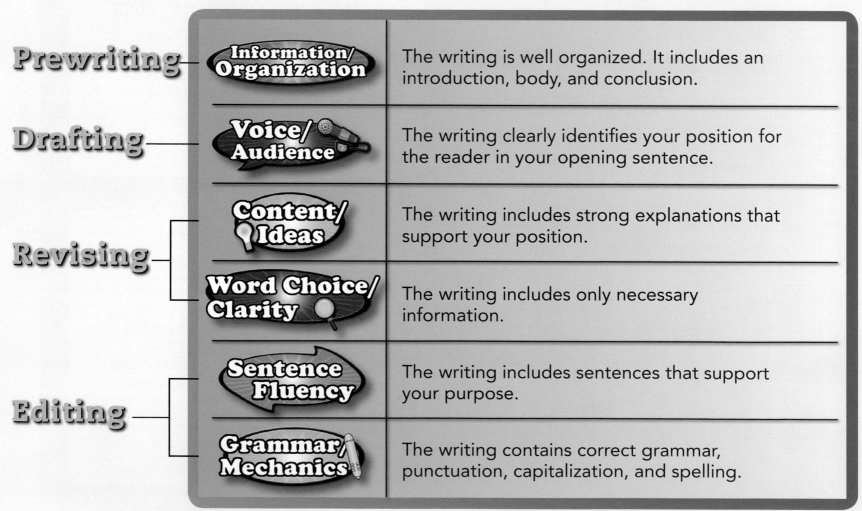

Prewriting — **Information/Organization** — The writing is well organized. It includes an introduction, body, and conclusion.

Drafting — **Voice/Audience** — The writing clearly identifies your position for the reader in your opening sentence.

Revising — **Content/Ideas** — The writing includes strong explanations that support your position.

Word Choice/Clarity — The writing includes only necessary information.

Editing — **Sentence Fluency** — The writing includes sentences that support your purpose.

Grammar/Mechanics — The writing contains correct grammar, punctuation, capitalization, and spelling.

Persuasive Test Writing Time Management

Day 1	Day 2	Day 3	Day 4	Day 5
Learning Objectives				
Students will: • learn the components of the writing prompt.	Students will: • recognize the relationship of the scoring guide to the rubric and the six traits of writing. • read a writing prompt response model.	Students will: • apply the scoring guide to a writing prompt response model.	Students will: • apply the scoring guide to a writing prompt response model.	Students will: • learn how to budget their time during a writing test.
Activities				
• Discuss the components of the writing prompt (Student pages 370–371).	• Read and discuss the scoring guide chart (Student page 372). • Read the model (Student page 373).	• Read and discuss **Using the Scoring Guide to Study the Model** (Student pages 374–375).	• Read and discuss **Using the Scoring Guide to Study the Model** (Student page 376).	• Read and discuss **Planning My Time** (Student page 377).

WEEK 2

Day 1	Day 2	Day 3	Day 4	Day 5
Learning Objectives				
Students will: • learn to read and understand a writing test prompt for test writing. • apply the six traits of writing to the writing prompt.	Students will: • learn how to respond to the task in the writing prompt.	Students will: • learn how to choose a graphic organizer for the writing prompt.	Students will: • learn how to check the graphic organizer against the scoring guide.	Students will: • use the graphic organizer to begin a writing test response essay.
Activities				
• Read and discuss **Prewriting: Study the Writing Prompt** (Student pages 378–379).	• Read and discuss **Prewriting: Gather Information** (Student page 380).	• Read and discuss **Prewriting: Organize Ideas** (Student page 381).	• Read and discuss **Prewriting: Check the Scoring Guide** (Student pages 382–383).	• Read and discuss **Drafting: Write a Draft** (Student pages 384–385).

WEEK 3

Day 1	Day 2	Day 3	Day 4	Day 5
Learning Objectives				
Students will: • strengthen any explanations that seem weak.	Students will: • delete information that doesn't support their opinion.	Students will: • make sure each sentence supports their position.	Students will: • edit their writing test response for grammar and mechanics.	Students will: • review tips for writing for a test.
Activities				
• Read and discuss **Revising: Extend Writing** (Student page 386).	• Read and discuss **Revising: Clarify Writing** (Student page 387).	• Read and discuss **Editing: Check Sentences** (Student page 388).	• Read and discuss **Editing: Proofread Writing** (Student pages 389–390).	• Read and discuss **Test Tips** (Student page 391).

To complete the chapter in fewer days, teach the learning objectives and activities for two days in one day.

This planning chart, correlated to your state's writing standards, is available on-line at http://www.zaner-bloser.com/sfw.

PERSUASIVE test writing

Read the Writing Prompt

When you take a writing test, you'll be given a writing prompt. Most writing prompts have three parts:

Setup This part of the writing prompt gives you the background information you need to get ready to write.

Task This part of the writing prompt tells you exactly what you are supposed to write: a persuasive essay.

Scoring Guide This section tells how your writing will be scored. To do well on the test, you should make sure your writing does everything on the list.

Remember the rubrics you have been using? When you take a writing test, you don't always have all of the information that's on a rubric. However, the scoring guide is a lot like a rubric. It lists everything you need to think about to write a good paper. Like the rubrics you've used in this unit, many scoring guides are based upon the six important traits of writing:

- Information/Organization
- Content/Ideas
- Sentence Fluency
- Voice/Audience
- Word Choice/Clarity
- Grammar/Mechanics

Writing MODEL Prompt

Your community is trying to decide between adding a skateboard park in the empty lot adjacent to the city park or putting in more picnic tables. Some of the members of the community feel a skateboard park would be too dangerous, but others say there are plenty of picnic tables and a skateboard park would provide a safer alternative for all the kids in the community who like to skateboard.

Write a persuasive essay for members of your community stating your support for either the skateboard park or the new picnic tables.

Be sure your writing

- is well organized. Include an introduction, body, and conclusion.
- clearly identifies your position for the reader in your opening sentence.
- includes strong explanations that support your position.
- includes only necessary information.
- includes sentences that support your purpose.
- contains correct grammar, punctuation, capitalization, and spelling.

Introduce the Writing Prompt
Persuasive Writing

(Student pages 370–371)

Read through the three parts of a writing prompt with your students. As you read the description of each part of the writing prompt, read that part of the writing prompt from the model writing prompt shown on Student page 371. Explain that within the scoring guide part of the writing prompt, they will find traits similar to those they have seen in the rubrics throughout this chapter. Point out that just as a persuasive writing rubric comprises the qualities that compose a good persuasive writing piece, the scoring guide includes the qualities that make for a good persuasive writing test essay.

Differentiating Instruction

Support Explain that not all writing prompts will include all six of the writing traits shown in the box on Student page 370 but that students should think about each of these traits as they write for a test. Encourage them to memorize each of these important traits of writing. Have them write the name of each trait on one side of each of six index cards. On the back, have them write an example of what that trait refers to, in their own words. Have them review the traits and their descriptions so that they can memorize them.

Writing Traits
in the Scoring Guide

Let's take a look back at the scoring guide in the writing prompt on page 371. Not every writing prompt will include each of the six writing traits, but we can see that this one does. Take a look at the following chart. It will help you better understand the connection between the scoring guide and the writing traits in the rubrics you've been using.

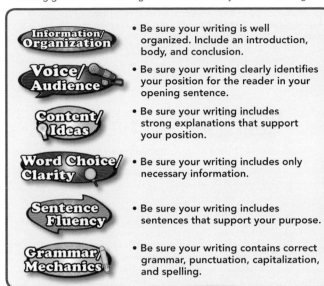

Information/Organization
- Be sure your writing is well organized. Include an introduction, body, and conclusion.

Voice/Audience
- Be sure your writing clearly identifies your position for the reader in your opening sentence.

Content/Ideas
- Be sure your writing includes strong explanations that support your position.

Word Choice/Clarity
- Be sure your writing includes only necessary information.

Sentence Fluency
- Be sure your writing includes sentences that support your purpose.

Grammar/Mechanics
- Be sure your writing contains correct grammar, punctuation, capitalization, and spelling.

Look at Sam Patel's essay on the next page. Did he follow the scoring guide?

372 Persuasive Writing ■ Persuasive Test

A Safe Place to Skate
by Sam Patel

By proposing a skateboard park to be built next to the city park, it's clear that members of our community realize that the large number of skateboarders who live here need a safe and accessible place to practice their sport. Although there are many people opposed to the skateboard park, I'd like to explain to you why I think this is a good idea.

First of all, our community's parks are there to provide enjoyment for the community and to promote the safety and welfare of the residents, and that should include skateboarders, too. Already, the park contains places to enjoy baseball, soccer, football, basketball, and tennis. But these days, skateboarding is just as popular. There is even a skateboard club in the community. These skateboarders need a place to go, yet there is not a place within our entire community that welcomes them.

Next, without a place that they can go to skateboard, many skateboarders use the street, which is not a safe alternative. I see many skateboarders riding along the streets and using curbs and stairways to practice their jumps. They also use plywood and other materials to build their own ramps, which do not look very safe at all. A skateboard park, though, would provide jumps that have been built with skateboarders' safety in mind. The many skateboarders who live in the community would not have to ride in the street and potentially get hit by cars.

Finally, although there are people in our town who want to add more benches, our park already contains enough benches and picnic tables. On the days that I have been to the park, including weekends, weekdays, and during the summer, when it is usually busiest, there have always been open benches and tables. It is clear to me that at this time we do not need additional benches.

Let's remember what our parks are here for, and let's put in something that will keep our skateboarders safe and address the needs of the many people enjoying this popular sport.

Persuasive Writing ■ Persuasive Test **373**

Writing Traits in the Scoring Guide
(Student pages 372–373)

Remind students that for each of the chapters in this unit, they were given a list of writing traits. The writing traits were the basis of the rubric that was used to assess and score their writing. Point out that the writing traits in the scoring guide are much like those found in the *Excelling* category of the rubric. Remind them that the *Beginning* column from the rubric listed qualities that did not meet the writing traits. As they review the writing prompt for their tests, they should think about meeting each of the traits shown in the writing prompt and about avoiding the qualities that would make for a *Beginning* score on a test or paper.

Ask a student volunteer to read the traits in the scoring guide on Student page 372.

Read the Model:
Writing Prompt Response

Point out that students will be studying strategies for test writing in this chapter. A good test contains the traits listed in the scoring guide. As they read through the model writing prompt response, "A Safe Place to Skate," have them look for the traits in the scoring guide.

Differentiating Instruction

Enrichment To further understand how the writing traits in the scoring guide relate to a rubric, have students create a four column rubric based on the writing traits for this persuasive writing test. Have them label the columns *Excelling, Achieving, Developing,* and *Beginning,* and provide descriptors in each column for each of the traits.

Using the Scoring Guide to Study the Model

Now let's use the scoring guide to check Sam's writing test, "A Safe Place to Skate." Let's see how well his essay meets each of the six writing traits.

Information/Organization
- The writing is well organized and includes an introduction, body, and conclusion.

Sam's essay is well organized. He includes an introductory paragraph, three paragraphs to support his opinion, and a conclusion paragraph to wrap things up. Here is Sam's conclusion.

Let's remember what our parks are here for, and let's put in something that will keep our skateboarders safe and address the needs of the many people enjoying this popular sport.

Voice/Audience
- The writing clearly identifies the writer's position in the opening sentence.

Sam states his point of view in the opening sentence. It's clear that he feels that the community's skateboarders need a safe and accessible place to practice their sport.

By proposing a skateboard park to be built next to the city park, it's clear that members of our community realize that the large number of skateboarders who live here need a safe and accessible place to practice their sport.

Content/Ideas
- The writing includes strong explanations that support the writer's position.

Sam gives strong explanations to support his view in favor of the skateboard park. For instance, he brings up the fact that without a designated skateboard park, the community's skateboarders have no safe alternatives.

Next, without a place that they can go to skateboard, many skateboarders use the street, which is not a safe alternative. I see many skateboarders riding along the streets and using curbs and stairways to practice their jumps. They also use plywood and other materials to build their own ramps, which do not look very safe at all. A skateboard park, though, would provide jumps that have been built with skateboarders' safety in mind.

Word Choice/Clarity
- The writing includes only necessary information.

Sam did a good job sticking to the topic. When he argues that there are already enough benches and picnic tables, he doesn't go into unnecessary details such as why he goes to the park—he sticks with what's important.

Finally, although there are people in our town who want to add more benches, our park already contains enough benches and picnic tables. On the days that I have been to the park, including weekends, weekdays, and during the summer, when it is usually busiest, there have always been open benches and tables. It is clear to me that at this time we do not need additional benches.

Using the Scoring Guide to Study the Model

(Student pages 374–376)

Explain that Student pages 374–376 show how the test writing model on Student page 373 meets all six traits of the rubric. Read each section with students. Then have students look through the test writing model for other examples of each trait.

Ask students if they agree with Leila's assessment of the writing test model. Have them explain why or why not. After you have gone through each section, ask the class how they would rate the test overall.

Remind students that when they are writing for a test, they should pay close attention to the writing traits in the scoring guide, to be sure they are meeting all of the traits.

Differentiating Instruction

Support To help students better understand how to clearly identify their position in an opening sentence, have them write an opening paragraph with their response to the following: *Do you think that students should be able to place stickers and other semi-permanent decorations on their lockers?* Remind students to include their position in the opening sentence as they craft their responses. Once they have completed the task, ask students to share their opening paragraphs by reading them aloud to the class. After a student reads his or her paragraph, ask others if they feel the student made his or her position on the issue clear.

Using the Scoring Guide to Study the Model

- The writing includes sentences that support the writer's purpose.

All of Sam's sentences support his purpose. For example, in the paragraph below, all of the sentences that follow the main topic support the idea in the main topic.

First of all, our community's parks are there to provide enjoyment for the community and to promote the safety and welfare of the residents, and that should include skateboarders, too. Already, the park contains places to enjoy baseball, soccer, football, basketball, and tennis. But these days, skateboarding is just as popular. There is even a skateboard club in the community. These skateboarders need a place to go, yet there is not a place within our entire community that welcomes them.

Grammar/Mechanics

- The essay has correct grammar, punctuation, capitalization, and spelling.

I think Sam did a great job with his grammar and mechanics. From what I can see, he did not make any serious mistakes in capitalization, punctuation, sentence structure, or spelling. Look at the section below. See any mistakes? Neither did I.

By proposing a skateboard park to be built next to the city park, it's clear that members of our community realize that the large number of skateboarders who live here need a safe and accessible place to practice their sport. Although there are many people opposed to the skateboard park, I'd like to explain to you why I think this is a good idea.

Planning My Time

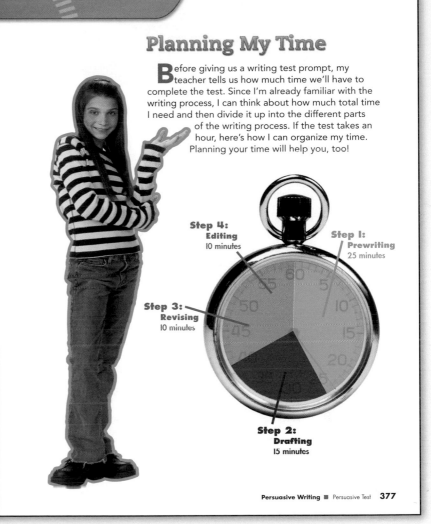

Before giving us a writing test prompt, my teacher tells us how much time we'll have to complete the test. Since I'm already familiar with the writing process, I can think about how much total time I need and then divide it up into the different parts of the writing process. If the test takes an hour, here's how I can organize my time. Planning your time will help you, too!

Step 4: Editing 10 minutes

Step 1: Prewriting 25 minutes

Step 3: Revising 10 minutes

Step 2: Drafting 15 minutes

Planning My Time
(Student page 377)

Remind students of the importance of organizing their time when they are planning for a test. Point out that when they take a writing test, they will have a limited amount of time. It is important to set aside blocks of time for each of the steps in the writing process to ensure that they successfully complete the test.

Ask a student volunteer to tell the class what Leila has devoted most of her test taking time to. **prewriting** Remind students that many students do poorly on writing tests because they begin writing before they have a plan and continue writing until they run out of time. Just as they have done in previous writing chapters, they need to spend time on prewriting. Stress to students the importance of including enough time to prewrite, revise, and edit.

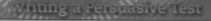

Writing a Persuasive Test

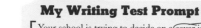 **Study the Writing Prompt**

Writing Strategy Study the writing prompt to be sure I know what to do.

When you take a writing test, study the writing prompt so you know just what you need to do. The writing prompt usually has three parts. Although the parts may not be labeled, you should be able to find them and label them on your own. Take a look at how I marked my writing prompt. First I found the setup, task, and scoring guide in the writing prompt. Then I circled key words in the setup and the task that tell what kind of writing I need to do. I circled the setup in purple and the task in red.

My Writing Test Prompt

Setup — Your school is trying to decide on a cover image and saying for this year's school yearbook. They want an image that will be visually appealing and a saying that will represent the school well.

Task — Come up with an idea for the cover of your school's yearbook and write a persuasive essay to convince the other students to agree with your choice.

Scoring Guide — Be sure your writing

- is well organized. Include an introduction, body, and conclusion.
- clearly identifies your position for the reader in your opening sentence.
- includes strong explanations that support your position.
- includes only necessary information.
- includes sentences that support your purpose.
- contains correct grammar, punctuation, capitalization, and spelling.

378 **Persuasive Writing** ■ Persuasive Test

Think about how the scoring guide relates to the six writing traits you've studied in the rubrics. All of the traits might not be included in every scoring guide, but you need to remember them all to write a good persuasive test.

 Information/Organization
- Be sure your writing is well organized. Include an introduction, body, and conclusion.

I'll begin my essay with an introductory paragraph. Then I'll write the body of my essay, and I'll finish with my conclusion.

 Voice/Audience
- Be sure your writing clearly identifies your position for the reader in your opening sentence.

I'll clearly state my position right away.

 Content/Ideas
- Be sure your writing includes strong explanations that support your position.

In order to make my argument strong, I will include good explanations in the body of my essay.

 Word Choice/Clarity
- Be sure your writing includes only necessary information.

As I write, I'll stay focused on what needs to be said. I'll reread my essay once I'm done to be sure I have included only necessary information.

 Sentence Fluency
- Be sure your writing includes sentences that support your purpose.

The sentences I use throughout my essay will be there for one reason: to support my purpose!

 Grammar/Mechanics
- Be sure your writing contains correct grammar, punctuation, capitalization, and spelling.

I'll read my essay once I have completed it to find and fix any spelling and grammar mistakes.

Persuasive Writing ■ Persuasive Test 379

Study the Writing Prompt
(Student pages 378–379)

Ask a student to read aloud Leila's words on Student page 378. Remind students of the importance of reading and understanding the writing prompt before they begin writing. Following the instructions set forth in the writing prompt is important when taking a test.

Ask students to state what type of writing Leila is being asked to do. **a persuasive essay** What type of background information does Leila need in order to write her persuasive essay? **The school is trying to decide on a cover image and saying for the yearbook. The image should be visually appealing, and the saying should represent the school well.**

Next, ask a student to read the scoring guide portion of the writing prompt. Review Student page 379 to show how each of the traits in the writing prompt relates to the six key areas of assessment. Have students look at how Leila thinks about each of the traits in the scoring guide. This is to ensure that she knows what she needs to do to succeed on the test even before she begins writing.

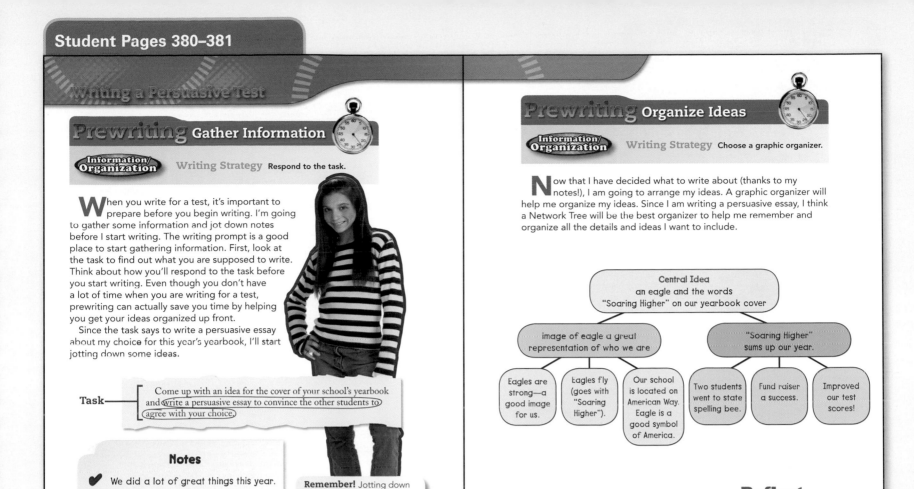

Gather Information and Organize Ideas

(Student pages 380–381)

Ask a student to read Leila's words on Student page 380. Note that Leila jots down notes to help her focus on what she is going to write. Because time is limited during a test, students may wish to brainstorm ideas about what they are going to write as they jot down their notes. Writing down the things that come to mind as they review the task can help them hone in on their topics.

Point out that even when writing for a test, students should organize their ideas using a graphic organizer. A Network Tree is one way for students to organize their notes for a persuasive essay for a writing test. Review Leila's Network Tree. Point out that the information Leila has included in her Network Tree is what she will be including in her essay.

Differentiating Instruction

English-Language Learners Graphic organizers are not only great tools for organizing information, but they also provide a visual image of the information students need to include in their writing tests. For English-language learners, graphic organizers can be especially helpful because they help students visualize what they need to do. During a writing test, students may wish to create a visual image of what they are supposed to do in addition to any graphic organizers they use to organize the information for their writing tests. Have students select and fill in a graphic organizer that lays out the details of the persuasive writing test from the writing prompt shown on Student page 378.

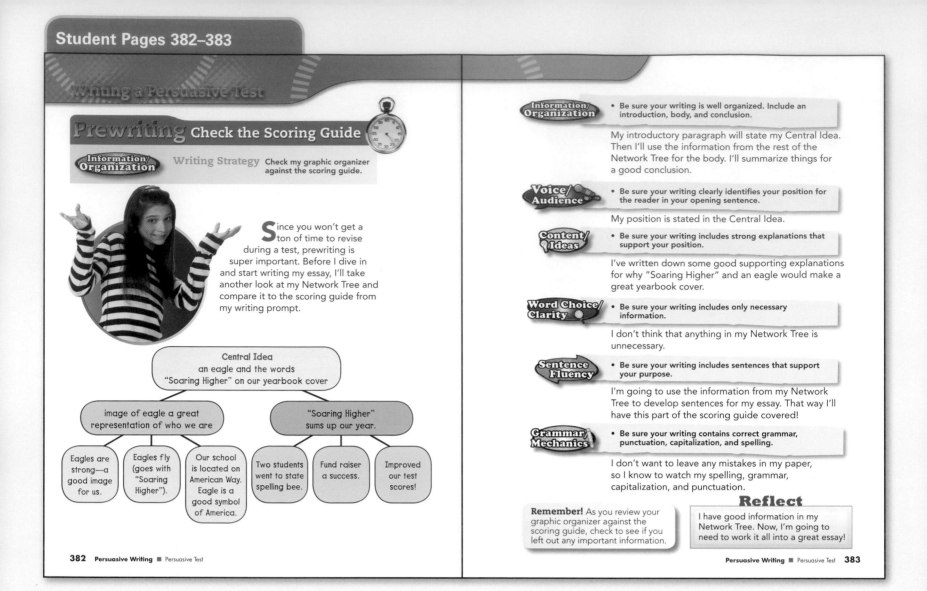

Check the Scoring Guide
(Student pages 382–383)

Ask a student to read Leila's words on Student page 382. Note that even though she has completed her graphic organizer, she is not yet ready to begin writing her draft. Instead, she uses this opportunity to review once more each of the traits in the scoring guide. She uses her Network Tree to compare what she has prepared against the traits in the scoring guide. Emphasize the importance of paying attention to the scoring guide throughout the test writing process. Point out that during this step of the test writing process, students may need to add informa-

tion or change information in their graphic organizers to meet the criteria set forth in the scoring guide portion of the writing prompt. Had Leila discovered, for instance, that she included unnecessary information, she could go back and make the changes on her Network Tree instead of on her draft.

Explain that while the graphic organizer helped Leila get her notes organized and meet some of the criteria in the scoring guide, she will still need to think about other parts of the scoring guide as she writes, including ensuring that her writing is free of grammatical and spelling mistakes.

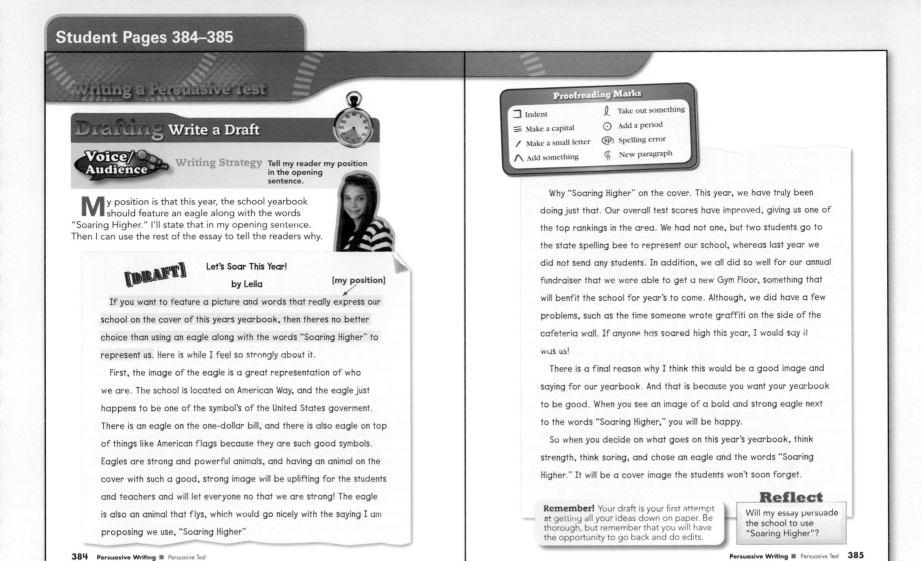

Drafting

(Student pages 384–385)

Remind students that even though Leila is writing for a test, her draft does not need to be perfect at this stage. As long as students leave time during the test taking process for revising and editing, the draft should be used to get their ideas on paper. Explain that students will want to leave space between the lines of their essays so that they will have room to make changes and additions later. Point out that in many cases, the edited draft is the final version of the test essay. Remind them, too, that is important to write neatly, even in the draft stage. The test evaluator needs to be able to read what they have written.

Ask students to read Leila's words on Student page 384. As she writes her draft, she keeps in mind the trait from the scoring guide that instructs her to state her position in the opening sentence. Have a student read Leila's opening sentence aloud. Ask the class whether they feel Leila has done a good job of stating her position.

Discuss Leila's draft. Have students refer back to her graphic organizer to see how she included the informa-

tion she outlined in her Network Tree. Note that there are mistakes in the draft but that Leila has left time to revise and edit her draft.

Review the proofreading checklist with students. Point out that these marks will be helpful as they revise and edit their drafts.

Differentiating Instruction

Enrichment To practice stating one's position in the opening sentence, provide a sample persuasive essay to read aloud to the class. Delete the opening sentence and paragraph from the essay so that students hear only the body and conclusion. You may wish to make photocopies of the essay, with the lead paragraph deleted, so that students can refer to it more easily. Ask the students to use the information from the body and conclusion of the essay to create an opening sentence and lead paragraph that states the writer's position. Ask for student volunteers to read their paragraphs aloud.

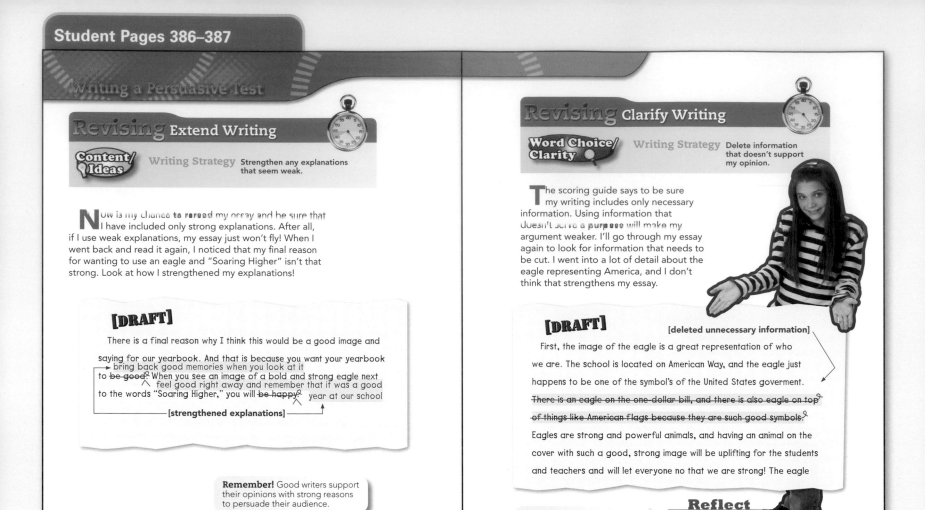

Revising

(Student pages 386–387)

Ask a student to read Leila's words on Student page 386 aloud. Note that the lines in the draft that say "you want your yearbook to be good" and "you will be happy" are vague and weak. Read aloud the sentences from Leila's draft after she made the revisions. Ask students whether they feel the revisions made the essay stronger.

Ask students if there are any other places in Leila's draft where they feel she could strengthen her explanations.

Next, ask a student to read Leila's words on Student page 387. Note that once again, Leila refers to the scoring guide as she completes her test. Review with students the sentence that Leila deleted, and ask students why they think this information did not belong in her essay. **Possible response: It is about the eagle as an American symbol and does not have to do with why it should be the school's symbol.**

Writing a Persuasive Test

Editing Check Sentences

Sentence Fluency **Writing Strategy** Make sure each sentence supports my purpose.

Now I'll go back through my essay, sentence by sentence, and determine whether each sentence is important in supporting my purpose for writing. Maybe this isn't the place to remind people of the graffiti incident!

[DRAFT]

Why "Soaring Higher" on the cover. This year, we have truly been doing just that. Our overall test scores have improved, giving us one of the top rankings in the area. We had not one, but two students go to the state spelling bee to represent our school, whereas last year we did not send any students. In addition, we all did so well for our annual fundraiser that we were able to get a new Gym Floor, something that will benfit the school for year's to come. ~~Although, we did have a few problems, such as the time someone wrote graffiti on the side of the cafeteria wall.~~

→ [deleted sentence that doesn't support my purpose]

Remember! Now's the time to edit out any sentences that aren't serving a good purpose in your essay.

Editing Proofread Writing

Grammar/Mechanics **Writing Strategy** Check my grammar, punctuation, capitalization, and spelling.

Always check your paper one last time. The scoring guide says to use correct grammar, punctuation, capitalization, and spelling. I always leave plenty of time to check for errors in these important areas.

[FINAL DRAFT]

Let's Soar This Year!
by Leila

If you want to feature a picture and words that really express our school on the cover of this year's yearbook, then there's no better choice than using an eagle along with the words "Soaring Higher" to represent us. Here is ~~while~~ *why* I feel so strongly about it.

First, the image of the eagle is a great representation of who we are. The school is located on American Way, and the eagle just happens to be one of the symbol's of the United States government. ~~There is an eagle on the one-dollar bill, and there is also eagle on top of things like American flags because they are such good symbols.~~ Eagles are strong and powerful animals, and having an animal on the cover with such a good, strong image will be uplifting for the students and teachers and will let everyone ~~no~~ *know* that we are strong! The eagle is also an animal that ~~flys~~ *flies* which would go nicely with the saying I am proposing we use, "Soaring Higher."

Remember! Even though you have read and reread your essay, you want to look at it carefully at this point to find and correct any mistakes.

Editing

(Student pages 388–390)

Write the following sentences on the board: *Tomato soup is great to have on cold days. Because it is hot, it warms you right up. It's also hearty and filling. It's good in the summer, too.* Ask students if any of the sentences seem unnecessary in an argument about why tomato soup is good on cold days. **the sentence, *It's good in the summer, too.*** Point out that it is important to ensure that every sentence supports your position when you are writing a persuasive essay.

Have a student read aloud Leila's words on Student page 388. Ask whether they feel that Leila made the right choice in deleting the sentence about the graffiti.

Remind students of the importance of allowing time to edit and proofread their writing before they submit a test. Have them look for errors as they proofread their drafts. Note that basic errors in sentence completeness, punctuation, and spelling will likely affect their scores more than minor errors.

Differentiating Instruction

Support To help students better understand how to strengthen explanations that seem weak, write the following on the board: *Keeping a travel journal is a great way to record memories from your vacation. You can write all about the trip and save special mementos. It will be nice to read later.* Ask students to rewrite the last sentence to make it stronger. **Possible response: Later, you can read your journal, and it will bring back all the fantastic memories from your trip.**

Student page 390

[FINAL DRAFT]

Why "Soaring Higher" on the cover? This year, we have truly been doing just that. Our overall test scores have improved, giving us one of the top rankings in the area. We had not one, but two students go to the state spelling bee to represent our school, whereas last year we did not send any students. In addition, we all did so well for our annual fundraiser that we were able to get a new gym floor, something that will benfit the school for year's to come. Although, we did have a few problems, such as the time someone wrote graffiti on the side of the cafeteria wall. If anyone has soared high this year, I would say it was us!

There is a final reason why I think this would be a good image and saying for our yearbook. And that is because you want your yearbook to be good. bring back good memories when you look at it When you see an image of a bold and strong eagle next to the words "Soaring Higher," you will be happy, feel good right away and remember that if was a good year at our school

So when you decide on what goes on this year's yearbook, think strength, think soaring, and chose an eagle and the words "Soaring Higher." It will be a cover image the students won't soon forget.

Reflect

There's just enough time for me to take one last look at the scoring guide to be sure I haven't missed anything.

390 Persuasive Writing ■ Persuasive Test

Student page 391

The test is complete! When you follow the right steps, it's not that difficult at all. Here are some helpful tips to remember when you write for a test.

TEST TIPS

1. **Study the writing prompt before you start to write.** Most writing prompts have three parts: the setup, the task, and the scoring guide. The parts probably won't be labeled. You'll have to figure them out for yourself!

2. **Make sure you understand the task before you start to write.**
   - Read all three parts of the writing prompt carefully.
   - Circle key words in the task part of the writing prompt that tell what kind of writing you need to do. The task might also identify your audience.
   - Make sure you know how you'll be graded.
   - Say the assignment in your own words to yourself.

3. **Keep an eye on the clock.** Decide how much time you will spend on each part of the writing process and try to stick to your schedule. Don't spend so much time on prewriting that you don't have enough time left to write.

4. **Reread your writing. Compare it to the scoring guide at least twice.** Remember the rubrics you have used all year? A scoring guide on a writing test is like a rubric. It can help you keep what's important in mind.

5. **Plan, plan, plan!** You don't get much time to revise during a test, so planning is more important than ever.

6. **Write neatly.** Remember, if the people who score your test can't read your writing, it doesn't matter how good your essay is!

Persuasive Writing ■ Persuasive Test **391**

Differentiating Instruction

Enrichment Explain that preparing for a writing test is different from preparing for tests such as math exams and vocabulary tests. Have students think about how they prepare for exams in other subjects, such as by preparing note cards with the information they need to remember, studying the content from their textbooks, and summarizing their notes. Then have them review the test taking tips on Student page 391. Have students come up with strategies for preparing for a writing test. You might suggest they include things such as getting a good night's sleep the night before or relaxing before the test to show students that preparation for a test often requires more than reviewing one's textbook. Have students share their ideas with the class.

Test Tips
(Student page 391)

Have students recall the lessons they learned in this chapter about preparing for and taking a test. Ask them what they think are important steps to remember when taking a writing test. **Possible responses: study the writing prompt; plan their time; save time for editing and revising** Read aloud the Test Tips on Student page 391.

Ask students how they feel now about taking a writing test. If some of your students are apprehensive about writing tests, remind them that they have already been studying all the skills they need to successfully complete a writing test. The lessons they have learned throughout the book have prepared them to do well on a test.

Books for Professional Development

Nickelsen, Leann. *Teaching Elaboration and Word Choice.* New York: Scholastic, 2001.

This book has easy and effective mini-lessons and activities that help students enrich and enliven their writing. It includes creative lessons on using lively verbs, colorful adjectives, specific nouns, and more.

Dean, Nancy. *Voice Lessons: Classroom Activities to Teach Diction, Detail, Imagery, Syntax, and Tone.* Gainesville: Maupin, 2000.

The author creates simple exercises that invite students to notice voice in writing. With intriguing quotes and discussion starters, students can talk about word choice, sentence structure, tone, etc. Instead of force-feeding students with heavy terminology and rote memorization of how grammar works, Dean helps create an environment in which students ask for the terminology in order to better express their thoughts.

Kanavy, Joan, and Susan Van Zile. *High-Interest Literature Units Survival: Teacher-Created Lessons and Activities That Use Favorite Novels to Motivate Kids to Read, Write, and Discuss.* New York: Scholastic, 2002.

This book helps instructors create meaningful literature units using five high-interest theme novels. It includes reading strategy mini-lessons, discussion and writing prompts, response projects, and creative activities for teaching literary elements.

Filipovic, Zlata, and Freedom Writers. *The Freedom Writer's Diary: How a Teacher and 150 Teens Used Writing to Change Themselves and the World Around Them.* Jackson: Main Street Books, 1999.

Woodrow Wilson High School in Long Beach, California, is the setting for this true story of how a first-year teacher named Erin Gruwell used both classic and socially conscious literature to inspire at-risk students to compose diaries describing their own fears and aspirations.

School-Home Connection

Dear Family,

In this chapter of *Strategies for Writers,* your child is learning to write a book review that compares and contrasts two books. As we study each genre of writing, we provide a list of reasons for writing in that particular genre. All writing has a purpose, and these authentic purposes help to shape the writing.

One of the reasons for writing book reviews is for your child to share his or her opinion. The book review is really just a well-organized written expression of that opinion.

One way that you can help your child form opinions about books is to encourage him or her to discuss the books he or she is reading or has read. Ask him or her about such things as

- **Plot:** What is the story about?

- **Characters:** Who are the main characters and what are they like? Does your child think the main character is weak or strong? Can he or she identify with the main character in any way?

- **Settings:** Where and when does the book take place? Did your child learn anything about the setting in which the book takes place?

- **Themes:** What are the main issues the book deals with? Has your child learned anything by reading the book?

- **General Opinion:** Did your child like or dislike the book and why? Ask your child to point out some of the things that make the book appealing or unappealing. Would he or she recommend the book to another person to read? Why or why not?

Getting your child to think about these issues as he or she reads a book will help him or her write book reviews. Thank you for your help in the writing process.

School-Home Connection

Dear Family,

Has your child ever presented you with a compelling argument about something that has managed to sway your opinion? Maybe it was to convince you to let him or her go to a friend's house or to allow him or her to finish homework before bed instead of right after school. In this chapter of *Strategies for Writers,* your child is focusing on reasoning skills as we learn to write a persuasive essay.

What makes a good persuasive essay? As with all of the writing genres we are exploring, we have set forth a list of traits that make up a good persuasive essay. These traits are as follows:

- The essay focuses on one issue. The essay is well organized with supporting details.

- The writer's opinion is convincingly stated at the beginning of the essay.

- Facts and reasons support the writer's opinion.

- The essay contains neutral words throughout.

- Question-and-answer sentence patterns help make the writer's case.

- Spelling, punctuation, and capitalization are correct. Pronouns all have clear antcccdents.

A well-written persuasive essay has the potential to change people's points-of-view, to inform others on a topic, and to turn a disagreement from a back-and-forth argument into a logical debate.

So next time your child wants to make a case for not doing the dishes one night, we hope you will encourage him or her to present a clear and logical argument with facts and reasons and neutral—not negative—words. This will help your child practice his or her reasoning skills that are helpful in writing a persuasive essay.

School-Home Connection

Dear Family,

In this chapter of *Strategies for Writers,* your child is learning how to write a persuasive business letter. This type of business letter is written for a purpose: to express an opinion and persuade the reader or readers to consider that opinion.

Your child will be learning about the elements of a business letter, including organization, correct form, businesslike tone, and supporting details. All of these elements help to make your child's argument stronger.

As with all genres of writing, we encourage your child to explore other reasons and ways to write and publish a business letter. One of the ways we suggest is writing a persuasive letter to their parents about something they would like changed. In this way, students will have the opportunity to practice their business letter writing skills and to present their opinions effectively.

The next time your child makes a request for change, we encourage you to ask him or her to write it in a persuasive business letter to you, complete with supporting facts and details. Ask him or her to structure the letter as they would a letter to a company, including using your name and address at the top of the letter, beginning with a greeting, and ending the letter with a proper closing and signature.

Once you have received the letter, review it with your child to see that he or she has explained the needed change in a businesslike tone and has clearly stated the purpose for writing the letter in both the opening and the closing paragraphs. Whether you choose to make the change or not is up to you, of course; what's more important is that your child has the chance to practice his or her skills at writing a business letter.

Once again, thank for your help in the writing process.

School-Home Connection

Dear Family,

In *Strategies for Writers,* we are giving students the tools they need to write well in a variety of genres. Good writing is one of the most important skills a student can have. Solid writing skills will serve your child well throughout his or her education and, indeed, throughout his or her life.

Sometimes when students are mired in the day-to-day details of completing schoolwork, they are not able to understand the practical applications of what they are learning. We encourage you to emphasize to your child how important it is to know how to represent himself or herself well in written communication. Here are some ways that writing well will be important in your child's life:

- It's practical. Students will need to write notes, instructions, and business letters throughout their lives. Even if your child does not follow a career that will require him or her to write letters and correspondence frequently, he or she will need writing skills to send out job letters and correspondence and to respond to e-mail on the job.

- It's thought-provoking. Writing can help your child formulate his or her thoughts and organize them logically.

- It's social. Written correspondence with friends and loved ones is even more prevalent today because of e-mail and messaging.

- It's relaxing. Writing in a journal is one way to express thoughts and feelings that may be hard to express in other ways.

Your support of your child's writing does make a difference! We hope that you will encourage your child to take an active and continued interest in writing well.

WRITER'S HANDBOOK

The Writer's Handbook will give you more help and some great hints for making your writing the best it can be. Use the Writer's Handbook any time you have more questions or just need a little extra help.

Table of Contents

Writer's Terms

Active Voice is writing that shows that the subject is doing the action.

Article is a piece of writing published in a magazine or newspaper.

Body is the main part of a writing piece.

Cause-and-Effect Chain is a graphic organizer that shows the reasons (causes) for specific events or results (effects).

Cause-and-Effect Relationship is the result of an action. One effect can have several causes, and one cause can have several effects.

Characters are people in a book, play, movie, or show.

Clichés are expressions used so often that they become stale or corny. (white as snow/black as night)

Climax is the most exciting or important moment in a story.

Colorful Words are words that create an exciting and clear picture in the reader's mind.

Common Words are words that most people understand. It is often easier for a reader to understand your writing if you replace jargon with common words.

Conclusion is the last paragraph of a long paper that ties up loose ends and summarizes main points.

Credible Source is a reliable place to obtain information that is accurate, trusted, unbiased, and up-to-date.

Detail Sentence is a sentence that supports the paragraph's main idea.

Details are facts, examples, and anecdotes that support a main idea.

Drama is something that makes a reader care deeply about a subject or a story.

Dull Words are words with general meanings that are not very exciting.

Encyclopedia is a reference book, or set of books, with information about many different topics.

Events are things that happen.

Exact Words are words that provide specific details about a topic or an event.

Exclamation is a sentence that expresses strong feeling.

Fact is a statement that can be proven to be true.

Five-Senses Chart is a chart that organizes information using the five senses (touch, taste, hear, see, smell).

Five W's Chart is a graphic organizer used to organize information by asking and answering What happened? Who was there? Why did it happen? When did it happen? Where did it happen?

Historical Event is an actual event in history.

Incident is something that happens.

Interesting Phrases are exciting phrases that make a reader want to know more.

Internet is an electronic source for information contained on Web sites.

Introduction is the first paragraph of a paper that states the main idea.

Lead Paragraph is the first paragraph in a long piece of writing.

Loaded Words are words that cause the reader to have a strong emotional reaction, whether positive or negative.

Metaphor is a comparison in which one thing is called another.

Network Tree is a chart that organizes information about a topic. The topic or opinion goes at the top, with the main ideas or reasons on the next level. The bottom level contains facts to support the main ideas or reasons.

Neutral Words are words that do not cause a strong emotional reaction.

Note Card is an index card used to write information about a topic.

Notes are information a writer gathers and writes down about a topic.

Opinion is a belief that cannot be proven to be true.

Writer's Terms continued

Order-of-Importance Organizer is an organizer that shows the main points about something in order of importance.

Outline is an organizational tool that shows the main idea and the supporting details of the paragraphs of an essay.

Overused Words are words that are vague or stale because they are used too many times.

Passive Voice is writing that shows that the subject is not doing the action.

Point of View is the perspective a writer uses to tell a story.

Professional Tone is a tone that is polite and formal.

Purpose is the reason for writing about a particular subject, for example, to inform, explain, entertain, or persuade.

Questions are sentences that ask something. Writers sometimes use questions to vary the tone in a writing piece.

Quotations are the exact words of a speaker.

Reason is an explanation behind an act, idea, or argument.

Relevant Details are pieces of information that help the reader understand the main points.

Response Journal is a notebook or other place where someone jots down his or her impressions about an experience, such as reading a book.

Run-on Sentences are compound sentences that are not joined correctly.

Sensory Details are details that relate to one of the five senses (seeing, hearing, feeling, smelling, tasting).

Sentence Fragment is a sentence that is missing a subject or a verb.

Sentence Pattern is the use of sentences to add impact to a letter or essay. For example, the question-and-answer sentence pattern is often used in persuasive essays.

Sequence Chain is a graphic organizer that shows steps or events in the order they happen.

Sincere Tone is when the writing sounds clear and honest.

Source is anything or anyone with information.

Spider Map is a chart that organizes information about a topic. A main point is written on each leg.

Story Map is a graphic organizer used to organize the setting, major and minor characters, plot and problem, major events, and outcome of a story.

Storyboard is a series of pictures. The pictures show the main events of a story in the order they happen.

Succinct is clear. Succinct writing doesn't contain unneeded words or phrases.

Supporting Facts are facts that support main points.

Thesis Statement is the sentence(s) that tells the purpose or main idea of an essay or report.

Time-Order Words are words that help show when different steps or events take place. They include words such as *after, during, first, second, third, until, meanwhile, next, soon, later, finally, then,* and *as soon as.*

Tone is how writing sounds.

Topic Sentence is the sentence in a paragraph that tells the main idea.

Transition Word or **Phrase** is a word or phrase that ties ideas together. It signals the reader that the writing is moving from one idea to another.

Venn Diagram is a chart with two overlapping circles that shows how things are similar and different. Ways the things are similar are described in the overlapping section. Ways the things are different are described in the outer part of each circle.

Visualize is to picture something in your mind.

Vivid Imagery is sensory words that create a clear picture for the reader.

Word Picture is a way of writing that uses descriptive words to help readers "see" the character or event as they read. When the writer paints word pictures, the writing becomes more interesting.

Writer's Handbook

Grammar / Mechanics

Sentence Structure

Simple sentence contains one subject and one predicate.

Compound sentence is made up of two **independent clauses** joined by a punctuation mark and a conjunction.

Complex Sentence is made up of one **independent clause** (or simple sentence) and at least one **dependent clause**. A dependent clause is a group of words that has a subject and a predicate but cannot stand on its own.

> **Dependent Clause:** while Shanna glued them to the poster
>
> **Independent Clause:** Tony cut out the letters
>
> **Complex Sentence:** Tony cut out the letters, while Shanna glued them to the poster.

Subject-Verb Agreement

The **subject** and its **verb** must agree in number.

> **Example:** The desk is full of paper.
> (Desk is **singular**; it requires the verb *is*.)
>
> **Example:** The astronauts in the rocket were ready to launch.
> ("Astronauts" is **plural**; it requires the verb *were*.)

Quotation Marks

Use **quotation marks** to separate a speaker's exact words from the rest of the sentence. Begin a **direct quotation** with a capital letter. Use a comma to separate the direct quotation from the speaker's name. When a direct quotation comes at the end of a sentence, put the end mark inside the last quotation mark. When writing a conversation, begin a new paragraph with each change of speaker.

> **Example:** Tim said, "My homework is done." He was hoping to go in-line skating before dinner.
> "You can go," his mom answered. "Just be back before dinnertime."

Parts of Speech

Verbs

Present, Past, and Future Tenses

Verbs can tell about the present, the past, or the future.

> **Example:** My friend **rides** down the hill. (present tense)
> **Example:** My friend **rode** down the hill. (past tense)
> **Example:** My friend **will ride** down the hill. (future tense)

Nouns

Common nouns name a person, place, or thing.

Proper nouns name a particular person, place, or thing.

Pronouns

A **pronoun** can replace a noun naming a person, place, thing, or idea. **Personal pronouns** include *I, me, you, we, us, he, she, it, they,* and *them.*

A **subject pronoun** takes the place of the subject of a sentence.

An **object pronoun** replaces a noun that is the object of a verb or a preposition.

Use a subject pronoun as part of a compound subject. Use an object pronoun as part of a compound object. To test whether a pronoun is correct, say the sentence without the other part of the compound subject or object.

> **Incorrect:** Rosco and him came with Jessica and we.
> **Correct:** Rosco and he came with Jessica and us.

An **antecedent** is the word or phrase a pronoun refers to. The antecedent always includes a noun.

> **Example: Joan** cleaned **her** room.

A possessive pronoun must match its antecedent. An antecedent and pronoun agree when they have the same number (singular or plural) and gender (male or female).

Indefinite pronouns replace a non-specific person, place, or thing. For example: *everyone, nobody, nothing, something,* and *anything.*

Writer's Handbook

Grammar / Mechanics continued

Appositives

An **appositive** is a phrase that identifies a noun. It follows the noun and explains it or gives more information about it. Appositive phrases may be short or long. Most appositives are separated from the rest of a sentence by commas. These appositives give more information about the nouns they describe.

> **Example:** Tara, my friend who figure skates, is traveling to Dallas.

Apostrophes

An **apostrophe** (') is used to form the possessive of a noun or to join words in a contraction.

Possessives show ownership. To make a singular noun possessive, add **'s**.

> **Example:** the girl**'s** book

To make a **possessive** form of a plural noun that ends in *s*, add only an apostrophe.

> **Example:** the dresses' belts

Some plural nouns do not end in *s*. To form possessives of these nouns, add **'s**.

> **Example:** children**'s** laughter

Homophones

A **homophone** is one of two or more words that have the same pronunciation but different spellings and different meanings. For example: *to, too, two* or *our, hour.*

APPENDIX

Table of Contents

Using the Mode-Specific Rubrics

Rubrics are central to instruction in *Strategies for Writers.* Each chapter includes a genre-specific rubric that guides students' writing and measures their performance on the six writing traits.

More general, mode-specific rubrics are included on the following pages. One rubric is included for each of the four writing modes: narrative, descriptive, expository, and persuasive. You may wish to duplicate these rubrics and use them as instruments to guide and assess students' writing both before (as a pretest rubric) and after (as a posttest rubric) instruction within that mode.

The writing traits on each of the rubrics are:

 **Information/Organization** meaning the way in which the writer chooses an appropriate topic, gathers information, and organizes the writing.

 **Voice/Audience** meaning the way in which the writer identifies, addresses, and relates to the audience intended for the writing.

 **Content/Ideas** meaning the way in which the writer includes relevant content and supporting information to flesh out the writing.

 **Word Choice/Clarity** meaning the way in which the writer chooses appropriate words to convey meaning and clarify writing.

 **Sentence Fluency** meaning the way in which sentence variety and patterns contribute to the flow of the writing.

 **Grammar/Mechanics** meaning the ways in which the writer observes grammar, usage, mechanics, and spelling guidelines.

Narrative Rubric

	Achieving ✓✓✓✓	Developing ✓✓✓	Excelling ✓✓	Beginning ✓
Information/Organization	Events follow one another in order.	Most events follow one another.	Some events follow one another.	Events need to follow one another.
Voice/Audience	The writer's voice connects with the audience.	The writer's voice connects with the audience most of the time.	The writer's voice sometimes connects with the audience.	The writer's voice needs to connect with the audience.
Content/Ideas	The writing contains all elements of narrative writing, including well developed characters, setting, and plot.	The writing contains most of the elements of narrative writing, and they are fairly well developed.	The writing contains some of the elements of narrative writing.	The writing needs all elements of narrative writing, such as characters, setting, and plot.
Word Choice/Clarity	Vivid wording and interesting details bring the writing to life.	The writing contains interesting details and some vivid wording.	The writing contains a few interesting details.	The writing needs vivid wording and interesting details.
Sentence Fluency	Sentence lengths and patterns vary to make the writing flow.	There is some variety in sentence patterns and length.	There is little variety in sentence patterns and length.	Sentences need to be varied to make the writing flow.
Grammar/Mechanics	The writing contains no errors in spelling, punctuation, grammar, or mechanics.	The writing contains very few errors in spelling, punctuation, grammar, and mechanics.	The writing contains some errors in spelling, punctuation, grammar, and mechanics.	The writing contains many errors in spelling, punctuation, grammar, and mechanics.

Descriptive Rubric

	Achieving ✓✓✓	Developing ✓✓✓	Excelling ✓✓	Beginning ✓
Information/ Organization	The description focuses on one topic. It is organized according to the five senses.	The description focuses on one topic. It is mostly organized around the five senses.	The description sometimes focuses on one topic and is loosely organized.	The description needs to focus on one topic and be organized around the five senses.
Voice/ Audience	The description captures the audience's attention and keeps it throughout.	The description gets the audience's attention and keeps it most of the time.	The description gets the audience's attention, but doesn't keep it.	The description needs to get the audience's attention.
Content/ Ideas	Many details make the description interesting.	Some details make the description interesting.	A few details make the description somewhat interesting.	The description needs details to make it interesting.
Word Choice/ Clarity	The description contains effective use of figurative language.	The description contains some figurative language.	The description contains little figurative language.	The description needs figurative language.
Sentence Fluency	Variety in sentence beginnings makes the description flow.	Some variety in sentence beginnings makes the description flow.	There is little variety in sentence beginnings to make the description flow.	The description needs variety in sentence beginnings.
Grammar/ Mechanics	The description contains no errors in spelling, punctuation, grammar, or mechanics.	The description contains very few errors in spelling, punctuation, grammar, and mechanics.	The description contains some errors in spelling, punctuation, grammar, and mechanics.	The description contains many errors in spelling, punctuation, grammar, and mechanics.

This page may be duplicated for classroom use.

Copyright © Zaner-Bloser, Inc.

Expository Rubric

	Achieving ✓✓✓	Developing ✓✓✓	Excelling ✓✓	Beginning ✓
Information/Organization	The writing focuses on one topic. It is well organized with an introduction, a body, and a conclusion.	The writing is focused on one topic. It is mostly organized.	The writing is sometimes focused on a topic. It is loosely organized.	The writing needs to focus on a topic and contain an introduction, body, and conclusion.
Voice/Audience	The tone of the writing is appropriate for the audience and the purpose.	The tone of the writing is appropriate most of the time.	The tone of the writing is sometimes appropriate.	The tone of the writing needs to be appropriate for the audience and the purpose.
Content/Ideas	The writing contains many facts and details about the topic.	The writing contains some facts and details about the topic.	The writing contains a few facts and details about the topic.	The writing needs facts and details about the topic.
Word Choice/Clarity	Effective use of signal/transition words clarifies ideas.	Signal/transition words sometimes clarify ideas.	Signal/transition words are rarely used to clarify ideas.	Signal/transition words are needed to clarify ideas.
Sentence Fluency	Sentences flow logically to reflect the purpose of the writing.	Most sentences flow logically.	Some sentences flow logically.	Sentences need to flow logically.
Grammar/Mechanics	The writing contains no errors in spelling, punctuation, grammar, or mechanics.	The writing contains very few errors in spelling, punctuation, grammar, and mechanics.	The writing contains some errors in spelling, punctuation, grammar, and mechanics.	The writing contains many errors in spelling, punctuation, grammar, and mechanics.

Persuasive Rubric

	Achieving ✓✓✓	Developing ✓✓	Excelling ✓✓	Beginning ✓
Information/ Organization	The opinion is stated clearly. The writing is organized to support the opinion.	The opinion is stated clearly. Most of the writing is organized to support the opinion.	The opinion is stated, but is not clear. Some of the writing is organized.	The opinion needs to be clearly stated. The writing needs to be organized.
Voice/ Audience	The writer uses a sincere and persuasive tone throughout.	The writer uses a sincere and persuasive tone most of the time.	The writer sometimes uses a sincere and persuasive tone.	The writer needs to use a sincere and persuasive tone throughout.
Content/ Ideas	Many reasons and facts support the writer's opinion.	Some reasons and facts support the writer's opinion.	A few reasons and facts support the writer's opinion.	Reasons and facts are needed to support the writer's opinion.
Word Choice/ Clarity	The writing contains clear wording throughout. There are no loaded words.	The writing is mostly clear and unbiased. There are very few loaded words.	The writing is sometimes clear and unbiased. There are some loaded words.	The writing needs to be clear and unbiased. It has many loaded words.
Sentence Fluency	Sentence patterns are effectively repeated for emphasis.	Sentence patterns are sometimes repeated for emphasis.	Sentence patterns are rarely repeated for emphasis.	Sentence patterns need to be repeated for emphasis.
Grammar/ Mechanics	The writing contains no errors in spelling, punctuation, grammar, or mechanics.	The writing contains very few errors in spelling, punctuation, grammar, and mechanics.	The writing contains some errors in spelling, punctuation, grammar, and mechanics.	The writing contains many errors in spelling, punctuation, grammar, and mechanics.

Eyewitness Account

Writing Strategies

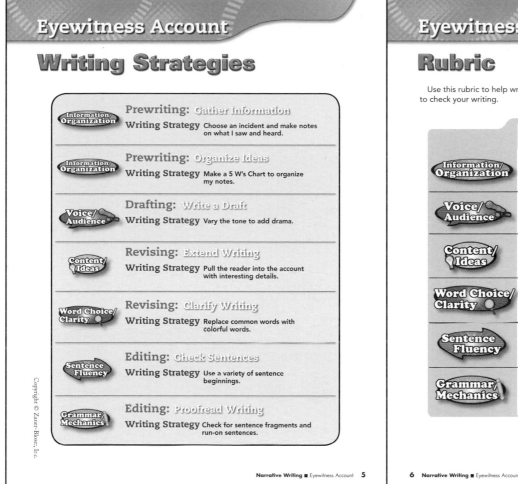

Information/Organization

Prewriting: Gather Information

Writing Strategy Choose an incident and make notes on what I saw and heard.

Information/Organization

Prewriting: Organize Ideas

Writing Strategy Make a 5 W's Chart to organize my notes.

Voice/Audience

Drafting: Write a Draft

Writing Strategy Vary the tone to add drama.

Content/Ideas

Revising: Extend Writing

Writing Strategy Pull the reader into the account with interesting details.

Word Choice/Clarity

Revising: Clarify Writing

Writing Strategy Replace common words with colorful words.

Sentence Fluency

Editing: Check Sentences

Writing Strategy Use a variety of sentence beginnings.

Grammar/Mechanics

Editing: Proofread Writing

Writing Strategy Check for sentence fragments and run-on sentences.

Narrative Writing ■ Eyewitness Account **5**

Eyewitness Account

Rubric

Use this rubric to help write your eyewitness account. Then, use it again to check your writing.

	Excelling ✓✓✓	Achieving ✓✓✓	Developing ✓✓	Beginning ✓
Information/Organization	The account focuses on one event. All of the 5 W's are included.	The account focuses on one event most of the time. Most of the 5 W's are included.	The account focuses on one event some of the time. Some of the 5 W's are included.	The account focuses on more than one event. Very few of the 5 W's are included.
Voice/Audience	The tone is varied and adds drama throughout.	The tone is varied in most areas and adds some drama.	The tone is sometimes varied but rarely adds drama.	The tone is not varied and does not add drama.
Content/Ideas	All details are interesting.	Most details are interesting.	Some details are interesting.	Very few details are interesting.
Word Choice/Clarity	Colorful and interesting words are used throughout.	Colorful and interesting words are used in most areas.	Colorful and interesting words are used in some areas.	Colorful and interesting words are used in very few areas.
Sentence Fluency	Many sentences begin with an interesting phrase or clause.	Several sentences begin with an interesting phrase or clause.	Most sentences begin in the same way—with the subject.	Nearly every sentence begins with the subject.
Grammar/Mechanics	There are no spelling or grammar errors and no fragments or run-ons.	There are a few spelling and grammar errors and a few fragments and/or run-ons.	There are several spelling and grammar errors and several fragments and run-ons.	There are many spelling and grammar errors and many fragments and run-ons.

6 Narrative Writing ■ Eyewitness Account

Writing an Eyewitness Account

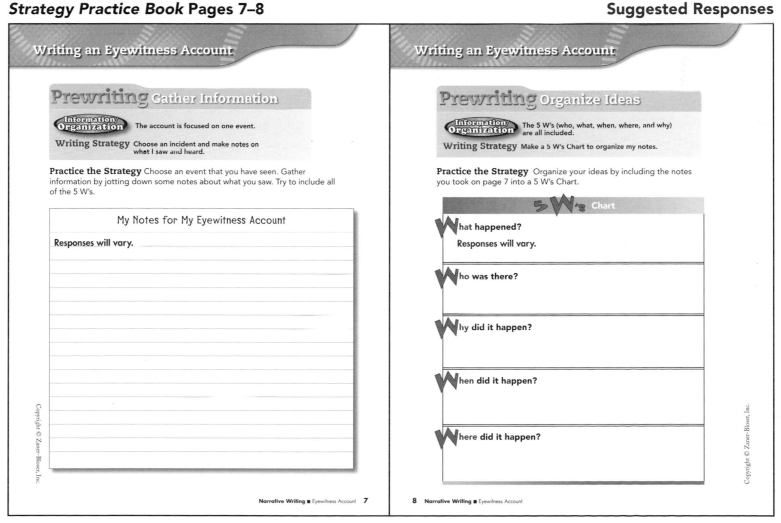

Prewriting Gather Information

Information/Organization The account is focused on one event.

Writing Strategy Choose an incident and make notes on what I saw and heard.

Practice the Strategy Choose an event that you have seen. Gather information by jotting down some notes about what you saw. Try to include all of the 5 W's.

My Notes for My Eyewitness Account

Responses will vary.

Narrative Writing ■ Eyewitness Account **7**

Writing an Eyewitness Account

Prewriting Organize Ideas

Information/Organization The 5 W's (who, what, when, where, and why) are all included.

Writing Strategy Make a 5 W's Chart to organize my notes.

Practice the Strategy Organize your ideas by including the notes you took on page 7 into a 5 W's Chart.

5 W's Chart

What happened?
Responses will vary.

Who was there?

Why did it happen?

When did it happen?

Where did it happen?

8 Narrative Writing ■ Eyewitness Account

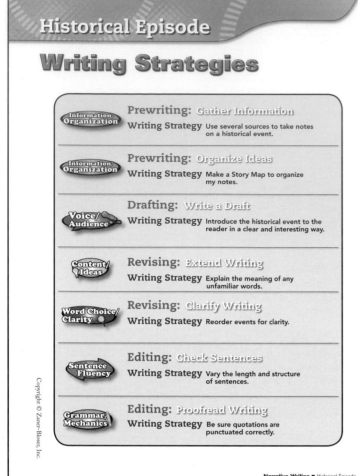

Historical Episode

Writing Strategies

Information/Organization	**Prewriting:** Gather Information
	Writing Strategy Use several sources to take notes on a historical event.

Information/Organization	**Prewriting:** Organize Ideas
	Writing Strategy Make a Story Map to organize my notes.

Voice/Audience	**Drafting:** Write a Draft
	Writing Strategy Introduce the historical event to the reader in a clear and interesting way.

Content/Ideas	**Revising:** Extend Writing
	Writing Strategy Explain the meaning of any unfamiliar words.

Word Choice/Clarity	**Revising:** Clarify Writing
	Writing Strategy Reorder events for clarity.

Sentence Fluency	**Editing:** Check Sentences
	Writing Strategy Vary the length and structure of sentences.

Grammar/Mechanics	**Editing:** Proofread Writing
	Writing Strategy Be sure quotations are punctuated correctly.

Narrative Writing ■ Historical Episode **9**

Historical Episode

Rubric

Use this rubric to help write your historical episode. Then, use it again to check your writing.

	Excelling ✓✓✓	Achieving ✓✓	Developing ✓	Beginning ✓
Information/Organization	The episode focuses on one historical event and is clearly organized.	The episode mostly focuses on one event. Most of the organization is clear.	The episode sometimes focuses on one event. Organization is not always clear.	The episode rarely focuses on one event. Organization is unclear.
Voice/Audience	The beginning directly relates to the event and captures the audience's interest.	The beginning directly relates to the event and is mildly interesting.	The beginning has some relation to the event but is not very interesting.	The beginning has little relation to the historical event.
Content/Ideas	All unfamiliar words are explained.	Many unfamiliar words are explained.	Some unfamiliar words are explained.	Few unfamiliar words are explained.
Word Choice/Clarity	The order of events is clear.	The order of events is mostly clear.	The order of events is somewhat clear.	The order of events needs to be clear.
Sentence Fluency	Many sentences vary in length and structure.	Some sentences vary in length and structure.	A few sentences vary in length and structure.	Almost all sentences are similar in length and structure.
Grammar/Mechanics	Spelling, punctuation, and capitalization are correct. Quotations are punctuated correctly.	There are few errors in spelling, punctuation, capitalization, or quotations.	There are some errors in spelling, punctuation, capitalization, or quotations.	There are many errors in spelling, punctuation, capitalization, or quotations.

10 Narrative Writing ■ Historical Episode

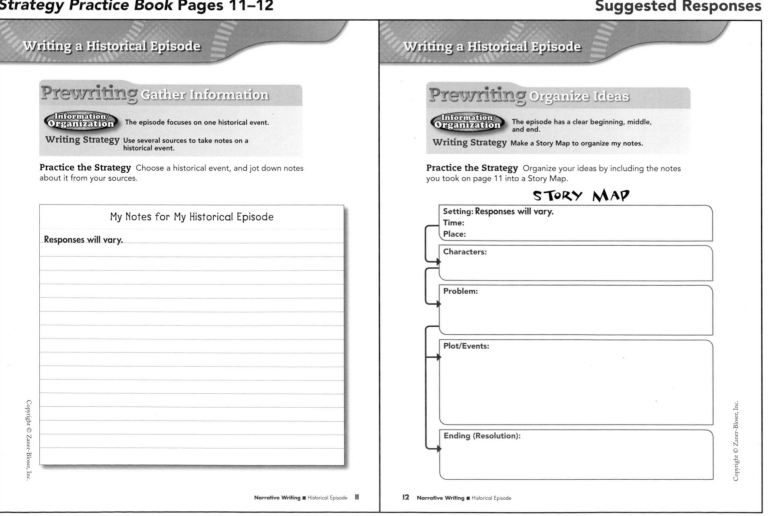

Writing a Historical Episode

Prewriting Gather Information

Information/Organization	The episode focuses on one historical event.

Writing Strategy Use several sources to take notes on a historical event.

Practice the Strategy Choose a historical event, and jot down notes about it from your sources.

My Notes for My Historical Episode

Responses will vary.

Narrative Writing ■ Historical Episode **11**

Writing a Historical Episode

Prewriting Organize Ideas

Information/Organization	The episode has a clear beginning, middle, and end.

Writing Strategy Make a Story Map to organize my notes.

Practice the Strategy Organize your ideas by including the notes you took on page 11 into a Story Map.

STORY MAP

Setting: Responses will vary.
Time:
Place:

Characters:

Problem:

Plot/Events:

Ending (Resolution):

12 Narrative Writing ■ Historical Episode

Short Story

Writing Strategies

Information/Organization — **Prewriting:** Gather Information
Writing Strategy Brainstorm characters and events to use in my story.

Information/Organization — **Prewriting:** Organize Ideas
Writing Strategy Make a Storyboard to organize my notes.

Voice/Audience — **Drafting:** Write a Draft
Writing Strategy Build the story to a climax to make it exciting for the audience.

Content/Ideas — **Revising:** Extend Writing
Writing Strategy Add sensory details to make the story come alive.

Word Choice/Clarity — **Revising:** Clarify Writing
Writing Strategy Replace overused words with more exact words.

Sentence Fluency — **Editing:** Check Sentences
Writing Strategy Use active voice to strengthen sentences.

Grammar/Mechanics — **Editing:** Proofread Writing
Writing Strategy Make sure indefinite pronouns are used correctly.

Copyright © Zaner-Bloser, Inc.

Narrative Writing ■ Short Story   **13**

Short Story

Rubric

Use this rubric to help write your short story. Then, use it again to check your writing.

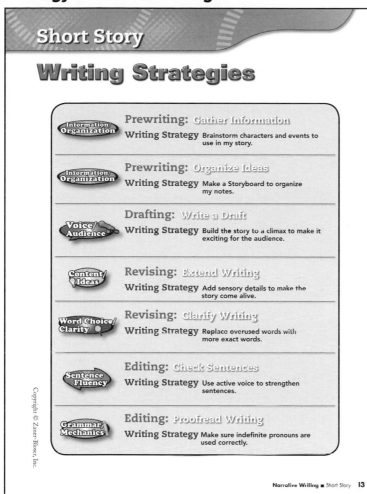

	Excelling ✓✓✓	Achieving ✓✓✓	Developing ✓✓	Beginning ✓
Information/Organization	The story focuses on the protagonist's problem. It is told sequentially.	The story mostly focuses on the protagonist's problem. Some events are out of sequence.	The story should focus more on the protagonist's problem. Many events are out of sequence.	The story does not focus on the protagonist's problem. The events are disorganized.
Voice/Audience	Tension builds well throughout the story, leading to an exciting climax.	Some tension builds throughout the story; the climax should be more exciting.	Mild tension builds throughout the story; the climax is weak.	Little tension builds throughout the story; the climax is missing.
Content/Ideas	Many sensory details bring the characters, setting, and events of the story to life.	Most sensory details are used to make the characters, setting, and events of the story seem real.	Some sensory details are used but not enough to make the story seem real.	Few sensory details are used.
Word Choice/Clarity	Many exact words make the writing powerful and vivid.	Some exact words are used, but the story still has some overused words.	There are few exact words and too many overused words.	The story needs exact words to make it vivid.
Sentence Fluency	Most sentences are written in active voice.	Many sentences are written in active voice.	Some sentences are written in active voice.	There are few sentences in active voice.
Grammar/Mechanics	Spelling, punctuation, and capitalization are correct. Indefinite pronouns are used correctly.	There are few errors in spelling, punctuation, and capitalization. Most indefinite pronouns are correct.	There are some errors in spelling, punctuation, and capitalization. Some indefinite pronouns are correct.	There are many errors in spelling, punctuation, capitalization, and indefinite pronouns.

Copyright © Zaner-Bloser, Inc.

14   Narrative Writing ■ Short Story

Writing a Short Story

Prewriting Gather Information

Information/Organization The story focuses on the protagonist's problem.
Writing Strategy Brainstorm characters and events to use in my story.

Practice the Strategy Think about short stories you might write, and gather information by jotting down possible characters and events that you think would be interesting to your readers.

My Notes for My Short Story

Responses will vary.

Copyright © Zaner-Bloser, Inc.

Narrative Writing ■ Short Story   **15**

Writing a Short Story

Prewriting Organize Ideas

Information/Organization The story is told sequentially.
Writing Strategy Make a Storyboard to organize my notes.

Practice the Strategy Organize your ideas by including the notes you took on page 15 into a Storyboard.

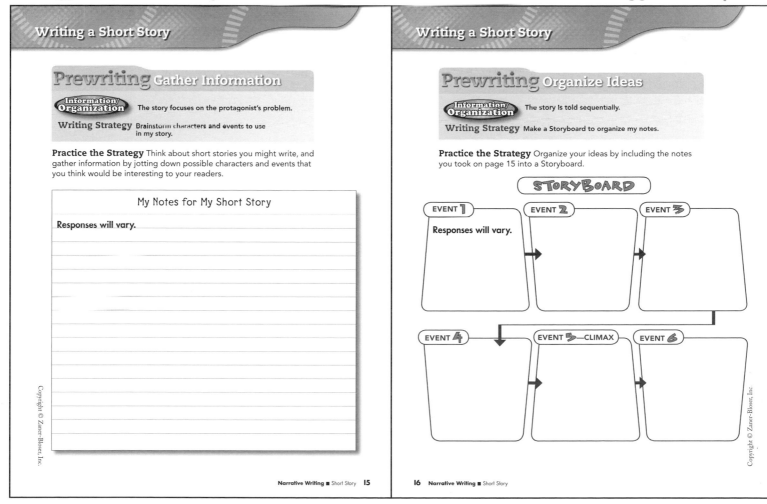

STORYBOARD

EVENT 1 — Responses will vary.
EVENT 2
EVENT 3
EVENT 4
EVENT 5 — CLIMAX
EVENT 6

Copyright © Zaner-Bloser, Inc.

16   Narrative Writing ■ Short Story

Descriptive Essay

Writing Strategies

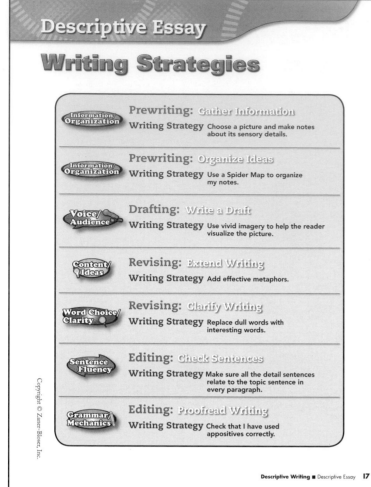

Information/Organization — **Prewriting:** Gather Information
Writing Strategy Choose a picture and make notes about its sensory details.

Information/Organization — **Prewriting:** Organize Ideas
Writing Strategy Use a Spider Map to organize my notes.

Voice/Audience — **Drafting:** Write a Draft
Writing Strategy Use vivid imagery to help the reader visualize the picture.

Content/Ideas — **Revising:** Extend Writing
Writing Strategy Add effective metaphors.

Word Choice/Clarity — **Revising:** Clarify Writing
Writing Strategy Replace dull words with interesting words.

Sentence Fluency — **Editing:** Check Sentences
Writing Strategy Make sure all the detail sentences relate to the topic sentence in every paragraph.

Grammar/Mechanics — **Editing:** Proofread Writing
Writing Strategy Check that I have used appositives correctly.

Copyright © Zaner-Bloser, Inc.

Descriptive Writing ■ Descriptive Essay **17**

Descriptive Essay

Rubric

Use this rubric to help write your descriptive essay. Then, use it again to check your writing.

	Excelling ✓✓✓	Achieving ✓✓✓	Developing ✓✓	Beginning ✓
Information/Organization	The essay is about one subject and is well organized.	The essay is mostly about one subject and is mostly well organized.	The essay is about more than one subject and is loosely organized.	The essay needs to be about one subject and needs to be organized.
Voice/Audience	The description is clear, vivid, and interesting.	The description is mostly clear, vivid, and interesting.	The description is fairly clear and interesting.	The description needs to be clear and interesting.
Content/Ideas	Metaphors are well chosen and add to the description.	Some metaphors are included and add to the description.	A few metaphors are included, but they are not well chosen.	The description needs metaphors.
Word Choice/Clarity	Lively, interesting words are used throughout the essay.	Many lively and interesting words are used in the essay.	Some lively and interesting words are used.	Few lively or interesting words are used.
Sentence Fluency	Each paragraph has a topic sentence supported by detail sentences.	Most paragraphs have a topic sentence supported by detail sentences.	Some paragraphs have a topic sentence supported by detail sentences.	Few paragraphs have a topic sentence supported by detail sentences.
Grammar/Mechanics	Spelling, punctuation, and appositives are correct.	There are few errors in spelling, punctuation, and appositives.	There are some errors in spelling, punctuation, and appositives.	There are many errors in spelling, punctuation, and appositives.

Copyright © Zaner-Bloser, Inc.

18 Descriptive Writing ■ Descriptive Essay

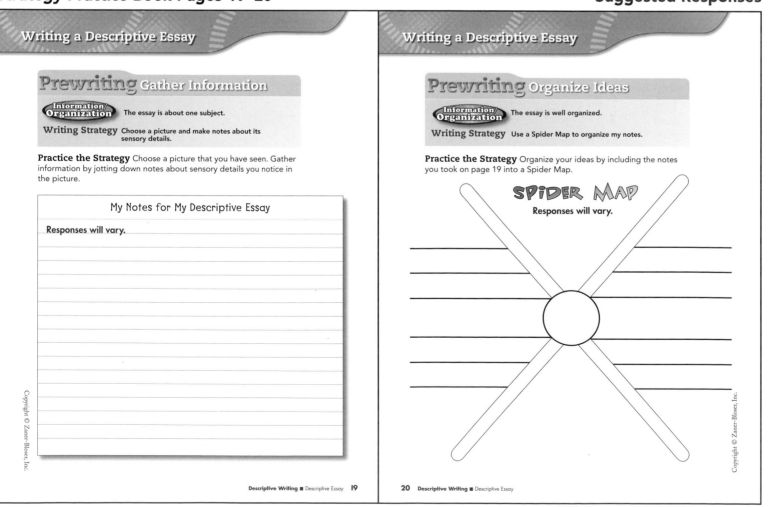

Writing a Descriptive Essay

Prewriting Gather Information

Information/Organization — The essay is about one subject.
Writing Strategy Choose a picture and make notes about its sensory details.

Practice the Strategy Choose a picture that you have seen. Gather information by jotting down notes about sensory details you notice in the picture.

My Notes for My Descriptive Essay

Responses will vary.

Copyright © Zaner-Bloser, Inc.

Descriptive Writing ■ Descriptive Essay **19**

Writing a Descriptive Essay

Prewriting Organize Ideas

Information/Organization — The essay is well organized.
Writing Strategy Use a Spider Map to organize my notes.

Practice the Strategy Organize your ideas by including the notes you took on page 19 into a Spider Map.

SPIDER MAP

Responses will vary.

Copyright © Zaner-Bloser, Inc.

20 Descriptive Writing ■ Descriptive Essay

Observation Report

Writing Strategies

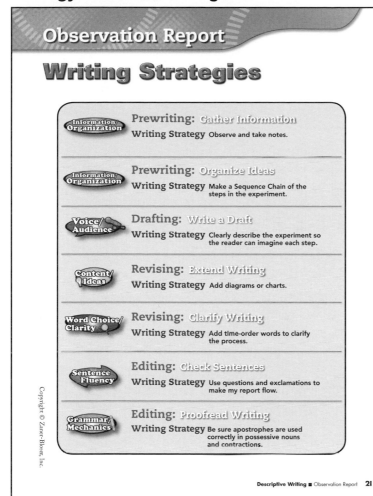

Information/Organization	**Prewriting:** Gather Information
	Writing Strategy Observe and take notes.

Prewriting: Organize Ideas
Writing Strategy Make a Sequence Chain of the steps in the experiment.

Drafting: Write a Draft
Writing Strategy Clearly describe the experiment so the reader can imagine each step.

Revising: Extend Writing
Writing Strategy Add diagrams or charts.

Revising: Clarify Writing
Writing Strategy Add time-order words to clarify the process.

Editing: Check Sentences
Writing Strategy Use questions and exclamations to make my report flow.

Editing: Proofread Writing
Writing Strategy Be sure apostrophes are used correctly in possessive nouns and contractions.

Copyright © Zaner-Bloser, Inc.

Descriptive Writing ■ Observation Report **21**

Observation Report

Rubric

Use this rubric to help write your observation report. Then, use it again to check your writing.

	Excelling ✓✓✓✓	**Achieving** ✓✓✓	**Developing** ✓✓	**Beginning** ✓
Information/Organization	The report is about an experiment, and the steps are described in order.	The report is about an experiment, and most steps are in order.	The report is mostly about an experiment, and some steps are in order.	The report needs to be about an experiment, and steps need to be in order.
Voice/Audience	The report describes all steps clearly for the reader.	The report describes most steps clearly.	The report mentions some of the steps.	The report needs to describe the steps in the procedure.
Content/Ideas	One or more informative diagrams or charts are included.	A diagram or chart is included.	A diagram or chart is included, but its purpose needs to be clearer.	The report needs to include diagrams or charts.
Word Choice/Clarity	Many time-order words make the order of events clear.	Some time-order words are used effectively.	A few time-order words are used effectively.	Few time-order words are used, and they are ineffective.
Sentence Fluency	Questions and exclamations make the report flow naturally.	Some questions and exclamations are included.	One or two questions or exclamations are used.	Questions or exclamations need to be used to make the report flow.
Grammar/Mechanics	Spelling, punctuation, and apostrophes are used correctly.	There are few errors in spelling, punctuation, and apostrophes.	There are some errors in spelling, punctuation, and apostrophes.	There are many errors in spelling, punctuation, and apostrophes.

Copyright © Zaner-Bloser, Inc.

22 **Descriptive Writing** ■ Observation Report

Writing an Observation Report

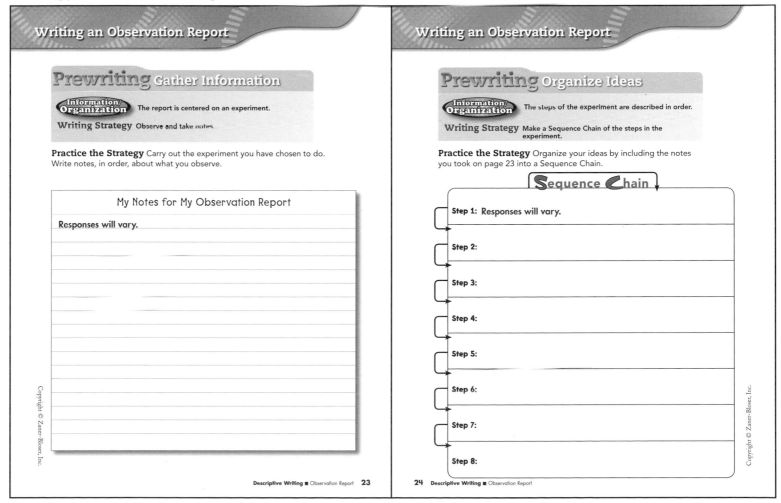

Prewriting Gather Information

Information/Organization The report is centered on an experiment.

Writing Strategy Observe and take notes.

Practice the Strategy Carry out the experiment you have chosen to do. Write notes, in order, about what you observe.

My Notes for My Observation Report
Responses will vary.

Copyright © Zaner-Bloser, Inc.

Descriptive Writing ■ Observation Report **23**

Writing an Observation Report

Prewriting Organize Ideas

Information/Organization The steps of the experiment are described in order.

Writing Strategy Make a Sequence Chain of the steps in the experiment.

Practice the Strategy Organize your ideas by including the notes you took on page 23 into a Sequence Chain.

Sequence Chain

Step 1: Responses will vary.

Step 2:

Step 3:

Step 4:

Step 5:

Step 6:

Step 7:

Step 8:

Copyright © Zaner-Bloser, Inc.

24 **Descriptive Writing** ■ Observation Report

Descriptive Article

Writing Strategies

Information/Organization

Prewriting: Gather Information

Writing Strategy Jot down some notes on my favorite spot in my neighborhood.

Information/Organization

Prewriting: Organize Ideas

Writing Strategy Use a Five-Senses Chart to organize my notes.

Voice/Audience

Drafting: Write a Draft

Writing Strategy Include word pictures to help the reader "see" my topic.

Content/Ideas

Revising: Extend Writing

Writing Strategy Add sensory details.

Word Choice/Clarity

Revising: Clarify Writing

Writing Strategy Replace clichés with interesting phrases.

Sentence Fluency

Editing: Check Sentences

Writing Strategy Repeat a sentence pattern to emphasize a point.

Grammar/Mechanics

Editing: Proofread Writing

Writing Strategy Make sure all the verbs are in the proper tense.

Descriptive Article

Rubric

Use this rubric to help write your descriptive article. Then, use it again to check your writing.

	Excelling ✓✓✓	Achieving ✓✓✓	Developing ✓✓	Beginning ✓
Information/Organization	The article is about a particular topic and is organized using the five senses.	The article is about one topic and is mostly organized.	The article is mostly about one topic and is somewhat organized.	The article is about several topics and could be better organized.
Voice/Audience	Vivid descriptions are used throughout to help readers "see" the topic.	Many vivid descriptions are used.	Some vivid descriptions are used.	Few vivid descriptions are used.
Content/Ideas	Many sensory details help readers experience the place fully.	Some sensory details help readers experience the place.	A few sensory details are included.	Sensory details need to be included.
Word Choice/Clarity	Fresh and interesting phrases are used to make the writing appealing.	Some fresh and interesting phrases are used to make the writing interesting.	A few interesting phrases are used, but there are some clichés.	The article needs interesting phrases. There are too many clichés.
Sentence Fluency	One or more sentence patterns are used effectively to emphasize a point.	Sentence patterns are repeated to emphasize a point.	A sentence pattern is repeated.	The article needs to repeat a sentence pattern.
Grammar/Mechanics	Spelling and punctuation are correct. Verbs are in the proper tense.	There are a few errors in spelling, punctuation, and verb tense.	There are several errors in spelling, punctuation, and verb tense.	There are many errors in spelling, punctuation, and verb tense.

Writing a Descriptive Article

Prewriting Gather Information

Information/Organization The article is about a particular topic.

Writing Strategy Jot down some notes on my favorite spot in my neighborhood.

Practice the Strategy Think about your favorite neighborhood spot. Jot down as many sensory details as you can think of.

My Notes for My Descriptive Article

Responses will vary.

Writing a Descriptive Article

Prewriting Organize Ideas

Information/Organization The article is organized using the five senses.

Writing Strategy Use a Five-Senses Chart to organize my notes.

Practice the Strategy Organize your ideas by including the notes you took on page 27 into a Five-Senses Chart.

Five-Senses Chart

Sight:
Responses will vary.

Sound:

Smell:

Touch:

Taste:

Summary

Writing Strategies

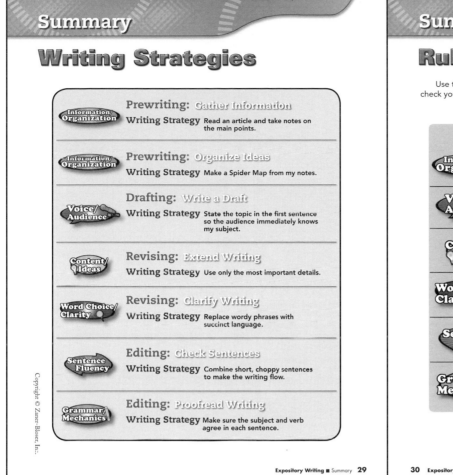

Information/Organization
Prewriting: Gather Information
Writing Strategy Read an article and take notes on the main points.

Information/Organization
Prewriting: Organize Ideas
Writing Strategy Make a Spider Map from my notes.

Voice/Audience
Drafting: Write a Draft
Writing Strategy State the topic in the first sentence so the audience immediately knows my subject.

Content/Ideas
Revising: Extend Writing
Writing Strategy Use only the most important details.

Word Choice/Clarity
Revising: Clarify Writing
Writing Strategy Replace wordy phrases with succinct language.

Sentence Fluency
Editing: Check Sentences
Writing Strategy Combine short, choppy sentences to make the writing flow.

Grammar/Mechanics
Editing: Proofread Writing
Writing Strategy Make sure the subject and verb agree in each sentence.

Copyright © Zaner-Bloser, Inc.

Expository Writing ■ Summary **29**

Summary

Rubric

Use this rubric to help write your summary. Then, use it again to check your writing.

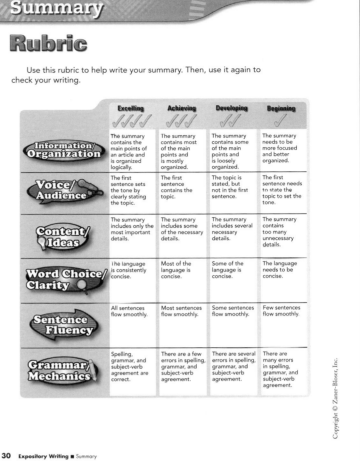

	Excelling ✓✓✓	Achieving ✓✓✓	Developing ✓✓	Beginning ✓
Information/Organization	The summary contains the main points of an article and is organized logically.	The summary contains most of the main points and is mostly organized.	The summary contains some of the main points and is loosely organized.	The summary needs to be more focused and better organized.
Voice/Audience	The first sentence sets the tone by clearly stating the topic.	The first sentence contains the topic.	The topic is stated, but not in the first sentence.	The first sentence needs to state the topic to set the tone.
Content/Ideas	The summary includes only the most important details.	The summary includes some of the necessary details.	The summary includes several necessary details.	The summary contains too many unnecessary details.
Word Choice/Clarity	The language is consistently concise.	Most of the language is concise.	Some of the language is concise.	The language needs to be concise.
Sentence Fluency	All sentences flow smoothly.	Most sentences flow smoothly.	Some sentences flow smoothly.	Few sentences flow smoothly.
Grammar/Mechanics	Spelling, grammar, and subject-verb agreement are correct.	There are a few errors in spelling, grammar, and subject-verb agreement.	There are several errors in spelling, grammar, and subject-verb agreement.	There are many errors in spelling, grammar, and subject-verb agreement.

Copyright © Zaner-Bloser, Inc.

30 Expository Writing ■ Summary

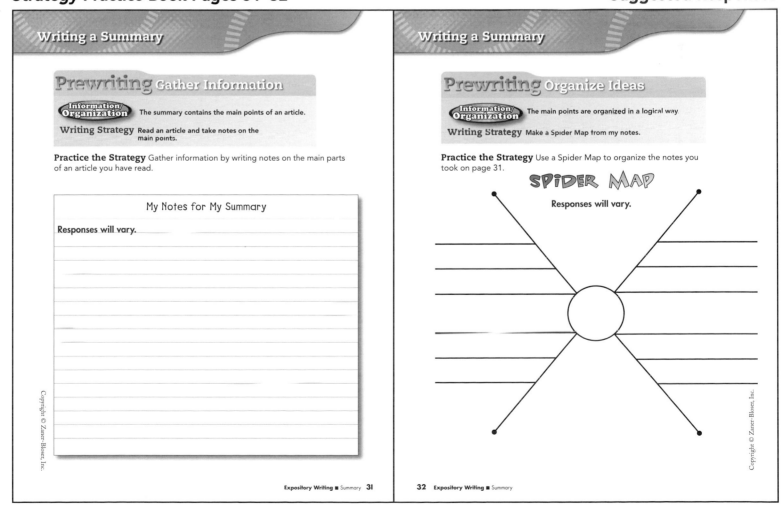

Writing a Summary

Prewriting Gather Information

Information/Organization The summary contains the main points of an article.

Writing Strategy Read an article and take notes on the main points.

Practice the Strategy Gather information by writing notes on the main parts of an article you have read.

My Notes for My Summary

Responses will vary.

Copyright © Zaner-Bloser, Inc.

Expository Writing ■ Summary **31**

Writing a Summary

Prewriting Organize Ideas

Information/Organization The main points are organized in a logical way.

Writing Strategy Make a Spider Map from my notes.

Practice the Strategy Use a Spider Map to organize the notes you took on page 31.

SPIDER MAP

Responses will vary.

Copyright © Zaner-Bloser, Inc.

32 Expository Writing ■ Summary

Cause-and-Effect Report

Writing Strategies

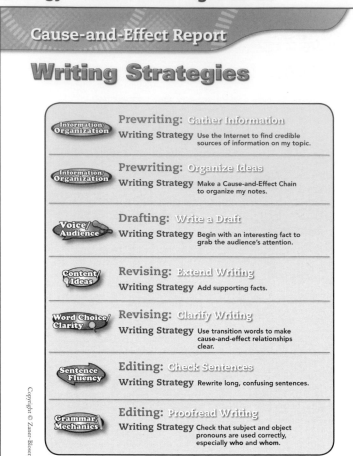

Information/Organization

Prewriting: Gather Information

Writing Strategy Use the Internet to find credible sources of information on my topic.

Information/Organization

Prewriting: Organize Ideas

Writing Strategy Make a Cause-and-Effect Chain to organize my notes.

Voice/Audience

Drafting: Write a Draft

Writing Strategy Begin with an interesting fact to grab the audience's attention.

Content/Ideas

Revising: Extend Writing

Writing Strategy Add supporting facts.

Word Choice/Clarity

Revising: Clarify Writing

Writing Strategy Use transition words to make cause-and-effect relationships clear.

Sentence Fluency

Editing: Check Sentences

Writing Strategy Rewrite long, confusing sentences.

Grammar/Mechanics

Editing: Proofread Writing

Writing Strategy Check that subject and object pronouns are used correctly, especially who and whom.

Cause-and-Effect Report

Rubric

Use this rubric to help write your cause-and-effect report. Then, use it again to check your writing.

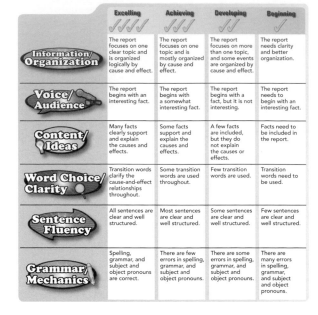

	Excelling ✓✓✓	Achieving ✓✓	Developing ✓✓	Beginning ✓
Information/Organization	The report focuses on one clear topic and is organized logically by cause and effect.	The report focuses on one topic and is mostly organized by cause and effect.	The report focuses on more than one topic, and some events are organized by cause and effect.	The report needs clarity and better organization.
Voice/Audience	The report begins with an interesting fact.	The report begins with a somewhat interesting fact.	The report begins with a fact, but it is not interesting.	The report needs to begin with an interesting fact.
Content/Ideas	Many facts clearly support and explain the causes and effects.	Some facts support and explain the causes and effects.	A few facts are included, but they do not explain the causes or effects.	Facts need to be included in the report.
Word Choice/Clarity	Transition words clarify the cause-and-effect relationships throughout.	Some transition words are used throughout.	Few transition words are used.	Transition words need to be used.
Sentence Fluency	All sentences are clear and well structured.	Most sentences are clear and well structured.	Some sentences are clear and well structured.	Few sentences are clear and well structured.
Grammar/Mechanics	Spelling, grammar, and subject and object pronouns are correct.	There are few errors in spelling, grammar, and subject and object pronouns.	There are some errors in spelling, grammar, and subject and object pronouns.	There are many errors in spelling, grammar, and subject and object pronouns.

Writing a Cause-and-Effect Report

Prewriting Gather Information

Information/Organization

The report focuses on one clear topic.

Writing Strategy Use the Internet to find credible sources of information on my topic.

Practice the Strategy Gather information by finding credible sources on the Internet and listing facts you find.

> ### My Notes for My Cause-and-Effect Report
>
> **Responses will vary.**

Writing a Cause-and-Effect Report

Prewriting Organize Ideas

Information/Organization

The report is organized in a logical cause-and-effect pattern.

Writing Strategy Make a Cause-and-Effect Chain to organize my notes.

Practice the Strategy Use a Cause-and-Effect Chain to organize the notes you took on page 35.

Cause-and-Effect Chain

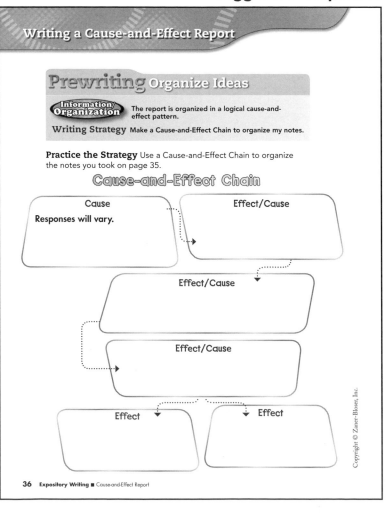

Cause
Responses will vary.

Effect/Cause

Effect/Cause

Effect/Cause

Effect

Effect

Research Report

Writing Strategies

Prewriting: Gather Information

Information/Organization

Writing Strategy Use an encyclopedia and at least two other sources to research my topic.

Prewriting: Organize Ideas

Information/Organization

Writing Strategy Make an Outline to organize my notes.

Drafting: Write a Draft

Voice/Audience

Writing Strategy Provide details to interest my audience.

Revising: Extend Writing

Content/Ideas

Writing Strategy Add a conclusion that summarizes the main points.

Revising: Clarify Writing

Word Choice/Clarity

Writing Strategy Change passive voice to active voice.

Editing: Check Sentences

Sentence Fluency

Writing Strategy Use a variety of lively, energetic sentences.

Editing: Proofread Writing

Grammar/Mechanics

Writing Strategy Make sure proper nouns and proper adjectives are capitalized correctly.

Copyright © Zaner-Bloser, Inc.

Expository Writing ■ Research Report **37**

Research Report

Rubric

Use this rubric to help write your research report. Then, use it again to check your writing.

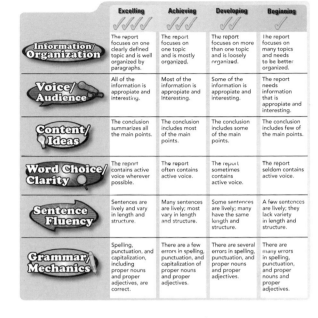

	Excelling ✓✓✓	Achieving ✓✓	Developing ✓✓	Beginning ✓
Information/Organization	The report focuses on one clearly defined topic and is well organized by paragraphs.	The report focuses on one topic and is mostly organized.	The report focuses on more than one topic and is loosely organized.	The report focuses on many topics and needs to be better organized.
Voice/Audience	All of the information is appropriate and interesting.	Most of the information is appropriate and interesting.	Some of the information is appropriate and interesting.	The report needs information that is appropriate and interesting.
Content/Ideas	The conclusion summarizes all the main points.	The conclusion includes most of the main points.	The conclusion includes some of the main points.	The conclusion includes few of the main points.
Word Choice/Clarity	The report contains active voice wherever possible.	The report often contains active voice.	The report sometimes contains active voice.	The report seldom contains active voice.
Sentence Fluency	Sentences are lively and vary in length and structure.	Many sentences are lively; most vary in length and structure.	Some sentences are lively; many have the same length and structure.	A few sentences are lively; they lack variety in length and structure.
Grammar/Mechanics	Spelling, punctuation, and capitalization, including proper nouns and proper adjectives, are correct.	There are a few errors in spelling, punctuation, and capitalization of proper nouns and proper adjectives.	There are several errors in spelling, punctuation, and proper nouns and proper adjectives.	There are many errors in spelling, punctuation, and proper nouns and proper adjectives.

Copyright © Zaner-Bloser, Inc.

38 Expository Writing ■ Research Report

Writing a Research Report

Prewriting Gather Information

Information/Organization

The report focuses on one clearly defined topic.

Writing Strategy Use an encyclopedia and at least two other sources to research my topic.

Practice the Strategy Use an encyclopedia and at least two other sources to research your topic.

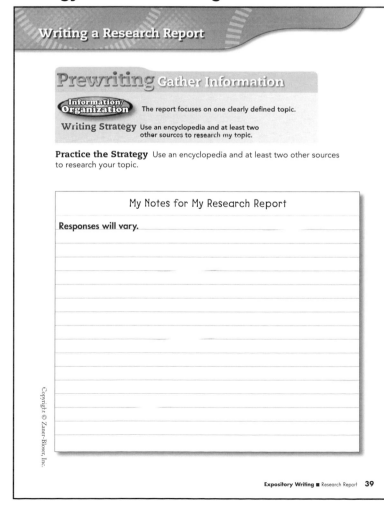

My Notes for My Research Report

Responses will vary.

Copyright © Zaner-Bloser, Inc.

Expository Writing ■ Research Report **39**

Writing a Research Report

Prewriting Organize Ideas

Information/Organization

The report is well organized with at least one or two paragraphs about each main point.

Writing Strategy Make an Outline to organize my notes.

Practice the Strategy Use an Outline to organize the notes you took on page 39.

Outline

I. **Responses will vary.**
　A.
　　1.
　　2.
　B.
　　1.
　　2.
II.
　A.
　　1.
　　2.
　B.
　　1.
　　2.
III.
　A.
　　1.
　　2.
　B.
　　1.
　　2.

Copyright © Zaner-Bloser, Inc.

40 Expository Writing ■ Research Report

Book Review

Writing Strategies

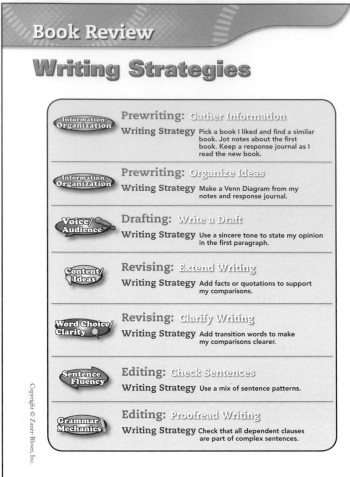

Information/Organization

Prewriting: Gather Information

Writing Strategy Pick a book I liked and find a similar book. Jot notes about the first book. Keep a response journal as I read the new book.

Information/Organization

Prewriting: Organize Ideas

Writing Strategy Make a Venn Diagram from my notes and response journal.

Voice/Audience

Drafting: Write a Draft

Writing Strategy Use a sincere tone to state my opinion in the first paragraph.

Content/Ideas

Revising: Extend Writing

Writing Strategy Add facts or quotations to support my comparisons.

Word Choice/Clarity

Revising: Clarify Writing

Writing Strategy Add transition words to make my comparisons clearer.

Sentence Fluency

Editing: Check Sentences

Writing Strategy Use a mix of sentence patterns.

Grammar/Mechanics

Editing: Proofread Writing

Writing Strategy Check that all dependent clauses are part of complex sentences.

Book Review

Rubric

Use this rubric to help write your book review. Then, use it again to check your writing.

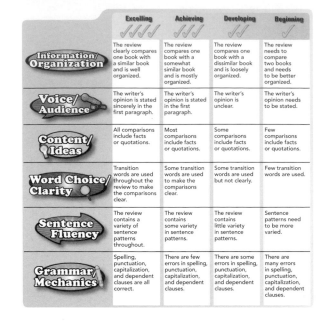

	Excelling ✓✓✓	Achieving ✓✓	Developing ✓	Beginning
Information/Organization	The review clearly compares one book with a similar book and is well organized.	The review compares one book with a somewhat similar book and is mostly organized.	The review compares one book with a dissimilar book and is loosely organized.	The review needs to compare two books and needs to be better organized.
Voice/Audience	The writer's opinion is stated sincerely in the first paragraph.	The writer's opinion is stated in the first paragraph.	The writer's opinion is unclear.	The writer's opinion needs to be stated.
Content/Ideas	All comparisons include facts or quotations.	Most comparisons include facts or quotations.	Some comparisons include facts or quotations.	Few comparisons include facts or quotations.
Word Choice/Clarity	Transition words are used throughout the review to make the comparisons clear.	Some transition words are used to make the comparisons clear.	Some transition words are used but not clearly.	Few transition words are used.
Sentence Fluency	The review contains a variety of sentence patterns throughout.	The review contains some variety in sentence patterns.	The review contains little variety in sentence patterns.	Sentence patterns need to be more varied.
Grammar/Mechanics	Spelling, punctuation, capitalization, and dependent clauses are all correct.	There are few errors in spelling, punctuation, capitalization, and dependent clauses.	There are some errors in spelling, punctuation, capitalization, and dependent clauses.	There are many errors in spelling, punctuation, capitalization, and dependent clauses.

Writing a Book Review

Prewriting Gather Information

Information/Organization The review compares one book with a similar book.

Writing Strategy Pick a book I liked and find a similar book. Jot notes about the first book. Keep a response journal as I read the new book.

Practice the Strategy Gather information by writing your book title below. Then list details and information that show your response to the book.

My Notes for My Book Review
Responses will vary.

Writing a Book Review

Prewriting Organize Ideas

Information/Organization The review is well organized so the comparisons between the two books are clear.

Writing Strategy Make a Venn Diagram from my notes and response journal.

Practice the Strategy Use a Venn Diagram to organize the notes you took on page 43.

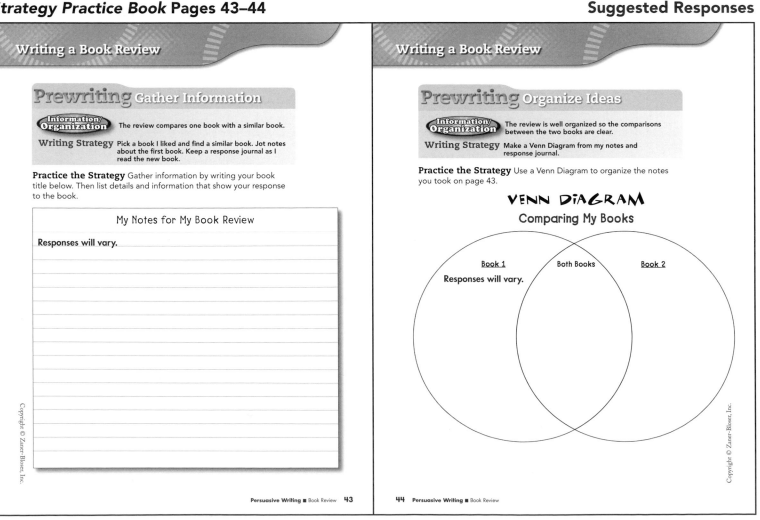

VENN DIAGRAM
Comparing My Books

Book 1   Both Books   Book 2

Responses will vary.

Persuasive Essay

Writing Strategies

Information/Organization
Prewriting: Gather Information
Writing Strategy Choose an issue and find information to support my opinion.

Information/Organization
Prewriting: Organize Ideas
Writing Strategy Use a Network Tree to organize my ideas.

Voice/Audience
Drafting: Write a Draft
Writing Strategy Begin by expressing my opinion in a convincing tone.

Content/Ideas
Revising: Extend Writing
Writing Strategy Add facts and reasons to support my opinion.

Word Choice/Clarity
Revising: Clarify Writing
Writing Strategy Replace loaded words with neutral words.

Sentence Fluency
Editing: Check Sentences
Writing Strategy Use question-and-answer sentence patterns.

Grammar/Mechanics
Editing: Proofread Writing
Writing Strategy Make sure each pronoun has a clear antecedent.

Copyright © Zaner-Bloser, Inc.

Persuasive Writing ■ Persuasive Essay **45**

Persuasive Essay

Rubric

Use this rubric to help write your persuasive essay. Then, use it again to check your writing.

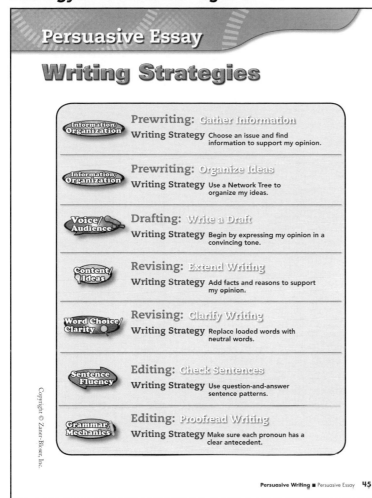

	Excelling ✓✓✓✓	Achieving ✓✓✓	Developing ✓✓	Beginning ✓
Information/Organization	The essay focuses on one issue and is well organized with many supporting details.	The essay focuses on one issue and has some supporting details.	The essay sometimes focuses on one issue and has a few supporting details.	The essay needs to be focused and to include supporting details.
Voice/Audience	The writer's opinion is convincingly stated at the beginning of the essay.	The writer's opinion is stated at the beginning of the essay.	The writer's opinion is stated in the body of the essay.	The writer's opinion needs to be stated at the beginning of the essay.
Content/Ideas	Facts and reasons support the writer's opinion throughout.	Facts and reasons support the writer's opinion most of the time.	Facts and reasons support the writer's opinion some of the time.	Few facts and reasons support the writer's opinion.
Word Choice/Clarity	The essay contains only neutral wording.	The essay contains mostly neutral wording.	The essay contains some neutral wording.	The essay contains little neutral wording.
Sentence Fluency	A question-and-answer sentence pattern is used very effectively.	A question-and-answer sentence pattern is used well.	A question-and-answer sentence pattern is used occasionally.	The essay needs question-and-answer sentence patterns.
Grammar/Mechanics	Spelling, punctuation, capitalization, and pronouns are correct.	There are few errors in spelling, punctuation, capitalization, and pronouns.	There are several errors in spelling, punctuation, capitalization, and pronouns.	There are many errors in spelling, punctuation, capitalization, and pronouns.

Copyright © Zaner-Bloser, Inc.

46 Persuasive Writing ■ Persuasive Essay

Writing a Persuasive Essay

Prewriting Gather Information

Information/Organization
The essay focuses on one issue.
Writing Strategy Choose an issue and find information to support my opinion.

Practice the Strategy Gather information by writing your opinion below. Then list details to support your opinion.

My Notes for My Persuasive Essay
Responses will vary.

Copyright © Zaner-Bloser, Inc.

Persuasive Writing ■ Persuasive Essay **47**

Writing a Persuasive Essay

Prewriting Organize Ideas

Information/Organization
The essay is well organized with supporting details.
Writing Strategy Use a Network Tree to organize my ideas.

Practice the Strategy Use a Network Tree to organize the notes you took on page 47.

Network Tree

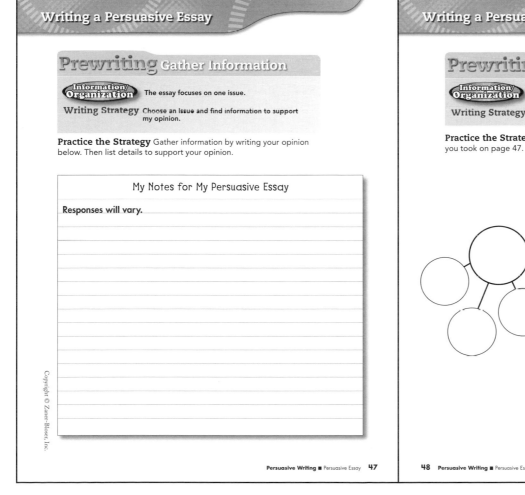

Opinion:
Responses will vary.

Copyright © Zaner-Bloser, Inc.

48 Persuasive Writing ■ Persuasive Essay

Business Letter

Writing Strategies

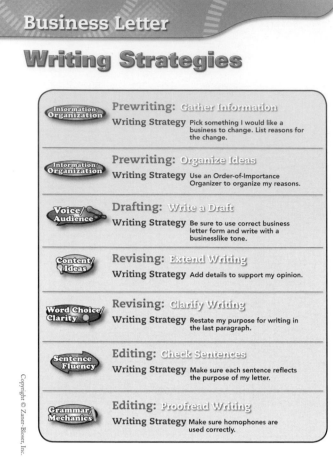

Information/Organization

Prewriting: Gather Information

Writing Strategy Pick something I would like a business to change. List reasons for the change.

Information/Organization

Prewriting: Organize Ideas

Writing Strategy Use an Order-of-Importance Organizer to organize my reasons.

Voice/Audience

Drafting: Write a Draft

Writing Strategy Be sure to use correct business letter form and write with a businesslike tone.

Content/Ideas

Revising: Extend Writing

Writing Strategy Add details to support my opinion.

Word Choice/Clarity

Revising: Clarify Writing

Writing Strategy Restate my purpose for writing in the last paragraph.

Sentence Fluency

Editing: Check Sentences

Writing Strategy Make sure each sentence reflects the purpose of my letter.

Grammar/Mechanics

Editing: Proofread Writing

Writing Strategy Make sure homophones are used correctly.

Copyright © Zaner-Bloser, Inc.

Persuasive Writing ■ Business Letter **49**

Business Letter

Rubric

Use this rubric to help write your business letter. Then, use it again to check your writing.

	Excelling ✓✓✓	Achieving ✓✓	Developing ✓✓	Beginning ✓
Information/Organization	The letter stays focused, and points are organized in order of importance.	The letter stays focused, and many points are organized.	The letter is somewhat focused and organized.	The letter needs to be more focused and better organized.
Voice/Audience	The overall tone is always businesslike.	The overall tone is mostly businesslike.	The overall tone is somewhat businesslike.	The overall tone is seldom businesslike.
Content/Ideas	Many clear and relevant details support the writer's opinion.	Some clear and relevant details support the writer's opinion.	A few relevant details support the writer's opinion, but they are not clear.	Clear and relevant details need to support the writer's opinion.
Word Choice/Clarity	The purpose for writing the letter is clearly restated in the last paragraph.	The purpose for writing is restated in the last paragraph.	The purpose for writing is restated in another paragraph.	The last paragraph needs to restate the purpose for writing the letter.
Sentence Fluency	Every sentence reflects the purpose of the letter.	Most sentences reflect the purpose of the letter.	Some sentences reflect the purpose of the letter.	Few sentences reflect the purpose of the letter.
Grammar/Mechanics	Spelling, punctuation, capitalization, and homophones are used correctly.	There are few errors in spelling, punctuation, capitalization, and homophones.	There are some errors in spelling, punctuation, capitalization, and homophones.	There are many errors in spelling, punctuation, capitalization, and homophones.

Copyright © Zaner-Bloser, Inc.

50 Persuasive Writing ■ Business Letter

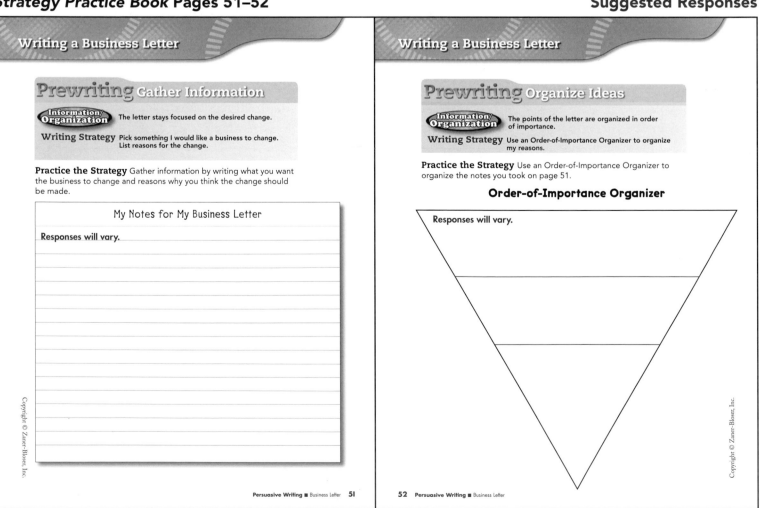

Writing a Business Letter

Prewriting Gather Information

Information/Organization The letter stays focused on the desired change.

Writing Strategy Pick something I would like a business to change. List reasons for the change.

Practice the Strategy Gather information by writing what you want the business to change and reasons why you think the change should be made.

My Notes for My Business Letter

Responses will vary.

Copyright © Zaner-Bloser, Inc.

Persuasive Writing ■ Business Letter **51**

Writing a Business Letter

Prewriting Organize Ideas

Information/Organization The points of the letter are organized in order of importance.

Writing Strategy Use an Order-of-Importance Organizer to organize my reasons.

Practice the Strategy Use an Order-of-Importance Organizer to organize the notes you took on page 51.

Order-of-Importance Organizer

Responses will vary.

Copyright © Zaner-Bloser, Inc.

52 Persuasive Writing ■ Business Letter

Scope and Sequence

Writing Genres	K	LEVEL A	LEVEL B	LEVEL C	LEVEL D	LEVEL E	LEVEL F	LEVEL G	LEVEL H
Adventure Story					●				
Biographic Sketch		●			●	●		●	●
Book Report		●		●	●	●	●		●
Cause-and-Effect Report							●	●	
Character Sketch					●				
Compare-and-Contrast Essay/Paper	●		●		●	●			
Contemporary Story					●				
Descriptive Essay/Paper		●	●	●		●	●		●
Descriptive Sentence/Paragraph	●	●	●	●	●				
E-mail								●	
Editorial					●			●	●
Eyewitness Account							●		
Fable			●			●			
Factual Report			●	●	●				
Folktale	●			●					
Geographic Description								●	
Historical Fiction/Episode							●	●	●
How-to Essay/Paper			●	●	●	●			●
Invitation	●								
Letters: Friendly, Business		●	●	●	●	●	●	●	●
List	●								
Mystery						●			
Observation Report				●		●	●	●	●
Once Upon a Time Story	●								
Personal Narrative	●	●	●	●	●	●		●	●
Persuasive Essay/Paper		●	●	●	●	●	●		
Persuasive Paragraph				●					
Persuasive Speech			●						●
Poem	●								
Problem-Solution Essay			●	●					
Recipe	●								
Research Report		●				●	●	●	●
Short Story							●		
Summary							●	●	
TV Commercial Script									●
Web Site Review								●	

Graphic Organizers	K	LEVEL A	LEVEL B	LEVEL C	LEVEL D	LEVEL E	LEVEL F	LEVEL G	LEVEL H
Attribute Chart			●		●	●		●	
Cause-and-Effect Chain						●	●	●	●
Character Chart								●	
Fact-and-Opinion Chart			●						

Scope and Sequence (continued)

	K	LEVEL A	LEVEL B	LEVEL C	LEVEL D	LEVEL E	LEVEL F	LEVEL G	LEVEL H
Graphic Organizers (continued)									
5 Senses Chart			●				●		
5 W's Chart; 3 W's Chart				●			●	●	●
K-W-S Chart								●	
Main Idea Table				●	●			●	●
Network Tree			●	●	●	●	●		
Observation Chart				●				●	
Opinion Chart		●	●					●	
Order-of-Importance Organizer					●		●		
Outline					●	●	●	●	●
Persuasion Map								●	●
Problem-Solution Frame				●				●	●
Pros-and-Cons Chart						●		●	●
Sequence Chain/Order Chain			●	●	●	●	●		●
Spider Map				●	●	●	●		
Storyboard		●	●			●	●		●
Story Frame									●
Story Map			●	●	●	●	●	●	●
Support Pattern						●			
Timeline					●				●
Venn Diagram		●	●				●		
Web		●	●	●	●	●		●	●
Writing Readiness Strategies									
Alphabet Review	●	●							
Big Books	●	●							
High-Frequency Words	●	●							
Left-to-Right Concept	●	●							
Letter Formation	●	●							
Letter Recognition	●	●							
Making Sentences	●	●							
Making Words	●	●							
Phonics	●	●							
Spacing	●	●							
Sound-Letter Correspondence	●	●							
Top-Bottom Concept	●	●							
Word Families	●	●							
Writing Strategies									
Adding Dialogue/Quotations	●			●	●	●	●	●	●
Adding Figurative Language						●	●	●	●
Adding or Rewriting Details/Facts/Examples		●	●	●	●	●	●	●	●
Adding Transition/Signal Words		●	●	●	●	●	●	●	●

Writing Strategies (continued)

	K	A	B	C	D	E	F	G	H
Assessing Personal Experience/Knowledge		●	●	●	●	●	●	●	●
Assessing Personal Interests		●	●	●	●	●	●	●	●
Clear Beginning, Middle, End; Introduction, Conclusion	●	●	●	●	●	●	●	●	
Correcting Sentence Fragments/Run-Ons/Confusing Sentences			●	●	●	●	●	●	●
Deleting Unnecessary or Confusing Information/Wordy Phrases		●	●	●	●	●	●	●	
Determining Audience	●	●	●	●	●	●	●	●	●
End Notes, Bibliography								●	●
Generating Ideas/Statements/Questions	●	●	●	●	●	●	●	●	
Interviewing				●	●	●	●	●	●
Listing	●	●	●	●	●	●	●	●	●
Making Notecards							●	●	●
Paraphrasing								●	●
Recognizing and Developing Parts of Genre	●	●	●	●	●	●	●	●	●
Recognizing and Using Genre Conventions	●	●	●	●	●	●	●	●	●
Reordering Sentences/Paragraphs		●	●	●	●	●	●	●	●
Replacing Vague/Loaded/Cliché Language				●	●	●	●	●	●
Restating Opinion, Purpose		●	●	●	●	●	●		●
Rewriting Unclear/Confusing/Incorrect Information		●	●	●	●	●	●	●	●
Selecting a Topic		●	●	●	●	●	●	●	●
Syntax of Oral Language	●								
Taking Notes	●	●	●	●	●	●	●	●	●
Thesis Statement						●	●	●	
Topic and Detail Sentences		●	●	●	●	●	●	●	●
Using Appropriate Text Structure	●	●	●	●	●	●	●	●	●
Using Appropriate Voice/Tone/Point of View		●	●	●	●	●	●	●	●
Using a Thesaurus			●		●	●	●	●	●
Using Exact/Precise/Interesting Words		●	●	●	●	●	●	●	●
Using Graphic Organizers to Generate Draft		●	●	●	●	●	●	●	●
Using References/Resources		●	●	●	●	●	●	●	●
Visual Aids/Illustrations	●	●	●	●	●	●	●	●	●
Writing Effective Sentences	●	●	●	●	●	●	●	●	●
Writing Paragraphs		●	●	●	●	●	●	●	●

Sharing Writing

	K	A	B	C	D	E	F	G	H
Author's Circle	●			●	●				
Big Books	●	●			●				
Mail to Appropriate Person or Publication		●	●	●	●	●	●	●	●

	K	LEVEL A	LEVEL B	LEVEL C	LEVEL D	LEVEL E	LEVEL F	LEVEL G	LEVEL H
Sharing Writing (continued)									
Multimedia Presentation						●	●	●	●
Observation Journal						●			
Part of a Display		●	●	●			●	●	●
Perform as Play/Newscast/Commercial				●					●
Post on Web Site		●	●	●	●	●		●	●
Post on Bulletin Board	●	●	●	●	●		●	●	●
Present as Speech or Read Aloud		●	●	●	●	●	●		●
Publish for Class Library	●	●	●	●	●	●			
Publish in Class or School Newspaper/Collection/Magazine/Newsletter/Journal/Diary		●	●		●	●	●	●	●
Record on Audiotape				●					
Send as E-mail								●	
Time Capsule						●			
Travel Brochure					●				
Grammar, Usage, and Mechanics									
Active and Passive Voice							●	●	●
Adjectives	●		●	●	●	●	●	●	●
Adverbs					●	●	●	●	●
Apostrophes	●		●	●			●	●	
Appositives					●		●	●	●
Capitalization	●	●	●	●	●	●	●	●	●
Clauses						●	●	●	●
Complete Sentences	●	●	●	●	●		●	●	●
Conjunctions			●			●	●	●	●
Contractions			●				●	●	
Dangling Modifiers								●	
Double Negatives						●		●	
Easily Confused Words/Homophones				●	●		●	●	
Introductory Verbal Phrases									●
Letters: Friendly, Business	●	●		●	●	●	●	●	●
Nouns: Plural, Possessive	●		●	●	●	●	●	●	
Pronoun Forms/Antecedents			●		●	●	●	●	●
Punctuation	●	●	●	●	●	●	●	●	●
Quotations/Dialogue	●			●	●	●	●	●	●
Sentence Patterns		●	●	●	●	●	●	●	●
Sentences: Complex							●	●	●
Sentences: Compound				●			●	●	●
Sentences: Fragments			●	●	●	●	●	●	●
Sentences: Run-Ons			●	●	●	●	●	●	●
Subject-Verb Agreement				●	●	●	●	●	●
Verb Forms/Tenses		●		●	●		●	●	●

Teacher Notes

Teacher Notes

Teacher Notes

Teacher Notes